Material Culture and (Forced) Migration

Material Culture and (Forced) Migration

Materialising the transient

Edited by

Friedemann Yi-Neumann, Andrea Lauser, Antonie Fuhse and Peter J. Bräunlein

UCLPRESS

First published in 2022 by
UCL Press
University College London
Gower Street
London WC1E 6BT

Available to download free: www.uclpress.co.uk

Cover illustration: *Headless Bodies* (2018) by the Afghan artist Ali Sadeqi (based in Mashhad, Iran). We thank Maliheh Bayat Tork for her efforts to realise this cooperation.

A CIP catalogue record for this book is available from The British Library.

ISBN: 978-1-80008-162-8 (Hbk.)
ISBN: 978-1-80008-161-1 (Pbk.)
ISBN: 978-1-80008-160-4 (PDF)
ISBN: 978-1-80008-163-5 (epub)
ISBN: 978-1-80008-164-2 (mobi)
DOI: https://doi.org/10.14324/111.9781800081604

SPONSORED BY THE
Federal Ministry of Education and Research

This publication is funded by the German Federal Ministry for Education and Research (BMBF).

Contents

List of figures

List of contributors

Rachel Barber is a doctoral student in social sciences at CIESAS Occidente in Guadalajara, Mexico, where she currently studies the labour identities constructed around artisanal work. In her master's thesis, published by the Universidad de Guadalajara, she studied North American retirees in Chapala, Mexico and the relation between their folk art consumption and their sociocultural adaptation. She is interested in the topics of material culture, social change and the anthropology of work, as well as opportunities to incorporate documentary and audiovisual methods into ethnographic studies.

Peter J. Bräunlein holds an extracurricular professorship in the study of religion from the University of Bremen, and master's and doctoral degrees in cultural anthropology from the University of Freiburg. He conducted extensive fieldwork on indigenous cosmologies and Catholicism in the Philippines, and did research on material religion in museums. He has taught at various universities in Germany and was a senior researcher in the project 'On the materiality of (forced) migration' in Göttingen from 2019 to 2021. His areas of interest and research are South East Asia, Europe, material religion, migration, museology, film and media studies, and ghosts, spirits and the uncertainties of modernity.

Louise Fowler is a Post-Excavation Manager at MOLA (Museum of London Archaeology). She is an archaeologist with 15 years' experience in development-led archaeology, and has directed numerous multi-period excavations within London. She has developed exhibitions and provided curatorial support for the London Mithraeum, winner of the Best Public Presentation of Archaeology award at the 2018 British Archaeological Awards. She has co-authored several archaeological site monographs, including *Doctors, Dissection and Resurrection Men* (2014, with Natasha Powers). She has interests in archaeological methodology, interfaces between art and archaeology, and urban archaeology, and leads MOLA's participation in the Dzhangal Archaeology Project.

Antonie Fuhse holds a PhD in social anthropology from the University of Göttingen. From 2019 to 2021 she was the scientific coordinator of the project 'On the materiality of (forced) migration' at the University of Göttingen. She has carried out fieldwork in Germany among early-career researchers from India. She has worked on mobility and temporality, multiple belonging, aspirations and the life course. Together with Elfriede Hermann she edited the volume *India beyond India: Dilemmas of belonging*. In 2021, she published her PhD thesis with the title *Mobilität und Zeitgestaltung: Junge Wissenschaftler*innen aus Indien und ihre biographische Navigation zwischen Gegenwart und Zukunft.*

Nada Ghandour-Demiri holds a PhD in politics from the University of Bristol and has research experience in academia, as well as in the humanitarian and development sectors. She is currently working at UNICEF, as Reporting and Monitoring Expert. During the research and writing of the chapter she co-authored for this book she was the Monitoring, Evaluation, Accountability and Learning Manager at the Danish Refugee Council in Greece.

Yaatsil Guevara González holds a PhD in sociology from the Bielefeld Graduate School in History and Sociology. She is a research fellow at the Department of Anthropology and African Studies at Johannes Gutenberg University Mainz. She studied anthropology and holds a master's in regional studies. Her research focuses on refugee studies, forced displacement, gender and the anthropology of everyday life. She has also conducted research on radicalisation, extremism and Muslim minorities in Europe. Her research combines different disciplines such as anthropology, sociology, human geography, and area and gender studies. Her doctoral research focused on Honduran refugees and their everyday life strategies of coping with their stranded mobility on Mexico's southern border. She has conducted ethnographic research in Mexico, Central America, the USA and Germany.

Elena Höpfner, MA, was a teaching assistant at Free University Berlin in 2019–20, and has been a PhD candidate at the Technical University of Dortmund and a junior researcher at the Institute for Employment Research (IAB) in Nuremberg (Germany) since 2020. In 2018, she received the Young Talent Award of the German Sociological Association (DGS) for her master's thesis *Menschen auf der Flucht und die Bedeutung ihrer Dinge: Eine gegenstandsbezogene Theoriebildung im doppelten Sinne* (Refugees and things: a grounded theory and material culture approach).

She is currently working on job seeking and the labour market availability of young single mothers on basic income support.

Andrea Lauser is Professor in the Department of Social and Cultural Anthropology, Georg August University, Göttingen, Germany. She works in the context of transnational mobility on questions of power, gender, and generational changes, as well as lived religion and aesthetics, visions of the future and anthropological methods. From 2011 to 2015 she was the spokesperson for the research programme on the 'Dynamics of religion in South East Asia' (www.dorisea.net) and since 2018 she has been coordinating the research network 'On the materiality of (forced) migration' (materialitaet-migration.de).

Sarah Mallet is a post-doctoral researcher at the Pitt Rivers Museum at the University of Oxford, currently working on the museum's programme of research on African restitution. Her previous work focused on the materiality of migration. She co-curated the major temporary exhibition 'Lande: The Calais "Jungle" and beyond' at the Pitt Rivers Museum and co-authored the book of the same title with Dan Hicks.

Petros Passas holds a PhD in anthropology from the Sapienza Università di Roma. He currently works as Head of Programme for the Danish Refugee Council in Colombia, and previously held the same role in Greece.

Georgina Ramsay is an Assistant Professor in the Department of Anthropology at the University of Delaware. Her work focuses on displacement, broadly conceived, and she has worked with refugees resettled in Australia, refugees in Uganda, displaced people in the Democratic Republic of the Congo, and people experiencing homelessness in the USA. Her work has examined displacement in terms of temporality, labour exploitation, sovereignty and existential dislocation. Her current projects explore how displacement emerges from racialised legacies of extraction and dispossession, intensified through emergent political, economic and environmental insecurities. Her book, *Impossible Refuge: The control and constraint of refugee futures*, was published in 2018.

Ayşe Şanlı is a PhD student in anthropology at Brown University. She is interested in the intersections of migration, materiality and material culture, borders and (il)legality. Her doctoral research explores migrants' daily material practices in Sicily, and the politics of border-making within the broader context of the 'refugee crisis' in the Mediterranean.

Özlem Savaş is a research fellow in comparative cultural and social anthropology at European University Viadrina, Frankfurt. She has worked as an assistant professor at Bilkent University and has held fellowships at Bard College Berlin, Humboldt University, the Brandenburg Centre for Media Studies and the University of Konstanz. She has carried out and published ethnographic research on Turkish diasporic material cultures in Vienna, affective digital media spaces of new migration from Turkey, and social media practices of self and lifestyle in Turkey. Her current ethnographic research explores contemporary exilic atmospheres in Berlin with a special focus on the affective culture of post-Gezi migration from Turkey.

Magdalena Suerbaum is a post-doctoral researcher at the Interdisciplinary Center for Gender Studies at Bielefeld University, Germany. She has carried out fieldwork among Syrian refugees in Egypt and among migrants in Germany who arrived during the so-called refugee crisis. Her work focuses on gendered and classed approaches to forced displacement, experiences of motherhood in contexts of migration, and migrants' legal and bureaucratic encounters. Her current project deals with child-rearing, educational choices and intergenerational relationships among Syrian parents in Turkey and Germany. She is the author of *Masculinities and Displacement in the Middle East: Syrian refugees in Egypt* (I.B. Tauris, 2020). Magdalena holds a PhD in gender studies from the School of Oriental and African Studies in London.

Maike Suhr is a research associate at the Department of Media Management at Bauhaus-Universität Weimar, Germany. Her research interests include transnationalism, migration and its materiality, and journalism in the post-migrant society. Currently she is working in a research project on novel organisational forms in journalism, funded by the German Research Association (DFG), and investigates in her dissertation the chances and pitfalls for diversity in an altered media landscape. Before this, she studied communication at the University of Arts Berlin and worked at the transcultural project space bi'bak for several years.

Maruška Svašek is Professor of Anthropology at Queen's University Belfast, UK. Her main research interests include migration, material culture, art and emotions. In the last 10 years, her work has brought these strands together, exploring the mobility and agency of humans, artefacts and images in an era of intensifying globalisation, transnational connectivity and environmental change. Her publications include *Ethnographies of Movement, Sociality and Space* (2018, with Milena Komarova), *Creativity in Transition* (2016, with Birgit Meyer), *Emotions and Human Mobility* (2012), *Moving Subjects, Moving Objects* (2012), *Anthropology, Art and Cultural Production* (2007), *Postsocialism* (2006) and *Mixed Emotions* (2005, with Kay Milton).

Simon Turner is Associate Professor at the Centre for Advanced Migration Studies, University of Copenhagen. He works on forced displacement, diaspora, conflict and humanitarianism in the African Great Lakes region, and on Europe. At present he is engaged in a project on 'carceral junctions' in European refugee policies and another on everyday humanitarianism in Tanzania. He is the author of *Politics of Innocence: Hutu identity, conflict and camp life* (Berghahn, 2010), the editor of *What is Camp?* (special issue of *Journal of Refugee Studies*, 29(2), 2016) and the co-editor of *Stuckness and Confinement: Reflections on life in ghettos, camps and prisons* (special issue of *Ethnos*, 84(1), 2019) and *Invisibility in African Displacements: From structural marginalization to strategies of avoidance* (Zed Books, 2020).

Andrea Verdasco holds a PhD in anthropology from the University of Copenhagen. Her work has mostly focused on young unaccompanied refugees 'coming of age' in the context of Denmark and how they construct a sense of belonging and social relations in the uncertainties of their situation. Before her PhD, she worked alongside UNICEF Mozambique and the UNICEF Office of Research and IOM Tanzania as a researcher and practitioner on child protection in the context of migrant youth. More recently, she conducted research on loneliness and precarious housing conditions among international students and old-age pensioners in Australia. Her current interests lie in exploring how refugee mothers negotiate deservingness to a family life in the context of different European welfare states.

Friedemann Yi-Neumann is a research fellow on the migration exhibition project MOVING THINGS (University of Göttingen). Previously, he was a scientific coordinator at the Institute of Social and Cultural Anthropology at the University of Göttingen in the BMBF research project 'On the materiality of (forced) migration'. In addition, he held a position in the Mobile Worlds research project (Goethe University Frankfurt). Yi-Neumann examines the relevance of material culture in the forced migration context. His main research interests are material culture, forced migration and post-migration, asylum reception, dispossessions, homes, everyday life, phenomenology and urban anthropology.

Preface

This edited volume's point of departure was the research project 'On the materiality of (forced) migration' (MatMig). Funded by the German Federal Ministry of Education and Research,[1] the project is a collaboration between the Institute for Social and Cultural Anthropology at the University of Göttingen, the exhibition agency Die Exponauten (Berlin), and Museum Friedland.

This volume grew out of contributions presented at two conferences: the online conference 'Materializing the Transient: Ethnographies and museums in the study of (forced) migration', which was organised by the editors and hosted by the MatMig research project[2] in May 2020, and a panel entitled 'The materiality of migration: From "bare necessities" to "promising things"', which was organised by Antonie Fuhse and Andrea Lauser (University of Göttingen) and Sarah Mallet (Pitt Rivers Museum, University of Oxford), and was part of the 16th conference of the European Association of Social Anthropologists (EASA), held online in July 2020. Early versions of the chapters in this volume were presented at one or the other of these two conferences. We would like to extend our sincere thanks to all those who participated in the conferences, including those whose contributions are not included in this volume, for taking part in the stimulating and constructive discussions.

We are grateful to the anonymous reviewers for their careful reading of the manuscript and their suggestions for improvements. And we would like to thank our student assistants – Miriam Kuhnke and Hannah Mohr – for their invaluable assistance in preparing this book.

Notes

1 Federal Ministry of Education and Research (Bundesministerium für Bildung und Forschung, BMBF); funding line: 'Language of objects' ('Sprache der Objekte'); project term: summer 2018–winter 2022.

2 https://materialitaet-migration.de/en/conference/ (accessed 10 August 2021).

Introduction
From 'bare life' to 'moving things': on the materiality of (forced) migration

Andrea Lauser, Antonie Fuhse, Peter J. Bräunlein and Friedemann Yi-Neumann

This introduction aims to show how a material culture approach can add valuable insights to the field of migration research. To do so, the central findings of the material turn in the social sciences are summarised and linked to migration research. The contributions in this volume provide an in-depth understanding of multiple, and sometimes conflicting, conceptions and engagements with things beyond their cultural or political fixations and problematic association with certain individuals or groups. Grasping things beyond their 'meaning' in a merely symbolic sense is a vital aim of the book. This approach makes it possible to consider the remarkable ability of things to stir both positive and negative affects and emotions, and to facilitate belonging, relatedness and place-making. Drawing on these conceptions, the volume offers methodological innovations as well as critical reflections on contemporary object-oriented approaches in migration research.

Contemporary social life under the conditions of global capitalism is fundamentally determined by things. This human–thing relationship seems quasi-natural. Things are, of course, essential in carrying out necessary functions in everyday life: to communicate, to provide protection against heat and cold, to prepare food, to maintain one's health. Some things carry promises: emotional closeness, the promotion of self-expression, the acquisition of prestige. Bureaucratic things – a piece of paper, a passport – decide one's fate. Things can trigger desire, despair, joy and a whole range of other emotions. Things may be functional, may have a personal value, may be charged with emotion, may be political, and they can, very often, be transformed into something else entirely. But one's relationship to things, so often taken for granted, is challenged by the conditions of flight and migration. Firstly, people on the move need to develop new ways of living – a process that requires fundamental renegotiations of ties to people *and* material objects. Secondly, one's quasi-natural relationship to things is challenged when an entitlement to them is contested. When from September 2015 increasing numbers of refugees came to Germany, calls for donations of clothes attracted a broad response. However, with the donations, debates started about the appropriateness of certain things being in the hands of refugees (Pellander and Kotilainen 2017), and these debates touched upon fundamental issues of power and boundary-drawing between refugees, migrants and citizens of a nation state (see, for example, Spencer and Triandafyllidou 2020; Gaibazzi et al. 2017; Holmes and Castañeda 2016). In other words: Who is entitled to an iPhone 7 or a pair of Nike trainers? Whose life is bare enough to receive help? What things are really necessary? Under the 'normal' circumstances of life, such questions are rarely asked, but they do refer to our fundamental relationship to things.

The chapters in this volume are based on qualitative and ethnographic research in a range of geographical areas and migratory contexts. The specific circumstances inform the chapters' focus on various materialities and people's active engagement with things. The chapters show how local political and material infrastructures shape materiality and how, in turn, people engage with things, (re)appropriate them, adapt and thus shape their social and material environment.

Despite the various regional foci, all of these case studies have been conducted at a time when migration has moved to the centre of global public, political and scholarly attention. The war in Syria and the following mass out-migration, the clandestine border crossings at the Mexico–USA border and the push-back of people at borders all over the world have again sparked debates about the distinction of people into refugees and migrants, the former understood as forced to leave their home countries, the latter assumed to have left voluntarily (Hamilakis 2016, 122). The use of the term '(forced) migration' in the title and introduction to this volume was part of a conscious decision to include chapters that focus on different forms of human movement, from the study of forced migration and displacement to the analysis of retirement migration. The chapters are tied together by a focus on materiality that is influenced by the specifics of the migration context. Nevertheless, we want to point out that migration, however defined and categorised, is not the exclusive explanatory factor for people's experiences and material practices (Bakewell 2008) and that the basic findings in this volume are relevant to the study of human mobility in general.

Our aim is to combine migration research with suggestions from the material turn, a term which covers a rather broad spectrum of theory. We dedicate a major part of this introduction to the material turn, looking in particular at the concept of 'object agency' and exploring concepts from material culture studies that may be relevant to migration research.

In the process of thinking migration consistently through things, we – and the other authors of this volume – also became aware of the centrality of temporality, spatiality and emotion. As these factors form a kind of common thread that runs through the volume, we pay analytical attention to them in the introduction to each part. This also applies to another challenge: methodology in a material approach to migration.

Before presenting the theoretical and conceptual framework of this volume, we turn to a story documented by two members of our research team, Samah Al Jundi-Pfaff and Katharina Brunner. The story nicely illustrates the goals we are pursuing here, and our understanding of the multiple ways in which things matter and transform.

The piece of cloth

0.1 The piece of cloth which Wael donated to Museum Friedland. © Samah Al Jundi-Pfaff, 2019.

In the beginning, the piece of cloth depicted in Figure 0.1 was a whole blanket. It was 2012, two weeks after the Syrian revolution had broken out, and Wael was living with his grandmother in Homs, while his family had been displaced to an area near Banias. As he was in danger of being 'captured' by the police and forced to serve in the military, Wael's grandmother gave him a few things to have ready, just in case: a pillow, a jar of makdous (stuffed, cured aubergines) and the blanket. The situation was changing constantly, and Wael was forced to move to his parents' in Banias. He took the blanket with him.

In Banias, he used the blanket as an extra bedcover, especially at night-time. But his situation didn't improve there: he would not be able to postpone military service. In August, shortly after Ramadan, he fled Banias. This time he went to Lebanon, where his uncle lived. For the journey, his mother prepared a bag of clothes, including warm pullovers, some food and the blanket. As a reminder of his grandmother, the blanket was of great importance to him. At his uncle's place, he was offered a mattress to sleep on, but only one blanket to cover him during the night. So Wael used the blanket from his grandmother to cover the mattress he slept on: it had found its next use, as a bedsheet.

After two months at his uncle's place, Wael moved with a cousin from Tripoli to Qubeh in Lebanon. At that time, the two couldn't find a room or place to rent, so they decided to sleep in a shop which had no electricity and nothing to cover the window. Here the blanket became a curtain.

In May 2013, Wael moved to Turkey to join a friend. At the time, his friend was living in a shop with 20 other people. There Wael used the blanket to cover not the mattress but the ground, where it provided protection from the cold, dirty floor. While in Turkey, Wael moved to five different shops and the blanket was used variously as a curtain, a carpet and, at times, a blanket.

There was a turning point after he moved to Istanbul. After all the stations the blanket had been through, it had become extremely dirty, a hole had grown bigger and bigger, and it was becoming increasingly difficult to clean. So Wael made a bold decision: he decided to cut one of the blanket's corners off – and to take only that with him. How did Wael feel when he cut it off? Was he not sad to take only a small piece of the blanket with him, after all those times it had been so helpful? Wael explained his thinking: 'I'm going to keep moving and moving and moving. And it is so dirty. It is so

> difficult to have it in my bag, so the only way will be to just preserve a piece of it, as a souvenir of my grandma.' He left the rest of the blanket with his friends in Turkey, so at least they would be able to benefit from its numerous possible uses. Having arrived in Friedland, Wael decided to donate the piece of the blanket to the Friedland Museum. But he said he did not feel sad to leave it there; rather, he understood it as a way of expressing his appreciation to his grandmother and her contribution to his journey to Germany.
>
> How is the rest of the blanket being used by Wael's friends today? Although we can only guess at its possible uses, we can be sure that there is not one single answer to that question, but rather a multitude of them.
>
> (Adapted from Al Jundi-Pfaff and Brunner 2020)

Wael's story shows the possible transformations an object can go through, from a blanket to a curtain to a carpet and, finally, to a keepsake (see also Stockhammer 2017). As the blanket changed its functions and form, and as a constant reminder of his grandmother, it offered Wael a certain continuity. The blanket provided a connection to the people he left behind and to those he met along the way; a part of his place-making activities along the way, it is now an object in storage in a migration museum. This story illustrates the complexity of even the most common and nondescript materiality, and provides the point of departure for the theoretically charged discussions that follow.

From 'bare life' to moving things

Expressions such as 'bare survival' are common in politicians' speeches and media when it comes to refugees. In academia, too, 'bare life' and 'bare existence' are common terms. A similar separation resonates in legal thinking: the obligation to protect life extends only to life itself – 'bare life' – and not to material possessions. The principle of 'naked' or 'bare' life is from legal philosophy, but it goes far beyond jurisprudence; it informs common-sense thinking and thus how to regard those who manage to survive, to save their 'bare lives'. However, if one takes this phrase literally, contradictions and confusions become apparent, revealing the necessary connection(s) between 'naked life' and material things. In media images, we do not see naked people in refugee camps and on the high seas: we see people with clothing, toddlers with soft toys, young men with backpacks and broken shoes. Wael's story is not one of 'no things' but actually shows how a mundane thing can take shape and transform in various ways, and through these changes, its relevance changes too. In short, talking about 'bare life' as a legal asset only captures part of the precarious existence all too often linked with migration and flight.

When we talk about 'life in a state of exception' and 'bare life', the reference to Giorgio Agamben's *homo sacer* project becomes obvious, even inevitable (Agamben 1998). Agamben is a much-cited and much-criticised author whose ideas are nevertheless stimulating, and were an important starting point for our project, and for several chapters in this volume.

In the ancient legal form of the *homo sacer*, the holy man, Agamben discovers a marginal figure who is simultaneously outside and inside the legal system: 'The sacred man is the one whom the people have judged on account of a crime. It is not permitted to sacrifice this man, yet he who kills him will not be condemned for homicide' (Agamben 1998, 71).[1] For Agamben, the function of *homo sacer* is highly relevant to modernity, as he shows through the example of the Nazi concentration camps. A person who stands outside both secular and sacral law is therefore subject to a twofold exception, which can be understood as an act of inclusive exclusion. This 'holy' life, which Agamben uses synonymously with 'naked' or 'bare' life – the only life that a refugee is entitled to in common-sense Western thinking – is a life in a permanent state of exception, a concept introduced by the German philosopher Carl Schmitt in the 1920s. Agamben, referring to the Nazi concentration camps, claims that the essence of the camp is the materialisation of the state of exception.

Agamben seeks to demonstrate a structural connection between legalisation and disenfranchisement, arguing that communities are biopolitically constituted precisely through the process of 'inclusive exclusion'. Adam Ramadan (2013) has provided a substantial critique of Agamben's paradigm of camps as 'spaces of exception' and a producer of bare life (see also Turner 2015). He argues that Agamben's model is limited, as it cannot explain the specific social, political, material and regional landscapes in which camps emerge. Through a series of examples, Ramadan illustrates the fact that camps can be fundamentally different in form and character. In his contribution to this volume, Simon Turner notes that the issue is not the agency–non-agency dichotomy in which the academic debate concerning camps is often framed, but rather 'it is the exceptional character of the camp that at once depoliticises and hyper-politicises the space of the camp'. Other scholars have criticised Agamben's concept for its inability to explain everyday camp life (Cooper-Knock 2017), for its Eurocentricity, and for its failure to address local perspectives on power and sovereignty (Owens 2009; Svirsky and Bignall 2012; Blunt 2013).

Although Agamben's central claims are heavily debated, his concept of the camp remains productive insofar as it calls for corrections and challenges academics to reflect on the materiality of life events such as flight and migration. In other words, Agamben forces scholars to take a stand. The reduction of the migrant subject to a being deprived of all agency, the assertion that camps are places of a permanent state of exception, and the assumption of migrant exceptionalism – including the significant role that migrants play in urban development and in diverse societies (Vertovec 2007; Çağlar and Glick Schiller 2018) – have all been challenged in various ways. Above all, however, the Agamben paradigm calls for empirical research that comes close to the reality of migrating people's lives.

The 'material turn': moving things in perspective

A fundamental ambition of anthropology is to empower the perspective of actors. Conventionally, it is people who produce meaning, and ethnographic research has therefore focused on human actors. But the 'material turn' shifts this focus: things are no longer (just) products of culture, but co-producers of culture and society.

Since this focus on materiality began to emerge in the social and cultural sciences in the 1980s, diverse research on the perspectives and agency of objects – that is, letting the objects speak – has been carried out. The 'material turn', as it became known, began with a critique of dualistic figures of thought, in particular the mind–matter, subject–object duality. The anthropologist Daniel Miller, who has provided significant impetus to the material turn, suggests expanding the traditional study of objects, which focused on the production, function and symbolic value of objects, in the direction of the subject–object relationship emerging in modern mass culture (Miller 2008). Miller criticises structuralism, Marxism, semiotics and symbolic anthropology for failing to take the three-dimensionality and palpability of things seriously. These heuristic lenses render artefacts little more than representations of immaterial quantities such as society, social relations and identity, and as a result, the material world is interpreted as nothing but signs, symbols and ideas (Hicks 2010, 53). In his research on clothing, housing, and mobile phone and internet use, Miller pursues the thesis that people only become cultural subjects through the appropriation of things (Miller 2008, 287). In his work, the Hegelian notion of self-creation is an important guiding principle: through active handling of the world of things, people internalise and incorporate culture, that is, social structures, ideas, norms, values and patterns of action. The premise of Miller's book *Stuff*, in which he elaborates his concept of material culture studies, is that things make people as much as people make things (Miller 2009). Over the past two decades, interest in material culture has grown substantially in the social sciences, as has the willingness to adopt a fundamentally different analytical perspective which Henare, Holbraad and Wastell (2006) call 'thinking through things'. Indeed, 'thinking through things' has led to a shift in the direction of research and theoretical work, with researchers now trying to understand how things matter and what they are in a certain context.

With the material turn, one classic anthropological and sociological text, in particular, demands rereading: Marcel Mauss's *The Gift* ([1923/1924] 2002). For Mauss, every gift demands a counter-gift: the gift and the person are intermingled. This almost universal rule of reciprocity between taker and giver is triggered by things, which thus become social actors. This insight has a tangible meaning when we look, for example, at the practice of sending transnational parcels, an important social element in the context of migration (cf. Mata-Codesal and Abranches 2018).

One of the most important figures in the material turn was Arjun Appadurai with his anthology *The Social Life of Things* (1986). In it, Appadurai reflects on the origin of value attribution to things and goods and asks: why do we desire certain things? For Appadurai, people assign value to things through the processes of exchange and consumption. Bronislaw Malinowski (1922), in his study of the Trobriand Kula ring – the classic anthropological example of ascribing value to, desiring and exchanging things – was primarily interested in the people-to-people relationships behind the exchange process. But Appadurai changes the perspective. For him, people enter into a relationship with things, and in so doing they, in a sense, awaken the identity of an object. While consumption is the expression of one's relationship to the world, that is not the whole story:

> Even if our own approach to things is conditioned necessarily by the view that things have no meanings apart from those that human transactions, attributions, and motivations endow them with, the anthropological problem is that this formal truth does not illuminate the concrete, historical circulation of things. For that we have to follow the things themselves.
>
> (Appadurai 1986, 5)

As they did in pre-modern societies, things in the sociocultural context of modern globalised societies have a social life. With this thesis, Appadurai directs his attention to both the material and symbolic sides of exchange relationships between people, while at the same time tracing the movement of things through social, political and economic spheres.

An object-centred approach also poses a methodological challenge. Appadurai explains that one cannot do without a certain degree of 'methodological fetishism', which means 'returning our attention to the things themselves', because on the one hand we humans attribute certain properties and abilities to things, and on the other hand we concede a certain independence to 'things in motion'. This 'methodological fetishism' is a necessary corrective 'to the tendency to excessively sociologize transactions in things, a tendency we owe to Mauss' (Appadurai 1986, 5).

In 'The cultural biography of things: Commoditization as process' – a chapter in *The Social Life of Things* – Igor Kopytoff (1986) sees an analogy between person and thing: each has a biography, and each biography is individual, unique. Through the study of these biographies, Kopytoff argues, not only the processes of reification or the commodity character of an object, but also its shift between economic and cultural spheres in a society, can be better understood.

Kopytoff's focus on object biographies opens up, among other things, the possibility not only of examining things in their historical becoming, but also of looking at them as historical memories. A differentiation between 'object biographies' and 'biographical objects' has been a productive approach in a number of studies (see for example Csikszentmihalyi and Rochberg-Halton 1981). Through 'biographical objects' – objects intimately connected to a person's life – scholars can learn a lot about a person's story. Indeed, Janet Hoskins's *Biographical Objects* (1998) demonstrates how productive this perspective can be. This approach in turn connects to Marilyn Strathern's insight that the becoming of people and the becoming of things take place interdependently: material and social spheres are intertwined in her concept of 'distributed personhood'. Certain personal belongings – such as photos, cuddly toys or jewellery – are often significant parts of people's biographies (Strathern 1988; see Friedemann Yi-Neumann in this volume). The blurred line between human and object biography is discussed further in Part II of this volume, which focuses on methods.

In material culture research, especially as it is applied in the disciplines of archaeology and history, objects are used to access individual and also collective histories. Auslander and Zahra (2018) analyse material culture in the context of war, forced migration and the colonial era, exploring how rescued, looted, misappropriated, abandoned, found and recovered things live on in the aftermath of mass violence (see also Hicks 2020; Dziuban and Stańczyk 2020).

Things and agency

The realisation that the material world is inextricably intertwined with the social world of an individual or a collective may, at least initially, appear trivial. However, the epistemic potential and methodological consequences of this awareness have only begun to be fully developed with the material turn. Here, the long-established subject–object dichotomy is being increasingly called into question; and, inspired especially by Alfred Gell's *Art and Agency* (1998), talk of the 'objects as social agents' has become increasingly common. Gell is interested in neither the symbolic nor the aesthetic, but rather in art as a system of social action. Using the Malanggan carvings of New Ireland (Melanesia) as an example, Gell shows how the wooden figures become 'a kind of body which accumulates, like a charged battery, the potential energy of the deceased' (Gell 1998, 225). For Gell, a thing unfolds efficacy as a kind of channel for the craftsman's actions and intentions: the living thing thus becomes alive only in relation to its maker and those who look at and use it.

Other scholars take a more radical approach to the concept of object agency. Bruno Latour's actor–network theory should be mentioned here (Latour 2005). Latour asks: who or what kills – the person or the gun? But for Latour, the either/or perspective of the question misframes the action: the act of killing takes place not simply through the person or through the gun, but through the person–gun actor, consisting of the two actants (Latour 1999, 176–7).[2] Through the example, Latour is seeking to open our eyes to how human existence is interwoven with things at every turn. Things not only provide new possibilities of perception and knowledge, of surveillance and control, but also open up and restrict possibilities for action. Things interact with people – they too can be given subject status. For actor–network theorists, 'subject' here is to be equated not with being human, but with the pragmatic competence of 'originating courses of action, defining contexts as contexts of some kind, creating meanings and delineating available ways of life. Inasmuch as objects have this competence, they may be considered as intentional subjects' (Caronia and Mortari 2015, 403). Through this perspective, the apparently self-evident separation between the subject and the object disappears. This insight is consistent with numerous examples from anthropological research, as Hoskins points out: ‘In certain contexts, persons can seem to take on the attributes of things and things can seem to act almost as persons’ (Hoskins 2006, 74).

In this vein, Latour (2005) argues that the category of the social should not only be applied to interpersonal relations and the society of humans, but also be extended to relations between humans and things, and between things and other things. One approach should be to investigate the human–non-human networks which come together and act as a whole.

In the context of the ontological turn, object-centred theorising is being pushed further, not least with the aim of destabilising the prevailing anthropocentric view of the world. Levi Bryant’s ‘onticology’, for example, inspired by systems theory and cybernetics, assumes that being consists entirely of objects, properties and relations. Onticology speaks of a *Democracy of Objects* (Bryant 2011), in which objects of all kinds and at different scales exist equally without being reducible to other objects. People are, according to Bryant, ‘objects *among* the various types of objects that exist or populate the world, each with their own specific powers and capacities’ (Bryant 2011, 20, emphasis in original).

Theorists who see themselves as new materialists recognise things as having a life of their own in the material world, beyond human sociality and language. They argue that matter is ‘immanently active, productive, and formative’ (Shaviro 2015, 32.). As Karen Barad states, ‘Matter feels, converses, suffers, desires, yearns and remembers’ (quoted in Dolphijn and van der Tuin 2012, 48). In her work *Vibrant Matter*, Jane Bennett insists that things are not passive, but wield a generative power ‘as quasi agents of forces with trajectories, propensities, or tendencies of their own’ (2010, viii). She appreciates the generative powers and agential capacities within both organic and inorganic matter, and aspires ‘to articulate a vibrant materiality that runs alongside and inside humans to see how analyses of political events might change if we gave the force of things more due’ (Bennett 2010, viii.). From such a perspective, things are not merely metaphorically or symbolically alive, they are factually alive. This new vitalism or neo-animism can be considered a general feature of the new materialists’ ontology (Bräunlein 2019). Looking at new materialisms confronts us with radical forms of object-oriented, non-anthropocentric thinking. These approaches explicitly contradict social constructivist theories which claim that things only become things when people interact with them. Philosophical concepts that are emerging in the context of the ontological turn are the subject of lively debate. It is about attempts to project new world views and about the deconstruction of old ones. For anthropologists, the urgent question is how theoretical concepts can be implemented empirically. Or, conversely, how empirical, thing-centred research stimulates work on theory. Scholars of the new materialism call on scholars to always think in new relations, and it is this call which forms the conceptual basis of our approach in this volume: 'materialising' migration research.

In this section, we have identified the key concepts in the material turn for our key purpose: to explore (forced) migration by the use of material culture approaches. It should have become clear that the things surrounding us are not simply factors that should be taken into account *additionally* but that sociocultural relations, world views, feelings and aspirations are materially constituted in a fundamental way. In this context, we argue that an object-oriented approach has great potential in migration research. Such a lens is not exhausted by the study of material culture, but invites us to take radically different perspectives, opening up new ways to think in, about and through objects, and to look at the new relationships these perspectives open up.

Material culture in migration research

In migration research, a focus on the connection between the material world, human sensory perception and memory, and the social life of things and humans, has only gradually begun to emerge.

A notable precursor in this regard is the anthology *The Suitcase: Refugee voices from Bosnia and Croatia* (Mertus et al. 1997). Here, it is not theoretical or conceptual ambitions that guide the authors, but the possibility of making the voices of refugee women audible – hauntingly and poignantly – through narratives about the things they carried in their suitcases. Since the 1990s, suitcases have become ubiquitous objects in museum representations of migration around the globe (Baur 2009).

Pnina Werbner, who looks at the concept of diaspora and the related identity discourses in the arts and literature, is another forerunner in this area. In Werbner's work, commonly shared 'cultural preoccupations' come into view, such as 'tastes, cuisines, musics, sport, poetry, fashion and film' (Werbner 2005, 479). Another example is Ruba Salih (2003), who wrote an ethnography on Moroccan women in Italy and their home-making practices. Salih's conceptual focus, however, is on gender and transnationalism rather than material culture. Likewise, Katie Walsh's study of British expatriates in Dubai is concerned with home-making through a material culture lens. In focusing on a painting, a plastic bowl and a DVD, Walsh shows how fluid and multiple the concept of 'home as process' can be among expatriates (Walsh 2006).

In contrast to the aforementioned studies, Paul Basu and Simon Coleman have a decidedly conceptual focus, elaborated in 'Migrant worlds, material cultures', their introduction to a special issue of the journal *Mobilities* (Basu and Coleman 2008). Here, Basu and Coleman attempt to bring together material culture studies and migration studies. This suggestion is taken up by Kathy Burrell (2008a, 2008b), who writes about the movement and materiality of Polish migrants in the UK, looking at four key intersections: passports, car and coach journeys, suitcases, and laptops in airport lounges.

Özlem Savaş (2014) makes a vital contribution to the interconnected research fields of migration research and materiality by examining the repertoire and relevance of objects, home interiors and everyday aesthetics among Turkish migrants in Vienna. An anthropologist, Savaş portrays the emergence of a specific Turkish-Viennese 'taste diaspora' through a profound and systematic empirical analysis of transcultural entanglements and distinctions of materiality in migration.

Empirical studies looking at bureaucracies have also proved stimulating for thing-oriented migration research. Documents – visas and passports in particular – have not only a material but also a symbolic, affective and embodied relation to migrant existences (Mathur 2017). Matthew Hull (2012) focuses on the agency of such documents by studying urban governance in Pakistan as a material practice; Anna Tuckett (2018) examines the impact of bureaucratic paperwork on the precarious status of migrants in Italy; and a number of other studies look at the material culture of bureaucracy and its affective dimensions and socialities (e.g., Navaro-Yashin 2007, 2012; Yaron 2009; Cabot 2012; Laszczkowski and Reeves 2017; Borrelli and Andreetta 2019).

A programmatic approach aiming to broaden the perspective of migration research is pursued by Maja Povrzanović Frykman (2016a, 2016b). She proposes 'that research on migrants should not prioritise ideas and discourses of identity and belonging; rather, it should pay equal attention to the practices and lived experiences involving objects that migrants carry, send, receive and use across borders' (Povrzanović Frykman 2016a, 43). Here, Povrzanović Frykman brings Bourdieu's (1977) double-faced concept of habitus and hexis into focus. She refers to Ghassan Hage (2013), who interprets hexis as a kind of fusion 'between "having" (possessing an object) and "being" (capable of an activity that lends the sense of normalcy)', and emphasises how helpful this conceptualisation is in theorising material culture (Povrzanović Frykman

2016a, 48). For Povrzanović Frykman, the materiality of habitus is reflected in elementary activities such as preparing tea, coffee or meals. Fractures of habitus reflect existential changes due to migration conditions, and such fractures of habitus become visible when practices are examined. Povrzanović Frykman offers three theoretical impulses for an ethnographic, material approach to migration research: 'the presence of objects in another location, the continuity of practices perceived as normal, and the practice-based feeling of emplacement' (Povrzanović Frykman 2016a, 53).

In focusing on emotional dynamics, Maruška Svašek offers another important conceptual approach. She employs the terms 'transit', 'transition' and 'transformation' (2007, 2010, 2012a, 2012b) to grasp the different processes of object and subject mobility, namely the movement of people and things through time and space, the transit-related changes in the meaning, value and emotional efficacy of objects and images, and the transit-related changes of subjects (2012b, 5).

The archaeologist Philipp W. Stockhammer also looks at the processes of how things are transformed and changed: 'First, based on the continuously changing perception of the objects; second, the change of objects through time without human interference; third, the transformations of objects due to human practices' (Stockhammer 2017, 318). By focusing on diverging and contested perspectives, on material practices, and on changes, this perspective allows for a dynamic and transformative understanding of different dimensions of material culture that goes beyond symbolic fixations of 'the other'.

One researcher who has made an outstanding contribution to the dialogue between material culture studies and migration studies is Sandra H. Dudley. Her monograph *Materialising Exile: Material culture and embodied experience among Karenni refugees in Thailand* (2010) is based on an intensive ethnographic field study of refugees in a camp on the Thai border. Dudley's work is ground-breaking in its analytical connection between displacement and materiality, the effects and meaning of exilic objects, and the corporeality and emotionality of refugees. Using her engagement with displaced objects in museums, Dudley has developed a displacement anthropology which she outlines in *Displaced Things in Museums and Beyond* (2021). Here, Dudley aims to put the perspective of people in exile in parallel with the perspective of exilic objects themselves. Objects which have been dislocated or exiled and found their way into a museum become methodological respondents, and through this process agency, distinction and dignity become recognisable in people *and* things. In her work, insights into the relationships between humans and things are also gained through a combination of analytical perspectives: ritual studies, museum anthropology and material culture studies.

A number of works from the field of contemporary archaeology, especially those strongly influenced by material cultural studies, also offer significant theoretical and methodological approaches for looking at (forced) migration as material migration (e.g., Rathje and Murphy 2001; González-Ruibal 2019). These works are concerned with legacies and traces from the recent past. Archaeology has always been concerned with remnants and has developed its expertise in analysis, documentation and reconstruction of what remains. This expertise is now being applied to the field of contemporary forced migration. On escape routes and in camps, anthropological archaeologists recover objects such as bottles, food containers, clothing and shoes. These objects allow for the forensic reconstruction of survival and escape conditions, making existential states of emergency visible that are otherwise neglected and hidden from public view (see De León 2013, 2015; Squire 2014; Soto 2016; Hamilakis 2018; Blake and Schon 2019; Hicks and Mallet 2019; Tsoni 2020, and the contributions by Sarah Mallet and Louise Fowler and by Ayşe Şanlı in this volume).

Materialising migration studies: challenges and aspirations

In researching migration through material culture, these researchers are shifting the focus from 'identity-talk' to 'object-talk' in order to better understand the complexity of migrants' lives (Povrzanović Frykman 2016a, 54). As these studies show, taking materiality seriously opens up new methodological and analytical approaches and enables new perspectives in migration research. Studying camp and border infrastructures or the rule of paper in the bureaucratic system of border regimes, for example, allows us to rethink the governance of migration and attempts to control people's mobilities (Jansen 2013). Furthermore, using materiality as a lens allows us to focus on people's everyday practices and experiences, and on their relationships to humans, things and places. Thus, these approaches help reveal the processes and transformations of people and things, and their interrelationships. Studying moving objects shifts migrants' everyday transnational lives, their 'palpable connections' (Povrzanović Frykman and Humbracht 2013), and their senses, emotions and affects to the centre of scholarly attention.

The multiplicity of perspectives and approaches to the materiality of migration is also evident in this volume. This diversity is a reflection not only of the diversity of materiality itself, but also of external factors, including the disciplinary backgrounds of the researchers – anthropology, archaeology, sociology, curatorial studies – and the contexts of research. Although these diverse approaches and perspectives posed several challenges to the preparation of this volume, we see them as contributing to a more nuanced, in-depth understanding of multiple, and sometimes conflicting, conceptions and engagements of things in (forced) migration and beyond. In this volume, we aim not only to introduce the reader to multiple possibilities of applying materiality as a lens in migration research, and to the insights which the different approaches open up, but also to advance the general understanding of materiality and migration in the social sciences and humanities. Moreover, it is our ambition to consider how things matter beyond their 'meaning' in a merely symbolic sense.

The volume is in four parts, each offering a particular perspective on the materiality of migration: temporality, methods, emotions and relatedness, and place-making. Its thematic emphases are necessarily a selection; there are other topics that deserve to be explored in depth through an object-oriented perspective on migration, such as gender, age, religion, social class, and border and migration regimes. As the four parts draw on specific concepts and debates in different but interconnected strands of migration research, each will start with a short introduction, carving out the potentialities of adding materiality as a perspective, and outlining the related chapters in more detail. Here we give a brief overview of the book's structure.

Part I, 'Transient foundations: on materiality and temporality', differs slightly from the others in approach and structure. The two contributions in this part take a more conceptually informed starting point and introduce the reader to the concepts of 'temporal partitioning' (Ramsay) and 'carceral junctions' (Turner). Temporality is a decisive aspect of the relationship between materiality and (forced) migration, and it emerges as a recurring theme in each chapter in this volume. Thus, in including references to all chapters in the volume, this introduction provides insights into the interconnection between materiality and temporality from different perspectives.

Part II, 'Materialising methods: applying things in (forced) migration research', centres on methods and ethical challenges in material (forced) migration research. The contributions focus on archaeological approaches (Mallet and Fowler), the possibilities and constraints of using things in anthropological fieldwork (Höpfner, Yi-Neumann), and on objects in exhibitions on migration (Şanlı).

Part III, 'Moving things: objects, emotions and relatedness in (forced) migration', takes as its point of departure the double meaning of 'moving things': firstly as objects moving through space and time, and secondly as objects arousing emotions and affects. These chapters show how materiality enables the construction and continuation of relationships across space and time (Svašek, Savaş), how things transform into social relationships (Verdasco), and how things reflect not only uncertainty but also an enduring sense of belonging and hope for the future (Suerbaum, Suhr).

Part IV, 'Taking and making place: engaging things', centres on how people make places in different migratory contexts. From buying and collecting local popular art (Barber) to altering the physical landscape of camps (Ghandour-Demiri and Passas) to everyday routines and practices like cooking (Guevara González), these chapters show how people on the move shape places and build relationships with and through people and things.

Notes

1 Agamben refers to Pompeius Festus's 'De verborum significatu' (On the significance of words), in which the etymology of the term 'homo sacer' is explained.
2 'You are different with a gun in your hand; the gun is different with you holding it. You are another subject because you hold the gun; the gun is another object because it has entered into a relationship with you' (Latour 1999, 179).

References

Agamben, Giorgio. 1998. *Homo Sacer: Sovereign power and bare life*. Translated by Daniel Heller-Roazen. Stanford, CA: Stanford University Press.

Al-Jundi Pfaff, Samah and Katharina Brunner. 2020. 'The piece of cloth'. Accessed 11 August 2021. https://materialitaet-migration.de/en/objekte/the-piece-of-cloth/.

Appadurai, Arjun, ed. 1986. *The Social Life of Things: Commodities in cultural perspective*. Cambridge: Cambridge University Press.

Auslander, Leora and Tara Zahra, eds. 2018. *Objects of War: The material culture of conflict and displacement*. Ithaca, NY: Cornell University Press.

Bakewell, Oliver. 2008. 'Research beyond the categories: The importance of policy irrelevant research into forced migration', *Journal of Refugee Studies* 21(4): 432–53. https://doi.org/10.1093/jrs/fen042.

Basu, Paul and Simon Coleman. 2008. 'Introduction: Migrant worlds, material cultures', *Mobilities* 3(3): 313–30. https://doi.org/10.1080/17450100802376753.

Baur, Joachim. 2009. *Die Musealisierung der Migration: Einwanderungsmuseen und die Inszenierung der multikulturellen Nation* [The musealisation of migration: immigration museums and the staging of the multicultural nation]. Bielefeld: transcript Verlag.

Bennett, Jane. 2010. *Vibrant Matter: A political ecology of things*. Durham, NC: Duke University Press.

Blake, Emma and Robert Schon. 2019. 'The archaeology of contemporary migrant journeys in western Sicily', *Journal of Mediterranean Archaeology* 32(2): 173–94. http://dx.doi.org/10.1558/jma.40579.

Blunt, Robert W. 2013. 'Kenyatta's lament: Oaths and the transformation of ritual ideologies in colonial Kenya', *HAU: Journal of Ethnographic Theory* 3(3): 167–93. https://doi.org/10.14318/hau3.3.008.

Borrelli, Lisa Marie and Sophie Andreetta. 2019. 'Introduction: Governing migration through paperwork', *Journal of Legal Anthropology* 3(2): 1–9. https://doi.org/10.3167/jla.2019.030201.

Bourdieu, Pierre. 1977. *Outline of a Theory of Practice*. Translated by Richard Nice. Cambridge: Cambridge University Press.

Bräunlein, Peter J. 2019. 'Studying material religion from a non-anthropocentric perspective? Some considerations on new materialisms', *Material Religion* 15(5): 622–3. https://doi.org/10.1080/17432200.2019.1666582.

Bryant, Levi R. 2011. *The Democracy of Objects*. Ann Arbor, MI: Open Humanities Press.

Burrell, Kathy. 2008a. 'Managing, learning and sending: The material lives and journeys of Polish women in Britain', *Journal of Material Culture* 13(1): 63–83. https://doi.org/10.1177%2F1359183507086219.

Burrell, Kathy. 2008b. 'Materialising the border: Spaces of mobility and material culture in migration from post-socialist Poland', *Mobilities* 3(3), 353–73. https://doi.org/10.1080/17450100802376779.

Cabot, Heath. 2012. 'The governance of things: Documenting limbo in the Greek asylum procedure', *PoLAR: Political and Legal Anthropology Review* 35(1): 11–29. https://doi.org/10.1111/j.1555-2934.2012.01177.x.

Çağlar, Ayşe and Nina Glick Schiller, eds. 2018. *Migrants and City-Making: Dispossession, displacement, and urban regeneration*. Durham, NC, and London: Duke University Press.

Caronia, Letizia and Luigina Mortari. 2015. 'The agency of things: How spaces and artefacts organize the moral order of an intensive care unit', *Social Semiotics* 25(4): 401–22. https://doi.org/10.1080/10350330.2015.1059576.

Cooper-Knock, Sarah-Jane. 2017. 'Beyond Agamben: Sovereignty, policing and "permissive space" in South Africa, and beyond', *Theoretical Criminology* 22(1): 22–41.

Csikszentmihalyi, Mihaly and Eugene Rochberg-Halton. 1981. *The Meaning of Things: Domestic symbols and the self*. Cambridge: Cambridge University Press.

De León, Jason. 2013. 'Undocumented migration, use wear, and the materiality of habitual suffering in the Sonoran Desert', *Journal of Material Culture* 18(4): 321–45. https://doi.org/10.1177%2F1359183513496489.

De León, Jason. 2015. *The Land of Open Graves: Living and dying on the migrant trail*. Oakland: University of California Press.

Dolphijn, Rick and Iris van der Tuin. 2012. *New Materialism: Interviews and cartographies*. Ann Arbor, MI: Open Humanities Press.

Dudley, Sandra H. 2010. *Materialising Exile: Material culture and embodied experience among Karenni refugees in Thailand*. New York and Oxford: Berghahn Books.

Dudley, Sandra H. 2021. *Displaced Things in Museums and Beyond: Loss, liminality and hopeful encounters*. Abingdon: Routledge.

Dziuban, Zuzanna and Ewa Stańczyk. 2020. 'Introduction: The surviving thing: Personal objects in the aftermath of violence', *Journal of Material Culture* 25(4): 381–90. https://doi.org/10.1177%2F1359183520954514.

Gaibazzi, Paolo, Alice Bellagamba and Stephan Dünnwald, eds. 2017. *EurAfrican Borders and Migration Management: Political cultures, contested spaces, and ordinary lives*. New York: Palgrave Macmillan.

Gell, Alfred. 1998. *Art and Agency: An anthropological theory*. Oxford: Clarendon Press.

González-Ruibal, Alfredo. 2019. *An Archaeology of the Contemporary Era*. London: Routledge.

Hage, Ghassan. 2013. 'Eavesdropping on Bourdieu's philosophers', *Thesis Eleven* 114(1): 76–93. https://doi.org/10.1177%2F0725513612463036.

Hamilakis, Yannis. 2016. 'Archaeologies of forced and undocumented migration', *Journal of Contemporary Archaeology* 3(2): 121–39. http://dx.doi.org/10.1558/jca.32409.

Hamilakis, Yannis. 2018. 'Introduction: Archaeologies of forced and undocumented migration'. In *The New Nomadic Age: Archaeologies of forced and undocumented migration*, edited by Yannis Hamilakis, 1–19. Sheffield: Equinox.

Henare, Amiria, Martin Holbraad and Sari Wastell, eds. 2006. *Thinking through Things: Theorising artefacts ethnographically*. Hoboken, NJ: Taylor & Francis.

Hicks, Dan. 2010. 'The material-cultural turn: Event and effect'. In *The Oxford Handbook of Material Culture Studies*, edited by Dan Hicks and Mary C. Beaudry, 25–98. Oxford: Oxford University Press.

Hicks, Dan. 2020. *The Brutish Museums: The Benin bronzes, colonial violence and cultural restitution*. London: Pluto Press.
Hicks, Dan and Sarah Mallet. 2019. *Lande: The Calais 'Jungle' and beyond*. Bristol: Bristol University Press.
Holmes, Seth M. and Heide Castañeda. 2016. 'Representing the "European refugee crisis" in Germany and beyond: Deservingness and difference, life and death', *American Ethnologist* 43(1): 12–24. https://doi.org/10.1111/amet.12259.
Hoskins, Janet. 1998. *Biographical Objects: How things tell the stories of people's lives*. London: Routledge.
Hoskins, Janet. 2006. 'Agency, biography and objects'. In *Handbook of Material Culture*, edited by Christopher Tilley, Webb Keane, Susanne Koechler-Fogden, Mike Rowlands and Patricia Spyer, 74–84. London: Sage.
Hull, Matthew S. 2012. 'Documents and bureaucracy', *Annual Review of Anthropology* 41(1): 251–67. https://doi.org/10.1146/annurev.anthro.012809.104953.
Jansen, Stef. 2013. 'People and things in the ethnography of borders: Materialising the division of Sarajevo', *Social Anthropology* 21(1): 23–37. https://doi.org/10.1111/1469-8676.12001.
Kopytoff, Igor. 1986. 'The cultural biography of things: Commoditization as process'. In *The Social Life of Things: Commodities in cultural perspective*, edited by Arjun Appadurai, 64–91. Cambridge: Cambridge University Press.
Laszczkowski, Mateusz and Madeleine Reeves, eds. 2017. *Affective States: Entanglements, suspensions, suspicions*. Oxford: Berghahn Books.
Latour, Bruno. 1999. *Pandora's Hope: Essays on the reality of science studies*. Cambridge, MA: Harvard University Press.
Latour, Bruno. 2005. *Reassembling the Social: An introduction to actor-network-theory*. Oxford: Oxford University Press.
Malinowski, Bronislaw. 1922. *Argonauts of the Western Pacific: An account of native enterprise and adventure in the archipelagoes of Melanesian New Guinea*. London: George Routledge and Sons.
Mata-Codesal, Diana and Maria Abranches, eds. 2018. *Food Parcels in International Migration: Intimate connections*. Cham: Palgrave Macmillan.
Mathur, Nayanika. 2017. 'Bureaucracy'. In *The Cambridge Encyclopedia of Anthropology*, edited by Felix Stein, Sian Lazar, Matei Candea, Hildegard Diemberger, Joel Robbins, Andrew Sanchez and Rupert Stasch. Cambridge: Cambridge University Press. http://doi.org/10.29164/17bureaucracy.
Mauss, Marcel. [1923/1924] 2002. *The Gift: The form and reason for exchange in archaic societies*. Translated by W. D. Halls. London and New York: Routledge.
Mertus, Julie A., Jasmina Tesanovic, Habiba Metikos and Rada Boric, eds. 1997. *The Suitcase: Refugee voices from Bosnia and Croatia*. Berkeley: University of California Press.
Miller, Daniel. 2008. 'Material culture'. In *The SAGE Handbook of Cultural Analysis*, edited by Tony Bennett and John Frow, 271–90. London: Sage.
Miller, Daniel. 2009. *Stuff*. New York: Wiley.
Navaro-Yashin, Yael. 2007. 'Make-believe papers, legal forms and the counterfeit: Affective interactions between documents and people in Britain and Cyprus', *Anthropological Theory* 7(1): 79–98. https://doi.org/10.1177%2F1463499607074294.
Navaro-Yashin, Yael. 2012. *The Make-Believe Space: Affective geography in a postwar polity*. Durham, NC: Duke University Press.
Owens, Patricia. 2009. 'Reclaiming "bare life"? Against Agamben on refugees', *International Relations* 23(4): 567–82. https://doi.org/10.1177%2F0047117809350545.
Pellander, Saara and Noora Kotilainen. 2017. '(Not) looking like a refugee: Visual memories of refugeeness and the figure of "the iPhone man"'. Accessed 12 August 2021. https://www.law.ox.ac.uk/research-subject-groups/centre-criminology/centreborder-criminologies/blog/2017/06/not-looking.
Povrzanović Frykman, Maja. 2016a. 'Conceptualising continuity: A material culture perspective on transnational social fields', *Ethnologia Fennica* 43: 43—56.
Povrzanović Frykman, Maja. 2016b. 'Sensitive objects of humanitarian aid: Corporeal memories and affective continuities'. In *Sensitive Objects: Affect and material culture*, edited by Jonas Frykman and Maja Povrzanović Frykman, 79–104. Lund: Nordic Academic Press.
Povrzanović Frykman, Maja and Michael Humbracht. 2013. 'Making palpable connections: Objects in migrants' transnational lives', *Ethnologia Scandinavica: A Journal for Nordic Ethnology* 43: 47–67.

Ramadan, Adam. 2013. 'Spatialising the refugee camp', *Transactions of the Institute of British Geographers* 38(1): 65–77. https://doi.org/10.1111/j.1475-5661.2012.00509.x.

Rathje, William L. and Cullen Murphy. 2001. *Rubbish! The archaeology of garbage*. Tucson: University of Arizona Press.

Salih, Ruba. 2003. *Gender in Transnationalism: Home, longing and belonging among Moroccan migrant women*. London: Routledge.

Savaş, Özlem. 2014. 'Taste diaspora: The aesthetic and material practice of belonging', *Journal of Material Culture* 19(2): 185–208. https://doi.org/10.1177/1359183514521922.

Shaviro, Steven. 2015. 'Consequences of panpsychism'. In *The Nonhuman Turn*, edited by Richard Grusin, 19–44. Minneapolis: University of Minnesota Press.

Soto, Gabriella. 2016. 'Place making in non-places: Migrant graffiti in rural highway box culverts', *Journal of Contemporary Archaeology* 3(2): 174–95. http://dx.doi.org/10.1558/jca.31830.

Spencer, Sarah and Anna Triandafyllidou. 2020. *Migrants with Irregular Status in Europe: Evolving conceptual and policy challenges*. Cham: Springer Open.

Squire, Vicki. 2014. 'Desert "trash": Posthumanism, border struggles, and humanitarian politics', *Political Geography* 39: 11–21. https://doi.org/10.1016/j.polgeo.2013.12.003.

Stockhammer, Philipp W. 2017. 'Afterword: The pot and the archaeologist – changing each other in an (un-)happy marriage?' In *Mobility and Pottery Production: Archaeological and anthropological perspectives*, edited by Caroline Heitz and Regine Stapfer, 315–20. Leiden: Sidestone Press.

Strathern, Marilyn. 1988. *The Gender of the Gift: Problems with women and problems with society in Melanesia*. Berkeley: University of California Press.

Svašek, Maruška. 2007. *Anthropology, Art and Cultural Production*. London: Pluto Press.

Svašek, Maruška. 2010. 'Improvising in a world of movement: Transit, transition and transformation'. In *Cultural Expression, Creativity and Innovation*, edited by Helmut Anheier and Yudhishthir Raj Isar, 62–77. London: Sage.

Svašek, Maruška, ed. 2012a. *Moving Subjects, Moving Objects: Transnationalism, cultural production and emotions*. New York: Berghahn Books.

Svašek, Maruška. 2012b. 'Introduction: Affective moves: Transit, transition and transformation'. In *Moving Subjects, Moving Objects: Transnationalism, cultural production and emotions*, edited by Maruška Svašek, 1–40. New York: Berghahn Books.

Svirsky, Marcelo and Simone Bignall, eds. 2012. *Agamben and Colonialism*. Edinburgh: Edinburgh University Press.

Tsoni, Ionna Wagner. 2020. 'Trash/traces: Lives adrift along the border', *KONESH [on the politics of space and cultural interventions]* 2. Accessed 12 August 2021. http://www.diva-portal.org/smash/get/diva2:1450503/FULLTEXT01.pdf.

Tuckett, Anna. 2018. *Rules, Paper, Status: Migrants and precarious bureaucracy in contemporary Italy*. Stanford, CA: Stanford University Press.

Turner, Simon. 2015. 'What is a refugee camp? Explorations of the limits and effects of the camp', *Journal of Refugee Studies* 29(2): 139–48. https://doi.org/10.1093/jrs/fev024.

Vertovec, Steven. 2007. 'Super-diversity and its implications', *Ethnic and Racial Studies* 30(6): 1024–54. https://doi.org/10.1080/01419870701599465.

Walsh, Katie. 2006. 'British expatriate belongings: Mobile homes and transnational homing', *Home Cultures* 3(2): 123–44. http://dx.doi.org/10.2752/174063106778053183.

Werbner, Pnina. 2005. 'The materiality of late modern diasporas: Between aesthetics and "real" politics'. In *Les Diasporas: 2000 ans d'histoire*, edited by Lisa Anteby-Yemini, William Berthomière and Gabriel Sheffer, 469–87. Rennes: Presses Universitaires de Rennes.

Yaron, Hadas. 2009. '"Your papers or your life": The significance of documents in the life experiences of African refugees in Israel', *New Proposals* 3(1): 7–14.

Part I

Transient foundations: on temporality and materiality

Introduction

Antonie Fuhse

The two main chapters of Part I, 'Transient foundations', explicitly focus on the times and temporalities of migration and the interconnectedness of temporality and materiality. Before we take a closer look at the different approaches to time in migration studies, we would like to state that migrants' temporalities should not be understood or framed as essentially different than those of non-migrants (see Ramsay 2019). Global and local power relations shape time differently for people categorised along the lines of migration status, citizenship, gender, age and so on. Time as an analytical lens on the materiality of (forced) migration adds an important perspective on power and inequalities.

Alongside 'place' and 'space', 'time' is a heavily discussed topic in anthropology and the social sciences more generally. Here, we are not interested in summarising these various different views about the nature of time (see Gell 1992; Bear 2014, 2016; Adam 1990; Munn 1992; James and Mills 2005), but in starting simply with the assumption that time is multiple and thus the 'times of migration' (Cwerner 2001) are multifaceted. Since Saulo Cwerner (1999, 2001), amongst others, first advocated for a greater focus on time in migration studies over two decades ago, much research has been carried out. Today, the temporalities of migration have been approached from a number of different perspectives (Meeus 2012; Griffiths et al. 2013; Mavroudi et al. 2017; Baas and Yeoh 2019). Although it is impossible to draw sharp boundaries between the diverging ways time has been conceptualised in migration studies, we have identified three key threads which arise in the chapters that follow: time as a future(s) that is aspired to, hoped for or uncertain; time as a temporal experience; and time as reflected (and negotiated) in memory and nostalgia.

These approaches are, of course, interconnected. For example, aspirations for the future influence what kind of experiences people have in the present, and what people imagine for the future is inspired by memories of the past and by present experiences (see Griffiths 2014; Brun 2015, 24). We now turn to these three areas of research and relate them to our focus on materiality by connecting them to the chapters throughout this volume.

Future(s): aspirations and uncertainties

In many studies, migration or plans for migrating are directly related to how people try to shape their futures (Cole 2010; Vigh 2009). To be able to act, to invest in their current relationships and to form new ones, people need to be able to have some vision of their future, some idea of what will happen next in life (Griffiths et al. 2013; Griffiths 2014). Thus, the future is connected to issues of agency – and migration itself can be seen as 'an act of agency actively employed in order to break stasis and generate change' (Griffiths et al. 2013).[1] Studies in this area often apply concepts of aspiration, desire (Carling and Collins 2018; Collins 2017; Boccagni 2017) or imagination (Baas 2010; Salazar 2011). Carling and Collins point out that the term 'migration aspirations' has been used in several studies to describe 'the conviction that leaving would be better than staying' (Carling and Collins 2018, 915). As Georgina Ramsay argues in her chapter here, migration is thus related to one's lack or loss of prospects, to a desire to escape an uncertain future, and as a way to create 'futures of possibility'. A focus on aspirations, imaginations and hopes draws attention to the fact that the physical movement of people, either within or across borders, should not be the starting point for research on mobilities. According to Ramsay, researchers should look at the broader forces that 'produce migrants' and uneven access to futures of possibility, an issue that she describes through the concept of 'temporal partitioning'.

What people try to achieve by becoming mobile, what they imagine as the outcome or, as Baas phrases it, the 'arrival points' (2010, 6) of migration are grounded in the social context (Carling and Collins 2018) and, amongst other things, are shaped by ideas on what course life should take. Research shows that decisions to migrate, return or move on are connected to events in the lives of mobile people themselves and of those they are connected to (e.g. Findlay et al. 2015; Kirk et al. 2017; Robertson et al. 2018; Bailey 2009; Kõu et al. 2017; Fuhse 2021). Such important events include marriage, childbirth and retirement, as illustrated by Rachel Barber in this volume. In relation to one's life course, mobility is often discussed as an important marker of transition from youth to adulthood (Robertson et al. 2018, 203). Consequently, ideas of 'growing up' and becoming an adult are increasingly shaped by 'aspirations and imaginaries of transnational mobility' (Robertson et al. 2018, 204).

Looking further into the interrelationship between the future and mobility has brought forward another important theme in migration research: the inability to know or even anticipate the future. Researchers working with refugees and asylum seekers have shown how the temporal uncertainty created by migration policies also serve as a tool of governmentality and a technique of power (Griffiths 2014, 2005; Horst and Grabska 2015; Hicks and Mallet 2019). Here, the state and its immigration policy shape people's temporal frames and their (in)ability to gain control over their future or to plan and structure time in general (Anderson 2007; Robertson and Runganaikaloo 2014; Griffiths 2014; Robertson 2014; Brun 2015; Ramsay 2017; Thorshaug and Brun 2019). People categorised as refugees or asylum seekers often have no temporal frame and no control over the timing of events such as being granted a residence permit, being transferred to a particular place, or even being deported (Griffiths 2014; Brun 2015). They live in a state of 'protracted displacement' (Brun 2015; Brun and Fábos 2015) characterised by uncertainty, waiting, and feelings of being stuck, not only in place, but also in time (Jefferson, Turner and Jensen 2019) – they are, in other words, 'trapped in the present' (Brun 2015, 19).

Similarly, migrants often find themselves 'living temporary' or, expressed differently, of living with the knowledge that one may not be able to stay. Migrants may be stuck with a temporary status, they may lack perspectives in the host country, or they may plan to return or to move on (see Baas 2010; Robertson 2014). As Bailey et al. show, this temporariness can become a 'permanent temporariness' (Bailey et al. 2002, 139; Collins and Shubin 2015, 100). In this situation, migrants find themselves 'living in limbo' (Robertson and Runganaikaloo 2013, 2014; Cabot 2012), 'in between' (Baas 2010), or in a state of 'liminality'[2] (Griffiths 2014, 2003; Malkki 1992). Griffiths, for example, argues that this experience should not be understood as inherently negative, but can offer 'opportunities to enjoy freedom otherwise circumscribed' and outside of familial expectations (2014, 2003).

Materiality as a lens offers important insights into people's aspirations, hopes and outlooks for the future. A material object, the right passport or paperwork, can open up futures in other places, and the lack of these objects can limit a migrant's movements, force them to move on (again), or lead them to being deported or moved to another facility (Tuckett 2018). Material objects can signify an uncertain future or display the aspiration to create a life in a new context (see Magdalena Suerbaum, this volume).

There is an important interrelationship between temporality and materiality in humanitarian aid infrastructures. The 'crisis' narrative and its articulation in humanitarian aid strategies lacks a long-term perspective (Hicks and Mallet 2019; Ramsay 2019). Through it, the infrastructures that are constructed in the humanitarian sector are meant to be short-term fixes, rather than long-term, structural solutions (Hicks and Mallet 2019, 64; Turner in this volume). The materiality that results from this short-term thinking adds to migrants' feelings of temporariness. But as several chapters in this volume show, and as we will elaborate in the following pages, migrants are not just fixed in the short term, they also find ways to make a life in uncertainty and waiting, and these ways often centre on material practices.

Temporal experiences: waiting and stuckness

Everybody experiences time – as crawling when we're bored, as running when we need to finish something important, as the right time or the wrong time to do something. How people experience, perceive and understand time varies according to the different conceptualisations of time within and between societies (Gell 1992; Bear 2014, 2016), and along the lines of age, gender, social position and so on (Adam 1994, 503).

Movement is one of several factors in an individual's specific experience(s) of time, and we should therefore be cautious in discussing migrants' temporal experiences as essentially different from those of non-migrants (Ramsay 2019). Nevertheless, looking at the research on displacement, refugees and asylum seekers, it becomes apparent that many have similar temporal experiences: boredom (Brun 2015), waiting[3] (Griffiths 2014), being stuck (Jefferson et al. 2019). Focusing on different 'sites of confinement', like prisons and refugee camps, Jefferson, Turner and Jensen show how these places create 'stuckness' and how confinement is both spatial and temporal (2019, 2). They understand 'stuckness' as the way confinement is experienced, sensed and lived (2019, 2), and as 'the sense of not making progress, of not seeing a future' (Jefferson et al. 2019, 3). Similarly, Brun writes about waiting as 'a feeling of being out of sync with time' (2015, 24). Asylum seekers and refugees are often not allowed to work (Griffiths 2014, 1996) and thus their days 'lack content' (Brun 2015, 23). Another temporal experience that can be caused by movement is that of asynchronicity (Cwerner 2001, 22), a feeling of being out of touch with familiar temporal (and spatial) orientations and rhythms, and of living in 'strange' times (and places) (Cwerner 2001).

Mobile people are not just thrown into these temporal experiences. They develop different tactics to deal with these experiences and to try to shape their lives. Differentiating between forms of waiting (Gasparini 1995; Brun 2015; Griffiths 2014), researchers have shown that it is not necessarily passive, empty and negative, it can also be productive and active (Griffiths 2014, 1996; Brun 2015). In this volume, Simon Turner understands the act of waiting itself as agentic. Camps, he argues, do not completely preclude refugees from seeing a future; as 'carceral junctions' camps enable glimpses of possible futures through hope. Indeed, a number of authors use hope as a concept to show how people living in conditions of protracted displacement or confinement deal with their experiences (Brun 2015; Turner 2015; Jefferson et al. 2019), how they maintain a sense of potential (Brun 2015, 24), and how they give meaning and purpose to what they are experiencing in the present (Griffiths 2014, 1996).

A focus on materiality and on how migrants use material objects reveals how they experience and try to change and negotiate time. People living in camps build gardens and informal economies to create a sense of home or to find ways to pass the time (Nada Ghandour-Demiri and Petros Passas in this volume). The days in refugee accommodation are often structured by staff who decide when it is time to shower, to eat and to sleep. Around these timetables, refugees develop everyday material tactics and strategies, like taking care of the kitchen, or cooking to pass the time (chapters by Yaatsil Guevara González and Andrea Verdasco in this volume). Thus, material practices enable the establishment and continuity of familiar practices, of routines and rhythms in daily life (see Povrzanović Frykman and Humbracht 2013; Povrzanović Frykman 2016), and of means for coping with prolonged waiting and uncertainty.

Mobile phones, laptops and other technologies are used to bridge the spatial and temporal distance from relatives living far away and to create feelings of co-presence (Baldassar 2008; Baldassar et al. 2016), simultaneity and continuity. But these technologies also create distinct temporal experiences and affects; they call attention to distance when people communicate with family and friends in different time zones, or when connection issues show co-presence to be an illusion (Maruška Svašek in this volume; Svašek 2018).

Memory and nostalgia

A third perspective on time in migration studies emerges if we look into works on memory, nostalgia and mobility/migration (Hage 2010; Creet 2011; Tošić and Palmberger 2016; Passerini et al. 2020). In their introduction to the volume *Memories on the Move* (2016), Tošić and Palmberger show that movement and memory interplay in several ways: mobility provokes memory, and 'memory practices' – managing photographs, revisiting houses, return visits – enable people 'to make sense of and integrate experiences of (im)mobility across different times and places' (Tošić and Palmberger 2016, 5). Not unlike Hage (2010), they stress the active and enabling effects of nostalgia through concepts like 'memory work' (Tošić and Palmberger 2016, 6) and 'mnemonic practices' (Tošić and Palmberger 2016, 2). For Creet (2011, 3) and Lems (2016, 430), memory and nostalgia have the potential to re-create temporal continuity and stability. Thus, remembering and nostalgia are temporally ambiguous and are not exclusively associated with the past, as often understood in common-sense terms, but are practices that link people's past, present and future (Lems 2016, 430).

Materiality is crucial for mnemonic practices and for remembering. This remembering could take place, for instance, in the form of 'mnemonic objects' (Tošić and Palmberger 2016, 2) that are sometimes carefully chosen and sometimes re-evaluated during the journey (Elena Höpfner in this volume). Materiality also provides continuity in an otherwise unsettled life in Friedemann Yi-Neumann's chapter, in which a cuddly toy becomes a 'companion for life' for a woman in her early thirties.

We also see the opposite in several contributions to this volume: here, materialities and material practices change, things can become less important or left behind, become useless, are taken away. In the study of the materiality of migration these transformations should be considered and framed analytically, not least because the objects that are left behind, the life jackets, the shoes and the backpacks, are often the objects displayed in exhibitions on migration.

Apart from things brought from 'home', things that people purchase or receive in the process of migrating enable them to remember and to create possibilities for 'homely feelings' (Hage 2010, 419). Food is often one of the most important things in this regard (Hage 2010), as we see in the chapters by Andrea Verdasco, Yaatsil Guevara González and Özlem Savaş.

Another connection between the materiality of migration and memory is opened up in the chapter by the archaeologists Sarah Mallet and Louise Fowler. They look at the things that remain after refugee camps have been dismantled and use them to document what happened, to make visible what government narratives try to efface, and to focus attention on what is easily forgotten and neglected in political and collective memories. Like those by Maike Suhr and Ayşe Sanlı, Mallet and Fowler's chapter draws attention to the connection between the materiality of migration and how it is used in exhibitions to tell particular (hi)stories.

The temporal complexity of life, migration and materiality

This overview of approaches to time in migration studies and how these can be related to materiality is not exhaustive. Looking into the varied ways in which time has been approached in the context of migration studies makes it clear that time and materiality are manifold, and are interconnected in manifold ways: the outlook for the future informs material practices, and vice versa, and material practices and materialities signify people's aspirations and hopes, and shape their experiences of time. Material practices enable people to connect themselves to places, people and times, to structure the everyday, and to re-create continuity and familiarity. But, of course, these dynamics do not only hold true in the context of migration and mobility. We would therefore argue that adding temporality and the ability of materials to help signify, shape and create time contributes to a refined understanding of materiality in general. In Parts II–IV, this understanding is complemented by a focus on methodological approaches to materiality, the ability of materiality to stir affects and create relationships, and the roles of and connection between materiality and place-making.

Notes

1 Here, Melanie Griffiths is referring to works by Jennifer Cole (2010) and Daniel Mains (2007).
2 Referring, of course, to Arnold van Gennep (1960) and Victor Turner (1967).
3 For more works on waiting, see Hage (2009) and Janeja and Bandak (2018).

References

Adam, Barbara. 1990. *Time and Social Theory*. Philadelphia: Temple University Press.
Adam, Barbara. 1994. 'Perceptions of time'. In *Companion Encyclopedia of Anthropology*, edited by Tim Ingold, 503–26. Abingdon: Routledge.
Anderson, Bridget. 2007. 'Battles in time: The relation between global and labour mobilities', Working Paper 55, COMPAS Centre on Migration, Policy and Society, University of Oxford.

Baas, Michiel. 2010. *Imagined Mobility: Migration and transnationalism among Indian students in Australia*. London and New York: Anthem Press.

Baas, Michiel and Brenda S. A. Yeoh. 2019. 'Introduction: Migration studies and critical temporalities', *Current Sociology* 67(2): 161–8. https://doi.org/10.1177/0011392118792924.

Bailey, Adrian J. 2009. 'Population geography: Lifecourse matters', *Progress in Human Geography* 33(3): 407–18. https://doi.org/10.1177%2F0309132508096355.

Bailey, Adrian J., Richard A. Wright, Alison Mountz and Ines M. Miyares. 2002. '(Re)producing Salvadoran transnational geographies', *Annals of the Association of American Geographers* 92(1): 125–44. https://doi.org/10.1111/1467-8306.00283.

Baldassar, Loretta. 2008. 'Missing kin and longing to be together: Emotions and the construction of co-presence in transnational relationships'. In *Transnational Families and Emotions*, edited by Maruška Svašek, special issue of *Journal of Intercultural Studies*, 29(3): 247–66. https://doi.org/10.1080/07256860802169196.

Baldassar, Loretta, Mihaela Nedelcu, Laura Merla and Raelene Wilding. 2016. 'ITC-based co-presence in transnational families and communities: Challenging the premise of face-to-face proximity in sustaining relationships', *Global Networks* 16(2): 133–44. https://doi.org/10.1111/glob.12108.

Bear, Laura, ed. 2014. *Doubt, Conflict, Mediation: The anthropology of modern time* (special issue). *Journal of the Royal Anthropological Institute* 20: vii–ix, 3–186.

Bear, Laura. 2016. 'Time as technique', *Annual Review of Anthropology* 45(1): 487–502.

Boccagni, Paolo. 2017. 'Aspirations and the subjective future of migration: Comparing views and desires of the "time ahead" through the narratives of immigrant domestic workers', *Comparative Migration Studies* 5 (art. 4): 1–18. https://doi.org/10.1186/s40878-016-0047-6.

Brun, Cathrine. 2015. 'Active waiting and changing hopes: Toward a time perspective on protracted displacement'. In *Uncertainty and Displacement*, edited by Cindy Horst and Katarzyna Grabska, special issue of *Social Analysis* 59(1): 19–37. https://doi.org/10.3167/sa.2015.590102.

Brun, Cathrine and Anita Fábos. 2015. 'Making homes in limbo? A conceptual framework', *Refuge* 31(1): 5–17. https://doi.org/10.25071/1920-7336.40138.

Cabot, Heath. 2012. 'The governance of things: Documenting limbo in the Greek asylum procedure', *PoLAR: Political and Legal Anthropology Review* 35(1): 11–29. https://doi.org/10.1111/j.1555-2934.2012.01177.x.

Carling, Jørgen and Francis L. Collins. 2018. 'Aspiration, desire and drivers of migration', *Journal of Ethnic and Migration Studies* 44(6): 909–26. https://doi.org/10.1080/1369183X.2017.1384134.

Cole, Jennifer. 2010. *Sex and Salvation: Imagining the future in Madagascar*. Chicago, IL, and London: University of Chicago Press.

Collins, Francis L. 2017. 'Desire as a theory for migration studies: Temporality, assemblage and becoming in the narratives of migrants', *Journal of Ethnic and Migration Studies* 44(6): 964–80. https://doi.org/10.1080/1369183X.2017.1384147.

Collins, Francis L. and Sergei Shubin. 2015. 'Migrant times beyond the life course: The temporalities of foreign English teachers in South Korea', *Geoforum* 62: 96–104. https://doi.org/10.1016/j.geoforum.2015.04.002.

Creet, Julia. 2011. 'Introduction: The migration of memory and memories of migration'. In *Memory and Migration: Multidisciplinary approaches to memory studies*, edited by Julia Creet and Andreas Kitzmann, 3–26. Toronto: University of Toronto Press.

Cwerner, Saulo Brilmann. 1999. 'The times of migration: A study of the temporalities of the immigrant experience'. Unpublished PhD thesis, University of Lancaster.

Cwerner, Saulo Brilmann. 2001. 'The times of migration', *Journal of Ethnic and Migration Studies* 27(1): 7–36. https://doi.org/10.1080/13691830125283.

Findlay, Allan, David McCollum, Rory Coulter and Vernon Gayle. 2015. 'New mobilities across the life course: A framework for analysing demographically linked drivers of migration', *Population, Space and Place* 21(4): 390–402. https://doi.org/10.1002/psp.1956.

Fuhse, Antonie. 2021. *Mobilität und Zeitgestaltung: Junge Wissenschaftler*innen aus Indien und ihre biographische Navigation zwischen Gegenwart und Zukunft*. Göttingen: Göttingen University Press.

Gasparini, Giovanni. 1995. 'On waiting', *Time & Society* 4(1): 29–45. https://doi.org/10.1177%2F0961463X95004001002.

Gell, Alfred. 1992. *The Anthropology of Time: Cultural constructions of temporal maps and images*. Explorations in Anthropology. Oxford: Berg.

Griffiths, Melanie. 2014. 'Out of time: The temporal uncertainties of refused asylum seekers and immigration detainees', *Journal of Ethnic and Migration Studies* 40(12): 1991–2009. https://doi.org/10.1080/1369183X.2014.907737.

Griffiths, Melanie, Ali Rogers and Bridget Anderson. 2013. 'Migration, time and temporalities: Review and prospect', COMPAS Research Resources Paper, March, COMPAS Centre on Migration, Policy and Society, University of Oxford.

Hage, Ghassan, ed. 2009. *Waiting*. Carlton, Victoria: Melbourne University Press.

Hage, Ghassan. 2010. 'Migration, food, memory, and home-building'. In *Memory: Histories, theories, debates*, edited by Susannah Radstone and Bill Schwarz, 416–27. New York: Fordham University Press.

Hicks, Dan and Sarah Mallet. 2019. *Lande: The Calais 'Jungle' and beyond*. Bristol: Bristol University Press.

Horst, Cindy and Katarzyna Grabska. 2015. 'Flight and exile: Uncertainty in the context of conflict-induced displacement', *Social Analysis* 59(1): 1–18. https://doi.org/10.3167/SA.2015.590101.

James, Wendy and David Mills, eds. 2005. *The Qualities of Time: Anthropological approaches*. Oxford: Berg.

Janeja, Manpreet K. and Andreas Bandak, eds. 2018. *Ethnographies of Waiting: Doubt, hope and uncertainty*. London: Bloomsbury Academic.

Jefferson, Andrew, Simon Turner and Steffen Jensen. 2019. 'Introduction: On stuckness and sites of confinement', *Ethnos* 84(1): 1–13. https://doi.org/10.1080/00141844.2018.1544917.

Kirk, Kate, Ellen Bal and Sarah Renee Janssen. 2017. 'Migrants in liminal time and space: An exploration of the experiences of highly skilled Indian bachelors in Amsterdam', *Journal of Ethnic and Migration Studies* 43(16): 2771–87. https://doi.org/10.1080/1369183X.2017.1314600.

Kõu, Anu, Clara H. Mulder and Ajay Bailey. 2017. '"For the sake of the family and future": The linked lives of highly skilled Indian migrants', *Journal of Ethnic and Migration Studies* 43(16): 2788–805. https://doi.org/10.1080/1369183X.2017.1314608.

Lems, Annika. 2016. 'Ambiguous longings: Nostalgia as the interplay among self, time and world', *Critique of Anthropology* 36(6): 419–38. https://doi.org/10.1177%2F0308275X16654549.

Mains, Daniel. 2007. 'Neoliberal times: Progress, boredom, and shame among young men in urban Ethiopia', *American Ethnologist* 34(4): 659–73. https://doi.org/10.1525/ae.2007.34.4.659.

Malkki, Liisa. 1992. 'National geographic: The rooting of peoples and the territorialization of national identity among scholars and refugees', *Cultural Anthropology* 7(1): 24–44. https://doi.org/10.1525/can.1992.7.1.02a00030.

Mavroudi, Elizabeth, Ben Page and Anastasia Christou, eds. 2017. *Timespace and International Migration*. Cheltenham: Edward Elgar Publishing.

Meeus, B. 2012. 'How to "catch" floating populations? Research and the fixing of migration in space and time', *Ethnic and Racial Studies* 35(10): 1775–93. https://doi.org/10.1080/01419870.2012.659272.

Munn, Nancy D. 1992. 'The cultural anthropology of time: A critical essay', *Annual Review of Anthropology* 21: 93–123. https://doi.org/10.1146/annurev.an.21.100192.000521.

Passerini, Luisa, Milica Trakilović and Gabriele Proglio. 2020. *The Mobility of Memory: Migrations and diasporas across European borders*. New York: Berghahn Books.

Povrzanović Frykman, Maja. 2016. 'Conceptualising continuity: A material culture perspective on transnational social fields', *Ethnologia Fennica* 43: 43–56.

Povrzanović Frykman, Maja and Michael Humbracht. 2013. 'Making palpable connections: Objects in migrants' transnational lives', *Ethnologia Scandinavica: A Journal for Nordic Ethnology* 43: 47–67.

Ramsay, Georgina. 2017. 'Incommensurable futures and displaced lives: Sovereignty as control over time', *Public Culture* 29(3(83)): 515–38. https://doi.org/10.1215/08992363-3869584.

Ramsay, Georgina. 2019. 'Time and the other in crisis: How anthropology makes its displaced object', *Anthropological Theory* 20(4): 385–413. https://doi.org/10.1177%2F1463499619840464.

Robertson, Shanthi. 2014. 'Time and temporary migration: The case of temporary graduate workers and working holiday makers in Australia', *Journal of Ethnic and Migration Studies* 40(12): 1915–33. https://doi.org/10.1080/1369183X.2013.876896.

Robertson, Shanthi, Anita Harris and Loretta Baldassar. 2018. 'Mobile transitions: A conceptual framework for researching a generation on the move', *Journal of Youth Studies* 21(2): 203–17. https://doi.org/10.1080/13676261.2017.1362101.

Robertson, Shanthi and Anjena Runganaikaloo. 2014. 'Lives in limbo: Migration experiences in Australia's education–migration nexus', *Ethnicities* 14(2): 208–26. https://doi.org/10.1177%2F1468796813504552.

Salazar, Noel B. 2011. 'The power of imagination in transnational mobilities', *Identities: Global Studies in Culture and Power* 18(6): 576–98. https://doi.org/10.1080/1070289X.2011.672859.

Svašek, Maruška. 2018. 'Ageing kin, proximity and distance: Translocal relatedness as affective practice and movement'. In *Affect in Relation: Families, places, technologies*, edited by Birgit Röttger-Rössler and Jan Slaby, 31–49. Abingdon: Routledge.

Thorshaug, Ragne Øwre and Cathrine Brun. 2019. 'Temporal injustice and re-orientations in asylum reception centres in Norway: Towards critical geographies of architecture in the institution', *Fennia* 197(2): 232–48. http://dx.doi.org/10.11143/fennia.84758.

Tošić, Jelena and Monika Palmberger. 2016. 'Introduction: Memories on the move – experiencing mobility, rethinking the past'. In *Memories on the Move: Experiencing mobility, rethinking the past*, edited by Monika Palmberger and Jelena Tošić, 1–16. London: Palgrave Macmillan.

Tuckett, Anna. 2018. *Rules, Paper, Status: Migrants and precarious bureaucracy in contemporary Italy*. Stanford, CA: Stanford University Press.

Turner, Simon. 2015. '"We wait for miracles": Ideas of hope and future among clandestine Burundian refugees in Nairobi'. In *Ethnographies of Uncertainty in Africa*, edited by Elizabeth Cooper and David Pratten, 173–92. Basingstoke: Palgrave Macmillan.

Turner, Victor. 1967. *The Forest of Symbols: Aspects of Ndembu ritual*. Ithaca, NY, and London: Cornell University Press.

van Gennep, Arnold. 1960. *The Rites of Passage*. Translated by Monika B. Vizedom and Gabrielle L. Caffee. London: Routledge & Kegan Paul.

Vigh, Henrik. 2009. 'Wayward migration: On imagined futures and technological voids', *Ethnos* 74(1): 91–109. https://doi.org/10.1080/00141840902751220.

1

Materialising transformative futures

Georgina Ramsay

Introduction

Your house is on fire. What 10 items do you select to escape with? What is closest to you? What is most important? What is irreplaceable?

So goes an activity that is taught in introductory anthropology classrooms: a hypothetical, designed to get students to critically analyse and reflect on the objects they interact with most and the objects they hold most dear, from the safety of a classroom. It is an exercise that encourages students to think about how the materiality of their worlds reflects their sense of personal identity as well as broader patterns of consumption, accumulation and inequality. But for migrants the hypothetical is often a lived reality. The house on fire is a metaphor for the manifold forces that are pushing and pulling people to move across the globe: economic precarity, political instability, family reunification, generalised violence and insecurity, climate change and environmental disaster. The world is already on fire, and migrants – particularly the unprecedented 80 million people who are, at the time I am writing this, estimated by the United Nations High Commissioner for Refugees (UNHCR) (2020) to be living in a situation of displacement – are the smoke, the warning signal of imminent danger. They are already burned and burning in a world in which it is the most vulnerable who suffer the consequences.

The materiality of migration is an invitation and provocation to think through a world in which it has become normalised, accepted even, that students in a classroom in one part of the world – albeit increasingly closeted and debt-accumulating, probably taught by an underpaid, precarious academic (Navarro 2017) – have an opportunity to discuss global inequalities as a hypothetical while others live them. The student who contemplates their 10 most proximal, important and irreplaceable items contrasts bitterly with the migrant who, depending on the manner and circumstances of their movement, may lose even the most precious material vestiges of background, history and self. The asylum seeker flushes a passport down the toilet in an airport, then destroys the only photograph of family they have with them to ensure that their journey cannot be traced (see Khosravi 2010; Shire 2016). A fire in a refugee camp destroys the few possessions a migrant family have managed to accumulate after fleeing war and violence (see Howden 2020). A resettled refugee, struggling to pay rent in a city they have been relocated to, is evicted, their second-hand furniture abandoned as they ask themselves (see Couch 2011): what next?

But migration is not all loss and violence. Remaking these material worlds is of vital importance for people who have crossed a border and settled in a foreign land, whether they bring with them a shipping container of possessions or the clothes on their back (Brun and Fábos 2015; Dudley 2011; Larsen 2011). It is through objects that people can remake a sense of home, or revive the affects of an older one, across a distant geography. Materiality is a powerful force in the lives of migrants. This is one of the reasons why those spaces – prisons – euphemistically named 'detention centres', 'immigration holding', 'reception camps' amongst others, are so often designed to be depersonalised and depersonalising (Oesch 2019). Prevented from accessing or attaining personal items, migrants within them are constrained from being able to settle and assert themselves materially within these spaces. Even in the ambiguous temporal worlds of camps, where migrants may spend months, years, or even decades, migrants walk a tenuous line between 'making' home and expecting that, at any time, the materials they have used to create that home may be removed or destroyed (Mould 2018). Their home is never their own.

The materiality of transience, then, is political. But while it is tempting to focus on the material life of migrants and migration in terms of their alienation, I want to suggest here that it is through attention to the ways in which migrants coexist with, create meaning through, and especially imagine futures in terms of, materiality that we can bring migrants into a locus of shared humanity, a condition that transcends their migration status and migration experiences. Like so many others across the globe navigating precarity and its various forms of social and economic impoverishment (Tsing 2015), many migrants are aspiring to – indeed seeking – the stability and solidity of a settled life: a home, a daily routine, proximity to family and friends, a clear path to education and employment: put simply, a certain tomorrow. It is these temporal rhythms, as much as political, legal and spatial contexts, that migrants – particularly refugees and asylum seekers – are alienated from (Griffiths 2014; Rotter 2016).

My aim in this chapter is to bring our work on materiality, migration and transience into conversation with temporality. Specifically, I take a zoomed-out view of migration, particularly South to North migration, to explore how global inequalities of aspiration and accumulation structure personal motivations to migrate as well as structural forces of dislocation. I argue that we should not see migration as an exceptional experience of transience. Rather, migration should be seen as an expected response to what I call the *temporal partitioning* that has privileged the futures of some at the expense of the futures of others. Contrary to popular understandings, migration is not the problem to be solved; migrants, and would-be migrants, see movement and mobility as one possible solution to the larger problem of stratified futures. Migration is the smoke billowing from the flames of the real problem, namely global inequality, an object which is much more slippery and difficult to address and contain than migrants themselves.

I will develop this argument in four parts. Throughout, I draw on 10 years of ethnographic data that I have collected with migrants and would-be migrants, mostly from the Democratic Republic of Congo (DRC). Some of the data I refer to here has been collected within the DRC (fieldwork conducted in 2019), other data has been collected with refugees in Uganda (fieldwork conducted in 2013) and resettled refugees in Australia (fieldwork conducted across 2012–14). In the first section of this chapter, 'Futures of decline', I describe the shared condition of precarity, instability and probable deterioration that so many of us, including people I have conducted fieldwork with, are feeling acutely in our contemporary lives. In the second section, 'Temporal partitioning', I describe how political and geographic bordering processes reflect an attempt to preserve the aspirational futures of some at the expense of others. In the third section, 'Material paradoxes', I use a case study of the mobile phone to trace how narratives of advancement produce displacement but also create, potentially, the means to overcome temporal partitioning. In the last section, 'Analytical brackets and anthropological complicity', I call for anthropologists to use critical reflexivity in how we bracket out our objects of study, or else we risk making our research complicit in reinforcing these partitioning logics as natural. We must ourselves move beyond migration as the distinct problem, and consider instead how migrants themselves see mobilisation as transformative possibility, no matter how unlikely or potentially lethal these journeys towards futures of possibility may seem.

Futures of decline

During a car ride in Bukavu, a large city that straddles the DRC–Rwanda border, in July 2019, Joseph, a research informant and friend, took a phone call from his sister, who was living in a refugee settlement, Nakivale, in Uganda. Joseph was trying to control the steering wheel on a road teeming with other cars, motorcycles, people walking, and market wares set out on blankets, and so the conversation with his sister was a short but loud exchange over the speaker of his phone, jiggling in his lap. She was checking in about when to expect a friend, who was coming to Nakivale to deliver new fabric to her; her husband worked as a tailor in the settlement. Soon, Joseph assured her. He would call and find out. From the back seat of the car, his six-year-old daughter Marie uttered an excited but mostly incoherent greeting to her aunt.

When the short conversation was over, there were a few long seconds of silence. Marie returned to a book that she had stashed away. Joseph turned to me and said that he would go there, to Nakivale, one day soon: not to visit, to live. This surprised me, I admit. Not only was Joseph not exactly 'refugee' material according to the UNHCR definition – his life in Bukavu was not under imminent threat of persecution – he was also one of the people I knew in the city who were relatively comfortable in the DRC. He was partway through building a house, he had his own car. He could afford to send his children to the local school. They did not want for food. Having been to the Nakivale refugee settlement in Uganda myself some years earlier, and knowing that life there is not easy, I asked him why he would ever want to 'give up' his life in Bukavu for the sake of becoming a refugee.

He laughed, knowing that what he proposed sounded silly: like going backwards. He assured me he would keep the small material wealth he had accumulated in Bukavu within his family; it did not belong wholly to him, but was already shared with and amongst kin. So too were the anticipated rewards of seeking refugee status in Uganda to be felt by more than just Joseph. The aim of a proposed move to Uganda was, first, to access better education for his children, but secondly, and more importantly, to get the family out of Africa altogether. Joseph was not naïve: he knew the likelihood of being selected for refugee resettlement was extremely low. But by trying he was at least incrementally increasing the likelihood of someone in his extended family being selected, and, in his mind, it only takes one family member being resettled to solicit others to follow. Besides, moving would be doing *something*. Even though Joseph was doing a lot to provide support for his family, he felt that there would always be a ceiling, a limit, for people like him: ordinary Congolese people. He would always be blocked from a stable future. All he could expect in Congo was, in his words, 'deterioration'.

While it may seem absurd that a person would migrate from a situation of relative stability to live in a refugee camp, on the basis of the slim (and diminishing) possibility of resettling elsewhere, what is important to note about Joseph's situation is how utterly unexceptional it is. His seeming stability is illusory, and he knows it. The context of his world in the DRC is 'deterioration'. Part of that bleak prediction is specific to the situation of the DRC, of course. The country exists in popular culture in the Western world only through tropes of the 'heart of darkness' – imagined and represented as a wild place, unparalleled in savagery and violence (Kabamba 2010). The postcolonial period has only enhanced that reputation (see also Mbembe 2001). The two wars that took place in the DRC in the 1990s and into the 2000s are not known for the estimated six million people who died (Coghlan et al. 2006), but instead came to be defined by the words of a United Nations officer who, in 2010, described the war-affected regions of the country as 'the rape capital of the world', thereby capturing sensationalist media headlines across the globe (BBC 2010). Coverage of the 2019 outbreak of Ebola in the country – while I was conducting ethnographic research – only fed this sensationalist view. Western media highlighted outlier tales of doctors in rural villages being injured or murdered for trying to treat Ebola patients while largely ignoring the fact that the country managed to safely and effectively manage the outbreak through an efficient contact-tracing programme, adherence to patient isolation programmes, education about transmission, and implementation of a vaccine.

What was more defeating to Congolese people I worked with during this time than the possibility of contracting Ebola was the likelihood of living the remainder of their lives in grinding poverty. Having gone years – decades – without what they saw as adequate governance and social, economic and medical infrastructure, people I spoke with had very little optimism about living out the future in their country. Many described how, over their lifetime, they had witnessed the visible deterioration of their societal services in the DRC: the roads that had once been surfaced now disintegrating into dust, the hospitals that once served all now charging more and more money, the rise in rural-to-urban migration creating population density in cities, making an already limited employment market even more competitive. Every person I spoke to expressed a desire to leave the country, if they could. Some, like Joseph, made plans to leave. What their stories told me, however, was that it was not the supposed 'dark' savagery of the DRC that drove their migration. Rather, it was aspirations towards futures of material security.

The migration imaginaries and present realities of people like Joseph, and the ways in which these reveal at once the absolute ordinariness of transience, instability and insecurity as a ubiquitous condition of our time and the spectacular violences of global partitioning that produce such conditions and enable them to become ordinary. In recent times, the conditions of everyday life have radically transformed everywhere because of the impact of the novel coronavirus, Covid-19. Our worlds – the materiality of our lives – rapidly constricted in 2020, for some literally, to a house, an apartment, even a single room. What has been relentlessly termed 'our new normal' in popular media has forced many into a caged existence. Yet for some these cages are not a new normal but a condition of everyday life. Restricted mobility is the structure that enables the domestication and submission necessary for processes of extraction, dispossession and accumulation of resources to continue, with the wealth gained from these accessible to only an elite, uncaged, few (Hage 2017). As Catherine Besteman (2019, 2020) has argued, the world is divided into North and South in a way that restrains and cages whole continents of people, actively preventing them from being included in the material and imaginative worlds of prosperity enjoyed by others.

But not all is lost. The 'ruins' of capitalism leave remnants and traces of possibility (Tsing 2015), and it is through these that those same caged people seek to establish futures on their own terms. The Covid-19 pandemic has not created a new normal of economic precarity, constrained mobility and political instability: it has only revealed these conditions, and expanded how they are felt and by whom. People like Joseph have been managing such situations for a long time. His sense of a future decline is not exceptional, nor exclusive to the DRC, and his motivation to transcend the borders of his caged existence, in which he is restricted to what he sees as a future of poverty and decline, can tell us much about making a way through these moments, and the necessity of diminishing – rather than enforcing – borders in order to do that.

Temporal partitions

Nonetheless, during the Covid-19 pandemic many of us had to learn to wait, and specifically to wait in the face of an uncertain future. For those of us who work with migrants, the stuckness that restricted mobility and seeded uncertainty worldwide in 2020 seemed somewhat ironic, a little sardonically painful. For so many, it was a new experience. Even while denouncing border regimes that constrain freedom of movement, we – researchers of mobility – too often took our own freedom for granted, or wielded it guiltily. We held our passports up at the border so that we could interview those without one. The 'new normal' of immobility was, of course, not truly a blanket, in that it covered and constrained in uneven ways, entrenching older inequalities. While many hoped fervently that immobility was only temporary, others have lived with that suffocation as a defining feature of life for a very long time.

Nonetheless, one of the most significant effects of the Covid-19 pandemic is that it has revealed the illusion of a linear temporal trajectory. The myth of modernisation is that societies move with forward momentum, towards infinite growth and absolute advancement (Koselleck 1988). This imagined linearity of time and progress has always been just that – an illusion – and one whose seeming constancy in the Global North has generally relied on the exploitation of people and resources in and from the Global South. What Covid-19, and its interconnected political and economic effects, have demonstrated, brutally and viscerally, is the fragility of advancement and the possibility of worlds gone backwards: as Joseph, in the section above, describes it, 'deterioration'. Of course, there have been other events that have similarly shaken the (Western) world's sense of temporal progression – the 2008 global financial crisis is one example (Roitman 2013); the September 2001 terrorist attacks in the United States are another (Butler 2004). It is yet to be seen what the long-term impact of the Covid-19 pandemic will be on how people and nations imagine their futures, but one thing is certain: the pandemic arrived at a time when the unevenness of trickle-down economies was already being felt in nations where it had served as a future promise, and when people were feeling economic pressures and funnelling these future anxieties into polarising politics and misguidedly blaming the 'Other', the migrant, for the failure of economic growth. Then, as now, the partitions between North and South were in the process of violent enforcement (Andersson 2014a; Besteman 2019; De Genova 2014). The pandemic has revealed – not created – the contemporary condition of precarity and the likely futures of decline. And so the central question that initially guided my thinking for this chapter has shifted in the light of the pandemic, only slightly, but nonetheless importantly. While I sought, before, to ask the question, 'What would it mean to conceptualise the possibility of a future of decline?', I now ask, 'What does it mean to live this as a reality?'

Such questions are relatively new within societies that have lived within a bubble of enlightenment assumptions that the passage of time equates to development, progress and growth. As Reinhardt Koselleck (1988) recognised in his conceptual history of time, the futures of modernity that have been imagined by European and American states are oriented towards the idea of a future that is empty and open. In that vein, futures are an opportunity for growth, a resource to cultivate. But the twenty-first century has brought with it events that challenge such narratives of uninterrupted progress. New situations of 'crisis' have emerged: events like terror attacks, global financial downturns, unprecedented numbers of refugees, political upheaval, and – yes – public health threats have punctuated the imaginary of unlimited future progress. As Janet Roitman (2013) suggests, these cycles of crisis production have a function; they are rendered into points of societal reflection that stir new social and political developments, often those which legitimate enhanced governance techniques. And so the trajectory of forward momentum, and the illusion of infinite advancement, are restored.

The 2015 refugee 'crisis' is a case in point. The year 2015 saw the largest number of displaced people since World War II, and significantly with unprecedented numbers of people seeking entry into and asylum in European nations (Albahari 2015). For context, there have been earlier mass displacements of refugees and migrants, but rarely have these so-called 'flows' of people entered Europe on this scale. Western media labelled this mass displacement a crisis, but depending on the media outlet it was less a humanitarian crisis of displaced people in need than a security crisis of threatening brown bodies entering predominantly white spaces. This was not a crisis for the migrants who had been forced to leave their homes, then, it was a crisis for the European nations receiving them (De Genova 2017; Hage 2016). The various border fortifications and exclusionary migration policies that were ushered in in the wake of the 'crisis' show how the label functions as an artificial 'break' in a narrative (see also Roitman 2013), demanding an urgent response with no great attention to the longitudinal forces and future impacts of quick policy, beyond preserving the global partitions of North–South, white–brown, exploiter and exploited, which restore the illusory narrative of future progress.

What gets missed in a normative reading of time as a vector of advancement is that futures of progress are only possible for a privileged few, and made possible by actively limiting, repressing, stagnating and emptying out the future of others (Povinelli 2011). Filling the futures of powerful states in the Global North with technological advancements, for example, requires the exploitation of the resources and wealth of the Global South, and the maintenance of a system of colonial extraction and accumulation by dispossession that has been in motion for centuries. While those processes were enabled by the *geographical* partitioning of the globe into those countries that colonised and those that were colonised – the stratified futures of the twenty-first century lead to what I call *temporal partitioning*.

By 'temporal partitioning', I mean the differential futures that are both a product of entrenched global inequalities and a requirement that they remain so. Some people who benefit from global systems of exploitation are able to imagine and pursue futures of prosperity; those who are exploited, to varying degrees, remain stuck in a persistent present, unable to advance and focused on survival. They are bereft of a 'capacity to aspire' (Appadurai 2007), since their opportunities are so limited. These temporal partitions map onto physical partitions between Global North and South (Besteman 2019), class differences (Harvey 2004) and racialised 'invisible' borders (Khosravi 2010). While these uneven futurities may not be obvious to those who are benefiting from them, they are palpable to the Congolese people whose futures are those that are stuck, limited, emptied out in front of them as the resources from their country are mined away. I will now turn to a case study of a material object, the mobile telephone, and describe how its production in the twenty-first century traces not only the contradictions of our globalised world, but also the migration imaginary.

Material paradoxes

The first time I pulled my iPhone out in front of Nyomanda, her attention turned to it, eyes narrowed. I was typing notes into my phone when she said, 'You know, that comes from my country.' I paused. Hesitant. 'Yes,' I responded eventually. 'The minerals inside,' she added. I didn't really know how to respond then, in 2012 when this conversation took place in a living room in Australia, far from the DRC; I am still unsure now. The phone was more than just a product of exploitation, it was a materialised symbol of a vast global supply chain and its embedded inequalities that had led her and her family to become refugees from the DRC, but which had sheltered my life enough that I could pay the exorbitant amount of money to buy the finished product. Shaking her head, Nyomanda told me that her country, Congo, is the richest in the world, but that its people are the poorest.

The war that ultimately forced Nyomanda and her family to leave Congo in 1999 was not the direct result of conflict over mining territory; nonetheless, like other refugees from the DRC I have conducted research with, she sees it as a crucial factor in why there was, and continues to be, such significant corruption, political turmoil and governance issues in the east of the country, where she is from. Our conversation took place just as smartphones, like my iPhone, had begun to burgeon in popularity and be taken up for widespread use. After fleeing Congo, Nyomanda and her family had spent almost a decade as refugees in Uganda, before being resettled by the UNHCR in Australia, where I met her. While our first meeting was somewhat tense, Nyomanda and I eventually became friends, family-like. In 2013, I accompanied her to Uganda, where we lived with her family members – still refugees living there – while I conducted research with refugees both in camps and in Kampala, the capital city.

In 2013, the smartphone technologies that were being produced from the raw minerals mined in their country were not yet widespread amongst Congolese refugees. Nonetheless, there was still enough media content about the West available – in addition to often exaggerated stories of prosperity from friends and family members who had migrated, seemingly backed up by occasional remittances of money – for many refugees I talked with to fantasise about migrating to Europe, North America or Australia. But within a few short years, the internet capacity of smartphones and their widespread uptake amongst people in refugee situations would not only lead many to fantasise about such onward migration journeys, but enable some to pursue them. Through increased access to the internet, more real-time information about routes, and tips, became available to would-be travellers. Some of the people I met in Uganda in 2013 had family members or acquaintances – mostly young men – who would later attempt the northern journey towards the Mediterranean Sea, their sights set on futures in Europe.

Within the migration imaginary, the desire to reach a country elsewhere – usually in Europe, North America or Australia – does not necessarily reflect a pull towards the cultures and people associated with those places (Salazar 2011). The pull of a croissant, or a Foster's beer, is not that strong. For people I worked with, the desire to leave Africa is more pragmatic (see Bredeloup 2013; Vigh 2009). They seek escape from the seeming inevitability of a future of decline; they want an opportunity to transcend futures in their country of birth that they saw as ceilinged, partitioned, limited. Many seemed to overestimate the possibility of achieving stability and prosperity in the Global North while underestimating the affective dissonance of migrating into a different, and often hostile, cultural context in which they would become the stranger (see also Jackson 2008).

Nyomanda, again, reminded me of this paradox of migration. She was particularly frustrated one afternoon when a flurry of bills arrived in the post. Opening the post, sighing in frustration, she vented her feelings to me: 'You think that we like it here?', 'here' being Australia, where she had been resettled through the UNHCR as a refugee. 'Do you?' I asked her, seriously. She paused. 'It is *okay*.' 'Just okay?' She told me that life here was not how she had imagined it from a refugee camp in Africa. 'Here it is bills, bills, bills. The children are bad, no respect. The neighbours don't talk to each other. People look at us.' This was not the first time Nyomanda and I had a conversation like this, nor the last. She and other resettled refugees from Congo that I conducted fieldwork with had described their frustrations with living in Australia, where they were, despite their best efforts, still comparatively poor and also struggling with racism directed towards them. They missed the affective feel of the lives they had in Africa: the easy sociality between neighbours, the taste of fresh meat and vegetables, the daily routines centring on family more than on work. 'But if we could take the things from here,' Nyomanda added, 'the education, the houses, the hospitals, the government, and take it there, that would be good. That would be better. That is what we want.' The point of migration, for Nyomanda, was not to renounce Africa or become 'Australian', but to find security and stability for herself and her family. If she could have done that within the social and cultural worlds of the DRC, she would have. She did not feel that it was possible, and part of that impossibility rests on the long-term impacts of decades of colonial and neocolonial interventions, fragile governance systems, and conflicts erupting from disputes over the lands from which resources are extracted for foreign companies that feed that wealth into advancing the economies and lives of people in their own nations.

While most of the people I was told about who were attempting to reach Europe would not make it to that destination – the perils and expense of the journey being too great – one thing was certain: some Congolese people were not willing to wait aimlessly for some external force to take charge of the direction of their life. They were engaging in what Henrik Vigh (2010) terms 'social navigation', that is, speculating about their futures, weighing odds within constrained circumstances, and eventually taking actions, small and large, to navigate these complexities towards a hopefully better, more liveable, life (see also Kuschminder 2020). My fieldwork in 2019 revealed a stark departure in attitudes towards migration from those I had found in work I had completed only a few years earlier in 2013, when refugees would painstakingly apply for resettlement to a third country through the UNHCR, even though the great majority were unlikely ever to be selected. Smartphone technology had given people I met a powerful tool in their social navigation kits: through phones, they could have more contact with – actually see – the lives of friends living in the Global North, unfolding so differently from their own, and could engage in more intensive planning and strategising of migration routes, with enhanced access to public information from others – strangers – who had mapped out those journeys before them (see also Gillespie et al. 2018). Many Congolese people were actively contemplating – and some were undertaking – independent journeys, in the hope of migrating to a country on their own terms. The mobile smartphone became a symbol of possibility, of forward momentum.

But, as Nyomanda signalled in the conversation I recounted earlier, the mobile phone is also a symbol of ongoing oppression for Congolese people, or, more specifically, a symbol of what she termed 'eaten' or stolen potential.[1] The effects of the extraction processes that are necessary to produce digital technologies contribute to the core mechanisms of conflict, land dispossession, corruption and environmental change that create displacement within and from the DRC in the first place (Kelly 2014; Laudati 2013; Verweijen 2017). Technological advancement in the twenty-first century has maintained a long legacy of predatory processes of extraction and accumulation by dispossession (Harvey 2004), which have seen global elites – Congolese and foreign alike – create capital from the raw minerals that have been mined from the country.

There is a road that local people call the 'road of shame', which begins on the Congolese side of the border between Rwanda and the DRC, leading into the city of Bukavu. Coming from Rwanda, with surfaced roads, orderly traffic, clean streets, and relatively few people milling about, entering Congo on this road – officially it is 'President Mobutu Avenue' – feels practically anarchistic. The buildings alongside it could be either dilapidated leftovers from the Belgian colonial period or newer, half-finished constructions – either way, many of the buildings are worn and scaffolded; the distinction between in progress and in decay is blurred. Refuse litters the street, a couple of small fires burn up some of it in piles outside buildings. Many adults and children walk along the road – few people have cars here – the latter in visibly dirty clothes; but then again, the unsurfaced road makes it difficult for anything or anyone to stay clean for long. For the few minutes during which one drives on that road, away from the border, it feels that all of the problematic tropes of poverty and Africa have come to life (Kabamba 2010): these are the kind of one-dimensional imaginaries of Africa I warn my students about, coming to surround me in the flesh, at least on the surface.

But the people who live here are not relics of another time, frozen in a proto-industrialised, under-developed bubble (Fabian 1983; see also Andersson 2014b). Separated by borders, both physical and political, these multiple realities – impoverished worlds and worlds of prosperity – exist in the same moment; the prosperity of the one comes from the exploitation of and extraction from the other. My Congolese friends know this; they often talk about foreign actors, working in collaboration with Congolese elites, who pillage the riches of the country and deprive the people who live there. When I ask one Congolese woman, Janvier, what she thinks the future holds for her, she responds, as many others do, 'My future … My future is the future of this country.' That is not a hopeful statement, given that she later describes the current state of the country – echoing Joseph's sentiments – as 'It is deterioration.'

Shahram Khosravi (2019) has challenged us to consider the question, 'What does it mean to see the border from the other side?' From the 'other side' of the border within the DRC, it feels as if a person travels across five, fifteen, fifty years of deterioration. The lie of time as a sequential – and inevitably progressive – trajectory is exposed. Joseph explained to me why the road is called the 'road of shame' by locals. When the Belgians colonised this part of the Congo it was surfaced. But in the neocolonial wake of corrupt government after corrupt government and conflict after conflict, the road has been left to go to ruin, 'like us', I am told, abandoned not just by a national government that still maintains the boundaries of a nation that was carved out at the Berlin conference of 1884–5, but also by the rest of us: each of us has, in all probability, used products that have been acquired through a global supply chain that begins with the extraction of material wealth from the DRC.

Materiality is at the core of these deteriorated futures, these futures of decline. Amongst the most notorious – but far from the only – mineral mined in this region is coltan, from which three separate materials are extracted that are sold to electronics manufacturers (Mantz 2008; Smith 2015). Practically every digital capacitor, laptop screen, even tin wiring, includes components that are sourced from the DRC. While we might see the technologies produced from these materials mined in Congo as markers of advancement, Congolese people, at least those I know, have been excluded from this trajectory of seeming progress, of forward momentum. Just as there is no paved road out of Bukavu, for people from this region there is no paved road towards the future. People in this part of Congo live – and have lived – the reality of a future of decline.

Analytical brackets and anthropological complicity

Perhaps it is strange that I should, while contributing to a book with migration at its core, discuss the global supply chains that are complicit in making life feel impossible, and futures uncertain, for many people in the DRC. I am talking about these topics because it is crucial that we, as researchers, cease to begin our research *at* the border encounter, as if the migrant came into being in and through those spaces. Too often, we analyse the refugee without attention to war; we explore migration without focusing on the forces of insecurity that propel it, or on the global networks that are implicated in these forces.

I want to conclude by arguing against the tendency in anthropology to engage in epochal thinking when it comes to migration, amongst other topics, specifically the kind of epochal thinking that brackets out migration as a period of liminality, of being betwixt and between fixed and stable categories of legal status, national identity and belonging (see Çağlar 2016, 2018; Ramsay 2017, 2019). Such liminality implies linearity; it assumes that migration neatly maps onto a temporal trajectory of rupture and resolution. Thus, while our focus on the violences that occur during the transience of migration might be well intentioned, by bracketing these violences within the singular frame of migration spaces – borders, camps, detention centres, amongst others – we may be inadvertently abstracting migration from the broader forces of global partitioning that produce migrants in the first place. We begin with migrants and their crisis of transience; we do not begin with the forces that create migrants.

I am calling, here, for anthropologists and social scientists working in contexts of migration to reimagine our methodological, theoretical and analytical brackets. While thick descriptions of how life unfolds in distinct spaces of migration are undoubtedly important, they can only tell us so much when it comes to understanding the broader global forces that make these kinds of spaces possible. While migrants do experience exceptional violence, these violences occur precisely because the movement of migrants threatens the partitions that maintain established power structures (Besteman 2020). When we do not contextualise the violence of migration and displacement within a more expansive frame, we risk making our analysis complicit in reproducing those bordering processes (see Cabot 2019). We cannot reproduce the crisis narrative without reinforcing its function as a technique of governance (Roitman 2013). Focusing on migration as the problem, we are suggesting that resolution lies in the very legal apparatuses that establish borders as important political signifiers in the first place. These are logics that migrants themselves often do not follow, yet we imagine their salvation through them.

My argument here is not new. Liisa Malkki (1995) developed a similar line of argument, recognising that displacement does not neatly map onto national categories. But in 2015 a so-called 'crisis' of displacement occurred, and despite much excellent critical work challenging the sensationalism of crisis narratives in studies of migration (see for example Andersson 2014a; Cabot 2019; Lems et al. 2020; Vigh 2008), it is still rare to see anthropologists connecting these situations of mass displacement to the broader forces of global dispossession that create them. Recently, work has begun to analyse migrants and citizens within the same frame, recognising that they often share overlapping concerns and insecurities. Building on formative work from Andreas Wimmer and Nina Glick Schiller (2002), which critiqued the ways in which social science research so often assumes the nation as a basis of bounded analysis, Bridget Anderson (2019) has called for 'methodological de-nationalism', that is, for the distinction between migrant and citizen to be approached more critically in social science research, given that we are living during a time when the protections provided to citizens are being stripped away. Notwithstanding the very real privilege of legal status that makes life more liveable for those with citizenship, the Covid-19 pandemic and other situations of precarity have shown just how many of us across the globe are only one disaster away from the kinds of instability that propel migration. Citizenship is no longer an automatic basis of care and protection, if indeed it ever was.

It is through epochal thinking, whether that be the kind of thinking that unconsciously brackets migrants into a different time from the researcher (Andersson 2014b; Çağlar 2016; Fabian 1983; Ramsay 2019) or the kind that defines them by a legal status (Malkki 1995), that anthropologists and other social researchers replicate the dehumanisation of migrants that is normalised elsewhere. We reduce them to abstractions, and figures, assuming that there is a 'migrant' story beyond the more fundamental human struggle for a liveable life. It is only this depersonalisation of migrants that leads to their becoming regarded as a vague but powerful threat to the societies they have entered or attempted to settle in.

As an *idea*, the futurity of migrants and migration can be depicted and understood by the societies that receive them in anxious terms, as harbingers of difference, change and insecurity. As *materialised beings*, migrants can be related to as humans, with aspirations – home, education, employment and family – similar to those of any other person. The example of a centre for asylum seekers established in the middle of a village in rural Denmark – comprising the only local childcare centre – documented by Zachary Whyte, Birgitte Romme Larsen and Karen Fog Olwig (2018; see also Whyte, Larsen and Schaldemose 2018) shows the significance of materiality for an understanding of the shared humanity of migrants. Even as debates about migration in the Danish media reflected increasing polarisation, people in this village, confronted with the proximity of asylum seekers and the need to interact with them as fully materialised human beings, led these Danish locals to be more accepting and understanding of asylum seekers: they shared 'mutuality', as those researchers put it.

It is a political move to recognise that migrants materially coexist in the same ways as non-migrants; it is a political move to recognise that migration is, often, an attempt to attain or preserve the safety and opportunity of material stability that others receive (seemingly) automatically at birth. We must come to see the futurity of migrants not as a threat to the projected futures of a nation and its citizens, but as a means to transform the bordered lives and temporal partitions that make global inequality a status quo.

But if we continue to exceptionalise displacement we are not only abstracting the displaced as objects who seemingly exist in a different liminal time of stuck futures, we are failing to recognise that such temporalities are increasingly typical in twenty-first-century precarious life across the globe. The eighty million people currently living in a situation of displacement suggest that displacement is more ubiquitous than exceptional. Moreover, with climate change, political instability and economic insecurity uprooting lives with increasing intensity, there is a need to begin addressing migration as an expected outcome and condition of contemporary life and migrants as humans seeking the same safety and stability that increasingly partitioned nations in the Global North are seeking to preserve, often through violent border regimes. If we reframe the temporality of displacement in that vein, we can see that migration itself is not the problem; rather, migration represents the transformative potential of collapsing and overcoming the temporal and geographic partitions that empty out the futures of some for the benefit of others.

No number of borders or amount of prevention through deterrence policies can solve the blatantly uneven life experiences across (and also within) these divides, which have been brought into even sharper focus through widespread access to mobile technologies and the internet. People can now visualise the lives that they are prevented from accessing. They will attempt – and are attempting – to rectify these vast inequalities, and ultimately to reclaim future possibility even if that means taking on present suffering. As Joseph told me on another occasion, while I was conducting fieldwork in the DRC in 2019, 'We will become refugees.' His aspiration certainly reframes the conventional understanding of refugee status as an inherently vulnerable condition of externality from the nation-state systems that provide protection and care to citizens.

For people like Joseph, becoming a refugee is not about a politico-legal status, it is about re-entering the world without the baggage of foreclosed futures. He would not be a refugee from the country of the DRC, he would be a person displaced from the dominant temporal rhythms of extraction and dispossession, seeking to reinsert himself elsewhere in these timescapes or, ideally, to create possible new tempos and rhythms outside of these. At a time when we are all, potentially, confronted with immobility and the potential reality of a future of decline, we can take the migration imaginaries of people like Joseph, who have endured such conditions for a long time, as signs of transformative potential, not simply as hopes for migration, but as hopes of collapsing and transforming the structures of division that make migration necessary for a future in the first place.

Note

1 It should be noted that many Congolese people view working in or adjacent to the mining industries in the DRC as a significant source of economic potential. I did not find so many people in my study who voiced these opinions but they are established in the literature, and it is important to recognise the role of mineral industries in stimulating local economies in the DRC (see Smith 2015; Mantz 2008).

References

Albahari, Maurizio. 2015. 'Europe's refugee crisis', *Anthropology Today* 31(5): 1–2. https://doi.org/10.1111/1467-8322.12196.

Anderson, Bridget. 2019. 'New directions in migration studies: Towards methodological de-nationalism', *Comparative Migration Studies* 7 (art. no. 36): 1–13. https://doi.org/10.1186/s40878-019-0140-8.

Andersson, Ruben. 2014a. *Illegality, Inc.: Clandestine migration and the business of bordering Europe*. Oakland: University of California Press.

Andersson, Ruben. 2014b. 'Time and the migrant other: European border control and the temporal economics of illegality', *American Anthropologist* 116(4): 795–809. https://doi.org/10.1111/aman.12148.

Appadurai, Arjun. 2007. 'The capacity to aspire: Culture and the terms of recognition'. In *Cultural Politics in a Global Age: Uncertainty, solidarity, and innovation*, edited by David Held and Henrietta L. Moore, 29–35. Oxford: Oneworld.

Besteman, Catherine. 2019. 'Militarized global apartheid', *Current Anthropology* 60(S19): S26–S38.

Besteman, Catherine. 2020. *Militarized Global Apartheid*. Durham, NC: Duke University Press.

BBC. 2010. 'UN official calls DR Congo "rape capital of the world"'. Accessed 14 August 2021. http://news.bbc.co.uk/2/hi/africa/8650112.stm.

Bredeloup, Sylvie. 2013. 'The figure of the adventurer as an African migrant', *Journal of African Cultural Studies* 25(2): 170–82. https://doi.org/10.1080/13696815.2012.751870.

Brun, Cathrine and Anita Fábos. 2015. 'Making homes in limbo? A conceptual framework', *Refuge: Canada's Journal on Refugees* 31(1): 5–17. https://doi.org/10.25071/1920-7336.40138.

Butler, Judith. 2004. *Precarious Life: The powers of mourning and violence*. New York: Verso.

Cabot, Heath. 2019. 'The business of anthropology and the European refugee regime', *American Anthropologist* 46(3): 261–75. https://doi.org/10.1111/amet.12791.

Çağlar, Ayse. 2016. 'Still "migrants" after all those years: Foundational mobilities, temporal frames and emplacement of migrants', *Journal of Ethnic and Migration Studies* 42(6): 952–69. https://doi.org/10.1080/1369183X.2015.1126085.

Çağlar, Ayse. 2018. 'Chronotopes of migration scholarship: Challenges of contemporaneity and historical conjuncture'. In *Migration, Temporality, and Capitalism: Entangled mobilities across global spaces*, edited by Pauline Gardiner Barber and Winnie Lem, 21–41. Cham: Palgrave Macmillan.

Coghlan, Benjamin, Pascal Ngoy, Flavien Mulumba, Colleen Hardy, Valerie Nkamgang Bemo, Tony Stewart, Jennifer Lewis and Richard Brennan. 2006. 'Mortality in the Democratic Republic of Congo: An ongoing crisis'. New York: International Rescue Committee. Accessed 30 August 2020. https://www.rescue.org/sites/default/files/document/661/2006-7congomortalitysurvey.pdf.

Couch, Jen. 2011. '"My life just went zig zag": Refugee young people and homelessness', *Youth Studies Australia* 30(2): 22–32.

De Genova, Nicholas. 2014. 'Extremities and regularities: Regulatory regimes and the spectacle of immigration enforcement'. In *The Irregularization of Migration in Contemporary Europe: Detention, deportation, drowning*, edited by Yolande Jansen, Robin Celikates and Joost de Bloois, 3–14. London: Rowman & Littlefield.

De Genova, Nicholas, ed. 2017. *The Borders of 'Europe': Autonomy of migration, tactics of bordering*. Durham, NC: Duke University Press.

Dudley, Sandra. 2011. 'Feeling at home: Producing and consuming things in Karenni refugee camps on the Thai-Burma border', *Population, Space and Place* 17(6): 742–55. https://doi.org/10.1002/psp.639.

Fabian, Johannes. 1983. *Time and the Other: How anthropology makes its object*. New York: Columbia University Press.

Gillespie, Marie, Souad Osseiran and Margie Cheesman. 2018. 'Syrian refugees and the digital passage to Europe: Smartphone infrastructures and affordances', *Social Media + Society* 4(1): 1–12. https://doi.org/10.1177%2F2056305118764440.

Griffiths, Melanie B. E. 2014. 'Out of time: The temporal uncertainties of refused asylum seekers and immigration detainees', *Journal of Ethnic and Migration Studies* 40(12): 1991–2009. https://doi.org/10.1080/1369183X.2014.907737.

Hage, Ghassan. 2016. 'État de siège: A dying domesticating colonialism?', *American Ethnologist* 43(1): 38–49. https://doi.org/10.1111/amet.12261.

Hage, Ghassan. 2017. *Is Racism an Environmental Threat?* Cambridge: Polity.

Harvey, David. 2004. 'The "new" imperialism: Accumulation through dispossession', *Socialist Register* 40: 63–87.

Howden, Daniel. 2020. 'Moria: Anti-shelter and the spectacle of deterrence'. In *Structures of Protection? Rethinking refugee shelter*, edited by Tom Scott-Smith and Mark E. Breeze, 57–70. New York: Berghahn.

Jackson, Michael. 2008. 'The shock of the new: On migrant imaginaries and critical transitions', *Ethnos* 73(1): 57–72. https://doi.org/10.1080/00141840801927533.

Kabamba, Patience. 2010. '"Heart of Darkness": Current images of the DRC and their theoretical underpinning', *Anthropological Theory* 10(3): 265–301. https://doi.org/10.1177/1463499610372248.

Kelly, Jocelyn T. D. 2014. '"This mine has become our farmland": Critical perspectives on the coevolution of artisanal mining and conflict in the Democratic Republic of the Congo', *Resources Policy* 40: 100–8. https://doi.org/10.1016/j.resourpol.2013.12.003.

Khosravi, Shahram. 2010. *'Illegal' Traveller: An auto-ethnography of borders*. Basingstoke: Palgrave Macmillan. doi:10.1057/9780230281325.

Khosravi, Shahram. 2019. 'What do we see if we look at the border from the other side?', *Social Anthropology* 27(3): 409–24. https://doi.org/10.1111/1469-8676.12685.

Koselleck, Reinhart. 1988. *Critique and Crisis: Enlightenment and the pathogenesis of modern society*. Oxford and New York: Berg.

Kuschminder, Katie. 2020. 'Before disembarkation: Eritrean and Nigerian migrants' journeys within Africa', *Journal of Ethnic and Migration Studies* 47(14): 3260–75. https://doi.org/10.1080/1369183X.2020.1804192.

Larsen, Birgitte Romme. 2011. 'Drawing back the curtains: The role of domestic space in the inclusion and exclusion of refugees in rural Denmark', *Social Analysis* 55(2): 142–58. https://doi.org/10.3167/sa.2011.550208.

Laudati, Ann. 2013. 'Beyond minerals: Broadening "economies of violence" in eastern Democratic Republic of Congo', *Review of African Political Economy* 40(135): 32–50. https://doi.org/10.1080/03056244.2012.760446.

Lems, Annika, Kathrin Oester and Sabine Strasser. 2020. 'Children of the crisis: Ethnographic perspectives on unaccompanied refugee youth in and en route to Europe', *Journal of Ethnic and Migration Studies* 46(2): 315–35. https://doi.org/10.1080/1369183X.2019.1584697.

Malkki, Liisa H. 1995. 'Refugees and exile: From "refugee studies" to the national order of things', *Annual Review of Anthropology* 24: 495–523. https://doi.org/10.1146/annurev.an.24.100195.002431.

Mantz, Jeffrey. 2008. 'Blood diamonds of the digital age: Coltan and the eastern Congo', *Global Studies Review* 4(3): 12–14.

Mbembe, Achille. 2001. *On the Postcolony*. Berkeley: University of California Press.

Mould, Oliver. 2018. 'The not-so-concrete Jungle: Material precarity in the Calais refugee camp', *Cultural Geographies* 25(3): 393–409. https://doi.org/10.1177/1474474017697457.

Navarro, Tami. 2017. 'But some of us are broke: Race, gender, and the neoliberalization of the academy', *American Anthropologist* 119(3): 506–17. https://doi.org/10.1111/aman.12888.

Oesch, Lucas. 2019. 'The politics of temporariness and the materiality of refugee camps'. In *Arrival Infrastructures: Migration and urban social mobilities*, edited by Bruno Meeus, Karel Arnaut and Bas van Heur, 229–48. Cham: Palgrave Macmillan. http://dx.doi.org/10.1007/978-3-319-91167-0.

Povinelli, Elizabeth A. 2011. *Economies of Abandonment: Social belonging and endurance in late liberalism*. Durham, NC: Duke University Press.

Ramsay, Georgina. 2017. 'Incommensurable futures and displaced lives: Sovereignty as control over time', *Public Culture* 29(3): 515–38. https://doi.org/10.1215/08992363-3869584.

Ramsay, Georgina. 2019. 'Time and the other in crisis: How anthropology makes its displaced object', *Anthropological Theory* 20(4): 385–413. https://doi.org/10.1177/1463499619840464.

Roitman, Janet. 2013. *Anti-Crisis*. Durham, NC: Duke University Press.

Rotter, Rebecca. 2016. 'Waiting in the asylum determination process: Just an empty interlude?', *Time & Society* 25(1): 80–101. https://doi.org/10.1177%2F0961463X15613654.

Salazar, Noel B. 2011. 'Tanzanian migration imaginaries'. In *Migration and Culture*, edited by Robin Cohen and Gunvor Jónsson, 673–87. Cheltenham: Edward Elgar.

Shire, Warsan. 2016. 'Home'. Accessed 14 August 2021. https://www.facinghistory.org/standing-up-hatred-intolerance/warsan-shire-home.

Smith, James H. 2015. '"May it never end": Price wars, networks, and temporality in the "3 Ts" mining trade of the Eastern DR Congo', *HAU: Journal of Ethnographic Theory* 5(1): 1–34. https://doi.org/10.14318/hau5.1.002.

Tsing, Anna Lowenhaupt. 2015. *The Mushroom at the End of the World: On the possibility of life in capitalist ruins*. Princeton, NJ: Princeton University Press.

United Nations High Commissioner for Refugees. 2020. 'Figures at a glance'. Accessed 9 August 2020. https://www.unhcr.org/en-us/figures-at-a-glance.html.

Verweijen, Judith. 2017. 'Luddites in the Congo? Analyzing violent responses to the expansion of industrial mining amidst militarization', *City* 21(3–4): 466–82. https://doi.org/10.1080/13604813.2017.1331567.

Vigh, Henrik. 2008. 'Crisis and chronicity: Anthropological perspectives on continuous conflict and decline', *Ethnos* 73(1): 5–24. https://doi.org/10.1080/00141840801927509.

Vigh, Henrik. 2009. 'Wayward migration: On imagined futures and technological voids', *Ethnos* 74(1): 91–109. https://doi.org/10.1080/00141840902751220.

Vigh, Henrik. 2010. 'Motion squared: A second look at the concept of social navigation', *Anthropological Theory* 9(4): 419–38. https://doi.org/10.1177%2F1463499609356044.

Whyte, Zachary, Birgitte Romme Larsen and Karen Fog Olwig. 2018. 'New neighbours in a time of change: Local pragmatics and the perception of asylum centers in rural Denmark', *Journal of Ethnic and Migration Studies* 45(11): 1953–69. https://doi.org/10.1080/1369183X.2018.1482741.

Whyte, Zachary, Birgitte Romme Larsen and Mona Schaldemose. 2018. 'The role of rural grocery stores in refugee reception', *Forced Migration Review* 58: 24–5.

Wimmer, Andreas and Nina Glick Schiller. 2002. 'Methodological nationalism and beyond: Nation-state building, migration and the social sciences', *Global Networks* 2(4): 301–34. https://doi.org/10.1111/1471-0374.00043.

2

Camps as vessels of hope

Simon Turner

Introduction

Refugee settlements, shelters, hotspots, etc. are often the favourite means for authorities – be it states, UN agencies or NGOs – to deal with mobile populations that are seen as matter out of space (Kreichauf 2018). With their clearly demarcated borders, monotonous housing and grid-like infrastructures, they stick out like a sore thumb, and give us the impression of being exceptional spaces. Often, those who inhabit them do so against their will; they are forced into the confinement of the camps, where their lives are put on hold while they wait for others to make decisions on their futures. We would assume that the camp as a place of waiting and confinement surely leads to a sense of stuckness for those who are forced to live there. However, we should not let the aesthetics of the camp – its straight lines and monotonous housing – lead us to assume that life in the camps is simply set on standby. Similarly, we should not assume that the official objective of confinement – of stopping movement – is achieved. Empirical ethnographic studies reveal that life in camps is more complex (Bochmann 2018; B. Jansen 2011; McConnachie 2014; Ramadan and Fregonese 2017). While camps might at first sight signal immobility, they may also act as junctions for onward mobility. They may be perceived – and used – as stepping stones or waiting rooms for onward mobility. This is what my colleagues and I have termed 'carceral junctions': places that simultaneously incarcerate and connect.[1] Related to this, we must not assume a link between physical immobility and existential stuckness, just as we must not equate mobility with freedom and agency (Bissell 2007; Jefferson et al. 2019).

In the following, I will unpack the concepts of confinement, stuckness and (im)mobility in relation to camps. Central to my chapter will be adding temporality to a debate that easily lends itself to spatial analyses. I will discuss how questions of anticipation – both in the sense of hope and in the sense of anxiety – qualify the sense of stuckness, arguing that stuckness is a question of whether or not one is able to see possible futures.

Carceral junctions

Since the publication of Giorgio Agamben's *Homo Sacer* in 1998, his thoughts about the camp have been a source of inspiration and contestation in studies of concrete refugee camps, detention centres and other sites of confinement. On the one hand, scholars have been inspired by his ideas of 'bare life' and sovereign power to try to understand the nature of contemporary encampments of migrant populations, whether irregular migrants, asylum seekers or rejected refugees (Diken and Laustsen 2006; Edkins 2000; Minca 2015). Meanwhile, a number of studies have emerged that counter Agamben's conceptualisation of the camp, arguing – often from an empirically based or ethnographic point of view – that refugees do not become 'bare life', and that life goes on in the camp (Bochmann 2018; Oesch 2017; Owens 2009; Maestri and Hughes 2017; Redclift 2013). Irit Katz calls it 'Between *Bare Life* and *Everyday Life*' (Katz 2017). Nando Sigona has, for instance, introduced the concept 'campzenship' to illustrate that a form of citizenship takes place within the camps (Sigona 2015). Adam Ramadan argues from his studies in the Palestinian refugee camps in Lebanon that these camps are spaces of resistance and (political) struggle and not just exceptional spaces of bare life (Ramadan 2013). However, we must be careful not to make a false opposition between Agamben's philosophical conceptualisation of the camp as the nomos of our time and the empirical evidence that shows that refugees have 'agency' despite the camp, and conclude that Agamben is therefore wrong. Rather, I argue that it is the exceptional character of the camp that at once depoliticises and hyper-politicises the space of the camp (S. Turner 2016b). In other words, it is the camp itself that creates these new subjectivities.

Others – inspired by new materialism – have been exploring the materiality of the camp to understand how the camp both constrains inhabitants and creates new possibilities. Abourahme (2015) in particular makes this argument. By exploring assemblages of people, ideas and things, he shows how things – in his case cement – have the capacity to spill over and to create unintended consequences that are neither the planned outcomes of juridico-political plans nor the result of heroic resistance. Meiches characterises the camp, as opposed to, for instance, the prison, by its elasticity, because it can be swiftly redesigned for new tasks, and claims that this elasticity makes it ripe for new forms of adaptation and resistance (Meiches 2015, 3). In their study of housing modules, built for Bosnian refugees in Denmark with the explicit aim of being modular, flexible and mobile, Whyte and Ulfstjerne found that the infrastructures left traces of their histories, even when repurposed (Z. Whyte and Ulfstjerne 2020). Similarly, Ghandour-Demiri and Passas in this volume argue that camps (in Greece) rely on former material infrastructures that allow, but also constrain, adaptations and transformations in different ways. I elaborate on the materiality of the camp below.

By seeing the camp as both carceral and a junction, I seek to expand upon this approach. While the camp obviously creates limits and exclusions, it also allows and creates movement of various kinds. The movement of bodies, hopes and structures through the camp, and the bringing together of different actors and rationalities at the junction, are productive in the Foucauldian sense, that new subjectivities may emerge at these junctions. In other words, while much of the literature on camps has criticised Agamben's understanding of the camp by showing empirically that the camp is, indeed, complex and ambiguous (Holzer and Warren 2015; B. Jansen 2011; Oesch 2017; Sigona 2015), I believe that the idea of the carceral junction is a way of understanding where this resistance, agency or politics comes from. The carceral junction as a concept holds within it both aspects of the camp, and is therefore able to explain the fact that camps have these apparently contradictory characteristics. While the carceral may explain the structures that create and control the camp, the junctions on the other hand might help explain why such subjectivities emerge, without falling into idealised ideas of agency and resistance from below.

Junctions are places where the traveller pauses, ponders, and takes his or her bearings, before making the next move. But junctions are also interfaces, places where two streams of traffic meet. And these interfaces can be productive of new subjectivities and new trajectories. Agier uses the term 'carrefours' (crossroads) to suggest that camps are places of cosmopolitan intersection (Agier 2014, 19). I observed this concretely in the refugee camps in Tanzania, when refugees told me that they had learned from other nationalities in the camp. The Burundian refugees claimed that they had learned from the Rwandans to be more assertive, which helped them in their business activities in the camp and in playing tricks with the UNHCR. Likewise, I observed that they were learning the jargon of international NGOs, in order to find a new position in the camp. They were convinced that their contact with the Rwandans and their experience from the camp would help them in their future political struggles (S. Turner 2010). The junction can in other words be a crossroads where different groups meet – like streams of traffic – and mingle. It can, however, be a junction where different 'levels' and rationalities intersect, such as the refugees passing through the camp, the NGO staff working there and the police controlling the camp.

The concept 'carceral junctions' is a means to come to terms with the paradoxical nature of the camp, as I try to go beyond the either/or understanding of the camp, that is, either confinement or mobility, either structure or agency, either Agamben's state of exception or a space of new political subjectivities. The key point is that camps are *at once* sites of confinement *and* junctions that connect and enable mobility; they are *at once* sites of state sovereignty *and* junctions where migrants navigate, evade and negotiate these enactments to reach other destinations. The concept thus challenges common-sense dichotomies of confinement/freedom, mobility/immobility and structure/agency, in a bid to understand the policies of encampment and refugee mobility as more than opposing processes.

In the following I unfold this understanding of the camp as a carceral junction by following the spatiality and the temporality of the camp. Because the most immediate defining characteristic of the camp is its unique and exceptional spatiality, this has been well described in the literature, and I will instead devote most of this chapter to the temporal aspect of the camp in my search for an understanding of the paradoxical nature of the camp.

Confining spaces

As mentioned above, we cannot simply assume a link between mobility and certain forms of liberated subjectivity. Recent debates in carceral geography that combine geography and prison studies have grappled with the relationship between forced immobility and agency, challenging received wisdoms on the subject. While camps are not prisons, there are certainly overlaps in the ways in which they confine those living in them (Jefferson et al. 2019). Similarly, scholars have argued that the boundaries between the criminal justice system and immigration enforcement systems have increasingly become blurred (Bosworth and Guild 2008; Drotbohm and Hasselberg 2015). According to D. Moran et al. (2013), we are witnessing the enrolment of increasingly diverse places, such as immigration detention centres, homes, hospitals, ghettos and camps, as carceral landscapes.

Carceral geographers have sought to destabilise the categories through which confinement is typically understood (D. Moran et al. 2013). Mobility itself, they argue, can be punitive and has always been an element of routines within prisons: forced movement from the cells to common rooms to the exercise yard, and movement between prisons (D. Moran 2015). As Nick Gill puts it, 'mobility is perfectly commensurate with confinement and has been used as a constituent element of confinement within prisons for many years' (Gill 2013). Similarly, Jennifer Turner and Kimberley Peters (2017) argue that we must explore what they term 'carceral mobilities'.

In order to understand this ambiguity between movement and confinement, we might look at the materiality of the camp. Inspired by Deleuze and Guattari's (1987) theories on assemblages, Benjamin Meiches makes a compelling argument on the emergence of camps, beyond what he terms the anthropocentric bias of seeing camps as merely derivative of social structures (Meiches 2015, 3). Assemblages of human and non-human actants have created the camp. He focuses on three 'singularities' by which the capacities of materials have enabled the emergence of camps: the invention of barbed wire, new kinds of colonial warfare that sought to target a population in need of 'humane treatment', and the growth of a transport system, capable of providing the logistics of such population concentrations outside cities. 'The combination of these capacities made the camp an ideal machine for combining the capacities of barbed wire, transit, and war to produce a new highly mobile form of political control capable of converting a dispersed mass into a governable population' (Meiches 2015, 485). The result is that camps are transient: they are easily established and easily changed or dismantled. Their task is not to discipline and produce docile bodies (as in Bentham's panopticon) but to contain and to give shelter in a malleable, flexible manner. The paradoxical nature of the camp is that it is elastic and mobile while also stopping movement and creating concentrations of people.

In sum, camps are 'elastic' and transient, and their purpose is more to concentrate populations than to discipline them. But they are also carceral, as 'the camp functions as a machine for converting molecular flows into stable molar "concentrations"' (Meiches 2015, 487). And while the camp may be carceral, carceral geography warns us not to assume a link between being stuck in space and being existentially stuck. To elaborate on this question, we must turn to the temporality of the camp.

Waiting

Space is clearly central to how we may approach confinement and stuckness: camps are clearly visible in space with their straight lines and their fences. The language we use is spatial, movement linking to agency, and stillness linking to social death. But there are also temporal metaphors in common language about confinement. Stuckness is associated with waiting and wasting time, as we see in the English expression for being in prison, 'doing time'. To be stuck is both spatial and temporal.

In the words of the architect Charlie Hailey (2009, 4), 'Just as they are lodged spatially between the open and the closed, camps exist between the temporary and the permanent. From the outset, camps are understood as having a limited, although sometimes indeterminate, duration.'

Refugee camps are by definition temporary; they are never meant to remain where they are permanently. In practice, however, camps may become quasi-permanent, and, more importantly, their temporary nature remains undecided in the sense that neither those in charge of establishing the camps nor those who inhabit them know how long the camp will remain or for how long the individual refugee will stay in the camp.

While large numbers of refugees reside in camps, none of the three durable solutions favoured by UNHCR – repatriation, resettlement and local integration – mentions camps, which means that millions of displaced persons live in situations that are deemed non-viable by those who are in charge of them. These situations in which the temporary becomes permanent – akin to Agamben's idea of a 'permanent state of exception' – are given the contradictory term 'protracted refugee crisis' by humanitarian organisations in charge of the camps.

Time in camps is often portrayed by those who live in them as time on standby, as if time stood still in the camp while moving relentlessly on outside it, creating a fear of being left behind and becoming out of touch. I heard this again and again when I did my fieldwork in a refugee camp: 'We are left behind. We are losing out.' One of the most striking characteristics of camps is the way in which the control of time is taken away from people. In other words, the unfreedom of their confinement is often more temporal than spatial. This affects the sense of having or not having a future which is essential to the strategies that they adapt in the present. What seems at stake is the individual's ability (or lack of it) to imagine a future, and to propel themselves towards such a future.

A central debate in the literature on waiting is whether it is somehow disempowering for those who are forced to wait, or whether waiting may be perceived as active and productive. In his critique of the mobilities turn in geography, Bissell argues that this literature privileges mobility over stasis. 'It is somehow "better", culturally, economically and politically, to be mobile than immobile' (Bissell 2007, 280). As a consequence, 'waiting is a universal experience' (Bournes and Mitchell 2002, in Bissell 2007, 283), and this experience is negative. Inspired by Henri Lefebvre's neo-Marxist ideas about time, the mobilities school perceives waiting as 'a product of bureaucratic appropriation of everyday life' (J. Moran 2004, quoted in Bissell 2007, 282). From a more Foucauldian point of view, Auyero (2011) shows how forcing the poor to wait may be perceived as a way of exercising power and disciplining subjects.

While waiting is related to disempowerment and precarity (just as forcing others to wait can be a means of exercising power), there are other sides to waiting that have been explored by geographers and anthropologists in recent years. Craig Jeffrey's work on 'time-pass' and chronic waiting among urban Indian youth is one of the best examples of exploring the everyday workings of waiting, rather than assuming its 'negative' effects (Jeffrey 2008, 2010). He argues that 'waiting must be understood not as the capacity to ride out the passage of time or as the absence of action, but rather as an active, conscious, materialized practice in which people forge new political strategies' (Jeffrey 2008, 957; 2010). In her ethnography of Guliston, a Tadjik village from where most of the adult men have migrated to Russia, Ibañez Tirado (2018) has similarly attempted to reconcile structure and agency in the act of waiting. She shows that the activities and interactions that take place in Guliston, while the inhabitants are engaged in strategies of waiting for relatives to return, create socialities and relations of care, contributing 'to the production of Guliston as a dynamic place at the centre of a circulation of care' (Ibañez Tirado 2018, 329).

Authors such as Jeffrey and Ibañez Tirado show how people 'get on' with everyday activities while waiting. Those who are left behind do not just sit down and wait, even though they might talk about time as empty, dead or on standby. I found similar dynamics taking place in the refugee settlement in Tanzania and among Burundian refugees, staying without papers on the outskirts of Nairobi. From my point of view as the outside observer, I could register activities taking place, filling the empty time of the camp with sociality, politics and entrepreneurship. According to this sociological perspective, the refugees were actively engaged in trading in food rations and goods, smuggled across the border. They built churches, mosques and schools. They were engaged in party politics and fighting the regime that had forced them to flee. Meanwhile, they would always emphasise that their lives were on standby and the camp was just a temporary stopover.

This tension between actively appropriating the place of enforced waiting on the one hand while discursively maintaining the temporariness of the situation on the other hand was even more evident in Nairobi. In Nairobi I found two very different groups of Burundians. One group was settled in the multicultural areas of Pumwani and California Estate where they spoke Swahili and blended into the local, informal economy as hairdressers, tailors and the like. They were not waiting but working on becoming part of East Africa's most cosmopolitan city (S. Turner 2015). The other group lived in Kawangware and around Dagoretti Corner where other rural immigrants had recently settled on the outskirts of the city. When I asked them how they survived, their response would be, 'We live off miracles.' I knew that they received remittances from relatives in Europe and occasional support from relatives in the camps. They also received stipends of some sort from churches. Finally, they had odd jobs such as teaching French. However, they had no interest in becoming embedded in this city. For them it was simply a stepping stone or what Jansen has called a portal (B. Jansen 2008) to somewhere else. In other words, it was important for these refugees to be waiting rather than settling in. The active act of waiting gave them access to better futures elsewhere (S. Turner 2016a).

While scholars like Ibañez Tirado and Honwana (2012) show how waiting time can be filled with activity and agency, I argue that the act of waiting is agentic in itself. In her ethnography of internally displaced persons (IDPs) in Tbilisi, Georgia, Cathrine Brun makes similar observations (Brun 2015). She explores what she calls 'agency-in-waiting', thus dispelling the idea that people who are waiting are stripped of agency. Jeffrey makes a similar argument when arguing that waiting becomes a political strategy. It might seem that I am thus retaining the opposition between mobility as productive and empowering and immobility as wasted, disempowering time. However, my argument is that our critique of the dichotomy between mobility and immobility should not result in the notion that waiting time is like any other time, erasing the exceptional qualities of waiting time. I argue that in some cases, waiting in the present – without filling waiting time with meaning here and now – is a strategy to move towards a desired future. The refugees in Nairobi perceived their present as a sacrifice that was an investment in future options.

The temporality of the camp can thus be explored at three levels. First is the conceptual level of speed and stasis, as explored in the mobilities literature. Camps represent spaces of low velocity, where travel grinds to a halt, creating situations of waiting. There are strong similarities here to Agamben's ideas of the camp as a space of exception, creating *homini sacri*. Second is the level of practice, where we can observe what actually takes place in the camp and confirm that agency is not missing. This is similar to the many critiques that have been made of Agamben's work from a sociological, empirical point of view (Katz, Ramadan, Sigona, Owens) and to the literature on waiting as practice. Finally is the level of emic perceptions where the other two levels merge while, importantly, being kept conceptually apart. This is where waiting is taken up as a strategy in itself. This level is similar to the critique I have launched elsewhere, namely that refugee camps are at once depoliticised, exceptional spaces and hyper-politicised and that this is not just the result of heroic agency but an effect of the depoliticisation (S. Turner 2016b).

Perhaps a way out of the conundrum is to remember the words 'to' and 'for', which often follow 'wait', when exploring waiting. I might agree that waiting or 'waithood' (Honwana 2012) is interesting to explore as a social practice in itself. However, by focusing solely on the practice of waiting, we forget that people usually wait *for* something to happen or wait *to* do something or go somewhere. In other words, waiting is future-oriented and oriented towards change. It is towards the futures that we now turn.

Camps as vessels towards futures

In the permanently temporary time of the camp, imagining a future, planning one's life trajectory and acting accordingly in the present becomes seriously challenged. Bourdieu argues that to anticipate is to assess the forthcoming (à venir) in a pre-reflexive manner. It is to have a 'sense for the game' and, if we remain in the metaphor of the game, it is to place oneself where one expects the ball to be in the near future. 'This means that the objective probabilities are determinant only for an agent endowed with the sense of the game in the form of the capacity to anticipate the forth-coming of the game' (Bourdieu 2000, 211). In other words, one's practical knowledge – one's habitus – must be in line with the game in order to predict the immediate future. If one cannot predict the forthcoming future – as he observes among the lumpenproletariat of the French banlieues – one cannot play the game and flounders between unrealistic optimism (I am going to be a football star) and despair (it doesn't matter what I do in the present, I don't have a future anyway). From Bourdieu we might therefore conclude that life in the camps leads to social death because there is no future.

Georgina Ramsay (2017) engages with the relationship between sovereignty, futures and displacement and makes the convincing argument that we might understand particular forms of sovereignty as based on control over futures. This temporal sovereignty produces 'a temporal state of exception: a condition of living in a social tense that does not correspond to the hegemonic timescapes of the governing structures' (Ramsay 2017, 532). Such temporal states of exception, she argues, can create a condition of bare life in which one's lack of control over time makes it hard to make assumptions about the future.

Bourdieu and Ramsay nicely demonstrate how being able to foresee a future and act accordingly is essential to subjectivity and control over one's own social being. Similarly, not being able to see a future may lead to social death and existential stuckness (Jefferson et al. 2019). However, insecurity and uncertainty may create new opportunities to imagine new potential futures. In an edited volume, *Ethnographies of Uncertainty in Africa* (Cooper and Pratten 2015), the authors argue that uncertainty – produced by neoliberal reforms, flight and conflict – opens up possibilities of alternative imaginaries of the future. In other words, the situations that might rip the certainty about futures away from under your feet may also be the situations that provide new openings for alternative futures. Susan Whyte terms this acting in the present in relation to an unknown future being in the 'subjunctive mode' (S. Whyte 2005). For individuals to remain socially alive they need to be able to imagine a meaningful future for themselves. This is where the concept of hope enters the picture: hope as a means to anticipate a future and act accordingly in the present in situations of uncertainty and unpredictability.

Anthropological studies of hope and aspirations have often been conducted in situations of crisis or conflict (Da Col and Humphrey 2012; Kleist and Jansen 2016; Pedersen 2019). Stef Jansen distinguishes between transitive hope, as hope that has objects ('I hope that my asylum application will go through next month'), and intransitive hope, as hopefulness or affect ('I am hopeful that the future will be better') (S. Jansen 2014). Many scholars – including myself – have similarly approached hope as intransitive and have especially regarded hope as related to uncertainty and indeterminacy. Inspired by Ernst Bloch's (1986) ideas of hope as future-oriented and hence indeterminate, they claim that we may use hope as a lens to understand and explore anticipation alongside how individuals orient themselves towards unknown futures, rather than simply build on their pasts. Bloch's understanding of hope as 'concrete utopia' helps us beyond the transitive–intransitive divide. 'Concrete Utopia ... is anticipatory rather than compensatory. It reaches forward to a real possible future, and involves not merely wishful but will-full thinking .... Concrete utopia embodies what Bloch claims as the essential utopian function, that of simultaneously anticipating and effecting the future' (Levitas 1990, 15). Concrete utopias anticipate and effect the future; they do not just wait for them, and reality does not just consist of what is but also of what is becoming (Levitas 1990, 17). Hope in the shape of concrete utopias thus brings the future into the present as a realm of possibility.

In situations of precarity and uncertainty, such anticipation is increasingly difficult but also increasingly important. Susan Whyte's concept of living in the 'subjunctive mood' – where one positions oneself in relation to unknown futures 'as if' one knew – describes well the anticipatory practices of 'reaching forward' towards possible futures in such circumstances. There is a danger in these anthropological studies of hope that we celebrate the ingenuity of the individual's ability to hope and aspire in situations of marginality and precarity and thereby ignore the structural injustices and limitations to which they are subjected, as Bourdieu reminds us. By giving refugees in camps agency and hope, we risk ignoring the fact that camps are incarcerating, confining and limiting their opportunities. Once again, we see the ambiguous nature of camps – also in relation to temporality and future-making. Being existentially stuck is not just about spatial stuckness – it is equally (perhaps even more) about temporal stuckness, the inability to imagine a future – and to plan accordingly. Camps seriously challenge the ability to see a future, but they do not completely prevent it. Through hope, refugees in camps are able to get glimpses of futures – for better or for worse – and are able to act accordingly, avoiding social death and gaining some kind of agency.

Rather than perceiving this agency as an expression of heroic resistance to the camp, I propose that the camp itself may act as a vessel of hope. Being in a camp is to be in the 'in-between', which is spatially neither here nor there and temporally cut off from the past and the future. And just as being neither here nor there may lead to 'anywhere', so being cut off from the past and from a pre-given future may open possibilities of other – better – futures. The camp therefore on the one hand forces its inhabitants to live in what seems an interminable present while on the other it affords glimpses of hope, of concrete utopias into which one must lean forward.

Conclusion

In this chapter I have tried in very general terms to investigate what makes up a camp and to push some of our understandings of the camp – challenging common assumptions about the relationship between human mobility and agency and between confinement and social death.

The materiality of the camp limits the spatial mobility of the refugees. It confines and directs their movements, as they have to remain within certain limits, collect food and water in designated spaces, follow building regulations, and only trade in designated marketplaces. Often, the infrastructure is defined by health and fire hazards as well as the logistics of humanitarian assistance. However, the materials of the camp may also be repurposed by the refugees, thus creating what Abourahme (2015) calls a 'spill-over'. Holes in the fence, footpaths leading outside the camp, trading tarpaulins, all mark how the materials and the infrastructures spill over and no longer follow their original carceral functions. Characteristically, the blue and white UNHCR tarpaulins that are given to refugees for shelter become a dominant feature of the land- and cityscapes that surround the camp for miles.

By adding a temporal aspect, we perhaps become better equipped to understand the confining aspects of camps. It is the temporary nature of camps and the fact that they are 'permanently temporary' that makes them difficult places to live in.

Time in this sense is 'time to come': what will happen in the future? Will I be able to move on? Will I get my permit or not? It is the future that matters and agency lies in these anticipations of these unknown futures. Through hope and anxiety, refugees and migrants try to navigate and act in the present, however bad their present is.

Furthermore, I have proposed the idea of camps as carceral junctions because camps are places that incarcerate. They stop movement. They isolate and separate. But they also bring people together in new constellations, what Agier has called 'carrefours' (crossroads). Furthermore, they act as stepping stones for onward journeys, waiting rooms in which the traveller pauses and gets her bearings, and as points at which one's journey might take a turn. By proposing the idea of carceral junctions. I have tried to overcome the distinction between camps as structures and refugees as agency and explore how camps can produce both stasis and movement.

Note

1 https://amis.ku.dk/research/camp/ (accessed 14 August 2021).

References

Abourahme, Nasser. 2015. 'Assembling and spilling-over: Towards an "ethnography of cement" in a Palestinian refugee camp', *International Journal of Urban and Regional Research* 39(2): 200–17. https://doi.org/10.1111/1468-2427.12155.

Agamben, Giorgio. 1998. *Homo Sacer: Sovereign power and bare life*. Stanford, CA: Stanford University Press.

Agier, Michel. 2014. 'Introduction: L'encampement du monde'. In *Un monde de camps*, edited by Michel Agier, 11–28. Paris: La Découverte.

Auyero, Javier. 2011. 'Patients of the state: An ethnographic account of poor people's waiting', *Latin American Research Review* 46(1): 5–29. https://doi.org/10.1353/lar.2011.0014.

Bissell, David. 2007. 'Animating suspension: Waiting for mobilities', *Mobilities* 2(2): 277–98. https://doi.org/10.1080/17450100701381581.

Bloch, Ernst. 1986. *The Principle of Hope*. Cambridge, MA: MIT Press.

Bochmann, Annett. 2018. 'The power of local micro structures in the context of refugee camps', *Journal of Refugee Studies* 32(1): 63–85. https://doi.org:10.1093/jrs/fey018.

Bosworth, Mary and Mhairi Guild. 2008. 'Governing through migration control: Security and citizenship in Britain', *British Journal of Criminology* 48(6): 703–19. https://doi.org:10.1093/bjc/azn059.

Bourdieu, Pierre. 2000. *Pascalian Meditations*. Translated by Richard Nice. Stanford, CA: Stanford University Press.

Bournes, Debra A. and Gail J. Mitchell. 2002. 'Waiting: The experience of persons in a critical care waiting room', *Research in Nursing & Health* 25(1): 58–67. https://doi.org/10.1002/nur.10019.

Brun, Cathrine. 2015. 'Active waiting and changing hopes', *Social Analysis* 59(1): 19–37. https://doi.org:10.3167/sa.2015.590102.

Cooper, Elizabeth and David Pratten. 2015. *Ethnographies of Uncertainty in Africa*. Basingstoke: Palgrave Macmillan.

Da Col, Giovanni and Caroline Humphrey. 2012. 'Subjects of luck: Contingency, morality, and the anticipation of everyday life', *Social Analysis* 56(2): 1–18. https://doi.org/10.3167/sa.2012.560202.

Deleuze, Gilles and Félix Guattari. 1987. *A Thousand Plateaus: Capitalism and schizophrenia*. Translated by Brian Massumi. Minneapolis: University of Minnesota Press.

Diken, Bülent and Carsten Bagge Laustsen. 2006. 'The camp', *Geografiska Annaler: Series B, Human Geography* 88(4): 443–52. https://doi.org/10.1111/j.0435-3684.2006.00232.x.

Drotbohm, Heike and Ines Hasselberg. 2015. 'Deportation, anxiety, justice: New ethnographic perspectives', *Journal of Ethnic and Migration Studies* 41(4): 551–62. https://doi.org/10.1080/1369183X.2014.957171.

Edkins, Jenny. 2000. 'Sovereign power, zones of indistinction and the camp', *Alternatives: Global, Local, Political* 25(1): 3–25. https://doi.org/10.1177/030437540002500102.

Gill, Nick. 2013. 'Mobility versus liberty? The punitive uses of movement within and outside carceral environments'. In *Carceral Spaces: Mobility and agency in imprisonment and migrant detention*, edited by Dominique Moran, Nick Gill and Deirdre Conlon, 19–36. Farnham: Ashgate.

Hailey, Charlie. 2009. *Camps: A guide to 21st-century space*. Cambridge, MA: MIT Press.

Holzer, Elizabeth and Kamryn Warren. 2015. 'Humanitarian spectacles from below: A study of social connections in unsettled contexts', *Ethnography* 16(4): 482–502. https://doi.org/10.1177/1466138114562310.

Honwana, Alcinda M. 2012. *The Time of Youth: Work, social change, and politics in Africa*. Boulder, CO: Kumarian Press.

Ibañez Tirado, Diana. 2018. '"We sit and wait": Migration, mobility and temporality in Guliston, southern Tajikistan', *Current Sociology* 67(2): 315–33. https://doi.org/10.1177/0011392118792923.

Jansen, Bram. 2008. 'Between vulnerability and assertiveness: Negotiating resettlement in Kakuma refugee camp, Kenya', *African Affairs* 107(429): 569–87. https://doi.org/10.1093/afraf/adn044.

Jansen, Bram. 2011. 'The accidental city: Violence, economy and humanitarianism in Kakuma refugee camp, Kenya'. PhD thesis, Wageningen University.

Jansen, Stef. 2014. 'Hope for/against the state: Gridding in a besieged Sarajevo suburb', *Ethnos* 79(2): 238–60. https://doi.org/10.1080/00141844.2012.743469.
Jefferson, Andrew, Simon Turner and Steffen Jensen. 2019. 'Introduction: On stuckness and sites of confinement', *Ethnos* 84(1): 1–13. https://doi.org/10.1080/00141844.2018.1544917.
Jeffrey, Craig. 2008. 'Waiting', *Environment and Planning D: Society and Space* 26(6): 954–8. doi:10.1068/d2606ed.
Jeffrey, Craig. 2010. *Timepass: Youth, class, and the politics of waiting in India*. Stanford, CA: Stanford University Press.
Katz, Irit. 2017. 'Between *Bare Life* and *Everyday Life*: Spatializing Europe's migrant camps', *Architecture_MPS* 12(2): 1–20. https://doi.org/https://doi.org/10.14324/111.444.amps.2017v12i2.001.
Kleist, Nauja and Stef Jansen. 2016. 'Introduction: Hope over time – crisis, immobility and future-making', *History and Anthropology* 27(4): 373–92. https://doi.org/10.1080/02757206.2016.1207636.
Kreichauf, René. 2018. 'From forced migration to forced arrival: The campization of refugee accommodation in European cities', *Comparative Migration Studies* 6 (art. no. 7). https://doi.org/10.1186/s40878-017-0069-8.
Levitas, Ruth. 1990. 'Educated hope: Ernst Bloch on abstract and concrete hope', *Utopian Studies* 1(2): 13–26.
Maestri, Gaja and Sarah M. Hughes. 2017. 'Contested spaces of citizenship: Camps, borders and urban encounters', *Citizenship Studies* 21(6): 625–39. https://doi.org/10.1080/13621025.2017.1341657.
McConnachie, Kirsten. 2014. *Governing Refugees: Justice, order and legal pluralism*. Abingdon and New York: Routledge.
Meiches, Benjamin. 2015. 'A political ecology of the camp', *Security Dialogue* 46(5): 476–92. https://doi.org/10.1177/0967010615590752.
Minca, Claudio. 2015. 'Geographies of the camp', *Political Geography* 49: 74–83. https://doi.org/10.1016/j.polgeo.2014.12.005.
Moran, Dominique. 2015. *Carceral Geography: Spaces and practices of incarceration*. Farnham: Ashgate.
Moran, Dominique, Nick Gill and Deirdre Conlon, eds. 2013. *Carceral Spaces: Mobility and agency in imprisonment and migrant detention*. Farnham: Ashgate.
Moran, Joe. 2004. 'November in Berlin: The end of the everyday', *History Workshop Journal* 57(1): 216–34. https://doi.org/10.1093/hwj/57.1.216.
Oesch, Lucas. 2017. 'The refugee camp as a space of multiple ambiguities and subjectivities', *Political Geography* 60: 110–20. https://doi.org/10.1016/j.polgeo.2017.05.004.
Owens, Patricia. 2009. 'Reclaiming "bare life"? Against Agamben on refugees', *International Relations* 23(4): 567–82. https://doi.org/10.1177/0047117809350545.
Pedersen, Thomas R. 2019. 'Ambivalent anticipations: On soldierly becomings in the desert of the real', *Cambridge Journal of Anthropology* 37(1): 77–92. https://doi.org/10.3167/cja.2019.370107.
Ramadan, Adam. 2013. 'Spatialising the refugee camp', *Transactions of the Institute of British Geographers* 38(1): 65–77. doi:10.1111/j.1475-5661.2012.00509.x.
Ramadan, Adam and Sara Fregonese. 2017. 'Hybrid sovereignty and the state of exception in the Palestinian refugee camps in Lebanon', *Annals of the American Association of Geographers* 107(4): 949–63. https://doi.org/10.1080/24694452.2016.1270189.
Ramsay, Georgina. 2017. 'Incommensurable futures and displaced lives: Sovereignty as control over time', *Public Culture* 29(3 (83)): 515–38. https://doi.org/10.1215/08992363-3869584.
Redclift, Victoria. 2013. 'Abjects or agents? Camps, contests and the creation of "political space"', *Citizenship Studies* 17(3–4): 308–21. https://doi.org/10.1080/13621025.2013.791534.
Sigona, Nando. 2015. 'Campzenship: Reimagining the camp as a social and political space', *Citizenship Studies* 19(1): 1–15. https://doi.org/10.1080/13621025.2014.937643.
Turner, Jennifer and Kimberley A. Peters, eds. 2017. *Carceral Mobilities: Interrogating movement in incarceration*. Abingdon and New York: Routledge.
Turner, Simon. 2010. *Politics of Innocence: Hutu identity, conflict and camp life*. New York and Oxford: Berghahn Books.
Turner, Simon. 2015. '"We wait for miracles": Ideas of hope and future among clandestine Burundian refugees in Nairobi'. In *Ethnographies of Uncertainty in Africa*, edited by Elizabeth Cooper and David Pratten, 173–92. Basingstoke: Palgrave Macmillan.

Turner, Simon. 2016a. 'Staying out of place: The being and becoming of Burundian refugees in the camp and the city', *Conflict and Society: Advances in Research* 2(1): 37–51. https://doi.org/10.3167/arcs.2016.020106.

Turner, Simon. 2016b. 'What is a refugee camp? Explorations of the limits and effects of the camp', *Journal of Refugee Studies* 29(2): 139–48. https://doi.org/10.1093/jrs/fev024.

Whyte, Susan R. 2005. 'Uncertain undertakings: Practicing health care in the subjunctive mood'. In *Managing Uncertainty: Ethnographic studies of illness, risk and the struggle for control*, edited by Richard Jenkins, Hanne Jessen and Vibeke Steffen, 245–64. Copenhagen: Museum Tusculanum Press.

Whyte, Zachary and Michael Ulfstjerne. 2020. 'Flexible shelters, modular meanings: The lives and afterlives of Danish "refugee villages"'. In *Structures of Protection? Rethinking refugee shelter*, edited by Tom Scott-Smith and Mark E. Breeze, 211–33. New York and Oxford: Berghahn Books.

Part II

Materialising methods: applying things in (forced) migration research

Introduction

Friedemann Yi-Neumann

The research of material culture has taken a diverse range of methodological approaches and been influenced by a number of different disciplines, including social and cultural anthropology, sociology, and classical and contemporary archaeology (Hicks 2010).[1] This part will focus on anthropological and approaches, though. There is no coherent methodical approach to material culture in the social and cultural sciences. In 2020, Sophie Woodward published what could be considered the first application-oriented monograph on the topic by bringing together anthropological, archaeological and arts-based material culture research methods.

Woodward (2014, 00:09) argues that, methodologically speaking, 'material culture in itself isn't a method per se but ... what we might think about more as a kind of approach to research, ... to thinking about various different topics.' In this volume, we propose similarly candid and explorative perspectives on things: ranging from ethnographic to archaeological to curatorial phenomenological to praxeological perspectives, all seeking to explore how things matter, move and transform (forced) migrations, and to look at how these things are used, valued, worn and discarded, and how these things unite and bring together, and how they divide and separate. Rather than merely interpreting what things mean, it is vital that we understand the 'synthetic capability' (Geismar and Horst 2004, 6) of the material and its extreme flexibility in terms of social engagement and effect (Geismar and Horst 2004, 7). The perceptional, substantial and practical 'changeabilities' of things (Stockhammer 2020, 37–43) are in themselves significant, especially in (forced) migration research, where people have to renegotiate themselves, and their belongings, in new environments.

Daniel Miller (2010, 48; 2007, 24–5) has tenaciously refused to define what 'materiality' is, or how to research it, for this very openness is the great advantage of materiality, enabling ethnographers to look at things in countless ways (see also Dudley 2021, 11). At the same time, this sort of refusal to specify materiality or how it should be studied may be a reason for the lack of concrete methodological frameworks – except in archaeology – that is based on the anthropological assumption that any issues will somehow be resolved during ethnographic fieldwork.

Indeed, things can become especially fruitful research objects or subjects. If used unthinkingly or as supposedly intrinsic 'markers', however, they can become problematic objects for manifesting and essentialising 'knowledge' about 'others' (Galitzine-Loumpet 2020, 42). Nevertheless, using things ethnographically can have an unsettling potential, pushing researchers to reflect on their approaches, perspectives and assumptions and, above all, the relevance of things in a certain setting (see Elena Höpfner in this volume). In other words, migration scholars do not only follow things; they actively employ them, and change their courses, roles and (interim) destinations, for better or for worse.

However, people on the move do not simply bring belongings with them along infrastructures of movement such as cars, ships or streets, and by circumventing or crossing structures of partitioning such as borders; they also establish themselves in new environments and condition and assemble things in new ways by bringing them into 'contact' (see for instance Greenblatt 2009). Limiting material (forced) migration research to 'migrants and their possessions', therefore, is a methodological mistake since a profound perspective also has to take into account the social, cultural and political conditions and movements of migration (Römhild 2015).

Ethnographic approaches to things

The in-depth and comprehensive understandings of ethnographic approaches make them powerful in the study of material migrations and their broader conditions. (Material) ethnography is characterised by the employment of and experimention with a wide range of methods, including participation, observation, ethnographic interviewing, informal conversations and multi-sited research (Woodward 2020, 119; O'Neill 2012; Hamilakis and Anagnostopoulos 2009, 75), all based on the establishment of relationships of trusts with interlocutors. That being said, different methodological tools also provide different perspectives on things. I would like to present some material methods relevant to migration anthropology more generally, and to the contributions in this volume.

Things and biographies

One of the most commonly applied methodological concepts in material culture studies is undoubtedly *the (cultural) biography of things* (Kopytoff 1986; on biographical approaches, see Yi-Neumann, Chapter 4 in this volume). This approach seeks to understand the altering forms and social functions of material objects by examining their shifts between different social and economic spheres (for instance as gifts or commodities) in which the objects are re-embedded and can gain singular value. With his highly influential approach to *multi-sited ethnography*, George Marcus (1995) took up and extended the idea of a cultural biography of things, issuing the dictum *follow the things* (and the people, the metaphors, the stories and the conflicts). These five dictums have been – implicitly and explicitly – applied in many studies of (forced) migrations;[2] and today the concept of *following* has become a key component in the ethnographic toolkit for material culture approaches to forced migration, mobility and beyond (see for example Dudley 2021, and Şanlı in this volume).

The term 'biography' as a metaphor for keeping track of things has been criticised for various reasons by material culture scholars. However, the alternative terminologies that have been proposed have proven unwieldy.[3] Therefore, while the authors in this volume talk of the 'biographies of things', they do so with caution, understanding biography to mean open-ended, multi-directional, entangled, and transformative in a social (materiality) and substantial (material) sense.

While the 'biographies of things' approach facilitates a critical understanding of the shifts, recontextualisations and transformations of things on a societal and cultural level, the anthropologist Janet Hoskins's (1998) concept of *biographical objects* adds another dimension to the relationship between people and things. By examining biographical objects, Hoskins seeks to grasp how things become part of people's biographies through practical and mobile employment over time, and how these personal items are then used to express people's biographies in return (see also Miller 2010, 65). In the context of forced migration in particular, a number of journalists[4] and critical migration scholars (for example Alexandre-Garner and Galitzine-Loumpet 2020) have used biographical objects as a lens to look at the evolvement, movements and (bio)politics of human–thing ties.

Together, these biographical approaches allow researchers to comprehend not only the material shifts and transformations, along with practices, preceptions and movements, but also the conflation of humans and things over time. In the following section, we turn to approaches that are meant to unearth and verbalise the often unconscious attachments to things.

Object-based conversations

As the cornerstone of ethnographic fieldwork, participant observation is usually complemented by ethnographic interviewing to better understand the observed by contrasting and collating it with the spoken (Hahn 2013, 78–80). Ethnographic interviews are characterised by ongoing trustful relationships and a certain openness regarding the questions and course of conversations (Heyl 2007, 369). In such conversations, things can serve as multivocal 'prompts' and reference points.

While constructivist scholars have stated that all conversation participants (co)produce knowledge (Briggs 2007, 554), material anthropologists have underlined the active role of things in these conversations. This argument led anthropologists to conduct research (on forced migrations) from the point of view of the material objects themselves as a heuristic lens (Dudley 2021; Giaccardi et al. 2016; Henare et al. 2007). Things, they argue from experience, can have vigorous and surprising affects (Woodward 2020, 36). As things matter beyond words or signs of meaning (Auslander 2005; Hoskins 1998), it can be necessary for interviewers to pay attention to interlocutors' silences, their inability and sometimes refusal to express sensations, emotions and connections to things in words (Woodward 2020, 39–41). Object-based interviews focus not only on single, biographical or valuable possessions, but also on seemingly unimportant or insignificant things. The relevance of such things is often realised only when they become objects of attention and reflection, or when they spark irritations in the everyday. In this light, the nexus of affective unpredictability and consistency in things makes them methodologically promising to examine (Neumann and Hahn 2019, 41–2).

Researchers conducting material ethnographic research in the context of (forced) migration require, in particular, empathy, sensitivity and consideration. A lack of sensitivity or understanding can result in problematic transgressions of boundaries drawn by interlocutors, who are often denied privacy, certainty and consistency. Ethnographers have to comprehend and respect such boundaries, related as they are to specific research contexts, and not as things that need to be transgressed to 'unveil the truth' (Klingenberg 2019). Here, researchers should prioritise doing no harm to interlocutors, but also aim to go beyond that by developing collaborations beneficial to both parties (Mackenzie et al. 2007).

The underlying affective potency of things (Frykman and Povrzanović Frykman 2016) can become a severe challenge for researchers, sparking unpleasant or painful emotions. Possibly fearful and mistrustful, interlocutors may interpret a researcher's interest in personal possessions as a cover for their 'actual' intentions: gathering sensitive information (see Elena Höpfner in this volume). Moreover, asking for permission to record audio, to film or to take photos, and especially the term 'interview' itself, can be highly problematic in the context of an asylum centre. We, the MatMig researchers, avoided the word in our research in a German asylum reception centre.[5] In this context, our interlocutors connected the term 'interview' with the Federal Office for Migration and Refugees' stressful, fear-laden interrogations during asylum (application) procedures. In this light, it becomes clear why many camp or reception facility residents may not be eager to expose themselves to another 'interview'.

In general, forms and variants of conversations and exchanges about material objects have to be carefully adapted to research conditions on the ground. Not least in the face of the Covid-19 pandemic, this need to adopt new methods became (painfully) apparent to many anthropologists. I turn to some remote approaches now.

Material remote ethnography

The Covid-19 pandemic has proved to be a substantial challenge to the 'classic' anthropological means of establishing trust with interlocutors, the long-term field stay (Miller 2010, 11). People affected by the virus and the measures to tackle it have had to develop new routines and adapt to severely limited social interactions, interactions that are the basis of participant observation. Similarly, ethnographers have had to develop creative ways of studying the materiality of migration during the pandemic (see Maruška Svašek in this volume). Digital anthropology (see Miller 2018) is, of course, not new, and a number of works at least partly related to migration have been produced in the last few years (Miller et al. 2016; Whitehead and Wesch 2012; Hine 2000). Indeed, some digital anthropologists have explicitly elaborated the relationship between the virtual and material cultures (Pink et al. 2016a). This parallel between the virtual and the material may not come as a surprise, since things have also been conceptualised as 'bundles of relations' (Fowler and Harris

2015) and can therefore be studied in similar ways.[6] In other words, virtual space does not make things obsolete; rather, they remain research objects in the digital realm and, in this context, prompt other, new questions about how things are entangled and how they matter (Pink et al. 2016b, 59–78). Migration anthropologists have also examined the materiality of information and communications technologies (ICTs) and how they affect people's lives (e.g. Madianou and Miller 2012).

However, the pandemic has unveiled not only new urgencies and potentialities of digital fieldwork, but also the challenges it poses to established means of ethnographic research. Anthropologists are now forced to establish trust, personal relations and cooperation via ICTs (Palmberger and Budka 2020). Digital anthropological approaches have, almost overnight, developed from a marginal phenomenon into a key set of tools. While many analogue researchers struggle with the seemingly limited scope digital access entails, for others these circumstances have become an incentive to engage in dynamic and intense research through a plethora of different devices, apps and methods of (collaborative) data collection (Ramella et al. 2017). These engagements may differ, especially in terms of perception, but they are not necessarily inferior to conventional field research in terms of intensity, proximity and productivity (see Bayat Tork forthcoming). These remote tools are wide-ranging, from messenger and social media groups to text-based and visuals-based methods to digital diaries, story completion methods, and design/art/material-based approaches. Here, new issues about private and public realms can appear even though the fundamental anthropological task of collaborating with people (on the move) in depth and contextualising migrations by their material conditions remains similar. The use of ICTs in anthropology, though, requires the development and employment of considerate, creative and empathetic approaches to in-depth research, be it online or on the ground.

Translating, piling, assembling

In the course of migrations, things are 'brought over'. This does not mean, though, that they simply move unaltered from A to B. Rather, things are 'translated', recontextualised, and re-engaged in new environments as people struggle to establish themselves in new and often challenging (forced) migration contexts. These material shifts mean material transformations and appropriations (Basu and Coleman 2008, 327–8), even in quite precarious contexts. This process is related to the following question: to what extent do things remain what they were, or do they become new entities with new qualities when becoming embedded and used in new environments?

Forced migrants, in particular, are often confronted with the loss and destruction of their belongings. By applying archaeological methods to the examination of the material remains and structures destroyed in the Dzhangal ('Jungle') Camp in Calais, Sarah Mallet and Louise Fowler (in this volume) prove, illustrate and contextualise the extensive use of violence and destruction by police in clearing the camp. In reassembling the materialisation of border politics, they show how people are violently pushed to society's margins, and how their provisional shelters and infrastructures for survival are destroyed.

Material culture scholars have studied boundary-making in more ordinary, quotidian contexts as well. In her work on privacy, Christena Nippert-Eng (2010, 97–158) asks interlocutors to discuss quotidian things, like the contents of their handbag. In recontextualising these things, and by piling and shifting them, she unearths how things matter in relation to one another, and how people negotiate boundaries of privacy along and between them.

Thus, seeking to understand not only the relational relevance between things but also their categorisation can provide valuable insights. Visual documentation – photos, self-narrated video tours, mapping – of contexts and practices shows how things matter in and as constellative ties and boundaries (Woodward 2020, 74–84). Scholars who work on *home* or *home cultures* have contributed to an analytical understanding of the material constellations, relatedness and boundaries in (forced) migrations. Focusing on sensory and transformative assemblages and the rearrangement and appropriations of material objects allows for a thing-based analysis of power struggles, of strategies, of place-making and of a sense of home in transnational (forced) migrations and everyday lives (see Boccagni 2020, 2014; Dudley 2011; Bonfanti 2020; Şenoğuz forthcoming).

Reassembling material objects in museum displays is another form of recontextualising material culture. In the early 1980s, Daniel Miller (see Hicks 2010, 54–5) critiqued ethnoarchaeological approaches which fetishised archaeological objects by understanding them as tags standing for certain 'cultural groups'. Such representative claims are problematic because exhibits often become or became part of collections through random, bizarre and questionable means (Appadurai 2017, 402–5), to name an example. This critique is also relevant to discussions of and disputes over the frequently violent colonial 'appropriation' of material objects, for instance the role of ethnographic collections and the ways researchers and curators use(d) and (do not) reconstitute them (see for example Thomas 1991, 125–84; Clifford 1997, 197–219, 278–98; Basu 2017, 135–9; Hicks 2020).

Forced migration scholars, migrants and activists have also used material objects to 'queer' classical heritage institutions (see Mallet and Fowler, Şanlı and Suhr in this volume) by bringing materials seen as rubbish or waste into museums. In so doing, they seek to display the precarious realities of the border, and human rights violations, and to show how experiences and perspectives are multiple.[7] In a similar vein, engaging collections in participatory research has been considered an effective and viable tool for reflecting on issues, voids and the relevance of museum collections (Friberg and Huvila 2019). Others have challenged the institutional privilege of displaying 'original objects' and developed impressive curatorial answers in order to overcome this issue and democratise migration exhibitions.[8]

Summary

The anthropology of material culture is not a single method, but rather entails a wide range of adaptable approaches. In this introduction, I have presented a short overview of material culture methodologies relevant to engaged ethnographic research in the context of (forced) migrations. Biographical approaches allow for an understanding of the transformative entanglements of things and humans over time. Material culture's affective potential – for example by recognising the emotional significance of personal belongings – can stimulate and drive insightful conversations and interviews during ethnographic research. The use of ICTs and digital anthropology – especially in the context of Covid-19 – allows for ethnographic fieldwork with interlocutors on a daily basis, for engagement in their routines, as well as practical and quotidian material engagement over distance. Understanding and documenting assemblages, from borderlands to homes, allow for a detailed and profound personal, social and political form of contextualising (forced) migrations. At the same time, researchers are developing new assemblages such as museum displays, moving from ethnographic documentation to object-based forms of representation, which themselves become important subjects of research.

Contributions to Part II

Part II comprises contributions from diverse field sites: the hostile Lande camp environment in Calais, asylum reception facilities in Germany, Mediterranean border crossings in Lesvos, and museums. The chapters include creative and critical considerations of how migration scholars use things for their research. These ethnographic and qualitative migration approaches consider both the materials and their properties, as well as their effect on forced migrations and the (trans)formation of materials in and through use and movement, and their (lacking) representation.

The disciplinary backgrounds of the authors – sociology, anthropology, contemporary archaeology and curatorial studies – influence their perspectives on things and how they employ them in their object-based research. Material objects – clothing, soft toys, life jackets, tear gas canisters – become objects and tools of research, or museum displays. These things rarely matter alone, but also in relation to shifting environments and social practices: they are moved, collected, assembled, lost, confiscated or given away in the context of migration. The focus on things and the researchers' perspectives can provide alternative understandings of forced migrations and unfold disturbing, surprising and reflective insights on interrelations. Indeed, by looking at multiple fields and from differing perspectives, we hope to develop new angles on the personal and political dimensions of the materialities of forced migrations.

Elena Höpfner provides an unflinching and (self-)critical reflection on research on residents in asylum reception facilities in Germany and on their belongings. The sociologist focuses on eventualities and problems, ethical issues and the obstacles her object-oriented analysis faced in challenging research settings characterised by uncertainty, precarity, lack of privacy and mistrust. Höpfner refers to how academics use things as research tools. However, she also refers to the tactics her interlocutors developed to 'hide behind things' or to deny possessions to limit the disclosure of information. Here, she asks when and under which conditions such research is legitimate, and what it can actually show.

In another contribution based on ethnographic research in a German asylum reception centre, Friedemann Yi-Neumann provides a perspective on personal belongings and their shifting relevances during flight and during years of protracted displacement. Employing both well-known and less well-known theoretical concepts, the anthropologist proposes the concept of 'biographical horizons'. Through this lens, Yi-Neumann aims to articulate phenomenological and intersectional perspectives on biographical objects. The weight of such items takes form along relations of proximity and distance by which the (social) relations between people and things unfold.

Sarah Mallet and Louise Fowler focus on material culture at the infamous refugee camp in Calais, Dzhangal. By employing contemporary archaeological and anthropological methods, they provide evidence of the devastating consequences of racism and systematic state violence that are rarely noticed in public discourses, but which significantly shape border politics on the European continent. Considering two collections of objects that found their way to the Pitt Rivers Museum and became displays, the archaeologists cooperating with artists visualise the political and social dynamics that shape(d) the conditions in the camp where up to 10,000 forced migrants live(d) in the hope of making it to the UK and having a decent life.

Ayşe Şanlı's research is dedicated to the material culture of risky border crossings along the EU's Mediterranean border. As a member of a curatorial team, she considers how objects used to cross borders, like life jackets, can be used in archaeology and anthropology to display issues related to undocumented and forced migrations. By following things, their contested evaluations and their multiple lives, Ayşe provides an insightful multi-sited perspective on the 'transient matters' of forced migrations and their representation. Here, stuff considered 'trash' on Lesvos becomes a museum object in the USA. Between 'these two things', a whole variety of transnational personal, creative and political interrelations unfold.

Notes

1 Without doubt, science and technology studies (STS) and actor–network theory (ANT) have yielded important methodological insights in the last few decades. However, as material, culture-based inquiries into (forced) migrations rarely refer to STS and ANT systematically, and moreover the approaches focus on networks rather than on material objects themselves, I have taken the liberty of dispensing with the methodological contributions of STS in this short introduction.

2 See Petridou (2020) on life jackets and border crossings; Mata-Codesal and Abranches (2018) on food parcels in transnational migration; Stein (2015) on dispossession; Boccagni (2014) on remittances homes; and Rosales (2017) and Dudley (2002) on consumption.

3 See Stockhammer (2020, 40–1), 'itinerancy'; Hahn and Weiss (2013) and Joy (2009), 'itineraries'.

4 See, for example, pictures by Mollison (2015), or the articles by Paul (2017) and Zhang (2013).

5 This was raised by our colleague Malihé Bayat Tork and repeatedly discussed within the project team during the research phase.

6 Fowler and Harris (2015, 128) criticise the paradigm, though, as it fails to consider the material qualities as well as the historical emergence and persistence of things.

7 See, for instance, 'Transient matter: Assemblages of migration in the Mediterranean', from February 2020 (on-site and online), Haffenreffer Museum of Anthropology, curated by Yannis Hamilakis, L. Darcy Hackley, Sherena Razek and Ayşe Şanlı; 'Lande: The Calais "Jungle" and

beyond', Pitt Rivers Museum, Oxford, 27 April–29 November 2019, curated by Majid Adin, Shaista Aziz, Caroline Gregory, Dan Hicks, Sarah Mallet, Nour Munawar, Sue Partridge, Noah Salibo and Wshear Wali, https://www.prm.ox.ac.uk/event/lande (accessed 16 August 2021); 'The shores of Austria', from 19 September 2018, Volkskundemuseum Wien, curated by Yarden Daher, Alexander Martos, Negin Rezaie, Ramin Siawash, Niko Wahl, Sama Yasseen and Reza Zobeidi https://www.volkskundemuseum.at/theshoresofaustria (accessed 16 August 2021).

8 A well-known example is the global pop-up exhibition 'Hostile terrain 94', curated by Jason De León (University of California) and the Undocumented Migration Project team, https://www.undocumentedmigrationproject.org/hostileterrain94 (accessed 16 August 2021).

References

Alexandre-Garner, Corinne and Alexandra Galitzine-Loumpet, eds. 2020. *L'Objet de la migration, le sujet en exil.* Paris and Nanterre: Presses Universitaires de Paris Nanterre.

Appadurai, Arjun. 2017. 'Museum objects as accidental refugees', *Historische Anthropologie* 25(3): 401–8. http://dx.doi.org/10.7788/ha-2017-0306.

Auslander, Leora. 2005. 'Beyond words', *American Historical Review* 110(4): 1015–45. https://doi.org/10.1086/ahr.110.4.1015.

Basu, Paul 2017. 'Communicating anthropology: Writing, screening, and exhibiting culture'. In *The Routledge Companion to Contemporary Anthropology*, edited by Simon Coleman, Susan B. Hyatt and Ann Kingsolver, 124–43. New York: Routledge.

Basu, Paul and Simon Coleman. 2008. 'Introduction: Migrant worlds, material cultures', *Mobilities* 3(3): 313–30. https://doi.org/10.1080/17450100802376753.

Bayat Tork, Malihé. Forthcoming. 'Ethnography during the pandemic: Working paper on remote ethnography', unpublished manuscript.

Boccagni, Paolo. 2014. 'What's in a (migrant) house? Changing domestic spaces, the negotiation of belonging and home-making in Ecuadorian migration', *Housing, Theory and Society* 31(3): 277–93. https://doi.org/10.1080/14036096.2013.867280.

Boccagni, Paolo. 2020. 'At home in the centre? Spatial appropriation and horizons of homemaking in reception facilities for asylum seekers', HOMInG Working Papers 10–2020, ERC StG HOMInG, Università di Trento.

Bonfanti, Sara. 2020. '(Im)materiality'. In *Ethnographies of Home and Mobility: Shifting roofs*, by Alejandro Miranda Nieto, Aurora Massa and Sara Bonfanti, 39–66. Abingdon and New York: Routledge.

Briggs, Charles L. 2007. 'Anthropology, interviewing, and communicability in contemporary society', *Current Anthropology* 48(4): 551–80. https://doi.org/10.1086/518300.

Clifford, James. 1997. *Routes: Travel and translation in the late twentieth century*. Cambridge, MA, and London: Harvard University Press.

Dudley, Sandra H. 2002. 'Local identities and global flows of objects and images', *Oxford Development Studies* 30(2): 165–76. https://doi.org/10.1080/13600810220138276.

Dudley, Sandra. 2011. 'Feeling at home: Producing and consuming things in Karenni refugee camps on the Thai-Burma border', *Population, Space and Place* 17: 742–55. https://doi.org/10.1002/psp.639.

Dudley, Sandra H. 2021. *Displaced Things in Museums and Beyond: Loss, liminality and hopeful encounters*. Abingdon: Routledge.

Fowler, Chris and Oliver J. T. Harris. 2015. 'Enduring relations: Exploring a paradox of new materialism', *Journal of Material Culture* 20(2): 127–48. https://doi.org/10.1177%2F1359183515577176.

Friberg, Zanna and Isto Huvila. 2019. 'Using object biographies to understand the curation crisis: Lessons learned from the museum life of an archaeological collection', *Museum Management and Curatorship* 34(4): 362–82. https://doi.org/10.1080/09647775.2019.1612270.

Frykman, Jonas and Maja Povrzanović Frykman. 2016. 'Affect and material culture: Perspectives and strategies'. In *Sensitive Objects: Affect and material culture*, edited by Jonas Frykman and Maja Povrzanović Frykman, 9–28. Lund: Nordic Academic Press.

Galitzine-Loumpet, Alexandra. 2020. 'De/dans et de/hors: Objets et sujets dans la migration et l'exil'. In *L'Objet de la migration, le sujet en exil*, edited by Corinne Alexandre-Garner and Alexandra Galitzine-Loumpet, 35–49. Paris and Nanterre: Presses Universitaires de Paris Nanterre.

Geismar, Haidy and Heather A. Horst. 2004. 'Materializing ethnography', *Journal of Material Culture* 9(1): 5–10. https://doi.org/10.1177/1359183504041086.
Giaccardi, Elisa, Chris Speed, Nazli Cila and Melissa L. Caldwell. 2016. 'Things as co-ethnographers: Implications of a thing perspective for design and anthropology'. In *Design Anthropological Futures*, edited by Rachel Charlotte Smith, Kasper Tang Vangkilde, Mette Gislev Kjaersgaard, Ton Otto, Joachim Halse and Thomas Binder, 235–48. London and New York: Bloomsbury Academic.
Greenblatt, Stephen, ed. 2009. *Cultural Mobility: A manifesto*. Cambridge: Cambridge University Press.
Hahn, Hans Peter. 2013. *Ethnologie: Eine Einführung*. Frankfurt: Suhrkamp.
Hahn, Hans Peter and Hadas Weiss. 2013. 'Introduction: Biographies, travels and itineraries of things'. In *Mobility, Meaning and the Transformations of Things: Shifting contexts of material culture through time and space*, edited by Hans Peter Hahn and Hadas Weiss, 1–14. Oxford: Oxbow Books.
Hamilakis, Yannis and Aris Anagnostopoulos. 2009. 'What is archaeological ethnography?', *Public Anthropology* 8(2–3): 65–87. https://doi.org/10.1179/175355309X457150.
Henare, Amiria, Martin Holbraad and Sari Wastell, eds. 2007. *Thinking through Things: Theorising artefacts ethnographically*. Abingdon and New York: Routledge.
Heyl, Barbara S. 2007. 'Ethnographic interviewing'. In *Handbook of Ethnography*, edited by Paul Atkinson, Amanda Coffey, Sara Delamont, John Lofland and Lyn Lofland, 369–83. London and Thousand Oaks, CA: SAGE.
Hicks, Dan. 2010. 'The material-cultural turn: Event and effect'. In *The Oxford Handbook of Material Culture Studies*, edited by Dan Hicks and Mary C. Beaudry, 25–98. Oxford: Oxford University Press.
Hicks, Dan. 2020. *The Brutish Museums: The Benin bronzes, colonial violence and cultural restitution*. London: Pluto Press.
Hine, Christine. 2000. *Virtual Ethnography*. London: SAGE Publications.
Hoskins, Janet. 1998. *Biographical Objects: How things tell the stories of people's lives*. London: Routledge.
Joy, Jody. 2009. 'Reinvigorating object biography: Reproducing the drama of object lives', *World Archaeology* 41(4): 540–56. https://doi.org/10.1080/00438240903345530.
Klingenberg, Darja. 2019. 'Einblicke in migrantische Wohnungen: Erkenntniskritik und Repräsentationspolitik'. In *Das neue Zuhause: Haushalt und Alltag nach der Migration*, edited by Hans Peter Hahn and Friedemann Neumann, 159–80. Frankfurt and New York: Campus.
Kopytoff, Igor. 1986. 'The cultural biography of things: Commoditization as process'. In *The Social Life of Things: Commodities in cultural perspective*, edited by Arjun Appadurai, 64–91. Cambridge: Cambridge University Press.
Mackenzie, Catriona, Christopher McDowell and Eileen Pittaway. 2007. 'Beyond "do no harm": The challenge of constructing ethical relationships in refugee research', *Journal of Refugee Studies* 20(2): 299–319. https://doi.org/10.1093/jrs/fem008.
Madianou, Mirca and Daniel Miller. 2012. *Migration and New Media: Transnational families and polymedia*. Abingdon and New York: Routledge.
Marcus, George E. 1995. 'Ethnography in/of the world system: The emergence of multi-sited ethnography', *Annual Review of Anthropology* 24: 95–117.
Mata-Codesal, Diana and Maria Abranches, eds. 2018. *Food Parcels in International Migration: Intimate connections*. Cham: Palgrave Macmillan.
Miller, Daniel. 2007. 'Stone age or plastic age?', *Archaeological Dialogues* 14(1): 23–7. https://doi.org/10.1017/S1380203807002152.
Miller, Daniel. 2010. *Stuff*. Cambridge: Polity.
Miller, Daniel. 2018. 'Digital anthropology'. In *The Cambridge Encyclopedia of Anthropology*, edited by Felix Stein, Sian Lazar, Matei Candea, Hildegard Diemberger, Joel Robbins, Andrew Sanchez and Rupert Stasch, 1–16. Cambridge: University of Cambridge. http://doi.org/10.29164/18digital.
Miller, Daniel, Elisabetta Costa, Nell Haynes, Tom McDonald, Razvan Nicolescu, Jolynna Sinanan, Juliano Spyer, Shriram Venkatraman and Xinyuan Wang. 2016. *How the World Changed Social Media*. London: UCL Press. https://doi.org/10.14324/111.9781910634493.
Mollison, James. 2015. 'What they carried: Refugees' wordly [sic] possessions in pictures', *Telegraph*, 14 November. Accessed 17 August 2021. https://www.telegraph.co.uk/news/worldnews/europe/11993282/What-they-carried-Refugees-wordly-possessions-in-pictures.html?frame=3498110.

Neumann, Friedemann and Hans Peter Hahn. 2019. 'Between things: Situating (post)migration and material culture in social space'. In *Family and Space: Rethinking family theory and empirical approaches*, edited by Maya Halatcheva-Trapp, Giulia Montanari and Tino Schlinzig, 35–45. Abingdon: Routledge.

Nippert-Eng, Christena. 2010. *Islands of Privacy*. Chicago: University of Chicago Press.

O'Neill, Maggie. 2012. 'Making connections: Biography, art, affect and politics'. In *Moving Subjects, Moving Objects: Transnationalism, cultural production and emotions*, edited by Maruška Svašek, 178–200. New York and Oxford: Berghahn Books.

Palmberger, Monika and Philipp Budka. 2020. 'Collaborative ethnography in the digital age: Towards a new methodological framework'. Digital Ethnography Initiative, Department of Social & Cultural Anthropology, University of Vienna. Accessed 17 August 2021. https://digitalethnography.at/2020/11/13/collaborative-ethnography-in-the-digital-age-towards-a-new-methodological-framework/.

Paul, Joshua. 2017. 'The things they'll take: Refugees and their most precious possessions', *auburnpub.com*, 18 March. Accessed 17 August 2021. https://auburnpub.com/news/world/the-things-they-ll-take-refugees-and-their-most-precious/collection_a7ad148b-ab33-5407-8a4d-e08ccea4d84e.html#1.

Petridou, Elia. 2020. 'Refugee life jackets thrown off but not away: Connecting materialities in upcycling initiatives'. In *Exploring Materiality and Connectivity in Anthropology and Beyond*, edited by Philipp Schorch, Martin Saxer and Marlen Elders, 228–46. London: UCL Press.

Pink, Sarah, Elisenda Ardèvol and Débora Lanzeni. 2016a. *Digital Materialities: Design and anthropology*. London and New York: Bloomsbury Academic.

Pink, Sarah, Heather A. Horst, John Postill, Larissa Hjorth, Tania Lewis and Jo Tacchi. 2016b. *Digital Ethnography: Principles and practice*. Los Angeles, CA, and London: SAGE.

Ramella, Anna Lisa, Asko Lehmuskallio, Tristan Thielmann and Pablo Abend. 2017. 'Mobile digital practices: Situating people, things, and data', *Digital Culture and Society* 3(2): 5–18. http://dx.doi.org/10.14361/dcs-2017-0202.

Römhild, Regina. 2015. 'Jenseits ethnischer Grenzen: Für eine postmigrantische Kultur- und Gesellschaftsforschung'. In *Nach der Migration: Postmigrantische Perspektiven jenseits der Parallelgesellschaft*, edited by Erol Yıldız and Marc Hill, 37–48. Bielefeld: transcript Verlag.

Rosales, Marta V. 2017. 'Materiality, migration and cultural diversity'. In *Routledge Handbook on Consumption*, edited by Margit Keller, Bente Halkier, Terhi-Anna Wilska and Monica Truninger, 282–91. Abingdon and New York: Routledge.

Şenoğuz, H. Pınar. Forthcoming. 'Seeking normalcy at impossible homes: Uncertainty and tactics of dwelling among asylum seeking women in reception centers in Lower Saxony in Germany'. In *Gender, Flight, and Reception Policies: Gender processes of in/exclusion in Lower Saxony*, edited by Sabine Hess. Wiesbaden: Springer VS.

Stein, Rebecca L. 2015. 'Dispossession reconsidered: Israel, Nakba, things', *Ethnologie française* 45(2): 309–20.

Stockhammer, Philipp W. 2020. 'Doing/changing things/us'. In *Exploring Materiality and Connectivity in Anthropology and Beyond*, edited by Philipp Schorch, Martin Saxer and Marlen Elders, 36–50. London: UCL Press.

Thomas, Nicholas. 1991. *Entangled Objects: Exchange, material culture, and colonialism in the Pacific*. Cambridge, MA: Harvard University Press.

Whitehead, Neil L. and Michael Wesch. 2012. *Human No More: Digital subjectivities, unhuman subjects, and the end of anthropology*. Boulder: University Press of Colorado.

Woodward, Sophie. 2014. 'What is material culture?', *methods@manchester*, 26 August. Manchester University, YouTube. Accessed 17 August 2021. https://www.youtube.com/watch?v=yL01mxtRPhA.

Woodward, Sophie. 2020. *Material Methods: Researching and thinking with things*. London and Thousand Oaks, CA: SAGE.

Zhang, Michael. 2013. 'Portraits of refugees posing with their most valued possessions', *PetaPixel*, 21 March. Accessed 17 August 2021. https://petapixel.com/2013/03/21/portraits-of-refugees-posing-with-their-most-valued-possessions/.

3

Why should(n't) refugees be asked about their possessions? A research-ethical and methodological reflection on my fieldwork in a refugee shelter

Elena Höpfner

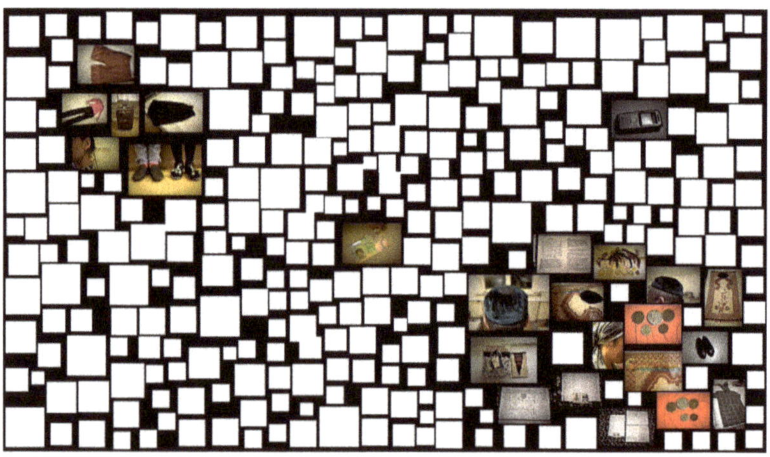

3.1 My own illustration composed of the photographed possessions present during the interviews and put in relation to other possessions that could not be photographed. © Elena Höpfner.

Introduction: 'You write about things? Why about things?'

In autumn 2015, I interviewed 10 residents of a Berlin initial recording facility for refugees, asking them about their personal background and experiences, their escape stories and their possessions. The research question I tried to answer with my field research was: What possessions do people take with them when they flee and what role do these possessions play en route?

I applied for a position as a volunteer Russian-German interpreter in a refugee shelter and presented my research project to the manager of the accommodation. With this employment I was able to visit people I met randomly during the open medical consultation hours, at their invitation. I told them about my research plans at the first meeting and asked if they were interested in participating. By means of a maximum contrast of cases (multiple-case-study), the greatest possible variance should be covered. My interview partners were six women and four men,[1] who were between 24 and 57 years old. I interviewed: people from different republics of Russia, Ukraine, Afghanistan and Egypt; people who travelled by plane, train, bus, car or boat, in a car boot or on foot; people who had wanted to leave for a long time and people who had made the decision the day before; people who fled because of ethnic and religious discrimination, state or domestic violence, political persecution, fear for the lives of family members or because of life-threatening illness. I talked with: self-employed people, workers, employees and housewives; people who travelled alone, or with other family members, children or strangers; people who had had some higher education, had nine years of schooling or were illiterate; people who described themselves as very wealthy, who had led an 'ordinary life' or had had almost nothing; people who loved old things, people who loved new things, people who did not care about things at all. Some interviewees remembered just one item, others named numerous items, in some cases over 60. As it is difficult to remember every little thing that was taken in a hurry, or acquired or disposed of during the escape, my work was limited to fragments, to those excerpts that remained in people's memories and were brought up during the conversations.

I conducted at least one object-related interview with each person and additional spontaneous conversations with some people (see Spradley 1979) about things and their experiences.[2] I interviewed the people where they wanted to talk to me: in their rooms, in other people's rooms or in the corridor of the accommodation. I also photographed certain things. One of the aims of my study was to convey the stories vividly. With the photographs I wanted to give readers a better idea of the things they brought with them and, at least two-dimensionally, of their materiality and corporeality (see also Bosch 2018). Object-related interviews are applied both to better understand the entanglement of subject–object relations and to design standard interviews more creatively (see S. Woodward 2020, 34). Thus, the focus of the analysis and reflection was on the meaning of things during the flight as well as in the interview situation. Sophie Woodward writes in her manual on material methods: '[T]he world is simultaneously material and social, as the things that surround us are an inseparable part of how our relationships to other people are mediated, and the environment, society and culture we live in' (S. Woodward 2020, 1).

Starting from these assumptions, I wish to examine each individual escape story as something that can only be understood holistically through the simultaneous consideration of its material and social components. This preliminary assumption might be, as I explain in the next section, decisive for the generation of important findings on forced migration and its many facets.

The benefits of material culture research in the context of forced migration

All kinds of objects were the subject of the interviews: means of transport, and buildings such as hospitals, police headquarters or border posts, petrol stations and boarding houses, but also smaller objects such as weapons and handcuffs or documents to be signed. These are things that already reveal a great deal about the causes and conditions of escape. Here I concentrated on personal things that had been once or were at the time of the interview in the possession of the interlocutors, because personal things seem to carry a greater significance for their owner than other things (Habermas 1996). And things selected from a larger set of personal things should have an even greater significance, for material culture research too. According to Depner (2015, 11), situations of upheaval break up the self-evident nature of human–thing relationships, making the potential and ambivalence of these relationships particularly evident. Bischoff and Schlör (2013) argue that in such selected personal belongings 'memories of lost homes, of being torn out and on the road, but also of arriving and experiencing heteronomous attributions of meaning in different cultural contexts, are symbolically condensed' (Bischoff and Schlör 2013, 10).[3] Likewise, I focus on the potential of personal things as the key to explaining processes of suffering and coping (see Bosch 2011). I would like to illustrate this with a case study.

The importance of personal things for understanding and objectifying forced migration

Me: And of the things you took with you, did anything make it to Germany?

Fawad: Oh yes, I had a document of identification from Holland with me. I wanted to have it with me, because this is a photo of me. It says that I was about twelve, thirteen years old. And I always liked it because it was a reminder for me of when I was so small. And this photo is very funny and I have that with me. That is with me at the moment . . . [Shows me the photo on the child ID.] Yes, that is quite an old photo. But that was also very dangerous at the Afghan border. And this is just a memory. . . . It has always been small . . . It's easy to bring it here. But I wanted to throw it away on the way where we met these Taliban. Because if they – if they saw that, I had a problem. Because this is a European identity card and they say I am a spy or something [unclear]. People who are not at all educated and who are somewhat educated, they are educated in such a way that they simply take everything in a negative way. And then I wanted to throw that away . . . (Höpfner 2019, 209)

Fawad was in his mid-twenties at the interview. He could already speak German well because he worked for German police in Afghanistan. In the refugee shelter he translated for other refugees. Fawad belonged to the group of interviewees who had taken very few things on the journey. With the help of paid people smugglers he travelled from Afghanistan via Pakistan to Iran, and from there to Turkey and Greece. The narrative on the identity card reveals a lot of interesting information. The criteria according to which this object was chosen as a companion during the escape become clear.

But although Fawad had been carrying the card with him for years, he didn't take it to Germany out of sheer habit or by chance. He decided to take it after he had subjected it to a re-evaluation. Fawad's flight represents a situation of upheaval that broke the naturalness of the relationship with his constant companion (see Depner 2015, 11). In this situation, the possession was consciously or unconsciously reassessed and practically examined (see Bischoff and Schlör 2013, 10).

Fawad's statement also shows that the identity card became a potential danger during the time he was being persecuted by the Taliban and lost its positive role for a short time. Fawad's first thought was to throw away something he had kept and carried for 13 years. Here it becomes clear that the role of things is not always stable, but can change on the run, when framework-giving cultural and political contexts change. Hiding or disposing of possessions that could provide clues to biography was a method of survival during the escape and of protection against external attribution, rejection or violence.

In the further course of the conversation, these acts were brought back to Fawad's memory and awakened memories that are condensed in this possession. In the narrative of his complex life story, the potential of and ambivalence in Fawad's relationship to his childhood identity card become apparent (see Depner 2015, 11). This possession combines negative and positive memories and is full of contradictory emotions, such as feelings of being torn out but also of resistance. The identity card has the characteristics of a '*Verlustsouvenir*' (souvenir of loss) (Habermas 1996, 278). On the one hand, it is linked to events that could plunge Fawad into another crisis. On the other hand, it has a potential to overcome crises, because it reminds us that they have been overcome.

Fawad's flight to Germany is one of many attempts to escape life in Afghanistan, and so the identity card was already a souvenir of loss long before he fled to Germany. The object had not only acquired its significance through flight. Because of forced migration it acquired a further biographical reference and reflects the biography of Fawad even more comprehensively (see also Yi-Neumann, Chapter 4 in this volume).

Flight is not only an exceptional situation in Fawad's life, but also a central theme of his biography. Fawad fled with his family to the Netherlands as a child. When he was a teenager, they were all deported back to Afghanistan. His flight does not mean leaving a homeland, but rather the search for a home lost 13 years ago, which is not clearly located territorially, but is so mentally and emotionally. The Dutch identity card is a symbol of this, of a place where he can live as a human. He considers Germany to be such a place. Thus, things on the run also embody wishes about and expectations of the destination country and thus become the motivation on the long journey. During the interview in Germany, it was a 'trophy' (see Habermas 1996, 279), reminding Fawad that he had not given up despite many defeats and that he had now arrived at his destination.

On his expired Dutch children's identity card, above his photo, the word 'Afgaanse' (Dutch for 'Afghan') is written in large letters, a foreign-determined attribution of meaning that places his identity in writing, and bindingly, in a place where he does not want to live. Fawad does not talk about that, and the many attempts to escape also show that such foreign attributions cannot dissuade him from his goal and cannot bind him to Afghanistan. What he sees in the identity card is tangible proof that he was once a 'European citizen' and still is in his heart. This object is an indication of his personal preferences, but also of non-affiliation or non-identification with a nation in which he was discriminated against by the majority society because of his religious affiliation.

The importance of things during interviews

As already made evident in the conversation with Fawad, the self-evident nature of things has turned out to be an opportunity in the context of the object interviews, especially when it came to talking about sensitive topics such as escape or the causes of escape. The circumstances and events that caused the respondents to flee, as well as the migration experience, were stressful or even traumatic. They are characterised by extreme interpersonal experiences. Very often these experiences are disturbing, hurtful or even life-threatening: persecution, abuse, blackmail, violence and discrimination come from people and make those affected leave their homes and flee from the threatening situation. Those seeking asylum find themselves in situations in which they are controlled, searched, interrogated, insulted or threatened by others. My fear was to confront my respondents with their traumatic experiences. To deal with this situation, I used the respondents' possessions as intermediaries between the respondents and their experiences and between the respondents and me.

Things as possible facilitation for a conversation

The potentials of object-based access as a facilitating and dynamic method for conducting interviews have been confirmed especially in those cases where the respondents still owned and wanted to show a relatively large number of things. Personal objects offered support and enabled the respondents to tell their stories without having to talk about themselves. By directing the questions towards things, I could often shift the focus from the person to the object and thus initiate a conversation, which could lead (in)directly to their speaking about their experiences. Not only talking about things, but their presence during the interview, as well as the photographing of them, dissolved the classic interview situation (in the sense of a stringing together of questions and answers) and opened up a more dynamic space (see also S. Woodward 2020). These interruptions led to a relaxed atmosphere in which the interlocutors could act and tell stories freely.

It was not always possible to interview people in their own rooms. However, where it was feasible, it proved to be a great advantage (see Hurdley 2010; Miller 2009; I. Woodward 2001; Kamptner 1991; Richins 1994). Some interlocutors did not speak in their (first) mother tongue during the interviews. It also often happened that I did not understand some words because they were from another language (for example Chechen, Arabic, Persian), or words were missing in the language of the conversation.[4] Often I was able to ask questions during the interview, but in some cases the meaning unfortunately remained unclear. In some cases, however, the things described could be taken out of the cupboard or wardrobe. In some situations things (such as photos of murdered relatives or of interviewees' own scarred body parts) were shown to illustrate without words the seriousness of a situation. In addition to the world of things, the world of bodies, for example of 'body things' (see Plessner 2015, 11), was able to provide a tangible remembrance of the extent of visible suffering and thus point to invisible pain. In cases of torture, abuse or illness, my interlocutors pointed to their own bodies – scarred wrists or backs, abnormally enlarged legs – as witnesses, and thus made their bodies into objects to mediate traumatic experiences.

Things as prompts and dynamic conversation anchors

My regular presence on site enabled me to visit people frequently as well as use ethnographic elements and was an important reason for the emergence of such situations as the interviews described above. In such contexts, possessions turned out to be important narrative prompts that reminded the interviewees of specific situations.

This was very present in Zaynap's case, for instance. Zaynap fled with her politically persecuted husband and her two children. They travelled from Dagestan via Moscow, Belarus and Poland to Germany. Organised escape helpers brought them to Berlin by car. Since the decision to flee was made very quickly, Zaynap only managed to pack a few personal things. Most of her possessions were bought en route. Her first response to the question of what she had taken from home was: 'I took nothing from home.' However, as I followed up and kept asking, she listed the following things: 'Telephone, money, passports and clothes.' The 30-minute conversation was almost exclusively about documents she had not received even though she needed them as proof that her husband had been persecuted. After this interview she often invited me for tea. On one of those days I asked her about her clothes: 'You said you took clothes with you, didn't you? What did they look like?' Zaynap replied, 'Normal, normal clothes!' She went to her wardrobe, took out the contents and put the clothes on the bed. Underneath all the skirts was a single pair of black jeans. This interested me immediately. I asked her why she had taken these jeans. 'We dressed up,' she said and laughed out loud. 'We wanted to pretend we were tourists to get across the border. We hadn't got a visa.' She said that she had bought a pair of jeans and a blouse at a market on the way. In a hotel in Belarus she took off her headscarf and exchanged her long skirt and black blouse for the purchased outfit. However, despite this 'disguise', they didn't manage to pass the border as tourists. The family had to identify themselves as 'refugees'. The adoption of global fashion trends (see Miller and Woodward 2012) served Zaynap as a way to adapt to different circumstances and to cross borders unnoticed and unobtrusively. The clothes, which had been treated as insignificant in the first conversation, hid important messages. They were a dynamic 'anchor' (see De Leon and Cohen 2005) for Zaynap's story. Focusing on them again at another time and in a more relaxed atmosphere prompted a full anecdote (see Höpfner 2019, 208). This conversation shows how fruitful it can be to tell stories from a fixed point, an object. I doubt that the question 'What was the time in Belarus like?' would have revealed so vividly Zaynap's strategy of escape, which in turn revealed her ideas about the world and what refugees or tourists look like.

Challenges and pitfalls: dealing with the insignificance and absence of things

Me: What other things could you take with you? What was important to you?

Marzhan: We did not take anything. What should we take? We had nothing to take.

I: Medicine, or ...?

Marzhan: We didn't take medicine. We didn't take anything.

Me: Clothes, food?

Marzhan: We didn't take any clothes.

Me: A mobile phone?

Marzhan: We didn't have a mobile phone either. We did not take anything. We came just like that.

Me: Not even any photos or beloved things?

Marzhan: Nothing, I tell you. I came here in this dress. And she [points at her daughter], she came like this. This is the only thing. Nothing, we took nothing at all. No telephone, nothing. We came and then they treated us medically here.

With this interview excerpt, I would like to discuss an important finding from my field research, namely that the material culture approach did not always provide easy access to the escape experiences of the people I interviewed in the refugee shelter, but at least as often risked blocking access. Marzhan from Chechnya, the oldest of the interviewees, who was in a very bad state of health, indicated that she was not able to pack anything. She suffered from a disease that caused an abnormal enlargement of her legs, and her heavy, sore body made the journey unbearable for her. She claimed to have been almost dead on arrival in Germany. Marzhan was the only one who maintained until the end of the field research that she had not taken anything with her. However, her case is not particularly striking compared to some others.

During the interviews it was confirmed that the choice of things in the escape context was very limited. Almost no one had sufficient time for a thorough selection or the possibility of deciding for or against certain personal possessions in the household. In contrast to a planned move, in some cases most things were taken away spontaneously or even by chance. For some of the interviewees the escape started from their 'homes', others were already in exile and could therefore not take things from home at all. A few had had their bag or one of their bags packed by other people. The ambivalence that things embody, namely of being at once existential in a human's life and at the same time a self-evident triviality, was evident in the interviews with the residents. This ambivalence brings with it many advantages, as I explained in the last section. In what follows, I wish to discuss the disadvantages of this characteristic, as well as other methodological challenges that became apparent during the research process through my use of the object-based approach.

'I took nothing'

The first challenge posed by this is the fact that, like Marzhan, almost all of my interlocutors answered 'Nothing' when asked what they took with them on their journey. It was only in the course of the interview (or in further conversations) that they mentioned some items. I was able to find some explanatory patterns for this response in a renewed analysis of the course of the interviews. Because things are taken for granted, it takes time to become aware of them and even more time to become aware of their meanings and translate them into words and stories, although this is never entirely possible because of their extralinguistic character (Auslander 2005). The answer 'nothing' can be seen as a way for respondents to secure time for reflection, in which case it would not be a real answer, but a strategy. This statement could also reflect the immense loss that humans have to take upon themselves in order to flee (see Höpfner 2018, 104). I doubt that such an answer would be so unanimous in a different interview context to the question of what people took on holiday or had with them when they moved to a new home.

Ryan-Saha (2015), who was also confronted with this answer when interviewing Bosnian refugees in Britain, terms 'this position of having "nothing", or of experiencing sudden and extreme material loss and current existential crisis, as "dispossession"' (Ryan-Saha 2015, 99). I also noticed that this response depended on what people associated with the words 'things' and 'taken' at first and also on their expectations about what I wanted to hear from them. The interlocutors and I had similar experiences and skills in common, such as the experience of migration, living in a shelter and, in many cases, the language. Nevertheless, it became clear in the interviews that because of visible privileges (see also Ozkul 2020), which unfortunately included or resulted in my migrant existence being invisible (in terms of the colour of my skin, my name, position, rights and language skills), I was seen as a representative of this country to which people had to justify their coming and their need for help.

The challenge to visualise fragments

Apart from the fact that none of the interlocutors had really taken 'nothing', I had to deal with the situation that almost half of my interlocutors could not or did not want to show things that could be photographed.

The fact that most or all things were no longer compactly stored in a bag or in a trouser pocket, as they had been when their owners were fleeing, but had been retained as evidence by various authorities, or stolen, lost, thrown away or used up, confronted my plan with methodological problems. Figure 3.1 is my answer to this fact, an attempt to show visually what I found out in research about things in the context of forced migration. At the beginning of the research, I pursued the intention of giving a better idea of the things, not only their names or terms and descriptions, and giving things and humans a platform to become visible. In my monograph, each possession was given its own page. But at the same time I wrote:

> Since no interviewee had sent or shipped a very large number of things to Germany before the escape, and since most of the things that could be taken were disposed of or used up on the escape route, there were few possessions that could be depicted in this work. So this work would have to contain many empty pages to draw attention to the emptiness and loss.
>
> (Höpfner 2018, 108)

Unfortunately, it is not possible in an anthology either to dedicate one page to each possession or to leave many pages empty. The illustration should show the rough relation between the things taken and the things left behind. Things taken, as well as the belongings of people who could bring more than others, would dominate the empirical results. The objects described in the interviews are not only fragments of entire households left behind, but also the totality of all possessions taken, lost, bought, disposed of, given and missing on the run. It is impossible to speak of a completeness of things in this context.

Openness of research

At this point I would like to refer to Marzhan's case. In the first interview the subject of possessions was cut off and at other meetings, in which she always wore the same dress, no objects were mentioned or addressed. In return, she talked in detail about her life under Soviet power, her experiences in Chechen hospitals and the persecution of her sons. Thus some of the potentials of the method depend not only on whether people like to talk about their possessions, but also on whether things are important to them or whether they have any at all. In general, this means not presupposing that possessions matter to the people who are the subjects of the research and therefore not asking what meaning things have for the respondents, but asking first of all whether they matter at all (see Marschall 2019, 14).

To researchers: what to be aware of when doing research on things in refugee accommodation

Following important research-ethical critiques of the anthropological or sociological view (Trouillot 2003; Boser 2006; Maiter et al. 2008; Reason and Bradbury 2008; Fernando 2014; Klingenberg 2018; Ozkul 2020),

I want to focus on two ethical pitfalls that were particularly important in my research and that are addressed in research with refugees.

A great challenge frequently mentioned in the literature on research on (forced) migration is the danger of 'retraumatization' (De Haene, Grietens and Verschueren 2010; Seedat et al. 2004). For this purpose, concrete questions about previous background and personal experiences during the escape should be avoided (see Miko-Schefzig and Reiter 2018; von Unger 2018; Narimani 2014). The question of the cause of escape was not only part of my interview, but the focus of my research. Even if the object-based approach generally made it easier to talk about what was experienced by shifting the focus to things, it was important to ask the question about the causes directly.[5] It felt strange to me to explain to people before the meetings that I was researching forced migration and things, and then only ask them about their personal items. The question about the causes and experiences would certainly hover above everything and create the feeling that I was not dealing openly with my subject. And even though I asked these risky questions, some people initially had the feeling that I was not really doing research on things. In fact, this question hovered over everything. Most of the people I met in the shelter had been preparing to justify their escape and prove their need for protection for a long time. The things in this study have shown this very clearly. During my research I rather had the feeling that the space created by the interviews was gratefully accepted by most of them. It was useful for the participants to reflect in a safe environment on what had happened (with a supportive researcher who emphasised that all statements would be anonymous).

I see a possible method of dealing with this dilemma in paying attention to and respecting the boundaries and signs of the interlocutors during the interviews and not digging deeper into the narratives on sensitive topics. As has already been explained, things were a great help in this.[6] The people talked about their things, and changed the focus of the narratives to themselves if they wanted to. Likewise, the persons could talk only about things, or not about things at all, if they preferred to talk about everything that happened to them without referring to specific personal possessions. In the interview analysis of this study I interpreted this respect for my limits and the limits of my interlocutors as a danger, as hiding behind the object-based method or behind the (thematised) objects and avoiding direct confrontation with sensitive issues (see Höpfner 2018, 110). In this research context, however, these set boundaries or conversational strategies should be understood as 'border markers' (Klingenberg 2018, 174). Klingenberg writes the following on the way people in camps handled defence strategies: 'I was less concerned with "overcoming" these boundaries in order to penetrate supposedly deeper into everyday life than with understanding them analytically as part of the field, vulnerability and positioning strategies of the actors and respecting them in terms of research ethics' (Klingenberg 2018, 174).

Another important research ethics-related aspect to be considered during and after the field research is the confidential use of the information. Most of the interlocutors relied on my promise to handle their data confidentially and this enabled an open handling of their experiences and personal matters, which, as I found out over time, was quite unusual among the residents. I was neither initiated nor affected and would soon leave the field again. In fact, I consider 'social inconsequence' (see Przyborski and Wohlrab-Sahr 2014, 48f.) to be an important potential of this relationship. And persons who are exposed to political or other persecution, in particular, must not be harmed by the researcher, for example by revealing their identity (see Krause 2016; Hugman, Pittaway and Bartolomei 2011; Pittaway, Bartolomei and Hugman 2010). This must always be taken into account when one is visualising things and the life stories that are intertwined with them.

Conclusion: object-based interviews as sensitive access to individual escape stories?

Talking about personal things made visible both their roles at the individual stages of the flight and the connections between life in the country of origin, the causes of escape and the expectations people had of the destination. Escape proved to be a process, which consisted of several stages that were neither independent of each other nor clearly demarcated, and it is in many cases difficult to distinguish escape from a 'previous' life.

Even though the focus on things often made conversations easier and inspired their owners to recount their strategies and world views in a more vivid and focused way, personal things were not important for all interlocutors. They often appeared as irrelevant, as trivialities, or simply were not there and not missed. Thus, before asking about the possessions and their significance for their owners, one must ask whether they have any relevance at all. This puts into question material culture as an easy and sensitive method of eliciting people's personal stories. In researching the phenomenon of forced migration with residents of a refugee shelter, one must also have the sensitivity not to talk about things. It is therefore necessary to consider how to deal with meaninglessness and absence of things in the context of such research. For me, depending on the situation and the person, this meant shifting the focus away from the things (back) to the person, if necessary: in other words, to do exactly what qualitative research is all about, namely to maintain an 'openness' throughout the research process to reflecting constantly on the limits and dangers of the applied research method.

Notes

1 In the interviews, people referred to themselves as man or woman.
2 At the beginning of the research only object interviews were planned. The ethnographic methods emerged automatically from the research situation and were used intuitively. As a result, my eyes remained closed to many ethnographically insightful situations, such as everyday dealing with things, and thereby becoming aware of the extent to which things brought along were still of everyday significance, of which things were newly appropriated or of how the material nature of the objects influenced the narrative of the interlocutors. Thus, the full potential of access was not realised. Because of time restrictions, I was not able to conduct further interviews.
3 Translations are my own, unless otherwise stated.
4 I was able to gain their confidence through my interpreting during medical examinations. In order not to lose the trust placed in me, I worked alone and did not involve any other person, such as a translator or a researcher from outside of the accommodation, in the research.
5 Of course, it is only justifiable if the physical and mental state of health of the interviewees, and the interview environment, allow it.
6 However, this approach does not generally prevent the risk of retraumatisation. Things can also unexpectedly represent the past in unpleasantly disturbing ways.

References

Auslander, Leora. 2005. 'Beyond words', *American Historical Review* 110(4): 1015–45. https://doi.org/10.1086/ahr.110.4.1015.

Bischoff, Doerte and Joachim Schlör, eds. 2013. *Exilforschung: Ein internationales Jahrbuch. Band 31: Dinge des Exils*. Munich: edition text + kritik.

Bosch, Aida. 2011. *Konsum und Exklusion: Eine Kultursoziologie der Dinge*. Bielefeld: transcript Verlag.

Bosch, Aida. 2018. 'Das Bild als Aktant: Theoretische und methodologische Implikationen des Visuellen'. In *Das Bild als soziologisches Problem: Herausforderung einer Theorie visueller Sozialkommunikation*, edited by Michael R. Müller and Hans-Georg Soeffner, 179–96. Weinheim: Beltz Juventa.

Boser, Susan. 2006. 'Ethics and power in community-campus partnerships for research', *Actions Research* 4(1): 9–21. https://doi.org/10.1177/1476750306060538.

De Haene, Lucia, Hans Grietens and Karine Verschueren. 2010. 'Holding harm: Narrative methods in mental health research on refugee trauma', *Qualitative Health Research* 20(12): 1664–76. https://doi.org/10.1177/1049732310376521.

De Leon, Jason Patrick and Jeffrey H. Cohen. 2005. 'Object and walking probes in ethnographic interviewing', *Field Methods* 17(2): 200–4. https://doi.org/10.1177/1525822X05274733.

Depner, Annemarie. 2015. *Dinge in Bewegung: Zum Rollenwandel materieller Objekte. Eine ethnographische Studie über den Umzug ins Altenheim*. Bielefeld: transcript Verlag.

Fernando, Mayanthi L. 2014. 'Ethnography and the politics of silence', *Cultural Dynamics* 26(2): 235–44. https://doi.org/10.1177/0921374014526025.

Habermas, Tilmann. 1996. *Geliebte Objekte: Symbole und Instrumente der Identitätsbildung*. Berlin: De Gruyter.

Höpfner, Elena. 2018. *Menschen auf der Flucht und die Bedeutung ihrer Dinge: Eine gegenstandsbezogene Theoriebildung im doppelten Sinne*. Wiesbaden: Springer VS.

Höpfner, Elena. 2019. 'Die Bedeutung der Dinge auf der Flucht', *Soziologie* 48(2): 205–12.

Hugman, Richard, Eileen Pittaway and Linda Bartolomei. 2011. 'When "do no harm" is not enough: The ethics of research with refugees and other vulnerable groups', *British Journal of Social Work* 41(7): 1271–87. https://doi.org/10.1093/bjsw/bcr013.

Hurdley, Rachel. 2010. 'The power of corridors: Connecting doors, mobilising materials, plotting openness', *Sociological Review* 58(1): 45–64. https://doi.org/10.1111/j.1467-954X.2009.01876.x.

Kamptner, Laura. 1991. 'Personal possessions and their meanings: A life-span perspective', *Journal of Social Behavior and Personality* 6(6): 209–28.

Klingenberg, Darja. 2018. 'Einblicke in migrantische Wohnungen: Erkenntniskritik und Repräsentationspolitik'. In *Das neue Zuhause: Haushalt und Alltag nach der Migration*, edited by Hans Peter Hahn and Friedemann Neumann, 159–80. Frankfurt: Campus.

Krause, Ulrike. 2016. 'Ethische Überlegungen zur Feldforschung: Impulse für die Untersuchung konfliktbedingter Flucht', Centre for Conflict Studies Working Papers 20, Zentrum für Konfliktforschung, Marburg. https://doi.org/10.17192/es2019.0015.

Maiter, Sarah, Laura Simich, Nora Jacobson and Julie Wise. 2008. 'Reciprocity: An ethic for community-based participatory action research', *Action Research* 6(3): 305–25. https://doi.org/10.1177/1476750307083720.

Marschall, Sabine. 2019. '"Memory objects": Material objects and memories of home in the context of intra-African mobility', *Journal of Material Culture* 24(3): 253–69. https://doi.org/10.1177%2F1359183519832630.

Miko-Schefzig, Katharina and Cornelia Reiter. 2018. 'Partizipatives Forschen im Kontext der Organisation Polizei: Ethisches Forschen mit vulnerablen Gruppen am Beispiel der Schubhaft', *Forum: Qualitative Social Research* 19(3) (art. no. 10). https://doi.org/10.17169/fqs-19.3.3142.

Miller, Daniel. 2009. *The Comfort of Things*. Cambridge: Polity.

Miller, Daniel and Sophie Woodward. 2012. *Blue Jeans: The art of the ordinary*. Berkeley: University of California Press.

Narimani, Petra. 2014. 'Zustimmung als Prozess: Informiertes Einverständnis in der Praxisforschung mit von Ausweisung bedrohten Drogenabhängigen'. In *Forschungsethik in der qualitativen Forschung: Reflexivität, Perspektiven, Positionen*, edited by Hella von Unger, Petra Narimani and Rosaline M'Bayo, 41–58. Wiesbaden: Springer VS.

Ozkul, Derya. 2020. 'Participatory research: Still a one-sided research agenda?', *Migration Letters* 17(2): 229–37. https://doi.org/10.33182/ml.v17i2.804.

Pittaway, Eileen, Linda Bartolomei and Richard Hugman. 2010. '"Stop stealing our stories": The ethics of research with vulnerable groups', *Journal of Human Rights Practice* 2(2): 229–51. https://doi.org/10.1093/jhuman/huq004.

Plessner, Helmuth. 2015. *Mit anderen Augen: Aspekte einer philosophischen Anthropologie*. Stuttgart: Reclam.

Przyborski, Aglaja and Monika Wohlrab-Sahr. 2014. *Qualitative Sozialforschung: Ein Arbeitsbuch*, 4th edition. Munich: Oldenbourg Verlag.

Reason, Peter and Hilary Bradbury, eds. 2008. *The SAGE Handbook of Action Research: Participative inquiry and practice*, 2nd edition. London and Thousand Oaks, CA: SAGE Publications.

Richins, Marsha L. 1994. 'Valuing things: The public and private meanings of possessions', *Journal of Consumer Research* 21(3): 504–21. https://doi.org/10.1086/209414.

Ryan-Saha, Eleanor. 2015. 'Repossession: Material absences, affective presences, and the life-resumption labors of Bosnians in Britain', *Social Analysis* 59(1): 96–112. https://doi.org/10.3167/sa.2015.590106.

Seedat, Soraya, Willem P. Pienaar, David Williams and Daniel J. Stein. 2004. 'Ethics of research on survivors of trauma', *Current Psychiatry Reports* 6: 262–7. https://doi.org/10.1007/s11920-004-0075-z.

Spradley, James P. 1979. *The Ethnographic Interview*. Belmont, CA: Wadsworth Cengage Learning.

Trouillot, Michel-Rolph. 2003. *Global Transformations: Anthropology and the modern world*. New York: Palgrave Macmillan. https://doi.org/10.1007/978-1-137-04144-9.

von Unger, Hella. 2018. 'Ethische Reflexivität in der Fluchtforschung: Erfahrungen aus einem soziologischen Lehrforschungsprojekt', *Forum: Qualitative Social Research* 19(3) (art. no. 6). https://doi.org/10.17169/fqs-19.3.3151.

Woodward, Ian. 2001. 'Domestic objects and the taste epiphany: A resource for consumption methodology', *Journal of Material Culture* 6(2): 115–36. https://doi.org/10.1177%2F135918350100600201.

Woodward, Sophie. 2020. *Material Methods: Researching and thinking with things*. London: SAGE.

4

From biographies to biographical horizons: on life courses and things in forced migrations

Friedemann Yi-Neumann

Introduction

What can the personal objects forced migrants bring with them tell about their biographies? Do ethnographies on biographical objects tend to focus on people's 'heroic' story of survival and on their things, and in so doing elide loss, dispossessions and fragmentation? How is it possible to present people's life courses and the life courses of their belongings without drawing these complex courses in line with one another?

This chapter attempts to answer these questions by considering the biographical objects of two women, Atiya and Zahra, who fled the war in Syria. Atiya brought with her the cuddly toy 'Rocky' and Zahra brought with her a metal bangle; both of them came from Syria across Turkey and on to Germany. Although both women were given the objects by close relatives and took them with them on their flight from war and kept them for the years in exile, the weight of the objects developed inversely over the years.

Atiya and Zahra's things and stories reveal not only the remarkable ways in which people can be, become or cease to be entangled with things, but also how such ties are violently fragmented or crumble imperceptibly. The stories of the women and their objects made me reflect on the flaws in my thinking and question my false assumption that biographical objects inherently take on increasing significance over time. Moreover, the bracelet and Rocky made me doubt some of the assumptions implicit in established paradigms around biographies and objects: the changing relevance of things here arises not merely from their shifts in social spheres, an underlying premise in many classic concepts (see Kopytoff 1986, 83–7), but also from how Atiya and Zahra perceive, use and adopt a position towards these things over time in changing precarious settings.

Objects and biographies in anthropology and beyond

In the anthropology of the 1980s, the social and cultural biographies of things became an important paradigm and an inherent part of material culture studies and its methodology (Tilley et al. 2006; Stahl 2010). Igor Kopytoff (1986) argued that things have to be understood through the processes of production, consumption and exchange in which they occupy changing roles. The biographical angle allows a comparison of how things accumulate relevance and how their influence on social lives changes over time (Gosden and Marshall 1999, 177; Stahl 2010, 156).

The idea of studying societies via material culture and its life courses did not start with Kopytoff, though. In 1929 the Russian constructivist Sergei Tret'iakov ([1929] 2006a, 61) developed his methodological concept of the 'biography of the object'.[1] He was an engaged writer and civic activist.[2] Through the biographical approach to things, Tret'iakov ([1929] 2006a, 59–60) sought to examine the interrelationship between personal experiences, emotions and things, as well as their societal forms of material assemblies. His approach offers an alternative to dominant forms of presenting characters and their capabilities to act at that time in the Soviet Union. These idealising depictions ascribed 'great deeds' to individualised, seemingly autonomous heroic characters, instead of considering them as joint material efforts (for example, in the production of consumer goods on the assembly line).[3] Tret'iakov's 'biography of the object' can be understood as an attempt to (re)contextualise the actor and his deeds in the material social world, in terms not only of material production but also of emotions. Emotions for the author are not merely individual, but a societal phenomenon that has a substantial impact on the creation of and relations to the material word around us ([1929] 2006a, 61–2). By proposing to investigate products such as bread, cotton, coal and steel, Tret'iakov states that neither their development and production nor their emotional attachment to these things is personal; rather, they are collectively shared in the biography of the object ([1929] 2006a, 62). These ideas, which the writer laid out in a few short pages, have been overlooked in the current anthropological debates on material culture.

In Kopytoff's (1986) work, this interrelationship between persons and things that Tret'iakov showed an interest in (from a societal perspective) is barely touched upon. However, the questions of how objects become intertwined with persons as biographies develop and how the line between possession and being becomes blurred became key issues for material anthropology (e.g. Strathern 1988; Hoskins 1998; Hage 2013). It is for this reason that the double localisation and transformation of the biography of an object as a social and personal material product seems to offer a promising lens. However, it is vital to reflect not only on entanglement but also on how (violent) separations matter (Hicks 2020, 28).

In her work on the constitution of personhood in Melanesia through gift giving, Marilyn Strathern (1988, 135, 338) showed that personhood is 'distributed' and that things can be considered part of a person. Personhood thus unfolds through human–object interaction. Gender can be understood as 'categorizations of persons, artifacts, events, sequences, and so on' (Strathern 1988, ix). It is vital to understand how these categorisations matter and materialise specific gender roles and social relations.

Alfred Gell (1998) argues for a similar understanding of persons, while he stresses more the agency of objects. People invest in things, like gifts or possessions; they keep and care for them, while these materialities take shape along histories and trajectories (Hoskins 1998, 192). Such dense interrelations can be considered the ground on which to tell life stories in depth. Things can help one to reflect and to learn about oneself, the conditions of life courses and migratory trajectories (Galitzine-Loumpet 2020), and they can ease strain caused by (the fear of) loss (see Böhme 2014, 350 on fetish).

Such changing social lives of things (Appadurai 1986) have been widely acknowledged. However, what led Arjun Appadurai to his ground-breaking examination of the material culture was that he felt that social aspects were overemphasised. In this regard, the return 'to things themselves' as a 'methodological fetishism' (Appadurai 1986, 5) offers an object-based correction of social theory.

Several scholars have argued that the term 'biography' is a problematic biological metaphor which suggests the birth and death of an object, and have proposed 'itinerary' (Hahn and Weiss 2013; see also Joy 2009, 543–4; for further debates see Burström 2014, 70–1) or 'itinerancy' (Stockhammer 2020, 40–1) as an anti-essentialist term instead. Others have emphasised the analogousness between things and living organisms through categories of growth or decomposition as a means of underlining the processual character of things themselves (Hallam and Ingold 2014; Herva 2005).

With Tret'iakov's transformative and multilayered concept in mind, I argue that the term 'biography' is not problematic in itself. Rather, what matters is how anthropologists employ this heuristic concept and how it frames the scopes of analyses; whom and what do scholars include in their object biographies, and which fragmentary, transformed and contested aspects are downplayed to tell more coherent stories (see for example Burström 2014, 72–3)?

Biographical objects and object biographies

At this juncture, it is important to differentiate between two different schools and two similar-sounding terms and concepts: 'biographical objects' and 'object biographies'. This distinction also has a disciplinary dimension.

Usually, historians, archaeologists and museologists trace back object biographies (e.g. Thompson 2017; Friberg and Huvila 2019; Wallen and Pomerance 2018).[4] The concept focuses on the trajectory of objects themselves through different historical and social contexts and migrations; I also consider Tret'iakov ([1929] 2006a) and Kopytoff (1986) to be representatives of this school. Although some scholars have argued that there has been a theoretical stagnation in the biographical concept(s) in recent years (see Burström 2014, 69), numerous object biographies – sometimes called 'life courses', '(non-human) life histories' or 'histories' (Hicks and Beaudry 2010; Joy 2009) – have been published.

In contrast, the term 'biographical objects' refers to things that are related to personal biographies. Janet Hoskins (1998), in an ethnography with that title, provided a key contribution in this regard. Rather than considering things to be icons of the self, Hoskins strikingly showed that biographical objects entail considerable (self-)reflexive potential, reflecting the shifting multivocal ties, positions and perspectives over time (Hoskins 1998, 112, 198; see also Gell 1998; Thomas 1991; Dudley 2018). The more 'references' are made to an object, the more biographical relevance this object may have for an individual (Habermas 1996, 279; Burström 2014, 78–9). Nevertheless, the strength of these references – or the 'weight' of a thing – is far from stable over time and under different social conditions. Do the established forms of representing the life courses of things and people undermine the complexity, dispossession and loss of items, and the situatedness of the narrations of these life courses? Whereas perspectives on 'object biographies' have dominated interdisciplinary debates on material, as an anthropologist I focus on the 'biographical objects' of interlocutors I encountered in my research.

The problem of linearity and representational consistency

One problem in many biographical presentations is that things are considered as continuous bearers of meaning in linear biographies (Joy 2009, 544; Burström 2014, 69, 77). This is a common issue despite frequent theoretical acknowledgement of de- and revaluations (see for example Thompson 2017), fragmentations, and the drastic and violent changes that shape things and the related human beings (Gosden and Marshall 1999, 176). Dan Hicks (2020, 26) argues that such linear stances enabled continuations of colonial representations through 'fixed objects' in museum contexts. Linearity, as a way of ignoring dispossession and fragmentations, has a highly political and ethical dimension, therefore.

However, consistencies in biographies are not merely an academic misrepresentation; they are actively (re-)created and matter in people's lives. As the psychologists Christin Köber and Tilmann Habermas (2017) have shown in a remarkable long-term study, these aspects have a constitutive effect for the individual who lays out and creates an object's biography by narration. Although consistency may be more evident in some life stories than in others, it would be a serious mistake to reproduce this apparent stability and importance of things ethnographically. Indeed, Alfred Gell (1998, 10–11) argues against a functionalist understanding of things in anthropological biography theory, in which things mainly have a passive function in a person's different biographical stages (Figure 4.1). Instead, he suggests comprehending things as social agents that (co-)exercise a certain agency through their qualities and therefore in the ways they are socially employed and framed.

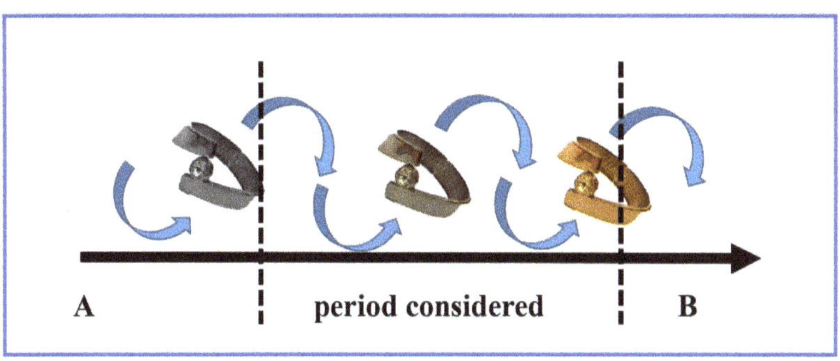

4.1 Linear scheme of object transformation in biographical process. © Friedemann Yi-Neumann, 2021.

I argue that the 'heroism' Tret'iakov criticised is apparent in many analyses of biographical objects. However, 'hero worship' here affects 'unique' material objects rather than persons. The hero-object may become decontextualised and, apparently against all odds, remain closely related to a person (see also Kopytoff 1986, 66; Joy 2009, 549; Burström 2014, 71). This phenomenon may also be understood as the negative turning of the methodological thing fetishism proclaimed by Appadurai. Translating Tret'iakov's ([1929] 2006a, 58) ideas to these anthropological works, one could provocatively state: 'The [object-]hero holds the [ethnography's] universe together.' Hence, scholars who set down life courses have to reflect carefully on the 'non-linear' (Joy 2009, 454) facets and the social conditions of the life courses of people and things.

Linear and consistent narratives tend to distort and embellish social and individual lives and movements (Joy 2009, 455). In such narratives, possessions remain somehow constant through different places and backgrounds in which they can become lost or replaced. Moreover, such accounts understate the complexity and fragmentation of life courses on the one hand, and overestimate the agency of both the person and the 'object heroes' on the other. Criticising the iconisation and symbolic reduction of museum objects, Appadurai (2017, 402) has stated that it is mandatory to pay attention to their complex and accidental biographies.

Furthermore, stories of fleeing individuals and the things they take with them are often those of the 'lucky survivor'.[5] Such presentations of the life course of humans and things are unable to grasp the massive structural violence and the temporal and material dispossession of forced migrations (see Hicks and Mallet 2019; Khosravi 2018) and, more generally, of precarious social classes (Ramsay 2019, 4; see also Brun, Fàbos and El-Abed 2017). The biographical objects in forced migrations are thus not only remnants of the initial dispossession through war (Chatty 2010), but also of repeated deprivations and structural devaluations by migration regimes and related capitalist economies (Ramsay 2019; Georgi 2019; Nieswand 2018).

In light of these critiques, one could ask what value material biographies have as a methodological tool for studying mobile, shifting and precarious life stories.

On biographical horizons

Fortunately, while the material biographical paradigms which I have discussed so far do have limitations, I would argue that they are not intrinsically problematic because they do enable convincing perspectives on in-depth human–object relations and allow social analysis and comparison. At the same time, it is important to underline that linearity and representational consistency remain issues in fieldwork and ethnographic writing.

Since I am addressing biographical objects, it is also essential to theoretically take the acting and sensing persons who are biographically entangled with things for granted. And this again requires some social, cultural and sensational embedding. The thoughts I will present in this regard are not new, but they reflect a paradigmatic shift in which itineraries are only one in a long line of considerations through which things take shape. One contribution of this chapter may be the use of a multilayered sensational lens for the analysis of biographical objects.

The phenomenologist Maurice Merleau-Ponty (1969, 67–8, 100) states that the perception of a thing is embedded in an open and explorative depth-horizon structure. The horizon unfolds where the perceiving body and the world encounter each other in degrees of proximities and distances, intensity, depth and difference (see also Ram and Houston 2015b). Sara Ahmed (2006, 55) has rephrased it this way: 'The horizon is not an object that I apprehend: I do not see it. It is what gives objects their contours .... Objects are objects insofar as they are within my horizon.' Merleau-Ponty's (2002, 346) aim is not to understand a thing amply or 'objectively' (something which he considers impossible in any case); rather, the precise understanding of things lies in the ways subjects interact with them bodily in the 'spectacle' of perception. For subjects or perceiving individuals, then, relations of proximity and distance shape not only their ties to the past but also their ties to their social and material environments (Rachamimov 2018, 165, referring to Libermann and Trope).

Tret'iakov ([1929] 2006a, 61) shows how emotional ties to objects are interwoven with their production, and the social practices this process implies. He underlines that the conditions of social production cross through different social classes and their dynamic material intersections. By urgently pressing for social contextualisation (of emotion and affect), Tret'iakov ([1929] 2006a, 61) paves the way for what are termed today intersectional methodologies (Ahmed 2006, 136–7; Ram and Houston 2015a, 4; Degnen and Tyler 2017). The aim of 'intersectional methodologies' is to consider the intimate and personal as well as the broader social tendencies of biographical objects. Here, it is difference that distinguishes things from their backgrounds during life paths. This difference is not merely visual, in terms of a shift from the visible realms

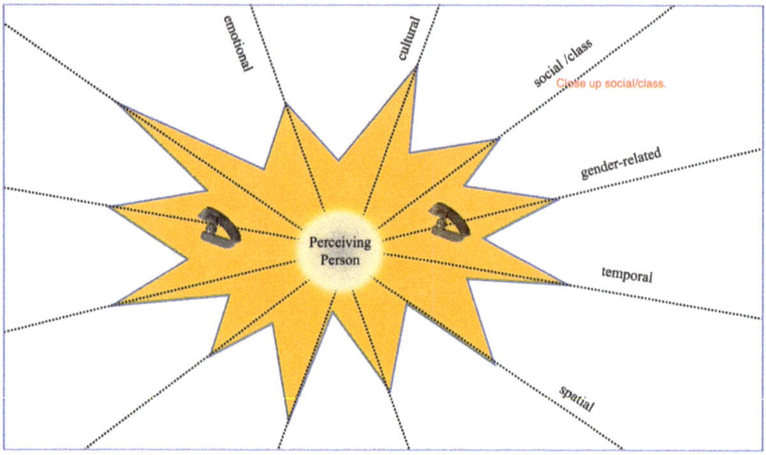

4.2 Horizon-related scheme of proximities and distances. The variables stand for different aspects of relations to biographical objects. © Friedemann Yi-Neumann, 2021.

to invisible ones, but also social, cultural, practical and personal, and it affects things and bodies in different ways (see for instance Ahmed 2007 on whiteness).

Rather than taking an unbroken spatiotemporal approach to studying biographical objects, I propose to look at them as a phenomenon within a perceptual horizon (Figure 4.2). The model is not meant as a rigid analytical template, but rather as an extensible attempt to illustrate the multiple variables in how an object is related to.

Shifting the position of an object along a particular variable alters its degrees of proximity to and distance from the perceiving person. The perceiver is affected by and takes a position towards biographical objects along the intersecting variables. In other words, one perceives a thing and reacts to it, appreciatingly, rejectingly, intensely, indifferently, etc. And it is this sensation and reaction towards a thing that decides how objects materialise in everyday life (Ahmed 2006, 28). Therefore, something can be spatially or temporarily distant and yet emotionally close, and vice versa. At the same time, others may consider these close emotional ties to a biographical object to be socially or culturally (in)adequate, for instance. Each variable entails the aspect of perception and ascription, both by the biographically entangled self and by social others. Biographical objects can thus be understood also by means of different angles or degrees within a horizon of bodily sensation. Out of these relations one is closely or distantly, intensely or faintly related to things. Whether and to what degree a subject (or an anthropologist) considers an object 'biographical' depends on the degree of proximity along the different axes of ties to it.

The horizontal degrees are co-constituted by various intersections. In order to avoid considering material matters as monadic ones, one has to consider their sociocultural embeddedness by means of an intersectional analysis that is located between an anthropological analysis of quotidian experiences and notions and a sociological angle on inequalities and exclusion (see Degnen and Tyler 2017, 36–7). The shifting relevance of things comes not only from shifting social spheres through exchange, for instance (see Kopytoff 1986), but also from entering another (socially positioned) perceptual horizon. This perceptional and intersectional lens is a valuable extension in understanding biographical objects. Specific personal relatedness to things does not often comply with the common normative and aesthetic conventions of a social field (Bourdieu 1984); such tensions around things may be fruitful to consider. As I will show, the material transformation of the object itself is related to but contingent upon its relevance in a perceptual horizon. The decay of an object itself does not necessarily mean declining importance, and persistence does not necessarily mean continuing relevance.

Some methodological aspects to consider

Before I continue to the empirical section of this chapter, I would like to present some methodological characteristics of biographical object research that are applicable to anthropological fieldwork or that it is necessary to reflect upon.

For migration research (and beyond), the material approach can be considered a way out of the problematic 'ethnic lenses' (Povrzanović Frykman 2016, 44; Neumann and Hahn 2019, 41) that may lead to one-sided 'cultural' orientations of researchers that bring about social disembedding of research findings. Hoskins (1998, 112) shows that biographical objects have a potential for personal reflections, both for interlocutors and for researchers. This capability lays the foundation for a differentiated understanding by unearthing complicated trajectories, social settings, ascriptions and importantly, the perceptional, biographical horizons in which biographical objects take shape.

There is another critical point to make in differentiating between emic and etic understanding of biographical objects. Sabine Marschall (2019, 7–8) has shown that, in some societies, there is not a concept or idea of keeping things (like inherited memory objects) for personal reasons. Biographical objects are therefore an anthropological framework and, correspondingly, not a universal but a particular cultural phenomenon. Thus, it is a chief task of ethnographic reflection to avoid such assumptions and to beware of methodologically producing a 'biographical spectacle' in an environment in which this relation to things does not exist in an emic sense.[6]

Biographical objects are often embedded and gain significance in specific material arrangements and alongside practical and narrative settings in which they become pertinent (Burström 2014, 73) and hold a special place in a living room or in a family story. This, too, relates to the idea of shifting social spheres and functions of things in their biographies (see Kopytoff 1986). 'Framing' can be situational (spontaneously during a conversation, for instance), yet also more durable (like giving a thing a specific place in a glass cabinet).

With changing sceneries, the (biographical) relevance of such objects may also change (see for instance Hurdley 2013, 81; Miller 2010, 65; Garvey 2002, 55). Scholars such as Nippert-Eng have used narrative and material (re)framings and rearrangements as productive material approaches in research (cf. Nippert-Eng 2010, 97–158).

Biographical objects can evoke unforeseeable affects. These open material encounters can unpack forgotten, hidden and unexpected associations and affordances (Burström 2014, 73; Frykman and Povrzanović Frykman 2016; Thomas 1991, 123; Gosden and Marshall 1999, 174; Woodward 2007, 172; Hurdley 2013, 6). This trait makes things methodically promising, not just for academics but also for creative writers (Lee Brien 2020), for instance. Things make the past sensible and tangible in other ways than narrations alone allow for (Auslander 2005).

The archaeologist Joshua Pollard (2004) has pointed out that material objects undergo a material transformation through decay, abrasion and fragmentation which profoundly affects societies as a whole (see also Auslander and Zahra 2018, 310 on the material effects of destruction in the Syrian civil war). This idea corresponds with Tret'iakov's ([1929] 2006a, 61) transformative understanding of biographies of things, both on a material and a social level. Therefore, looking at material alterations in things can be a crucial aspect of biographical research, since they also change the perception, use and evaluation – in other words, the characteristics – of things. I will refer to this phenomenon of material, personal and social transformation in two case studies of biographical objects.

Rocky, a companion for life

I will begin the ethnographic section of the chapter with one of the most impressive biographical objects I encountered during my research – Rocky (Figure 4.3). I came across Rocky when I interviewed its owner Atiya, a woman in her early thirties, together with my colleague Samah Al Jundi-Pfaff, in the Friedland Transit Camp in Germany in spring 2019.[7] Atiya, who comes from an Ismaili[8] family, grew up in the city of Salamiyah in the Hama governorate in Syria.

Rocky is extraordinary not only for the continuity of his daily usage, but also with respect to the intensity of his relationship with Atiya. The tie between Atiya and Rocky has remained strong and indeed has strengthened, over more than two decades. In this sense, he is a perfect example of a biographical object.

4.3 Rocky and Atiya. © Friedemann Yi-Neumann, 2019.

Rocky is now 24 years old. Atiya's mother tailored him out of the inner fabric and lining of a used jacket, and gave him to her as a gift (on no particular special occasion) when she was around 11 years old. Because of limited means, they could not afford many toys. With her father working in Lebanon, Atiya lived with her mother and siblings in Salamiyah. Rocky has a white body and face, brown arms, hair and ears, button eyes and a friendly grinning mouth stitched with red thread.

At first he did not have a name. But when Atiya started watching American television programmes she became fascinated by a place called Rocky Creek in Texas and named the teddy after the series. Subsequently, she learned about the movie character 'Rocky', which turned out to be a more common name; she finally decided to call him Rocky.

Atiya went to Homs and Damascus to study, and later on to Hama, where she worked as a pharmacy assistant in the national hospital. There she treated the wounded from the escalating civil war; many died in front of her eyes. One day she decided to escape the 'nightmare', as she called it.

Atiya left Syria hastily and went to Turkey – via Tripoli in Lebanon – in September 2015. At that time, it was still possible for Syrians to enter Turkey without a visa. She made it to Istanbul where she lived for over three years studying for a master's degree in economic policy, which she was unable to complete. Her time in Turkey was also experienced as a 'nightmare': she had various jobs there, and faced precarity, hostility and, as an atheist and an unveiled woman, gender-related harassment, amongst other forms of discrimination. These issues arose both in the Turkish and the Syrian communities, and along the tense and fractious political and ethnic lines of the civil war (Özkaya 2020), deep trenches that remain present in the German reception facilities.

Atiya decided to leave for Germany, where her sister was now living with her family. In February 2019, she travelled to Izmir in Turkey and went to Greece by speedboat. There were 30 people without life jackets on the boat which crossed the Aegean Sea. Luckily, there was no incident. Atiya went on to Athens, where she stayed for a few days. On her journey, she had only a small bag with her qualification certificates and Rocky. 'Besides that, I just brought some small things that are related to my memories,' she told us (interview 16 April 2019). These things included a *misbaha* (a prayer chain), which was a gift from a Syrian friend, and a tiny wooden cup her flatmate in Istanbul had given her to drink mate tea, the famous beverage from her hometown, and Atiya's favourite drink. The cup has now been left at her sister's home. On her second attempt, Atiya finally arrived in Germany with her belongings by plane in March 2019.

Atiya describes her relationship with Rocky as very close since he had also helped her to cope with social isolation and struggles between her and her sisters, long before she had left Syria. His place is in Atiya's bed. When her sister repeatedly asked Atiya why she would not throw Rocky away, she shouted at her 'How could I!' As Atiya explained in the interview while eyeing the patches, the sewn-up parts and the holes in the fragile fabric where the inner lining was coming out, 'It really is a part of me! As you can see, I tried to repair it many times, but everything falls apart … It is so old' (interview 16 April 2019).

Not only age but also the intensity of this relationship have found their expression in Rocky's material condition, both in terms of abrasion and holes and again in Atiya's attempts to preserve and keep Rocky together with the multiple repairs she has made and the stitching she has added. But Atiya also explained in detail her interrelatedness with Rocky and the specific forms of 'communication' that take place between her and him. Moreover, she explained why she considers him a companion and friend like no other person or thing, always aware of her 'oddness' and the incomprehension it causes in others. 'He doesn't cheat or leave me. In some way or another, I recognise he is me, or a part of me, he is just the other opinion of me,' she said in another conversation on 18 March 2020.

> Many people … talk to themselves. I do that a lot, with Rocky, it becomes easier; he is just a mirror that allows me to talk aloud to myself … I am 35 years old; he has been with me for more than 24 years. To be honest, I couldn't throw stuff away or remove stuff or people easily from my heart and life. I am a loyal person … I had other friends, pillars, but they couldn't move, [but] he stayed with me all the time … There is a writer called Youssef Ziedan,[9] he said something like … 'There is no sacred place by itself … Places gain sanctity from what we feel towards [them] …' The same [is true] for me, my feelings towards him [Rocky] are what makes him special. … For others, he is just a doll, ugly or lovely. For me, he is more …

This statement echoes a profound reflection by Atiya. She has also intently studied psychology for help in facing her personal struggles. At the same time, this points to how social environments react to her relation to Rocky, since Rocky's significance is not always easy to convey to others and not always readily accepted.

Relations yield and at the same time are based on a particular commitment. This is certainly true of the relationship Atiya has with Rocky. Atiya felt that she had failed to keep this commitment when she initially left Syria in 2015. That time she had left Rocky behind and could only be reunited with him one year later:

> When I went to Turkey … I did not take him with me, but really I missed him so much … Till now I keep feeling guilty because I left him for a year. Now and here I couldn't imagine my life without him. I still know he is a doll, but for me, it is a soul. I mean, I could buy another doll or bear, a pretty one, but it would be as if I had cheated on him and left him because he is old and ugly … In some way or another [it would be] as if I [had] abandoned my principles.

Being asked when she needed Rocky the most on her journey, Atiya replied that that time was here and now. Although the situation in Germany was different from that in Turkey, her striving to gain a foothold continues. As she struggles with another start in another country, with personal issues, with the feeling of social isolation, with pressure, and using all her energy to learn German as a third foreign language (after English and Turkish), Rocky remains a reliable companion. These conditions give Atiya the feeling that Rocky is now more vital than ever; to give Rocky away is simply unimaginable for her.

Zahra's bangle and some conceptual doubts

The biographical object I now turn to tells a different story. For me, this unobtrusive bangle (Figures 4.4 and 4.5) gave rise to some doubts about how anthropologists create narrations of people and their biographies.

This bangle belonged to a young woman I will call Zahra. Zahra, who was born in July 2000 in al-Hasaka in the north-eastern part of Syria, arrived with her Kurdish family in the Friedland Transit Camp at the end of November 2018. Coming on a UN resettlement plane they were able to bring some suitcases containing their belongings. Zahra's eldest brother had already settled in Germany. The family, after years of forced separation in the chaos of war and exile, was reunited.

Zahra's flight began in 2011, in the wake of the uprisings against the Syrian government that started that year in al-Hasaka city. Fearing that their sons – her brothers – would be drafted into the Syrian Arabic Army, her parents decided to leave. 'We wanted neither to kill nor to be killed,' Zahra's mother said in the interview. The family went to Turkey, first to Amouda, then to Gaziantep, and then on to Mersin. Zahra brought the bangle, as well

4.4 Zahra's bangle. Photo by Andrea Sorina Müller. © Friedemann Yi-Neumann, 2019.

4.5 Zahra wearing bangle and bracelet. © Friedemann Yi-Neumann, 2019.

as a bracelet, from Syria to Friedland and, when asked to tell us about an object important to her, decided to tell us about these possessions.

Zahra had been given the two items as gifts by her older sister over ten years earlier. Her sister had bought them on the Shar'i-Phalestin (or Palestine Street, a famous shopping street in al-Hasaka).

When Zahra looked at the bangle in Friedland, she said: 'I recall my childhood in Syria via these things. They are the memories of my country.' Zahra and her siblings described how their former home looked and the condition they had heard it was in now (parts of it had apparently been destroyed after they left), the building, the yard where they once played, the three older children sitting in front of the house as they used to do. She also related her flight from war and their exile in Turkey.

When asked how she would feel if she lost these items, Zahra said that it would be sad, since she had kept them all these years. What was interesting in this statement is that it refers to the effort she had made so far to keep them. But unlike Atiya and Rocky, she did not seem to consider herself intrinsically interwoven with the bangle and bracelet. In the conversation, while the objects functioned as a launching pad into her memories, her recollections were not closely related to these things. The bangle and bracelet, despite the trajectories and biographical aspects laid out in front of us, left Zahra and us a little bemused. The story of the thing was vague and offered far less emotional involvement and importance than what I implicitly expected. What could they say about now?

She told us that she wore the jewellery regularly in Turkey, but not in Friedland: 'It is not the right place to wear them.' The jewellery was for parties, and she therefore felt that the camp was not a proper place to wear them. In anticipation of the things to come and especially because a friend she had made in Friedland had left on the day of the interview, Zahra was not in the mood for partying.

The Friedland Transit Camp, where my colleague and I met her, is a place where the sense of belonging is fragile and uncertain. Visibly traumatised by war-related experiences, Zahra and her Kurdish family were facing an uncertain future, and they were anxious about it. Here, people who come with the UN resettlement programmes stay only for a short time. At the same time, however, it is a place to make new friends and have new experiences.

Another reason Zahra had stopped wearing the jewellery was that she felt it had gone a bit out of fashion. She felt that it did not suit her any more, since her time in exile was also one of coming of age and experiencing herself in new surroundings. Part of the process of adolescence is detaching oneself from some relationships via 'transitional objects' (Habermas 1999) and, I would add, detaching from things themselves. Soon she will have lived longer outside Syria than inside, and other possessions from that time are likely to lose some of their insignificance too. Perhaps, someday, they will become pertinent to her again.

While Zahra took the jewellery with her, her motives blurred during the flight and the years in exile. She spent most of the time with her family and could rely on social relations. Atiya had spent significant times in exile alone and became very reliant on her cuddly toy Rocky. Here lies a key difference between the two cases. Another reason for Zahra detachment from the bangle is undoubtedly her coming of age. It was now out of place, out of fashion, unsuitable for a young woman. Hence, efforts to explore its biography somehow remained superficial too. Sometimes the things brought along turn out to be incongruous. These items – at least initially – cannot be re-embedded in the new exilic environments and practices in ways that give their biographically accumulated weight relevance again.

Zahra decided to give the once-treasured bangle to the Friedland Museum collection, as she had visited the museum days before.[10] Given the uncertainty Zahra and her family were facing, where everything seemed undecided, I struggled to accept her offer. I felt that her apparent lack of relatedness to this thing was premature. Our conversation was one way of redefining this bond since it was still relevant as a gift from Zahra's sister, and as a thing she kept during the chaos of war in Syria and precarious times in Turkey. At the same time, it no longer suited her and had lost the importance it once had to her.

In the end, we agreed that the museum would add the bangle to its collection, but on a permanent loan basis, meaning Zahra could ask for it to be returned if she wanted to in the future. I came to realise that the museum was the perfect destination for an object that had become displaced over time, both holding it in due regard as a precious object, and allowing Zahra to be free of this increasingly unsuitable thing.

Analysis

I will now try to compare the two cases using the framework presented above, and to provide an understanding of the situations out of which these items became biographical objects more or less intimately entangled with their respective owners. Considering belongings alongside changing social and cultural backgrounds within perceptional horizons (Merleau-Ponty) is helpful for reflecting on the social positionality, personal relatedness and orientation of people who have fled during their life courses and routes. Following Tret'iakov, this specific materiality is socially produced here by everyday practice and sensational experience in precarious and transient contexts along fragmented biographical courses. These ties have to be considered in reference to shifting backgrounds, in which objects are perceived by their possessors, who take different positions towards them over time and also against the backdrop of the social environment they live in. This allows for an understanding of personal biographies and positionalities mediated by and negotiated between things.

The ethnographic material reflects a clear difference between Atiya and Zahra, the former a mature academic, and a highly reflective woman, and the latter a young woman who spent her teenage years in war and exile, and who has largely been deprived of education. Their ages and backgrounds affect their ability to describe and reflect on these biographical things and on their personal entangledness with them, but also on violent disruptions or gradual disentanglement.[11] Moreover, the fact that Zahra was with members of her family during our conversation partly explains her reticence in discussing the jewellery,[12] as did my presence as an older unfamiliar European male. Without my female Syrian colleague, Samah Al Jundi-Pfaff, I would certainly not have been able to interact with Zahra or other female interlocutors similarly (see Berliner and Falen 2008).

In Atiya's case, the history of Rocky tells us something not only about the creative and manual dexterity of her mother, but also about the social background and limited economic capacities of her family when she was growing up. The intensity and tenderness of the ties between mother and daughter are materially expressed in the lovingly done sewing, in the heavy wear and tear, and in Atiya's ongoing attempts to keep Rocky from, quite literally, falling apart (on 'overuse' see Ahmed 2019, 48–9). In reference to the horizon scheme the object is of high emotional value and existentially related to Atiya (perception) but not very well considered from a perspective on social status of maturity (ascription).

Zahra's bangle does not say much about the social position of her family. Considering the material and its processing, as well as the fact that it was a gift from her sister, one can assume that the item's quality is solid but the bangle was not extraordinarily expensive. The minor scuffs and oxidations on its edges suggest it was worn regularly. Although the bangle stayed stable physically, it did not do so emotionally, practically or socially during its course, as I had initially assumed it would.

Similarly to other events leading to forced migrations, the Syrian civil war conditioned what people could take with them; after all, people can only take things that are portable or transportable (see for example Wallen and Pomerance 2018, 249; Basu and Coleman 2008, 316). These circumstances represent a critical 'point of passage' (Star and Griesemer, 1989) at which most other belongings are left behind. For Atiya and Zahra, in the same way as for many others, situated decisions and randomness played a crucial role in which possessions they kept and took with them from the chaos of war in Syria and the precarious years they both had in Turkey. Atiya's luggage – a small backpack – and Zahra's family's luggage – several big suitcases – also illustrate the illegalised and legal ways to Europe, based on structural conditions, constraints and dispossessions. Illegality is thus reflected in the (kind of) things one is (un)able to keep (see Hicks and Mallet 2019).

Disrupted and changing environments, in the course of Atiya's and Zahra's flights and migrations, have also changed the things, their aesthetics and how they affect their possessors and the people around them. Under this conjuncture, they are also paralleled by judgements and renegotiations of what is perceived and conceived as a 'proper' thing for whom at which life stage and context.

The biographical objects are also gendered, that is to say, categorised by the social environments and their possessors. Zahra's jewellery is a female accessory, one that has lost some of its attractiveness as it has gone out of fashion but still retains value as it was a personal gift and therefore has a relationship status. In the case of Rocky, the gender aspect is more ambiguous; one could argue that during Atiya's adolescence, keeping of soft toys during adolescence and into adulthood became feminised. A man in his mid-thirties who sleeps with a cuddly toy, both in the Middle East and in Europe, may not be acting in line with heterosexual gendered norms. Atiya as a woman may dare to keep Rocky as she is perceived as a 'freak' by her family and others, and has come to accept her 'freakdom' to some degree.

This facet leads to another striking difference concerning the social proximity and distance between the two objects. To stick with the norms and aesthetics of her social environments, Zahra feels that her jewellery may become an obstacle, and she distances herself from it by not wearing it, something she admits only hesitatingly in front of her sister. It was in precisely this situation that my doubts arose about how much objects can tell us biographically about Zahra in that moment, when she had recently arrived in a reception facility in Germany, because she seemed to rely not on biographical objects but rather on her family and friends. The relatedness to the thing at this point stems more from the obligation of cherishing the sister's gift than from emotional relatedness to the object itself. Distancing herself from the unsuitable bangle also allows her to adapt herself and 'fit in' to the new environments and their aesthetics.

In contrast, Atiya keeps Rocky as close as possible, since she feels more distant from her social worlds, from the German and the Syrian communities there, and also, at least partly, from her family. And it is at these intersections that her emotions have their 'proper place' in Rocky (see also Tret'iakov above and Part III of this book). While excessive use and time have changed Rocky's appearance, he remains a source of reliability. This reliability is necessary since Atiya struggles in several ways, with her past traumas, and with the challenges of setting up a stable life as a refugee woman in her second place of exile, Germany. Rocky seems to be exceptionally important to her, perhaps now more than ever, and he has a remarkable continuity as a fetishised object (see Böhme 2014, 350ff.) that enables Atiya to cope with the loss or absence of loved ones.

Sara Ahmed has outlined a way of being related to things that comes close to the relationship Atiya has with Rocky. She writes: 'A queer affinity can be an affinity with the broken ... The broken can be queer kin. To offer a queer way of working ... is to start with the weighty, the heavy, the weary, and the worn' (Ahmed 2019, 226–7). Hardship and social exclusion can create a new form of kin, a term that seems to be more appropriate than exaggerated in this case (although neither Atiya or Rocky can be considered to be broken). In hostile environments, things from the past can become relevant or pertinent again; ties can be created, re-created, revived (see Levin 2014). Though they do not easily gain social acknowledgement or acceptance, queer ties, like those between a 35-year-old woman and her stuffed toy, can nevertheless lead to some form of self-assurance.

What can the museum's collection and the women's decisions to keep or to hand over an object tell us about its involvement or disengagement in personhood at its current biographical state? Zahra can give the jewellery to the museum as an act of abiding by the social rule of treating gifts appropriately while also giving an increasingly undesirable item away and – at the same time – adding value to this object through an anonymous staging of the gift and its itinerary. This is only possible because the emotional and practical references to the object have decreased to a certain degree. Giving Rocky away to an institution that keeps things in inaccessible storage vaults or showcases would be unthinkable to Atiya because of the suffering that such an amputation of part of her 'distributed personhood' would cause. At the same time, Atiya cannot absolve herself of the duty or caring for and being close to Rocky, while Zahra can discharge her duty by giving her bangle to the museum.

The German reception facility Friedland Transit Camp is the beginning of a new and uncertain but also promising life of new engagements for Zahra. At the same time, it appears as a site of continued existential struggle and social isolation for Atiya, with only rare glimpses of the joy, hope and ease which are apparent in Zahra's case. Personal belongings matter differently in these cases; while in the first the bangle tends to be a burden in everyday life, in the second the practical and emotional ties to the thing remain (or become more) intense and existential as a substitute for intimate ties. Life courses and length of relationships between persons and things are only two of many constitutional aspects that frame a subject's perceptual horizons and the part things play in bodily sensation, social practice, and finally personhood. Similarly, trajectories are only one facet amid multiple forms of proximities and distances, perceptions, practices and ascriptions out of which things relate to people. Even though Rocky and the bangle were brought over during flights from Syria and kept in exile, and then made their way to Germany, things developed in quite different directions. Moreover, the capability to keep and bring things over can be a matter of coincidence and luck but also reflect structural reasons for flight and migrations as well as the practices and sensations of personal belonging and being.

Conclusion

This chapter has discussed biographical perspectives on material culture by means of an ethnographic consideration of two women who fled Syria and of their personal belongings. By referring to established but also neglected biographical approaches to objects, their reflexive capabilities, and their limitations, this chapter seeks to unfold a phenomenological and intersectional perspective on biographical objects.

The innovation of this perspective is that it brings the concept of perceptional horizons into the realm of biographical approaches to material culture. Here, movements, time and space are only three aspects of a whole range of proximities and distances out of which biographical things take shape in open-ended perceptional horizons. While 'object biographies' considered the changing functions and relevancies of things along with shifts and exchanges between different social spheres in the course of their cultural biographies, in this chapter I have suggested that one can understand how 'biographical objects' matter within fields of bodily perception and social practice. Following Tret'iakov's long-forgotten consideration – that societies produce things and environments and ways of being related to them – allows for an alternative and transformative understanding of things, of their situatedness and the orientation of their owners. As the case studies show, biographical objects can develop quite different roles, despite comparable backgrounds and migratory paths. The material consistency of a thing does not inevitably mean durability of esteem, as happened with Zahra's bangle; material disintegration may diminish the social value of a thing but be a result of intense relatedness, as the tie between Rocky and Atiya so vividly reflects.

For a long time, the possessions that refugees bring with them have been considered persistent 'symbols of identity' or 'hardship' and problematically equated people with their belongings and considered them as others. Instead, this chapter explains forced migrations through biographical objects and the ways in which their possessors are related and oriented towards these objects in perceptional horizons. Focusing on sensations and ties around things allows one to reflect on the horizons of moving people's perceptions and their intersecting positionalities. Considering (forced) migrations as materially mediated shifts of proximity and distance enables a transformative understanding of perceptions and ascriptions, dispossessions and fragmentations, belongings and ties (across national borders and ethnic lines). Things do not merely stand for something; they run counter to intentions, wear, degrade, are patched and change physically in the eyes of beholders during biographical courses. These traits of the material can serve to present migrations in less iconic and more tangibly related ways.

Notes

1 Acknowledging the plural entanglement of objects and their biographies, I use the plural form 'object biographies' in the following.

2 Tret'iakov reported on a collective farm (kolchoze) in the Caucasus region. He strongly criticised urban intellectuals for their remoteness from the reality of working people, and considered them to be the 'real savages' and farmers to be elaborated experts. As a thing- and practice-oriented writer he considered himself a productive actor of Soviet modernisation and joined the kolchoze (Tret'iakov [1931] 2006b).

3 The sociologist Tobias Schlechtriemen (2016) pursues a comparable thought through his ANT-based analysis of heroisations.

4 The archaeologist Jody Joy (2009, 542) differentiates between a multi-scalar life-story approach and biographical approaches that focus on the human–thing interaction.

5 An aspect I cannot address here is the topic of accumulated dispossessions, the repeated experience of dispossession and how it biographically and habitually shapes the capabilities to act and how these lost possessions matter. I plan to develop this topic in further publications.

6 In the empirical cases presented here, biographical objects are noticeably an emic concept.

7 I am greatly indebted to Samah Al Jundi-Pfaff, my dedicated colleague from the Friedland Museum who enabled my access to the field and for her excellent translations. The interview with Atiya was conducted in Friedland on 16 April 2019.

8 The Ismailis are a broadly moderate branch of Shia Islam but also one of the most atheist ethnic communities in Syria. At present, approximately 1 per cent of the national population are Ismailis (Douwes 2011, 19). Salamiyah is 1 of their cultural centres in the country (Douwes 2011, 28–32).

9 Youssef Ziedan, born in 1958, is an Egyptian writer and professor of Arabic and Islamic sciences.

10 The museum, a cooperation partner in our 'On the materiality of (forced) migration' research project, encourages people to tell their own stories and the stories of their belongings. Sometimes people donate personal items to the collection.

11 I do not wish to claim here that self-awareness necessarily requires academic education; it can help as a tool of understanding but there is no direct link between formal education and self-awareness.

12 As the family was transferred the following day, I was not able to talk to Zahra again under different circumstances.

References

Ahmed, Sara. 2006. *Queer Phenomenology: Orientations, objects, others*. Durham, NC, and London: Duke University Press.

Ahmed, Sara. 2007. 'A phenomenology of whiteness', *Feminist Theory* 8(2): 149–68. http://doi.org/10.1177/1464700107078139.

Ahmed, Sara. 2019. *What's the Use? On the uses of use*. Durham, NC, and London: Duke University Press.

Appadurai, Arjun, ed. 1986. *The Social Life of Things: Commodities in cultural perspective*. Cambridge: Cambridge University Press.

Appadurai, Arjun. 2017. 'Museum objects as accidental refugees', *Historische Anthropologie* 25(3): 401–8. https://doi.org/10.7788/ha-2017-0306.

Auslander, Leora. 2005. 'Beyond words', *American Historical Review* 110(4): 1015–45. https://doi.org/10.1086/ahr.110.4.1015.

Auslander, Leora and Tara Zahra. 2018. 'Epilogue'. In *Objects of War: The material culture of conflict and displacement*, edited by Leora Auslander and Tara Zahra, 309–18. Ithaca, NY, and London: Cornell University Press.

Basu, Paul and Simon Coleman. 2008. 'Introduction: Migrant worlds, material cultures', *Mobilities* 3(3): 313–30. https://doi.org/10.1080/17450100802376753.

Berliner, David and Douglas J. Falen. 2008. 'Introduction to special section on men doing anthropology of women', *Men and Masculinities* 11(2): 135–44. https://doi.org/10.1177/1097184X08315090.

Böhme, Hartmut. 2014. *Fetishism and Culture: A different theory of modernity*. Translated by Anna Galt. Berlin and Boston, MA: De Gruyter.

Bourdieu, Pierre. 1984. *Distinction: A social critique of the judgement of taste*. Translated by Richard Nice. Cambridge, MA: Harvard University Press.

Brun, Cathrine, Anita H. Fàbos and Oroub El-Abed. 2017. 'Displaced citizens and abject living: The categorical discomfort with subjects out of place', *Norsk Geografisk Tidsskrift/Norwegian Journal of Geography* 71(4): 220–32. https://doi.org/10.1080/00291951.2017.1369458.

Burström, Nanouschka M. 2014. 'Things in the eye of the beholder: A humanistic perspective on archaeological object biographies', *Norwegian Archaeological Review* 47(1): 65–82. https://doi.org/10.1080/00293652.2014.909877.

Chatty, Dawn. 2010. *Displacement and Dispossession in the Modern Middle East*. Cambridge: Cambridge University Press.

Degnen, Cathrine and Katharine Tyler. 2017. 'Amongst the disciplines: Anthropology, sociology, intersection and intersectionality', *Sociological Review* 65(1_suppl): 35–53. https://doi.org/10.1177/0081176917693508.

Douwes, Dick. 2011. 'Modern history of the Nizari Ismailis of Syria'. In *A Modern History of the Ismailis: Continuity and change in a Muslim community*, edited by Farhad Daftary, 19–44. London: I.B. Tauris.

Dudley, Sandra H. 2018. 'Paku Karen skirt-cloths (not) at home: Forcibly migrated Burmese textiles in refugee camps and museums'. In *Objects of War: The material culture of conflict and displacement*, edited by Leora Auslander and Tara Zahra, 277–307. Ithaca, NY, and London: Cornell University Press.

Friberg, Zanna and Isto Huvila. 2019. 'Using object biographies to understand the curation crisis: Lessons learned from the museum life of an archaeological collection', *Museum Management and Curatorship* 34(4): 362–82. https://doi.org/10.1080/09647775.2019.1612270.

Frykman, Jonas and Maja Povrzanović Frykman. 2016. 'Affect and material culture: Perspectives and strategies'. In *Sensitive Objects: Affect and material culture*, edited by Jonas Frykman and Maja Povrzanović Frykman, 9–28. Lund: Nordic Academic Press.

Galitzine-Loumpet, Alexandra. 2020. 'De/dans et de/hors: Objets et sujets dans la migration et l'exil'. In *L'Objet de la migration, le sujet en exil*, edited by Corinne Alexandre-Garner and Alexandra Galitzine-Loumpet, 35–49. Paris and Nanterre: Presses Universitaires de Paris Nanterre.

Garvey, Pauline. 2002. 'Organized disorder: Moving furniture in Norwegian homes'. In *Home Possessions: Material culture behind closed doors*, edited by Daniel Miller, 47–68. Oxford and New York: Berg.

Gell, Alfred. 1998. *Art and Agency: Anthropological theory*. Oxford: Clarendon Press.

Georgi, Fabian. 2019. 'Toward fortress capitalism: The restrictive transformation of migration and border regimes as a reaction to the capitalist multicrisis', *Canadian Review of Sociology/Revue canadienne de sociologie* 56(4): 556–79. https://doi.org/10.1111/cars.12264.

Gosden, Chris and Yvonne Marshall. 1999. 'The cultural biography of objects', *World Archaeology* 31(2): 169–78. https:/doi.org/10.1080/00438243.1999.9980439.

Habermas, Tilmann. 1996. *Geliebte Objekte: Symbole und Instrumente der Identitätsbildung*. Berlin: De Gruyter.

Habermas, Tilmann. 1999. 'Persönliche Objekte und Bindungen im Prozeß der Ablösung vom Elternhaus'. In *Persönliche Objekte, Identität und Entwicklung*, edited by Urs Fuhrer and Ingrid E. Josephs, 109–33. Göttingen: Vandenhoeck and Ruprecht.

Hage, Ghassan. 2013. 'Eavesdropping on Bourdieu's philosophers', *Thesis Eleven* 114(1): 76–93. https://doi.org/10.1177/0725513612463036.

Hahn, Hans Peter and Hadas Weiss. 2013. 'Introduction: Biographies, travels and itineraries of things'. In *Mobility, Meaning and the Transformations of Things: Shifting contexts of material culture through time and space*, edited by Hans Peter Hahn and Hadas Weiss, 1–14. Oxford: Oxbow Books.

Hallam, Elizabeth and Tim Ingold, eds. 2014. *Making and Growing: Anthropological studies of organisms and artefacts*. Farnham and Burlington, VT: Ashgate.

Herva, Vesa-Pekka. 2005. 'The life of buildings: Minoan building deposits in an ecological perspective', *Oxford Journal of Archaeology* 24(3): 215–27. https://doi.org/10.1111/j.1468-0092.2005.00233.x.

Hicks, Dan. 2020. *The Brutish Museums: The Benin bronzes, colonial violence and cultural restitution*. London: Pluto Press.

Hicks, Dan and Mary C. Beaudry, eds. 2010. *The Oxford Handbook of Material Culture Studies*. Oxford and New York: Oxford University Press.

Hicks, Dan and Sarah Mallet. 2019. *Lande: The Calais 'Jungle' and beyond*. Bristol: Bristol University Press.

Hoskins, Janet. 1998. *Biographical Objects: How things tell the stories of people's lives*. New York and London: Routledge.

Hurdley, Rachel. 2013. *Home, Materiality, Memory and Belonging: Keeping culture*. Basingstoke and New York: Palgrave Macmillan.

Joy, Jody. 2009. 'Reinvigorating object biography: Reproducing the drama of object lives', *World Archaeology* 41(4): 540–56. https://doi.org/10.1080/00438240903345530.

Khosravi, Shahram, ed. 2018. *After Deportation: Ethnographic perspectives*. Cham: Palgrave Macmillan.

Köber, Christin and Tilmann Habermas. 2017. 'How stable is the personal past? Stability of most important autobiographical memories and life narratives across eight years in a life span sample', *Journal of Personality and Social Psychology* 113(4): 608–26. https://doi.org/10.1037/pspp0000145.

Kopytoff, Igor. 1986. 'The cultural biographies of things: Commoditization as process'. In *The Social Life of Things: Commodities in cultural perspective*, edited by Arjun Appadurai, 64–91. Cambridge: Cambridge University Press.

Lee Brien, Donna. 2020. 'Object biography and its potential in creative writing', *New Writing* 17(4): 377–90. https://doi.org/10.1080/14790726.2019.1659373.

Levin, Iris. 2014. '"This is for the children, the grandchildren ...": Houses of Moroccan migrants in metropolitan Tel Aviv', *Housing, Theory and Society* 31(1): 54–75. https://doi.org/10.1111/j.1470-6431.2009.00805.x.

Marschall, Sabine. 2019. '"Memory objects": Material objects and memories of home in the context of intra-African mobility', *Journal of Material Culture* 0(0): 1–17 (preprint). https://doi.org/10.1177/1359183519832630.

Merleau-Ponty, Maurice. 1969. *The Visible and the Invisible*. Translated by Alphonso Lingis. Evanston, IL: Northwestern University Press.

Merleau-Ponty, Maurice. 2002. *Phenomenology of Perception*. London and New York: Routledge.

Miller, Daniel. 2010. *Stuff*. Cambridge: Polity.

Neumann, Friedemann and Hans Peter Hahn. 2019. 'Between things: Situating (post)migration and material culture in social space'. In *Family and Space: Rethinking family theory and empirical approaches*, edited by Maya Halatcheva-Trapp, Giulia Montanari and Tino Schlinzig, 35–45. Abingdon: Routledge.

Nieswand, Boris. 2018. 'Border *dispositifs* and border effects: Exploring the nexus between transnationalism and border studies', *Identities* 25(5): 592–609.

Nippert-Eng, Christena. 2010. *Islands of Privacy*. Chicago: Chicago University Press.

Özkaya, Derya. 2020. 'Negotiating solidarity and conflict in and beyond the neighbourhood: The case of Gülsuyu-Gülensu, Istanbul'. In *Urban Neighbourhood Formations: Boundaries, narrations and intimacies*, edited by Hilal Alkan and Nazan Maksudyan, 199–217. Abingdon and New York: Routledge.

Pollard, Joshua. 2004. 'The art of decay and the transformation of substance'. In *Substance, Memory, Display: Archaeology and art*, edited by Colin Renfrew, Chris Gosden and Elizabeth DeMarrais, 47–62. Cambridge: McDonald Institute for Archaeological Research, University of Cambridge.

Povrzanović Frykman, Maja. 2016. 'Conceptualising continuity: A material culture perspective on transnational social fields', *Ethnologia Fennica* (43): 43–56. https://www.diva-portal.org/smash/get/diva2:1398316/FULLTEXT01.pdf.

Rachamimov, Iris. 2018. 'Small escapes: Gender, class, and material culture in great war internment camps'. In *Objects of War: The material culture of conflict and displacement*, edited by Leora Auslander and Tara Zahra, 164–88. Ithaca, NY, and London: Cornell University Press.

Ram, Kalpana and Christopher Houston. 2015a. 'Introduction: Phenomenology's methodological invitation'. In *Phenomenology in Anthropology: A sense of perspective*, edited by Kalpana Ram and Christopher Houston, 1–25. Bloomington: Indiana University Press.

Ram, Kalpana and Christopher Houston, eds. 2015b. *Phenomenology in Anthropology: A sense of perspective*. Bloomington: Indiana University Press.

Ramsay, Georgina. 2019. 'Time and the other in crisis: How anthropology makes its displaced object', *Anthropological Theory* 0(0): 1–29 (preprint). https://doi.org/10.1177/1463499619840464.

Schlechtriemen, Tobias. 2016. 'The hero and a thousand actors: On the constitution of heroic agency', *helden. heroes. héros* 4(1): 17–32. https://doi.org/10.6094/helden.heroes.heros./2016/01/03.

Stahl, Ann B. 2010. 'Material histories'. In *The Oxford Handbook of Material Culture Studies*, edited by Dan Hicks and Mary C. Beaudry, 150–72. Oxford and New York: Oxford University Press.

Star, Susan L. and James R. Griesemer. 1989. 'Institutional ecology, "translations" and boundary objects: Amateurs and professionals in Berkeley's Museum of Vertebrate Zoology, 1907–39', *Social Studies of Science* 19(3): 387–420.

Stockhammer, Philipp W. 2020. 'Doing/changing things/us'. In *Exploring Materiality and Connectivity in Anthropology and Beyond*, edited by Philipp Schorch, Martin Saxer and Marlen Elders, 36–50. London: UCL Press. https://doi.org/10.14324/111.9781787357488.

Strathern, Marilyn. 1988. *The Gender of the Gift: Problems with women and problems with society in Melanesia*. Berkeley and Los Angeles: University of California Press.

Thomas, Nicholas. 1991. *Entangled Objects: Exchange, material culture, and colonialism in the Pacific*. Cambridge, MA: Harvard University Press.

Thompson, Michael. 2017. *Rubbish Theory: The creation and destruction of value*, 2nd edition. London: Pluto Press.

Tilley, Chris, Webb Keane, Susanne Kuechler, Mike Rowlands and Patricia Spyer, eds. 2006. *Handbook of Material Culture*. London and Thousand Oaks, CA: SAGE.

Tret'iakov, Sergei. [1929] 2006a. 'The biography of the object', *October* 118: 57–62.
Tret'iakov, Sergei. [1931] 2006b. 'The writer and the socialist village', *October* 118: 63–70.
Wallen, Jeffrey and Aubrey Pomerance. 2018. 'Circuitous journey: The migration of objects and the trusteeship of memory'. In *Objects of War: The material culture of conflict and displacement*, edited by Leora Auslander and Tara Zahra, 248–76. Ithaca, NY, and London: Cornell University Press.
Woodward, Ian. 2007. *Understanding Material Culture*. London: SAGE Publications.

5

The Dzhangal Archaeology Project and 'Lande': two archaeological approaches to the study of forced migration

Sarah Mallet and Louise Fowler

Introduction

This chapter presents an archaeological investigation of the 'Jungle', the infamous refugee camp in Calais in northern France. We explore both the material dimension of contemporary migration and the new experimental regimes of state borderwork at Calais as enforced by the French and British states, and we have reimagined archaeology and anthropology as methods of making visible what would otherwise stay hidden by the politics of the present. Indeed, by examining the material culture of the camp through the lens of archaeology, our innovative approach accounts for the *longue durée* political, cultural, historical and social trends that led to ten thousand people living in this refugee camp in northern France from 2015 to 2016. We will present work on two different but complementary 'collections', which have been made to represent the camp in different ways: the first is the assemblage collected in the camp by photographer Gideon Mendel, which provided the material for his exhibition 'Dzhangal' at the Autograph ABP gallery in London in 2017, and the second is the collaboratively assembled collection which was on display at the Pitt Rivers Museum in 2019 as the major temporary exhibition 'Lande: The Calais "Jungle" and beyond'. We will discuss how the materials were examined, as well as our continuing work on how they are represented, both as an archaeological collection and as a museum display.

Through archaeological practices and methodologies, both the Dzhangal Archaeology Project and the 'Lande' exhibition have contributed to an understanding of the camp through the study of artefacts from the site to reveal the complex human networks in and around Calais. They have also allowed us to develop a reflexive approach to our methodologies for dealing with archaeological and museum collections. We argue that, by using the spaces of ethnography and the 'archaeology of the contemporary', we have provided new voices in our representation of forced migration in Europe today and we render visible the landscape of the UK/French border at Calais.

To begin, a note on terminology is necessary. In recent years, the distinction between 'refugees' and 'migrants' has dominated political debates (Edwards 2016). Refugees, fleeing war and persecution, are entitled to asylum and state protection as outlined in the 1951 United Nations Refugee Convention, while migrants are 'merely' seeking to better their economic prospects and should be sent back (Edwards 2016). The difference between 'refugees' and 'migrants' is often an attempt to defend xenophobia and anti-immigrant sentiment: the refugee is deserving of help, the migrant is not, although events in Greece in March 2020, when the government suspended asylum applications, suggest that refugees may soon not be deserving of help either (Edwards 2016; Hamilakis 2016; Rankin 2020). The issue of what to call people forced out of their countries has long been problematic and was addressed as early as 1943 by Hannah Arendt in her essay 'We refugees': 'In the first place, we don't like to be called "refugees". We ourselves call each other "newcomers" or "immigrants"' (Arendt [1943] 2007, 264). The term 'refugee' has also been criticised for its passiveness: it implies that people were pushed from their home, displaying no agency of their own (Greussing and Boomgaarden 2017; Brettell 2015). The term 'migrant' suggests a more active decision process, but one that borders on criminality (Hamilakis 2016). However, taking into account that so-called economic migrants often want to escape low-level warfare, extreme poverty, political instability, unrest or dictatorship, which all curtail life options, and climate catastrophe, it is debatable whether the distinction between 'refugee' and 'migrant' is relevant, or even appropriate. However, we would argue that the distinction should not be erased academically, as it remains significant in the Global North and shapes the political, cultural and social discourse about forced migrations (Ong 2003). It is also noteworthy that, when in a group, asylum seekers are likely to be viewed negatively as migrants, but individual and personal 'refugee' stories are likely to be viewed positively. From David Cameron to Donald Trump, notions of 'swarms', 'hordes' and ‘invasions’ have dominated the media and political discourse (Elgot and Taylor 2015; Zimmer 2019). We argue that this has an impact on how refugees and migrants are perceived, potentially explaining the shift of the ‘refugee’ from tolerated to ‘undesirable’, as seen in the EU’s reaction to the situation in the Mediterranean in February 2020 as numbers arriving from Turkey increased. The Greek Prime Minister Kyriakos Mitsotakis had previously described the people fleeing Turkey as ‘economic migrants’ (Smith 2019), and such a view was perhaps used to justify the violent response of the Greek state after the navy was seen attacking a boat full of people (Smith 2020).

Here, we will use ‘refugee’ for people whose refugee status has been legally recognised and ‘migrant’ for people whose status is unsettled. We will also use ‘forced migrant’ and ‘displaced population’, while recognising that the terms are problematic as they suggest a lack of agency in the decision to leave one’s homeland.

Contemporary archaeology

This investigation relies on the methods and practice of contemporary archaeology. Contemporary archaeology is a growing field within archaeology, engaging with the remains of the present and the recent past (Graves-Brown et al. 2013). It has brought an archaeological lens through which to view contemporary social problems, and through a process that makes the familiar strange it has made visible aspects of contemporary life which some might prefer were ignored or went undocumented. An interest in the potential of archaeology to address political and social problems has led to the establishment of a subfield of scholarship addressing contemporary borders and undocumented migration, demonstrated by an edited volume devoted to the topic which emerged from a forum in the *Journal of Contemporary Archaeology*, initially published in 2016 (Hamilakis 2018). Work has focused on camps (Dreyer 2001; Myers 2008; Burström 2009; Ramadan 2012; Kourelis 2018; Hicks and Mallet 2019), shelter (Fredriksen 2014; Caraher, Weber and Rothaus 2018; Kiddey 2020), border landscapes (De León 2015), and objects (Bergqvist Rydėn 2018; Breene 2018; Seitsonen, Herva and Kunnari 2018; Tyrikos-Ergas 2018). The Undocumented Migration Project, which investigates how the landscape is used by and against those who attempt to cross it, has been particularly influential. This project is a ‘non-profit research-art-education-media collective’, which encompasses countermapping, participant interviews and observation, material culture studies and public engagement to take an archaeological and anthropological approach to clandestine migration across the Mexico–USA border (De León 2012, 2013, 2015; Stewart et al. 2018).

The strength of using an archaeological framework or methodology to study forced migration is that it allows us to investigate the deep historical, social and cultural contexts that surround the presence of ten thousand people in a refugee camp in northern France in 2015 and 2016. The Jungle has often been seen as a symptom of the 'migration crisis' or 'refugee crisis'. The short temporal framing created by the use of the term crisis is problematic, however. It deflects attention from the social, political, economic and historical processes of which the present situation is a result, positioning the West as a solution to a problem that is perceived to arise elsewhere, and providing a justification for a polarised and contradictory military/humanitarian response, which combines riot police and tear gas on the one hand with appeals to charity on the other, a heavy military police presence being justified by the existence of a 'state of exception' (Agamben 1998). As a discipline, archaeology examines the entanglements between people, processes and materials; we argue that attempts in the Global North to evade the obligation to offer asylum have had a distinct material impact on the world.[1] Like the study of traditional heritage, the materiality of forced displacement is a window onto the temporal and spatial processes at play: the construction of walls everywhere in the world, the proliferation of border checkpoints and controls, the establishment of refugee camps and the complex transnational flow of materials between refugees, humanitarian and state actors, border guards and 'vigilantes' are all events shaping our world and our response to it. Investigating forced migration through the practices and methods of archaeology differs from other methodological approaches by allowing a focus on the 'physical manifestation of politics' (Herz 2013, 12). Herz points out that one of the principal ways of investigating refugee camps is 'as spaces of humanitarianism or a state of exception', but his focus is on 'understanding the camps as they are used by the population' simply by asking the question: 'How do people live in camps?' Similarly, archaeology asks how people lived in any given space and time, and by extending the focus beyond the camp archaeology can be an important tool for investigating the physical manifestation of the politics of forced migration.

Archaeology is a lens through which to study forced migration and, at the same time, a way of communicating with and engaging wider publics. The techniques and methods of archaeology – a discipline usually associated with the study of the deeper past – can be used to make the present unfamiliar and in so doing open a space in which new narratives can grow. Archaeology here is unapologetically used as a form of activism, and we argue that the materiality of forced migration forces us to face the shared humanity of those we leave to die at the borders of our nation states.

The UK border

In this chapter, we specifically investigate the situation around Calais in northern France, where the UK border has been relocated by treaty with France, first at the Channel Tunnel terminal at Fréthun under the Sangatte Protocol (1991) and then at the Port of Calais under the later Treaty of Le Touquet (2003). When Europe's Schengen Area removed many official border controls, Calais became, for those seeking to claim asylum in Britain, a place from which to make an irregular crossing, which has resulted in many informal camps located in and around the city. Calais thus became 'an intra-European laboratory for an EU-external border regime' (Müller and Schlüper 2018, 17, quoted in translation from the German in Hicks and Mallet 2019, 25). While the best-known 'Jungle' is arguably the one that dominated the media in 2015 and 2016, other informal camps also known as 'jungles' have been set up and dismantled in and around Calais ever since the 1980s (Agier et al. 2018; Hicks and Mallet 2019; Human Rights Observers Project 2019).

The UK government has always been involved with the 'management' of refugees in northern France. In 1999, a warehouse in Sangatte was transformed into a refugee centre and administered by the Red Cross, but it was closed in 2002 under pressure from the British Government during the negotiations for the Touquet Treaty (Tempest 2002). UK involvement increased financially in later years and in 2014 the mayor of Calais threatened to close the port if the British government did not provide support, as the number of refugees in and around the city had tripled. It was very much seen as a 'French problem' (Khomami 2014), but the UK government agreed to send a 9ft tall 'ring of steel' fence, which had been used for security at the NATO summit in Wales earlier that year (BBC 2014). While the 'ring of steel' did not survive the winter in northern France, it was agreed in late 2014, between Theresa May, the then Home Secretary, and Bernard Cazeneuve, her French counterpart, that the UK would spend £5 million per year for three years to secure the port (Khomami 2014). By August 2015, after the so-called 'refugee crisis' of the summer, another £9 million had been agreed (BBC 2015). This money was fully intended to go towards the securitisation of the border, as stated by the Minister of State for Immigration James Brokenshire during a parliamentary debate:

> We are not providing financial support for any day centres. Our financial support is *focused on security* at Calais and on *confronting the organised criminality* that seeks to take advantage of those trying to come to the UK. The juxtaposed controls absolutely benefit this country and we have no plans to change that.
>
> (Hansard 2015, our emphasis)

A freedom of information request to the Home Office confirmed that the money had been spent on fences (Calais Research 2016). However, the many kilometres of walls and fences being built across the city are not the only deterrent employed against migrants and refugees funded by UK taxpayers. Hostile 'tactics of exhaustion', designed to limit successful Channel crossings, have also been reported; amongst them are dispossession, destructions and sleep deprivation, including the routine use of tear gas, slashing tents with blades, spraying blankets with pepper spray, breaking mobile phones, sustained confiscations of shelter, clothing or property, and even the practice of taking one shoe from displaced people to limit their movements (Refugee InfoBus 2018). While these are reported by the charity organisations on the ground, the French state and police have denied having recourse to 'unreasonable force'. Even when these reports end up in the French or British news, and even when the EU Court of Human Rights intervenes, very little is actually done to combat such violence. Developments at Calais have taken place against the background of the UK government's 'hostile environment' policy, a suite of measures intended to reduce immigration figures and make life harder for illegal immigrants living in the UK, first announced by the then Home Secretary Theresa May in 2012. The UK 'hostile environment' in Calais has been deadly: from 1999 up to the time of writing, at least 292 people have died trying to cross the UK border in France, including 36 children (IRR 2020, 7).[2] Four people died in the Channel in the summer and autumn of 2019, making it a concern that the number could rise as many more people attempt to cross (Sánchez Dionis and Dearden 2019, 78; Sanderson 2019; Oberti 2019; AFP 2019). During the preparation of this chapter, on 24 November 2021, 27 people (including three children) drowned in the Channel when their boat sank. It is, to this date, the biggest loss of life recorded. It was later revealed that both French and British police were aware the boat was encountering difficulties but did not rescue the people on board.

The Calais 'Jungle'

It is against this landscape of a hard border that the 'Grande Jungle' of 2015 to 2016 emerged. Officially known as the Camp de la Lande, it was an attempt by the city of Calais to remove refugees from the town centre by 'tolerating' an encampment on the outskirts of the city. The camp grew quickly, and became known as the 'Jungle' after previous similar informal camps in and around the city. The name 'Jungle' comes from the Pashto *dzhangal*, which means 'woods'. While the camp itself does not survive today, the name 'Jungle' has persisted and now describes the living conditions of displaced people still in Calais.

While it is common for refugee camps to emerge alongside hard borders, the Calais 'Jungle' was unusual for many reasons: it grew with no oversight from the traditional state or humanitarian actors (Alaux 2015). Help Refugees, arguably one of the largest aid organisations in Europe today, was created specifically to address the situation in Calais. The camp grew organically and became an urban space with restaurants, mosques and churches, and attracted worldwide attention both as an active refugee camp in northern Europe and as a space of solidarity, hospitality and resilience, and at the same time one of tremendous violence (PEROU 2016; Agier et al. 2018). It existed on French soil, but outside France. Volunteers from over the world started pouring into the camp in September 2015, after the picture of Alan Kurdi, a three-year-old Syrian boy of Kurdish origin who drowned in the Mediterranean, became a symbol of the plight of refugees and Europe's cruel and dangerous border policies.

Displaced people at Calais came predominantly from Afghanistan, Sudan, South Sudan and Eritrea, all territories which had been under British administration during the later British Empire. Here, an archaeological approach allows us to go beyond discussions about asylum, which remain framed between the 'push and pull factors' of conflict or lifestyle, and instead to consider Calais over the *longue durée*, as a (post)colonial environment impacted by the enduring effects of militarist colonialism (Hicks and Mallet 2019).

The large 'Jungle' camp was cleared in two phases in 2016, the southern section in March (Chakelian 2016), and the rest in October. People still wishing to live in and make use of the landscape were not deterred by the dismantlement of the camp, and a new network of places to find Wi-Fi or food distribution, or to sleep and hide, was soon established. A city park was even used as a 'invisible church' for people to worship and conduct Mass (Hagan 2019). All of these have created a geography unknown and hidden to most 'legal' citizens, similar to the landscape that Kiddey (2017) described in her pioneering study of homelessness. State apparatuses are attempting to make this new geography invisible, but archaeology can render the invisible and the unrecorded visible, though this is not without its ethical issues (De León 2015). By investigating these landscapes through archaeological methods, we resist the injunction to look away and are forced to recognise the lives of the people who are constantly pushed into the margin of our societies (De León 2015, 3; Hicks and Mallet 2019, 31).

'Dzhangal', or an archaeology of the 'Jungle'

The Dzhangal Archaeology Project is a collaboration between the co-authors and the artist and photographer Gideon Mendel, which takes as its starting point an assemblage of objects collected by Mendel at the site of the Calais 'Jungle' camp, many of which were displayed in 2017 as part of his exhibition 'Dzhangal' at the Autograph ABP gallery in London (Figure 5.1). Our work was partly funded by Museum of London Archaeology (MOLA), and partly through two Knowledge Exchange Fellowships funded by TORCH (The Oxford Research Centre in the Humanities) and the Social Sciences Division at the University of Oxford.

5.1 Gideon Mendel's exhibition 'Dzhangal' at the Autograph ABP gallery in London, 2017. © Gideon Mendel.

Mendel's politically engaged art practice blurs disciplinary boundaries between art, journalism, activism and the gathering of data to confront people in the UK with the material culture of the 'Jungle'. As an artist, he is not alone in having incorporated the material culture of migration into his art practice. The 2019 Venice Biennale was dominated by debate about the ethics of exhibiting *Barca Nostra*, the wreck of a fishing vessel in which hundreds of migrants died, brought to the festival by the artist Christoph Büchel (Higgins 2019). The Chinese artist Ai Weiwei has also produced several artefact-based works on the theme of the current migration 'crisis' in Europe. In 2016 his team collected fourteen thousand abandoned life jackets from the Greek island of Lesvos and wrapped them around the columns of the façade of the Konzerthaus in Berlin, installing them the following year in the windows of the Kunsthal Charlottenborg in Copenhagen. Also in 2016, clothing, shoes and blankets from a camp at Idomeni in Greece were displayed as part of Ai's installation *Laundromat* at the Deitch gallery in New York, later exhibited in Doha, Qatar. In the UK, Arabella Dorman's installations *Flight* (created from life jackets and an inflatable vessel used in a journey to the Greek island of Lesvos) and *Suspended* (created from seven hundred items of refugee clothing salvaged from the same island) were both displayed in the nave of St James's church, Piccadilly, in London, the latter then moving to the cathedrals of Leicester and Canterbury (J. Jones 2015; Sherwood 2017). Such an approach is not limited to Europe. In the US, Thomas Kiefer secretly collected and later photographed the confiscated belongings of migrants apprehended while crossing the border between the USA and Mexico, while he was working as a janitor at a US Customs and Border Patrol processing facility in Arizona (Easter 2019).

These artists and others use real objects to lend a sense of authenticity and urgency to their work. Things, like photographs, can be seen as evidence, and perhaps, when we are ever more sensitive to the ways in which photography can play with truth, things at first appear to be something that cannot be manipulated so easily. But there are clearly difficulties with this assumption. Art installations of refugee material culture often focus on personal and emotive items such as clothing and shoes, which evoke the presence of an imagined and absent other. But the affectiveness of things also relies upon the knowledge, experience and beliefs of viewers. Tyrikos-Ergas (2018) has explored how life jackets elicit differing responses from different groups on Lesvos. Some installations of material culture uncomfortably echo museum displays created using the personal belongings taken from people sent to Nazi concentration camps, and they are often intended to function in a similar way, simultaneously providing historical proof and acting affectively, to elicit empathy (E. Jones 2001). There is also a danger that decontextualised displays of material culture, like much photography of suffering, can 'focus on the powerless, reduced to their powerlessness' (Sontag 2003, 70), removing agency and voice from those they claim to represent.

In some press reports and by his own assessment, Mendel's approach to his work was described as an archaeological one. His collecting sprang from a desire to treat the objects 'as if they were precious archaeological artefacts that might help us make sense of the complex relationships and politics of the place' (Mendel n.d., 2). He also adopted the aesthetic of archaeological reporting and antiquarian museum display for his photographs, arranging objects by functional category and in an orderly, regular layout. This process also raises uneasy and contradictory associations, which are explored in the book which accompanied the exhibition: 'Intentional as well is the collision with Euro-American traditions of collecting. The praxis of compiling physical evidence to account for "others", making sense of their difference and, thereby, of the collector's power to examine, name, bracket and administer, has a long and violent history' (Malaquais 2017, 74).

Mendel, however, has discussed his ordering as a way of according respect, and avoiding the potential for his images to be seen as a kind of 'ruin porn' (Gentleman 2017). The order he imposed can also be seen as an attempt to de-aestheticise. The troubling (and haunting) aspect of the images is that it is simply not possible to display these items in a gallery, away from their original context, and avoid aestheticising them in some way. Mendel's images *are* beautiful, and the objects he has chosen to photograph *do* include the kinds of obviously affective objects common to other art installations and displays of 'refugee material culture'. In this, they force the viewer to confront the paradoxical response of the West to a 'crisis' of our own making. The emotive and personal items such as toys, clothing and toothbrushes are there, but so too is other detritus of the camp: burnt fragments of pallets, scraps of tarpaulin, fragments of frayed bungee cord, tools and teargas canisters, elevated to monumental status.

The aim of our archaeological engagement with the assemblage collected by Mendel is twofold. Firstly, we believe an archaeological approach has the potential to contribute to an understanding of the human relationships characterising the 'migrant crisis' in Calais. Archaeology has more to offer than an invitation to empathise and an appreciation of the shared humanity that inheres in things which have been abandoned. This is not to suggest that the affective potential of objects is not important. An affective, emotionally engaged archaeology should be capable of challenging received histories and inspiring acts that lead to real social and political change (Perry 2018; 2019). However, qualified aspirations to objectivity and emotional responses can combine in ways that are nuanced and complicated. Emotive pleas may not necessarily lead to positive action, if at the same time they elicit feelings of helplessness and fear (Sontag 2003). Some degree of dispassion and distance also has a role to play in seeking political action and change.

Though the assemblage collected by Mendel could be used to create archaeological narratives about the lived experience of those who occupied the 'Jungle', to do so is not our goal. We believe that this can only be achieved by working directly with those who were there, and we recognise the emotional labour involved in repeating and reliving traumatic events and experiences. We would not, however, wish this to be taken as an abdication of our own responsibility to observe and to make visible to others the lived reality in the 'Jungle'. We are in agreement with Sontag, that 'So far as we feel sympathy, we feel we are not accomplices to what has caused the suffering' (Sontag 2003, 91). An archaeological approach has the potential to go beyond engendering feelings of sympathy or empathy, to help us explore the ways in which our own privilege is located on the same map (Sontag 2003, 92). In order to do this, we wish to expand the map both temporally and spatially, by considering the biographies of the things that have been collected, facilitating a consideration of how they were enmeshed within social, economic and political relationships that extended far beyond Calais.

Biographical approaches to material culture are well embedded in archaeological and anthropological practice (Kopytoff 1986; Holtorf 2002; Joy 2010; Schofield et al. 2020). These studies build on the belief that things are enmeshed in social relationships that change and develop over time, and that they have the potential to affect behaviour in humans. In the context of archaeologies of undocumented migration, De León (2013) has adopted a 'use-wear' approach to the study of material culture found in the Sonoran desert, combined with ethnographic interviews to appreciate the ways in which the bodies of border crossers are intimately involved with things. We are also interested in evidence for the use of things, but the concept of biography expands this over a longer timescale to incorporate evidence that may not be the result of a physical interaction occurring during the use of the object; it includes product labelling and evidence of point of manufacture, origin or sale, as well as the objects' 'afterlives' as part of an art installation.

Secondly, we wanted to find out what this material could tell us about the assumptions and processes of knowledge production in English development-led archaeology, as practised at MOLA. Such an aspiration is not as divorced from our wider project as it may at first seem. The archaeological past, including the narratives created through development-led projects, contributes to perceptions of local and national identity (Sommer 2017), and the heritage sector has often been complicit in the creation of narratives of rootedness that exclude more mobile ways of relating to the past (Harrison, Appelgren and Bohlin 2018). We wished to explore the ways in which methods and frameworks in the development-led sector lead us to prioritise and give voice to particular narratives as part of this process, and to silence other possible narratives.

Our work on the 'Dzhangal' assemblage began with a period of familiarisation, practically enabled by using both written records and photography. As we hoped to facilitate some conversations about the traditional methodologies of commercial archaeological practice, all staff at MOLA were given an opportunity to participate in the work. A standard recording process was designed for consistency, using a combination of photography and written description. The assemblage arrived at MOLA packed by the gallery, mostly in labelled plastic bags. These were photographed unopened, and then the bag was opened and its contents were ordered, photographed and recorded in a spreadsheet (Figure 5.2). As well as a brief description, participants were prompted to record systematically any obvious biographical evidence of the origin, manufacture, use and disuse of objects. We photographed the objects with a scale against a white background, using a digital SLR camera situated either directly overhead or obliquely, depending on the subject. Though this process bore some similarity to Mendel's art practice, it also replicated to some degree the approach taken at MOLA to the photography of finds from excavations. Finds processors photograph objects when registering them, prior to any conservation treatment, and these images are used primarily as a quick reference for those working on a project, as an aide-memoire for the moment when something was encountered, observed and recorded.

A total of 2,189 objects have been archaeologically recorded, and our work investigates what these materials can tell us about the camp, its inhabitants, the volunteers and the French and British response. Like traditional archaeological material, the Calais artefacts can help us understand what life was like in the camp and the journeys undertaken by those there, through objects such as a travelcard from Istanbul, or Italian 'tourist' ware (Figure 5.3). But attributing specific items to specific groups proved hard. We did not know, for example, whether the wallet from Italy was acquired during a journey by someone following one of the main routes taken by refugees and migrants through Europe to Calais, or

5.2 The authors with artist Gideon Mendel discussing the recording of tin cans, 2017. © MOLA.

if it was something donated, or if it belonged to a volunteer who had been to Italy on holiday. Charitable donations and the work of volunteers are also visible in the assemblage, specifically through a number of tins of food from British supermarkets and other items with British price tags and labels, which would have been transported from the UK (Figure 5.4).

Of particular interest has been the material evidence of violence at the UK border. Despite denials by both the French and British states about the violence in Calais, we have been able to record and document that this violence did occur. Out of 2,189 objects, we have recorded 550 fragments of tear gas canisters (Figure 5.5). Even taking into account a possible 'sample bias' in Mendel's collecting, these numbers tell a story of violence.

5.3 'ITALIA' tourist wallet. © MOLA.

5.4 Tin of organic red kidney beans labelled in English. © MOLA.

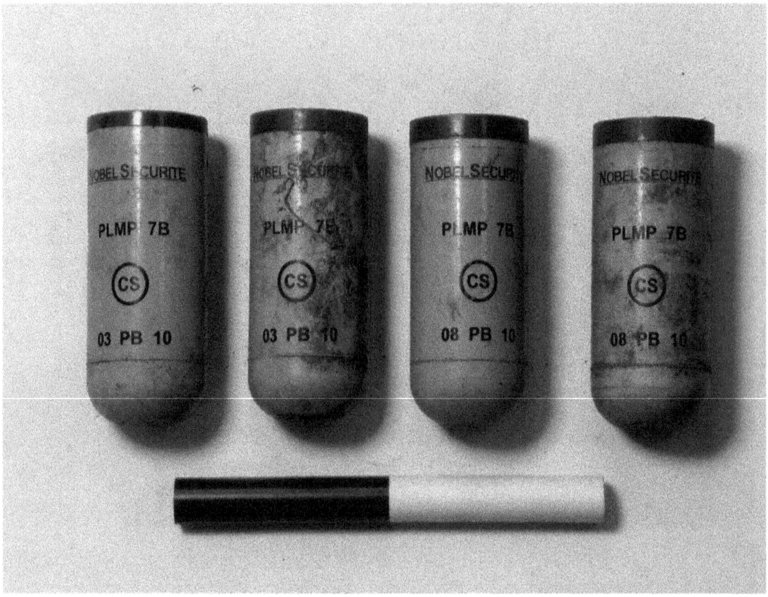

5.5 Tear gas canisters manufactured by Nobel Sport Sécurité. © MOLA.

There have been many reports of the use of tear gas against refugees, some even suggesting that up to two hundred canisters could be fired in a day (Hassoux and Labbé 2016) but the French state has always denied use of excessive force (Macron 2018). Maybe more importantly, the presence of these objects inside the camp contradicts the narrative that tear gas was mainly used to disperse migrants around the port. Indeed, the presence of the canisters in the camp would seem to indicate that '*lieux de vie*' (living spaces) were also targeted. The canisters range in date from 1993 to 2016 and come from two different French manufacturers (Nobel Sport Sécurité and SAE Alsetex), and it is worth asking whether legislation about the composition of tear gas changed in that timeframe, which would have effectively rendered the older tear gas illegal in the later years. What is striking, however, is that the production seemingly increased in the years 2015 and 2016 (possibly evidenced by the presence of much higher batch numbers), which could be due to both the situation in Calais and the situation at the site of a planned airport near Nantes where environmentalists occupied the land. But there is some evidence that the French state was investing in weaponry which might be connected specifically to Calais: the camp was dismantled – violently – a first time in March 2016. A month earlier, SAE Alsetex had won a €5.6 million contract to supply the French police with 'short-range ammunition' (Halissat 2019).

The 'Lande' exhibition

'Lande: The Calais "Jungle" and beyond' was a major temporary exhibition at the Pitt Rivers Museum in Oxford in 2019, of which co-author Sarah Mallet was a co-curator. The exhibition reassembled visual and material culture from the 'Jungle', as it existed in Calais between March 2015 and the demolition of October 2016, and is another example of contemporary archaeology and heritage methodologies being used to investigate contemporary forced migration. The project started after the camp was finally dismantled in October 2016, and was first articulated around the simple question 'What survives from the "Jungle"?' To answer, we contacted people who had spent time in the camp in order to discuss their experience and to ask whether they had kept anything from the site. The first groups we were in touch with were artists, journalists, academics and activists who had had a visible presence on social media (mostly Twitter and Facebook) and had documented their time in the camp. We also contacted local and international grassroots organisations that had been present in the 'Jungle', as well as some French official organisations. From these preliminary conversations, it was clear that keeping materials from the camp with the aim of documenting what had happened in northern France was common practice amongst those who had been there. Our initial network developed through word of mouth, until we reached close to three hundred people. The complex political landscape of the 'Jungle', with different competing forms of humanitarian approaches, meant that it was clear very early on that the exhibition would not have a straightforward narrative, but should, on the contrary, reflect the reality on the ground. It must be noted that attempts to contact the city of Calais, anti-'Jungle' groups and police officers were unsuccessful. While we did talk to people from the city of Calais about the project and the camp, these conversations remained anecdotal and did not inform the project. The lack of Calais 'voices' was not something that had been planned, but once it became obvious that there was no interest in exchanging with us, we decided to focus our attention on the local charities, volunteers, activists and refugees. From our initial network, we identified some people who were interested in participating further to constitute a co-curatorial group to discuss and select the objects that would be displayed in the exhibition. The team was made up of two archaeologists at the University of Oxford, a specialist in archaeology and endangered heritage, three refugees who had spent time in camps in northern France (both the 'Jungle' and Dunkirk), and two long-term activists, who had volunteered in the camp throughout the time it existed. One of the roles of the team was to select, from a long list of over two hundred objects, the material that was closest to their experiences of the camp, and the stories they wanted to tell in the museum space.

Throughout the process of co-curation, our work experimented with the ethnographic museum to make visible fragments of Europe's recent history. By reassembling images, objects, environments and words from the recent past, we bore witness to the human experiences of displaced people at the UK national border at Calais, which continue today. Indeed, one of the project aims was to bring attention to the current situation in Calais, where, despite the lack of a camp, close to one thousand people still live in dreadful conditions. We also facilitated donations to Help Refugees with a contactless donation point, which our visitors could use to donate £5 directly to the charity. The scheme was very successful and raised £5,100 in total.

It is also important, however, to address some of the more difficult questions that we were faced with. While one of the explicit aims of the project was to render the 'invisible visible', this approach is not without ethical concerns, and one of the most debated issues we faced concerned the visible faces in photographic materials, of which we had an enormous number (over thirty thousand photos at one point). As De León recognised during the Undocumented Migration Project, information and data collected by academics can be used by the police, border guards or the state against the very people we work with. While, in the case of Calais, the camp had ceased to exist and therefore anything that we 'collected' from the site could not be used against its residents, exposing people who had spent time in the camp remained a risk. Indeed, because of the Dublin III legislation pertaining to asylum, it is a requirement that refugees ask for asylum in the first EU member state or associated country that they reach (Home Office 2020). This is enforced through the fingerprinting of people on arrival in Italy and Greece (usually the ports of entry into Europe), but some people do manage to escape it. However, photographic evidence can also be used, so showing recognisable faces of people who had been in Calais would have damaged the chances of seeking asylum in Britain of those who had managed to cross the border. As Hamilakis (2016) points out, archaeology shares a love of records and documentation with border guards, and it is important for our work not to become part of the toolbox of the state borderwork. Beyond considerations of jeopardising people's asylum claims, there was also the issue of 'outing' people as having been in the 'Jungle' to a museum audience. While some of the people, such as our co-curators, wanted their stories told, others wanted to move on, and it would have been unethical to expose them. There were some conversations around the question of consent, especially with photographers, who felt that if the photo had been consented to, not showing it could be seen as an act of erasure, although it can be debated whether consent to have a picture taken equals consent to have it exhibited some years later. Along the same lines, not showing any faces in an exhibition about the life conditions of asylum seekers could be interpreted as dehumanising them. Therefore, a compromise was reached by not showing any faces in photographs, but showing drawings of people instead.

Our work also aimed to fight the erasure of the camp and to argue against it being framed as a crisis or emergency. By reassembling what was kept and what was made in the camp, we showed how the knowledge of the place endured by opening up a space for reflection, and we also resisted the dehumanising borderwork and violence at Calais and everywhere else.

Conclusion

The October 2016 demolition of the 'Jungle' sought to reduce a long-standing (post)colonial border situation to a crisis or emergency. It was thus an act of occlusion and silencing, in which physical erasure was akin to the redaction of a document. The place co-produced by displaced people, volunteers and activists was more than shelter. There were restaurants, shops, places for Muslim and Catholic worship, a school, a kindergarten, a library, a theatre and even a nightclub. In this respect the 'Jungle' was a place of hospitality and counter-building, in timber, tarpaulin and human lives, against the fences, tear gas and evictions. Building was an act of resistance against the border, bearing witness to how inequality and difference are produced through borderwork. When resistance takes the form of making something that leaves a trace that endures for a while and can be seen, and so can bear witness to the bulldozer, a potential space for an archaeology of the recent past opens up.

In this chapter, that archaeology takes two forms, but both make use of the methods of archaeology as a way of recording and bearing witness, and of communication. The methods of the Dzhangal Archaeology Project aspire to a kind of dispassionate observation, familiar within the more traditional archaeological work carried out within the UK development-led archaeology sector, which largely operates within frameworks that privilege scientific objectivity. But, far from being dehumanising, we argue that in this case a less passionate observation of these objects has afforded us an opportunity to give our attention to each object, in the same way we would for much older material, to give them a level of respect on a par with more ancient archaeological remains, and also to understand what it is about them that makes them work affectively. Seeing the material culture associated with border crossings as 'garbage' or 'trash' ignores the potential that these things have to inform a greater understanding of the experience of clandestine migration (De León 2013, 7; 2015). But these labels also serve to associate the material culture with the 'other', leading to the assumption that it should primarily be seen as the lost or discarded belongings of displaced people, that have nothing to do with 'us'. This perception can be reinforced by public encounters with this material culture in installations and artworks that are emotionally affective but fail to provide much, if any, context. However, through a strict co-curatorial process, an exhibition can also open up a space in which these objects are not seen as 'trash' but as part of our heritage. Both our national borders and our anthropology museums are Victorian technologies of ordering the world and formalising differences between people, but both are also unfinished and open-ended (post)colonial enterprises. Using the space of the museum to expose the excess of the border can be an effective way not only of allowing the narratives of refugees' lived experiences to grow out of the shadow of the political and media discourses of the Global North, but also of understanding the ways in which these things are enmeshed in a much wider set of social relations that include refugees and migrants and encompass a wider world of volunteers, charity workers, police and security forces, government agencies, artists, archaeologists, the general public and those who chose to donate their own possessions as a form of aid.

An archaeology of the material culture associated with forced migration should seek to move beyond the tropes of personal belongings as stand-ins for individual refugees' lives and experiences, to facilitate wider discussion and interrogation of the situation. The value of archaeology lies in its ability to give context. An archaeology of response, using a biographical approach, can centre other relationships and also help to critique and to disentangle the ways in which 'refugee material culture' is used to represent refugees in the present.

Notes

1 The 'right to seek and to enjoy in other countries asylum from persecution' is enshrined in the United Nations' Universal Declaration of Human Rights (United Nations 1948).

2 Two other people have died: a French man drowned trying to help a refugee who had fallen in a canal, and a Polish truck driver died trying to avoid a roadblock constructed by refugees near Calais. They did not die because they tried to cross the border, but, nevertheless, their deaths are a result of the militarisation of the UK border (IRR 2020).

References

AFP. 2019. 'Two migrants found dead on northern French beach', *Arab News*, 19 August. Accessed 19 August 2021. https://www.arabnews.com/node/1568881/world.

Agamben, Giorgio. 1998. *Homo Sacer: Sovereign power and bare life*. Translated by Daniel Heller-Roazen. Stanford, CA: Stanford University Press.

Agier, Michel, Yasmine Bouagga, Maël Galisson, Cyrille Hanappe, Mathilde Pette and Philippe Wannesson. 2018. *La Jungle de Calais*. Paris: Presses Universitaires de France.

Alaux, Jean-Pierre. 2015. 'Calais vaut bien quelques requiem', *Plein droit* 2015/1(104): 3–8. https://doi.org/10.3917/pld.104.0003.

Arendt, Hannah. [1943] 2007. 'We refugees'. In *The Jewish Writings*, edited by Jerome Kohn and Ron H. Feldman, 264–74. New York: Schocken Books.

BBC. 2014. 'UK offers NATO security fence to help Calais tackle migrants', BBC News, 7 September. Accessed 19 August 2021. https://www.bbc.co.uk/news/uk-29098641.

BBC. 2015. 'Calais migrant crisis: Theresa May signs deal with France', BBC News, 20 August. Accessed 19 August 2021. https://www.bbc.co.uk/news/uk-33992952.

Bergqvist Rydén, Johanna. 2018. 'When bereaved of everything: Objects from the concentration camp of Ravensbrück as expressions of resistance, memory, and identity', *International Journal of Historical Archaeology* 22: 511–30. https://doi.org/10.1007/s10761-017-0433-2.

Breene, Morgan Lynn. 2018. 'Reframing the Lampedusa cross: The British Museum's display of the Mediterranean migrant crisis'. In *The New Nomadic Age: Archaeologies of Forced and Undocumented Migration*, edited by Yannis Hamilakis, 167–75. Sheffield: Equinox.

Brettell, Caroline B. 2015. 'Theorizing migration in anthropology: The cultural, social, and phenomenal dimensions of movement'. In *Migration Theory: Talking across Disciplines*, edited by Caroline B. Brettell and James F. Hollifield, 3rd edition, 148–97. New York and Abingdon: Routledge.

Burström, Mats. 2009. 'Selective remembrance: Memories of a Second World War refugee camp in Sweden', *Norwegian Archaeological Review* 42(2): 159–72. https://doi.org/10.1080/00293650903351045.

Calais Research. 2016. 'Funding the border'. Accessed 19 August 2021. https://calaisresearch.noblogs.org/finances.

Caraher, William, Bret Weber and Richard Rothaus. 2018. 'Lessons from the Bakken oil patch'. In *The New Nomadic Age: Archaeologies of forced and undocumented migration*, edited by Yannis Hamilakis, 87–96. Sheffield: Equinox.

Chakelian, Anoosh. 2016. 'Demolishing purgatory: What happens to the refugees when Calais's "jungle" is destroyed?', *New Statesman*, 15 March. Accessed 19 August 2021. http://www.newstatesman.com/world/europe/2016/03/demolishing-purgatory-what-happens-refugees-when-calais-s-jungle-destroyed.

De León, Jason. 2012. '"Better to be hot than caught": Excavating the conflicting roles of migrant material culture', *American Anthropologist* 114(3): 477–95. https://doi.org/10.1111/j.1548-1433.2012.01447.x.

De León, Jason. 2013. 'Undocumented migration, use wear, and the materiality of habitual suffering in the Sonoran Desert', *Journal of Material Culture* 18(4): 321–45. https://doi.org/10.1177%2F1359183513496489.

De León, Jason. 2015. *The Land of Open Graves: Living and dying on the migrant trail*. Oakland: University of California Press.

Dreyer, J. 2001. 'Archaeology and the Anglo-Boer war (1899–1902): A report on the discovery of the black refugee camp and cemetery at Brandfort, Free State', *South African Journal of Ethnology* 24(4): 131–7.

Easter, Makeda. 2019. 'Border Patrol threw away migrants' belongings: A janitor saved and photographed them', *Los Angeles Times*, 2 December. Accessed 19 August 2021. https://www.latimes.com/entertainment-arts/story/2019-12-02/tom-kiefer-exhibition-el-sueno-americano.

Edwards, Adrian. 2016. 'UNHCR viewpoint: "Refugee" or "migrant" – which is right?' Accessed 19 August 2021. http://www.unhcr.org/uk/news/latest/2016/7/55df0e556/unhcr-viewpoint-refugee-migrant-right.html.

Elgot, Jessica and Matthew Taylor. 2015. 'Calais crisis: Cameron condemned for "dehumanising" description of migrants', *The Guardian*, 30 July. Accessed 19 August 2021. https://www.theguardian.com/uk-news/2015/jul/30/david-cameron-migrant-swarm-language-condemned.

Fredriksen, Aurora. 2014. 'Emergency shelter topologies: Locating humanitarian space in mobile and material practice', *Environment and Planning D: Society and Space* 32(1): 147–62. https://doi.org/10.1068%2Fd17912.

Gentleman, Amelia. 2017. 'Teddies and teargas canisters: What remained in the Calais camp', *The Guardian*, 30 December. Accessed 19 August 2021. https://www.theguardian.com/world/2016/dec/30/teddies-tear-gas-canisters-what-remained-calais-camp.

Graves-Brown, Paul, Rodney Harrison and Angela Piccini, eds. 2013. *The Oxford Handbook of the Archaeology of the Contemporary World*. Oxford: Oxford University Press.

Greussing, Esther and Hajo G. Boomgaarden. 2017. 'Shifting the refugee narrative? An automated frame analysis of Europe's 2015 refugee crisis', *Journal of Ethnic and Migration Studies* 43(11): 1749–74. https://doi.org/10.1080/1369183X.2017.1282813.

Hagan, Maria. 2019. 'Inhabiting a hostile environment: The sanitary politics of life at the post-camp Calais border', *Society and Space*. Published online 13 May. Accessed 19 August 2021. http://societyandspace.org/2019/05/13/inhabiting-a-hostile-environment-the-sanitary-politics-of-life-at-the-post-camp-calais-border.

Halissat, Ismaël. 2019. 'Alsetex: Depuis une explosion mortelle en 2014, des failles révélées et répétées', *Libération*, 26 December. Accessed 19 August 2021. https://www.liberation.fr/france/2019/12/26/alsetex-depuis-une-explosion-mortelle-en-2014-des-failles-revelees-et-repetees_1771159.

Hamilakis, Yannis. 2016. 'Archaeologies of forced and undocumented migration', *Journal of Contemporary Archaeology* 3(2): 121–39. https://doi.org/10.1558/jca.32409.

Hamilakis, Yannis, ed. 2018. *The New Nomadic Age: Archaeologies of forced and undocumented migration*. Sheffield: Equinox.

Hansard. 2015. House of Commons parliamentary debates, vol. 590, part no. 84, column 13, 5 January. Accessed 19 August 2021. https://publications.parliament.uk/pa/cm201415/cmhansrd/cm150105/debtext/150105-0001.htm.

Harrison, Rodney, Staffan Appelgren and Anna Bohlin. 2018. 'Commentary: Belonging and belongings: On migrant and nomadic heritages *in* and *for* the Anthropocene'. In *The New Nomadic Age: Archaeologies of forced and undocumented migration*, edited by Yannis Hamilakis, 209–20. Sheffield: Equinox.

Hassoux, Didier and Christophe Labbé. 2016. 'Gendarmes et CRS se préparent à jouer les farces de l'ordre', *Le Canard enchaîné*, 28 September.

Herz, Manuel. 2013. *From Camp to City: Refugee camps of the Western Sahara*. Baden: Lars Müller Publishers.

Hicks, Dan and Sarah Mallet. 2019. *Lande: The Calais 'jungle' and beyond*. Bristol: Bristol University Press.

Higgins, Charlotte. 2019. 'Boat in which hundreds of migrants died displayed at Venice biennale', *The Guardian*, 7 May. Accessed 19 August 2021. https://www.theguardian.com/artanddesign/2019/may/07/boat-in-which-hundreds-of-migrants-died-displayed-at-venice-biennale.

Holtorf, Cornelius. 2002. 'Notes on the life history of a pot sherd', *Journal of Material Culture* 7(1): 49–71. https://doi.org/10.1177%2F1359183502007001305.

Home Office. 2020. 'Dublin III regulation. Version 4.0. Transferring asylum claimants into and out of the UK where responsibility for examining an asylum claim lies with the UK or with another EU member state or associated state'. Accessed 19 August 2021. https://assets.publishing.service.gov.uk/government/uploads/system/uploads/attachment_data/file/909412/dublin-III-regulation.pdf.

Human Rights Observers Project. 2019. 'Forced evictions in Calais and Grande-Synthe: 1 August 2018–1 June 2019'. Accessed 19 August 2021. https://helprefugees.org/wp-content/uploads/2019/06/Forced-Evictions-in-Calais-and-Grande-Synthe-ENG-1.pdf.

IRR (Institute of Race Relations). 2020. 'Deadly crossings and the militarisation of Britain's borders'. Accessed 19 August 2021. https://irr.org.uk/wp-content/uploads/2020/11/Deadly-Crossings-Final.pdf.

Jones, Ellen Carol. 2001. 'Empty shoes'. In *Footnotes: On shoes*, edited by Shari Benstock and Suzanne Ferris, 197–232. New Brunswick, NJ: Rutgers University Press.

Jones, Jonathan. 2015. 'Flight by Arabella Dorman review: Relic of a rough crossing illustrates refugee crisis', *The Guardian*, 20 December. Accessed 19 August 2021. https://www.theguardian.com/artanddesign/2015/dec/20/flight-by-arabella-dorman-review-relic-of-a-rough-crossing-illustrates-refugee-crisis.

Joy, Jody. 2010. *Iron Age Mirrors: A biographical approach*. Oxford: Archaeopress.

Khomami, Nadia. 2014. 'British government pledges £12m to tackle "illegal immigration" from Calais', *The Guardian*, 20 September. Accessed 19 August 2021. https://www.theguardian.com/uk-news/2014/sep/20/uk-government-illegal-migrants-calais-twelve-million.
Kiddey, Rachael. 2017. *Homeless Heritage: Collaborative social archaeology as therapeutic practice*. Oxford: Oxford University Press.
Kiddey, Rachael. 2020. 'Reluctant refuge: An activist archaeological approach to alternative refugee shelter in Athens (Greece)', *Journal of Refugee Studies* 33(3): 599–621. http://dx.doi.org/10.1093/jrs/fey061.
Kopytoff, Igor. 1986. 'The cultural biography of things: Commoditization as process'. In *The Social Life of Things: Commodities in cultural perspective*, edited by Arjun Appadurai, 64–91. Cambridge: Cambridge University Press.
Kourelis, Kostis. 2018. 'If place remotely matters: Camped in Greece's contingent countryside'. In *The New Nomadic Age: Archaeologies of forced and undocumented migration*, edited by Yannis Hamilakis, 108–20. Sheffield: Equinox.
Macron, Emmanuel. 2018. 'Discours devant les forces de sécurité à Calais'. Accessed 19 August 2021. https://www.elysee.fr/emmanuel-macron/2018/01/16/discours-devant-les-forces-de-securite-a-calais.
Malaquais, Dominique. 2017. 'Forensics: Photography in the face of failure'. In *Dzhangal*, by Gideon Mendel, 73–4. London: GOST Books.
Mendel, Gideon. n.d. 'Dzhangal'. Accessed 19 August 2020. http://gideonmendel.com/dzhangal/.
Müller, Thomas and Uwe Schlüper. 2018. *Dynamiken der Jungles: Calais und das europäisch-britische Grenzregime*. Munich: bordermonitoring.eu.
Myers, Adrian T. 2008. 'Between memory and materiality: An archaeological approach to studying the Nazi concentration camps', *Journal of Conflict Archaeology* 4(1–2): 231–45. https:/doi.org/10.1163/157407808X382827.
Oberti, Charlotte. 2019. 'Iranian woman becomes first migrant to officially disappear in the Channel trying to reach England', *Info Migrants*, 16 August. Accessed 19 August 2021. https://www.infomigrants.net/en/post/18876/iranian-woman-becomes-first-migrant-to-officially-disappear-in-the-channel-trying-to-reach-england.
Ong, Aihwa. 2003. *Buddha is Hiding: Refugees, citizenship, the new America*. Berkeley: University of California Press.
PEROU, 2016. 'Atlas d'une cité potentielle'. Accessed 19 August 2021. http://www.urbanisme-puca.gouv.fr/IMG/pdf/CALAIS_16_PEROU_PUCA_INTRO_3.pdf.
Perry, Sara. 2018. 'Why are heritage interpreters voiceless at the trowel's edge? A plea for rewriting the archaeological workflow', *Advances in Archaeological Practice* 6(3): 212–27. https://doi.org/10.1017/aap.2018.21.
Perry, Sara. 2019. 'The enchantment of the archaeological record', *European Journal of Archaeology* 22(3): 354–71. https://doi.org/10.1017/eaa.2019.24.
Ramadan, Adam. 2012. 'Spatialising the refugee camp', *Transactions of the Institute of British Geographers* 38(1): 65–77. https://doi.org/10.1111/j.1475-5661.2012.00509.x.
Rankin, Jennifer. 2020. 'Greece warned by EU it must uphold the right to asylum', *The Guardian*, 12 March. Accessed 19 August 2021. https://www.theguardian.com/world/2020/mar/12/greece-warned-by-eu-it-must-uphold-the-right-to-asylum.
Refugee InfoBus. 2018. 'Police violence in Calais: Abusive and illegal practices by law enforcement officers, observations and testimonies: 1st November 2017–1st November 2018'. Accessed 19 August 2021. https://docs.wixstatic.com/ugd/5eb73a_ae875cd65dcc434588a7a69ed4cf3167.pdf.
Sánchez Dionis, Marta and Kate Dearden. 2019. 'Missing migrants project data: A global overview'. In *Fatal Journeys. Volume 4: Missing Migrant Children*, edited by Frank Laczko, Julia Black and Ann Singleton, 1–52. Geneva: International Organization for Migration. Accessed 19 August 2021. https://publications.iom.int/system/files/pdf/fatal_journeys_4.pdf.
Sanderson, Sertan. 2019. 'Migrant drowned trying to swim to UK', *Info Migrants*, 27 August. Accessed 19 August 2021. https://www.infomigrants.net/en/post/19102/migrant-drowned-trying-to-swim-to-uk.
Schofield, John, Kayleigh J. Wyles, Sean Doherty, Andy Donnelly, Jen Jones and Adam Porter. 2020. 'Object narratives as a methodology for mitigating marine plastic pollution: A new multidisciplinary approach, and a case study from Galápagos', *Antiquity* 94(373): 228–44. https://doi.org/10.15184/aqy.2019.232.

Seitsonen, Oula I., Vesa-Pekka Herva and Mika Kunnari. 2018. 'Abandoned refugee vehicles "in the middle of nowhere": Reflections on the global refugee crisis from the northern margins of Europe'. In *The New Nomadic Age: Archaeologies of forced and undocumented migration*, edited by Yannis Hamilakis, 139–55. Sheffield: Equinox.

Sherwood, Harriet. 2017. 'Artist hangs refugees' clothing in London church to highlight crisis', *The Guardian*, 13 December. Accessed 19 August 2021. https://www.theguardian.com/world/2017/dec/13/artist-arabella-dorman-refugees-clothing-london-church-highlight-crisis.

Smith, Helena. 2019. 'Greek PM: EU states must do more to share burden of hosting refugees', *The Guardian*, 4 October. Accessed 19 August 2021. https://www.theguardian.com/world/2019/oct/04/greek-pm-eu-states-must-do-more-to-share-burden-of-hosting-refugees.

Smith, Helena. 2020. 'Child dies off Lesbos in first fatality since Turkey opened border', *The Guardian*, 2 March. Accessed 19 August 2021. https://www.theguardian.com/world/2020/mar/02/child-dies-as-boat-carrying-migrants-capsizes-off-lesbos.

Sommer, Ulrike. 2017. 'Archaeology and nationalism'. In *Key Concepts in Public Archaeology*, edited by Gabriel Moshenka, 166–86. London: UCL Press.

Sontag, Susan. 2003. *Regarding the Pain of Others*. London: Penguin.

Stewart, Haeden E., Ian Osterreicher, Cameron Gokee and Jason De León. 2018. 'Surveilling surveillance: Countermapping undocumented migration in the USA–Mexico borderlands'. In *The New Nomadic Age: Archaeologies of forced and undocumented migration*, edited by Yannis Hamilakis, 42–57. Sheffield: Equinox.

Tempest, Matthew. 2002. 'Blunkett to face Chirac's "hardman" over Sangatte', *The Guardian*, 25 June. Accessed 19 August 2021. https://www.theguardian.com/politics/2002/jun/25/immigrationpolicy.immigrationandpublicservices.

Tyrikos-Ergas, George. 2018. 'Orange life jackets: Materiality and narration in Lesvos, one year after the eruption of the "refugee crisis"'. In *The New Nomadic Age: Archaeologies of forced and undocumented migration*, edited by Yannis Hamilakis, 121–6. Sheffield: Equinox.

United Nations. 1948. 'Universal Declaration of Human Rights'. Accessed 19 August 2021. https://www.un.org/en/about-us/universal-declaration-of-human-rights.

Zimmer, Ben. 2019. 'Where does Trump's "invasion" rhetoric come from?' *The Atlantic*, 6 August. Accessed 19 August 2021. https://www.theatlantic.com/entertainment/archive/2019/08/trump-immigrant-invasion-language-origins/595579.

6

Undocumented migration and the multiplicity of object lives

Ayşe Şanlı

The relationship between migration and museums is not new. It is possible to find migration museums around the world, with collections about emigration from or immigration to the country in question. These museum exhibitions include objects such as suitcases, keys, passports and letters. In recent years, however, a new kind of museum exhibition has emerged. These new exhibitions put contemporary forced migrations, the people who risk their lives and take perilous routes to cross borders, often without proper documentation, at the centre of global attention. While some exhibitions are comprised of art installations, others display the very objects that are found at border-crossing sites, such as backpacks, water bottles and life jackets.

Roughly speaking, museums are full of objects that have moved through space and time. In the past few decades, a growing number of scholars have become interested in exploring the 'social lives' of such objects, that is, the shifting significance of objects as they move from one sociocultural context to another. This method, called *object biographies*, has been applied in various case studies. Conventionally focused on a somewhat linear 'life' trajectory, the object biographies method has paid particular attention to the moments of production, exchange, transformation and disposal. This chapter discusses the extent to which the object biographies approach may be employed in the case of discarded objects displayed in exhibitions on contemporary forced migration. My question is what these objects tell us and how they pose new challenges to object biographies, rather than whether the object biographies approach is the best way to scrutinise these objects and exhibitions. In the following, I provide a brief history of the object biographies approach. I then give an overview of recent studies on migration and material culture, and the public display of objects carried by migrants while they are crossing borders. By bringing contemporary exhibitions on forced migration into the debate about object biographies, I suggest that objects may have *multiple lives*, each 'life' having its own sociocultural relevance and meaning.

Object biographies, itineraries, afterlives

In *The Social Life of Things: Commodities in cultural perspective*, Appadurai (1986, 3–5) suggests that commodities, like persons, have social lives, and that we should turn our attention to the things themselves, 'for their meanings are inscribed in their forms, their uses, their trajectories' (Appadurai 1986, 5). The object biographies approach has been adopted by a number of scholars in the past few decades to illuminate the sociocultural meanings attributed to objects. Earlier scholars contended that the moments of exchange and transformation are of particular importance for the objects' biographies. They argued that 'Commoditization is … a process of *becoming* rather than … *being*' (Kopytoff 1986, 73; emphasis added); that '*things-in-motion* … illuminate their human and social context' (Appadurai 1986, 5; emphasis added); and that 'transformations of person and object are tied up with each other' (Gosden and Marshall 1999, 169).

The object biographies approach has thus focused mainly on the moments of 'birth', exchange, transformation and 'death' of objects, and the significance of these moments in their contexts – an idea that can be traced back as far as Arnold van Gennep's *Rites of Passage* ([1909] 1960), in which social lives are framed as linear sequences of stages. This method has been both picked up and criticised by many scholars. Within the context of the museum, scholars pushed for a biographical approach and emphasised the displacements of museum objects as transformative moments full of possibilities (Dudley 2020). They have raised the question of scale and suggested two levels of biography for museum objects: the individual level and the collection level (Friberg and Huvila 2019). On the collective level, Alberti (2005) argued that museum objects followed similar trajectories: (1) provenance and acquisition, (2) being in the museum collection, (3) being on display. While some suggested that considering an entire museum collection as one object might provide a broader framework for the analysis of museum practices (Friberg and Huvila 2019), others have flagged that such homogenisation of diverse objects and their biographies bears the risk of privileging one 'typical life' over others (Joy 2009).

One major challenge to the object biographies approach stems from its particular dependence on terminology such as birth, death, reincarnation and afterlife, as these words often signify some sort of linearity (Hahn and Weiss 2013). Since objects continually move and transform over time and space, scholars alternatively offer the term *itineraries* (Hahn and Weiss 2013; Joyce 2015), meaning 'the routes by which things circulate in and out of places where they come to rest or are active' (Joyce 2015, 29). While object biographies restrict accounts of temporality and spatiality, *itineraries* aim to 'trace connections that are spatial, temporal, material, and consequential' (Joyce 2015, 37). Colwell (forthcoming), on the other hand, underlines the necessity of mapping the overlapping, shifting and competing meanings of objects as they travel across different cultural systems through time and space. He offers a theory of the *palimpsest*, which aims to add to the object biographies method by uncovering the processes of inscription and erasure. A palimpsest is a tablet or parchment from which writing has been partially or completely erased to make space for another text. Palimpsest theory thus investigates the ways in which the objects concurrently contain multiple meanings, layered on top of one another.

The next section illuminates the context in which the new exhibitions on contemporary undocumented migrations emerge. As we shall see, these exhibitions pose further challenges not only to conventional museum practices but also to the object biographies approach.

Undocumented migration on display

Since about the late 1990s, there has been an increasing interest in how material culture and migration converge. Scholars working on modern material culture (Rathje 1979), referring to the material traces of the recent past, have explored the interrelatedness of the movements of people and things (Basu and Coleman 2008). Scholars have enquired into the belongings of migrants, and other objects – not only in places of origin or destination but also in places of transit – for a better understanding of migrants' experiences. Such *biographical objects* (see Hoskins 1998; see also Yi-Neumann, Chapter 4 in this volume) include but are not limited to passports, cars and coaches, keys, suitcases, sofas, curtains, carpets, laptops and televisions (Burrell 2008; Miller 2008; O'Reilly and Parish 2017; Yuan 2014). Immigration and emigration museums all over the world display such objects of personal, social and political significance, aiming to evoke the difficulties of leaving 'home' and crossing borders (O'Reilly and Parish 2017; Ulz 2019).

Within this context, a growing body of scholarship, known as *archaeological ethnography* (Hamilakis 2011) or *the archaeology of the contemporary* (De León 2013; González-Ruibal 2019), focuses on materiality as a substantial part of clandestine border crossings, and offers a refreshed discussion on migration, borders and the state apparatus (see De León 2015; Hamilakis 2018; McGuire 2020; Stewart et al. 2018). The rich 'material culture' of undocumented migration, including objects carried by immigrants while crossing borders, such as backpacks, bottles, food containers, clothing, shoes, photographs and booklets, has drawn the attention of anthropological archaeologists (Blake and Schon 2019; De León 2013; 2015; Hamilakis 2018; Soto 2018b; Tyrikos-Ergas 2018). While such objects are often considered 'trash' by local and national authorities (see De León 2015; Hamilakis 2018; Soto 2018a), some researchers, activists and artists have taken a different approach and collected these objects for documentation, analysis and public display. Perhaps the most popular installation so far is Ai Weiwei's *Safe Passage*. The installation, consisting of thousands of life jackets from Lesvos, Greece, mounted on the classical Greek-style columns of notable buildings, has made appearances in Germany, Japan, Chile and the United States. These life jackets have become iconic objects that symbolise the perilous border crossings in the Mediterranean (and beyond). The Undocumented Migration Project, run by Jason De León and his team, put together dozens of backpacks along with media such as images and videos, and personal belongings, collected on the Mexico–USA border for the exhibition 'State of exception/Estado de excepción'. The Pitt Rivers Museum in Oxford hosted the exhibition 'Lande: The Calais "Jungle" and beyond', which offers an insight into the material world of the now destroyed informal refugee camp in Calais, France (see Mallet and Fowler in this volume; see also Hamilakis 2019). Most recently, Brown University's Haffenreffer Museum of Anthropology opened its doors with 'Transient matter: Assemblages of migration in the Mediterranean'.[1] This exhibition invites visitors to pay attention to the objects that crossed borders together with humans, as well as to different practices of art and agency by the migrants living in the camps of Lesvos – including the notorious Moria Camp which was destroyed by fire in early September 2020.

Exhibitions on contemporary forced migrations bring forward a number of interrelated questions and challenges. Some of these challenges stem from the conventional roles that the museums play, some from the social significance of the objects of display, and some from the publics of the exhibitions.

First, scholars have been raising questions regarding exhibition ethics (Gazi 2014) and pushing for a *critical museology* (Phillips 2007), or an *appropriate museology* (Kreps 2015). Museums have historically become sites of authority over the material aspects of cultures (Reynolds 1989, 112). The museums of anthropology especially have been considered centres of information on cultures they display (Karp 1991; Reynolds 1989). The didactic and instructional role attributed to museums facilitated the reproduction of 'social structures and [the] forging [of] imaginary communities. [Museums] establish who is located at the center and who is at the margin, what is valuable and authentic, and what is unworthy or fake' (Phillips 2007, 13–14). Additionally, the perception of curatorship as an expertise or a skill-requiring job often precludes possible conversations and co-curations (McLean 2011). Although some museums, as well as states,[2] have started to take steps towards decolonisation, restitution, social justice and better museum ethics, all these issues remain important challenges for museums as well as curators.

Second, the materials used in these exhibitions draw visitors' attention strongly to the experience of border crossing. This is partly because of the nature of the objects and belongings that later make their way to public display. Objects that populate such exhibitions are left behind for a reason: the object had fulfilled its function, or it was lost or forgotten, or the person who carried the object was caught by the border patrol, or they lost their life before making it to the other side of the border. Another commonly used material is photography from camps and makeshift shelters, documenting the impermanence and precarity of such places. While shedding light on the dire conditions that migrants face, such exhibitions carry the risk of telling a particular story rather than the migrant experience in its entirety. Despite their limits, there is a global interest today in exhibits and installations on contemporary undocumented migrations. Parallels can be drawn between the 'migration crises' happening in different parts of the world. For instance, the European Union's border protection policies are similar to Australia's policy on offshore processing of asylum claims and to the Prevention Through Deterrence policy employed by the United States at the USA–Mexico border, all of which strategically funnel migrants through the perilous routes. This brings up the challenge of publics. Although curators of such exhibitions aim to evoke feelings of empathy, understanding and solidarity with the migrants, this might not be a simple task, considering the diverse backgrounds and political opinions of the visitors.

On the multiplicity of object lives

The aforementioned challenges to the emerging exhibitions on forced migration prove the necessity of contextualising the objects on display. Object biographies may be a useful tool of analysis in this undertaking. Scholars have applied the object biographies method to different objects, both on an individual and on a collective level. They agree that the objects and their social meanings do not remain fixed as they move across time and space. However, contemporary undocumented migration and its material components pose new challenges to this approach. Although the object biographies approach conveniently creates a 'life' narrative for objects, this narrative simultaneously carries the risk of privileging one particular life of the object over other possibilities. Hence, I suggest that objects have *multiple lives* and that each 'life' has its own sociocultural relevance and meaning. The idea of *multiple lives* differs from the *itineraries* approach, too, in which the objects are considered to be at rest or active at different stages (see Joyce 2015). This activeness versus passiveness dichotomy is somewhat arbitrary, since the designation of activeness or passiveness is based on the interpreter's perspective.

Object lives are closely linked to the human and non-human entities that they interact with (Hill 2012, 5). Jody Joy emphasises the importance of the social relationship between humans and objects for object biographies (Joy 2009, 544). She maintains that objects can die many times, or live different simultaneous lives based on the spheres of relationships they are involved in (Joy 2009, 543). This idea underlies the multiplicity of object lives that I suggest here. A multiple-lives perspective may have several merits. Firstly, biographies of objects, like biographies of people, are doomed to be partial (Kopytoff 1986, 68). Acknowledging the multiplicity of the lives of an object may allow researchers to leave the omniscient object-biographer role aside. It also challenges scholars to reflect on the limits of their knowledge and the choices that they make (evaluating, privileging or ignoring certain aspects) while writing *a* (as opposed to *the*) biography of an object. Secondly, instead of following an object from 'birth' to 'death', the multiple-lives approach allows us to focus on a particular temporal, spatial and sociocultural context, and thus to take each 'life' on its own terms. This might produce more partial yet more informed stories, which, in turn, brings about the possibility of collaboration and of constructing more exhaustive biographies of objects. Last but not least, this approach allows us to consider not only the changing contexts but also the changing forms of the objects.

Let us take the example of one life jacket in Lesvos to elucidate how the objects may have multiple lives. Various materials are brought together to produce a life jacket; a migrant takes the life jacket and uses it for crossing the sea border; the life jacket is discarded upon arrival on the shore, collected from the shore and dumped in the 'Lifevest Cemetery' landfill, collected from the landfill, brought from Greece to the United States, and makes it to a museum as part of an exhibition. From the moment of their production as an indispensable part of the border-crossing experience, to being designated as 'trash', and to becoming objects of display in museums and elsewhere, these objects occupy multiple 'lives' as well as 'unlived' potentials, where their social interactions inform their meanings. However fragmentary this account may be, it demonstrates that in each 'life' stage there are drastic changes in the economic and use value of the object, as well as in the sociocultural context that surrounds it. The upcycled bags displayed in the 'Transient matter' exhibition are also intriguing examples of the multiplicity of object lives. These bags are made by migrants and volunteers in order to repurpose the discarded life jackets from 'trash' into something 'practical'. The life jackets, hence, have changed their physical form. Here, I maintain that it is possible to conceive the bag as a different facet of the biography of the life jacket: the partitioning and processing of the object engender a multiplication of its lives.

Concluding remarks

Appadurai (2017) characterises museum objects as 'accidental refugees'. Appadurai challenges the 'fixity' of objects in museums, where they tell a story or represent a culture, while the displacement and relocation of the objects themselves become almost irrelevant. He asserts that objects and humans as refugees have reverse conditions, as human refugees' stories are often about their displacement and relocation (Appadurai 2017, 407). However, it is equally possible to think about the reverse, in the sense that refugee humans are often wrongly stereotyped and become a 'fixity' in people's minds. This 'refugee objects' versus 'refugee humans' dichotomy is, furthermore, problematic: with regard to migration and objects carried by migrants, it is almost impossible to separate humans and their belongings. Migration, whether in the museum space or not, is all about the movement of both humans and objects. Moreover, in the strictly legal sense of the term, a 'refugee' is a person fleeing their home country owing to a well-founded fear of persecution.[3] Considering museum objects as accidental 'refugees' does not do justice to the people, their stories or their agency.

It is important to consider that most objects displayed in exhibitions related to forced migration accompany humans at a fleeting yet crucial moment in their lives. In many cases, the objects do not convey much information about their owners. Regardless of how iconic they may become, such objects should not be considered 'pure tools of representation' (Appadurai 2017, 402), for they do not represent a 'culture' or a 'way of living' in the conventional sense. Thus, following the multiplicity of object lives would mean a plethora of paths, perspectives and interpretations, each with a particular sociocultural and political context.

The COVID-19 pandemic introduced a new life and new ways of interaction for humans and objects (or, more generally, non-humans). It is possible to think that museums have conventionally been keeping objects 'in quarantine', only allowing certain forms of interaction between these objects and the visitors. The outbreak of the pandemic and the subsequent closures of museums have resulted in a new form of 'quarantine', whereby the objects are locked in galleries with extremely limited or no human interaction. On the other hand, many museums have focused on creating online versions of their exhibitions since the pandemic started, which creates a whole new virtual world where the objects can interact with a larger public – though in different ways – than ever before. Objects, like human beings, have changing lives in a changing world.

Acknowledgements

I would like to thank Yannis Hamilakis, Darcy Hackley and Sherena Razek, as our collaboration on the 'Transient matter' exhibition laid the groundwork for the ideas in this chapter. I would also like to thank Robert Preucel for his feedback on an earlier version of the chapter.

Notes

1 Curated by Yannis Hamilakis, L. Darcy Hackley, Sherena Razek and Ayşe Şanlı. The online version of the exhibition can be seen at https://blogs.brown.edu/transientmatter/ (accessed 20 August 2021).
2 Examples are France's Sarr–Savoy Report (Sarr and Savoy 2018) and the United States' Native American Graves Protection and Repatriation Act (NAGPRA) (National Park Service 2020).
3 The definition is from the 1951 Geneva Convention Relating to the Status of Refugees (UNHCR 2010).

References

Alberti, Samuel J. M. M. 2005. 'Objects and the museum', *Isis* 96(4): 559–71. https://doi.org/10.1086/498593.

Appadurai, Arjun. 1986. 'Introduction: Commodities and the politics of value'. In *The Social Life of Things: Commodities in cultural perspective*, edited by Arjun Appadurai, 3–63. Cambridge: Cambridge University Press.

Appadurai, Arjun. 2017. 'Museum objects as accidental refugees', *Historische Anthropologie* 25(3): 401–8. https://doi.org/10.7788/ha-2017-0306.

Basu, Paul and Simon Coleman. 2008. 'Introduction: Migrant worlds, material cultures', *Mobilities* 3(3): 313–30. https://doi.org/10.1080/17450100802376753.

Blake, Emma and Robert Schon. 2019. 'The archaeology of contemporary migrant journeys in western Sicily', *Journal of Mediterranean Archaeology* 32(2): 173–94. http://dx.doi.org/10.1558/jma.40579.

Burrell, Kathy. 2008. 'Materialising the border: Spaces of mobility and material culture in migration from post-socialist Poland', *Mobilities* 3(3): 353–73. https://doi.org/10.1080/17450100802376779.

Colwell, Chip. Forthcoming. 'A palimpsest theory of objects', *Current Anthropology*.

De León, Jason. 2013. 'Undocumented migration, use wear, and the materiality of habitual suffering in the Sonoran Desert', *Journal of Material Culture* 18(4): 321–45. https://doi.org/10.1177%2F1359183513496489.

De León, Jason. 2015. *The Land of Open Graves: Living and dying on the migrant trail*. Oakland: University of California Press.

Dudley, Sandra H. 2020. *Displaced Things in Museums and Beyond: Loss, liminality and hopeful encounters*. New York: Routledge.

Friberg, Zanna and Isto Huvila. 2019. 'Using object biographies to understand the curation crisis: Lessons learned from the museum life of an archaeological collection', *Museum Management and Curatorship* 34(4): 362–82. https://doi.org/10.1080/09647775.2019.1612270.

Gazi, Andromache. 2014. 'Exhibition ethics: An overview of major issues', *Journal of Conservation and Museum Studies* 12(1) (art. no. 4): 1–10. http://doi.org/10.5334/jcms.1021213.

Gennep, Arnold van. [1909] 1960. *The Rites of Passage*. Translated by Monika B. Vizedom and Gabriella Caffee. Chicago, IL: University of Chicago Press.

González-Ruibal, Alfredo. 2019. *An Archaeology of the Contemporary Era: The age of destruction*. Abingdon: Routledge.

Gosden, Chris and Yvonne Marshall. 1999. 'The cultural biography of objects', *World Archaeology* 31(2): 169–78. https:/doi.org/10.1080/00438243.1999.9980439.

Hahn, Hans Peter and Hadas Weiss. 2013. 'Introduction: Biographies, travels and itineraries of things'. In *Mobility, Meaning and the Transformations of Things: Shifting contexts of material culture through time and space*, edited by Hans Peter Hahn and Hadas Weiss, 1–14. Oxford: Oxbow Books.

Hamilakis, Yannis. 2011. 'Archaeological ethnography: A multitemporal meeting ground for archaeology and anthropology', *Annual Review of Anthropology* 40: 399–414. https://doi.org/10.1146/annurev-anthro-081309-145732.

Hamilakis, Yannis. 2018. 'Introduction: Archaeologies of forced and undocumented migration'. In *The New Nomadic Age: Archaeologies of forced and undocumented migration*, edited by Yannis Hamilakis, 1–19. Sheffield: Equinox.

Hamilakis, Yannis. 2019. 'Planet of camps: Border assemblages and their challenges', *Antiquity* 93(371): 1371–7. https://doi.org/10.15184/aqy.2019.163.

Hill, Kate. 2012. 'Introduction: Museums and biographies – telling stories about people, things and relationships'. In *Museums and Biographies: Stories, objects, identities*, edited by Kate Hill, 1–9. Woodbridge: Boydell Press.

Hoskins, Janet. 1998. *Biographical Objects: How things tell the stories of people's lives*. New York: Routledge.

Joy, Jody. 2009. 'Reinvigorating object biography: Reproducing the drama of object lives', *World Archaeology* 41(4): 540–56. https://doi.org/10.1080/00438240903345530.

Joyce, Rosemary A. 2015. 'Things in motion: Itineraries of Ulua marble vases'. In *Things in Motion: Object itineraries in anthropological practice*, edited by Rosemary A. Joyce and Susan D. Gillespie, 21–38. Santa Fe, NM: School for Advanced Research Press.

Karp, Ivan. 1991. 'Culture and representation'. In *Exhibiting Cultures: The poetics and politics of museum display*, edited by Ivan Karp and Steven D. Lavine, 11–24. Washington, DC, and London: Smithsonian Institution Press.

Kopytoff, Igor. 1986. 'The cultural biography of things: Commoditization as process'. In *The Social Life of Things: Commodities in cultural perspective*, edited by Arjun Appadurai, 64–91. Cambridge: Cambridge University Press.

Kreps, Christina. 2015. 'Appropriate museology and the "new museum ethics": Honouring diversity', *Nordisk Museologi* 2: 4–16. https://doi.org/10.5617/nm.3044.

McGuire, Randall H. 2020. 'The materiality and heritage of contemporary forced migration', *Annual Review of Anthropology* 49: 175–91. https://doi.org/10.1146/annurev-anthro-010220-074624.

McLean, Kathleen. 2011. 'Whose questions, whose conversations?' In *Letting Go? Sharing historical authority in a user-generated world*, edited by Bill Adair, Benjamin Filene and Laura Koloski, 70–9. Philadelphia, PA: Pew Center for Arts & Heritage.

Miller, Daniel. 2008. 'Migration, material culture and tragedy: Four moments in Caribbean migration', *Mobilities* 3(3): 397–413. https://doi.org/10.1080/17450100802376712.

National Park Service, US Department of the Interior. 2020. 'Native American Graves Protection and Repatriation Act'. Accessed 20 August 2021. https://www.nps.gov/subjects/nagpra/the-law.htm.

O'Reilly, Chiara and Nina Parish. 2017. 'Suitcases, keys, and handkerchiefs: How are objects being used to collect and tell migrant stories in Australian museums?', *Museums & Social Issues* 12(2): 99–114. https://doi.org/10.1080/15596893.2017.1386015.

Phillips, Ruth. 2007. 'The museum of art-thropology: Twenty-first century imbroglios', *RES: Anthropology and Aesthetics* 52: 8–19. https://doi.org/10.1086/RESv52n1ms20167734.

Rathje, William L. 1979. 'Modern material culture studies', *Advances in Archaeological Method and Theory* 2: 1–37.

Reynolds, Barrie. 1989. 'Museums of anthropology as centres of information'. In *Museum Studies in Material Culture*, edited by Susan Pearce, 111–18. London: Leicester University Press.

Sarr, Felwine and Bénédicte Savoy. 2018. 'The restitution of African cultural heritage: Toward a new relational ethics'. Translated by Drew S. Burk. Paris: République française, Ministère de la Culture. Accessed 20 August 2021. http://restitutionreport2018.com/sarr_savoy_en.pdf.

Soto, Gabriella. 2018a. 'Object afterlives and the burden of history: Between "trash" and "heritage" in the steps of migrants', *American Anthropologist* 120(3): 460–73. https://doi.org/10.1111/aman.13055.

Soto, Gabriella. 2018b. 'Place making in non-places: Migrant graffiti in rural highway box culverts'. In *The New Nomadic Age: Archaeologies of forced and undocumented migration*, edited by Yannis Hamilakis, 58–79. Sheffield: Equinox.

Stewart, Haeden Eli, Ian Osterreicher, Cameron Gokee and Jason De León. 2018. 'Surveilling surveillance: Countermapping undocumented migration in the USA–Mexico borderlands'. In *The New Nomadic Age: Archaeologies of forced and undocumented migration*, edited by Yannis Hamilakis, 42–57. Sheffield: Equinox.

Tyrikos-Ergas, George. 2018. 'Orange life jackets: Materiality and narration in Lesvos, one year after the eruption of the "refugee crisis"'. In *The New Nomadic Age: Archaeologies of forced and undocumented migration*, edited by Yannis Hamilakis, 121–6. Sheffield: Equinox.

Ulz, Melanie. 2019. 'Migration on display: Curatorial concepts and artistic approaches in France and Germany'. In *Handbook of Art and Global Migration: Theories, practices, and challenges*, edited by Burcu Dogramaci and Birgit Mersmann, 315–30. Berlin: De Gruyter.

UNHCR. 2010. 'Convention and Protocol Relating to the Status of Refugees'. Geneva: UNHCR. Accessed 20 August 2021. http://www.unhcr.org/3b66c2aa10.

Yuan, Yan. 2014. 'Acquiring, positioning and connecting: The materiality of television and the politics of mobility in a Chinese rural migrant community', *Media, Culture & Society* 36(3): 336–50. https://doi.org/10.1177%2F0163443713518575.

Part III

Moving things: objects, emotions and relatedness in (forced) migration

Introduction

Peter J. Bräunlein

In Part III, the contributions establish relationships between materiality, emotion and migration. This part is about 'moving' things in two meanings of the word: things that move through space and time, and things that trigger an emotional response.

The connection between things and emotions is obvious to anyone who does migration research. For example, packing a suitcase at the start of a trip is a well-known routine activity. In the context of flight and migration, however, the activity changes significantly. Each piece is carefully selected and fulfils not only practical but also emotional functions. Orvar Löfgren writes, '[p]acking and unpacking a suitcase means constantly negotiating ... tensions and paradoxes' (Löfgren 2016, 150). In writing this, Löfgren is asking how things transport hopes and dreams, traumatic experiences, and difficult-to-formulate feelings of abandonment and adventure.

In the study of the interconnection between migration, materiality and emotion, different key topics have emerged which are reflected in the following chapters. Three key strands are focused on here: the connection between the body, senses and memory; the affective spaces that are shaped by migrants or that have an influence on them; and the role of materiality in building and maintaining a sense of belonging and relatedness on the move.

We now look at findings from emotion research in relation to migration, then link the affective and material turns with migration research, before outlining how these topics are addressed in the chapters that follow.

Emotion and affect in migration studies

Similarly to the material turn, the affective turn has had an immense impact in the human sciences for around two decades (Massumi 2002; Clough and Halley 2007). This turn developed from a critique of the cultural-theoretical fixation on text, semiotics, discourse and especially 'representation'. Proponents of the affective turn question the primacy of language, focusing their attention on the pre- or non-linguistic capacities of humans. Thus, the body, the senses, and above all, feelings, moods, emotions and affects now come into play. When it comes to the question of where emotions and affects are anchored, not only history and the social sciences have their say, but also the neurosciences and philosophy. Anthropologists and sociologists are in debate with brain scientists and philosophers (Seigworth and Gregg 2010).

In the scholarly literature, including in migration research, the key terms are used inconsistently. Historians speak exclusively about the history of emotions (and not affects) (Reddy 2001; Matt 2011; Boddice 2018), while philosophers and social scientists accentuate affect and emotion differently. In many cases, the following distinction can be found in the literature: 'affect' is described among other things 'as felt bodily intensity that is: different from emotion and language; presocial, but not asocial; material or somehow pertaining to matter; dynamic and energetic; rife with possibilities to produce new and emergent phenomena' (McGrail, Davie-Kessler and Guffin 2013), whereas emotions are 'cultural interpretations' and 'everyday understandings of affects' with a distinct vocabulary that serves communication in the social world (Frykman and Povrzanović Frykman 2016, 14; Thrift 2008, 221).

This distinction between affect as precognitive and emotion as a culturally specific translation of affect has proved useful in the social sciences. The epistemic object 'emotion' becomes relevant as a medium of communication and thus becomes a relational concept. As a medium of communication, it is involved in social discourses. Thus, the pure emotion does not exist. Rather, 'discourses on emotion and emotional discourses as social practices' (Abu-Lughod and Lutz 1990, 1) are inseparably connected. Emotions, culturally bound and historically embedded, are better suited to become subjects of empirical research than affects. In this context, it seems useful to ask not what emotions *are*, but what they *do* (Ahmed 2004).

Inspired by Bourdieu's theory of praxis, the historian Monique Scheer speaks of 'emotional practices' as the object of investigation. This concept is built on the basic assumption that 'thought and emotion are embodied and understandable only in their social context' (Scheer 2012, 219). In a similar vein, Jonas Frykman and Maja Povrzanović Frykman argue in their introduction to the anthology *Sensitive Objects: Affect and material culture* (2016): 'As ethnologists and anthropologists we are interested in practices and lived experiences that are always historically embedded' (Frykman and Povrzanović Frykman 2016, 20). Integrating a focus on affects and materiality, they state: 'We therefore do not understand objects as having an *independent* affective "charge"' (Frykman and Povrzanović Frykman 2016, 20; emphasis original). Objects and affects are to be grasped through events or scenes, or as 'situated praxis', a concept that Frykman and Povrzanović Frykman attribute to Bourdieu (Bourdieu 1977; Frykman and Povrzanović Frykman 2016, 22).

Since the turn of the century, emotions have emerged in migration research in different thematic areas, including emotion management in transnational families (Baldassar 2007, 2008; Yeoh et al. 2005; Svašek 2008), the emotional effects of transnational long-distance communication (Panagakos and Horst 2006; Wilding 2006), emotion-laden returns to the 'home' country (Baldassar 2001; Lambkin 2008; Ramirez et al. 2007), home-making practices, and questions of belonging (Ahmed et al. 2003; Burrell 2008; Fortier 2000). Maruška Svašek is among the scholars who have done seminal work in this area (Svašek 2008, 2018; Svašek and Skrbiš 2007) and, importantly for this volume, has included materiality in her work on migration and emotion (2012a, 2012b).

In the following, I approach the relationship between materiality, migration and emotion through three interconnected fields of research: body, senses and memory; affective space; and relatedness.

Body, senses, memory

Both the material turn and the studies on emotion and affect have drawn attention to the body in terms of its materiality, its senses, and the interconnection between emotions and sensation (Massumi 1995; Frykman and Povrzanović Frykman 2016, 12–13; Parrott 2012). In asking what it feels like to be a refugee, Dudley (2010) argues that two kinds of 'feelings' have to be accounted for: 'the physical senses and the emotions, which are intrinsically linked and historically and culturally situated' (Dudley 2010, 3). To make this link plausible, Dudley develops the concept of 'aesthetics', understood by her not in the conventional terms 'of judgements of taste regarding art or beauty, but in its wider meaning of inter-linked sensory and emotional experience and preference'

(Dudley 2010, 3). Dudley shows in her research in a refugee camp in Thailand that the Karenni 'work hard and creatively to preserve a feeling of connection with real and imagined pasts' (Dudley 2010, 7). To give 'meaning' to their existence, they try to make their lives as normal as possible and make the place as familiar as the old. Establishing this connection between past and present, between familiar places and the foreign dwelling, requires 'a continual imaginative and cognitive movement between the camps and places of origin, the present and the past' (Dudley 2010, 7). Memory in multiple forms, then, is a central issue, for it is through memory that the past is maintained. Dudley sees memory and the senses as interlinked, and argues that the active recollection of memories themselves is a bodily experience (Dudley 2010, 8). Through their connection to the body, material objects like dress and food bring back particular feelings, and trigger re-experiences and physical sensations (Dudley 2010, 55). At the same time, these refugees use the objects to actively reshape their sensorial landscape and make the new place familiar (Dudley 2010, 57).

Memory is an important theme in several studies of migration, materiality and emotion. Maja Povrzanović Frykman analyses memory culture in the context of the wartime siege of Sarajevo in her 'Sensitive objects of humanitarian aid' (2016b). The documented stories are situated in a configuration of affective object relations, bodily remembering and storytelling. In this case, the objects that trigger memories are items needed to survive, which were flown in and distributed to wartime Sarajevo via an airlift. 'Sensitive objects' in this sense are more than just memory aids, they are 'sites of feeling'. Their significance lies in embodying the narrator's memory (Povrzanović Frykman 2016b, 90). Povrzanović Frykman shows how person–object interaction activates bodily memory, a process that is by no means reducible to cognition. Sensory experiences – smell, taste, touch – have a bridging function between then and now because 'senses engaged then retain a lingering affective dimension that is communicated in the narration now, and at the same time affects the person in the act of narration' (Povrzanović Frykman 2016b, 99). Biographical objects are of outstanding interest in the context of flight and migration (Yi-Neumann, Chapter 4 in this volume). They store memories and emotional experiences, can provide security in times of crisis and, moreover, form connections to friends and relatives. Without the physical-sensory dimension, the affective dimension, and ultimately the function of these objects, cannot be understood and described: biographical objects are touching and moving, in multiple ways.

In her study focusing on intra-African migration, Marschall introduces the term 'memory objects' for 'possessions without obvious mnemonic function that develop mnemonic characteristics over time and … through the experience of mobility and migration' (Marschall 2019, 254). Thus, she differentiates between memory objects and mementoes, which she understands as material artefacts that migrants intentionally take with them (Marschall 2019, 264). In her study, mostly utilitarian objects, like a belt or a comb, develop into memory objects and elicit memories when people use them. She emphasises that people's relationships to material objects are influenced by their socio-economic situation, their circumstances of mobility, and the context of migration (Marschall 2019, 265; see Svašek 2012b, 25). The other factors she highlights are the expectations of eventual return to the home country, and the individual disposition towards material objects and remembering (Marschall 2019, 266).

The works cited in this short overview show how, in interacting with the human body through the senses of touch, smell, sight and sound, material objects can trigger emotions and memories. These material objects can either be consciously chosen 'mementoes' to remember a former home or family members, or develop into 'memory objects' by provoking particular emotions and memories over time. People can then use these objects to actively and consciously produce a familiar sensuous geography (Rodaway 1994) and to '"make" home in displacement' (Dudley 2010, 57), issues we turn to in the following section.

Affective spaces and atmospheres

The connection between emotion research and spatial research – which was developed in a dialogue between the affective and spatial turns – still draws inspiration from Henri Lefebvre's epochal work *The Production of Space* ([1974] 1991). From a post-Deleuzian perspective, theorists of the affective turn show that 'affectivity can be studied in sites and spaces beyond the scope of the "human subject", his or her "subjectivity", or "psyche"' (Navaro-Yashin 2009, 12; see also Deleuze and Guattari 2004). These scholars have developed a new vocabulary, talking now of affective spaces, fields, geographies and atmospheres (Harris and Sørensen 2010, 150–1; Reckwitz 2012; Böhme 2014; Navaro-Yashin 2012; Edensor and Sumartojo 2015). That is, affects, previously confined to the inner spaces of the subject, are now located in outer spaces from which the subject is permeated.

Studies in migration research look into how particular places, such as domestic settings or camps, feel (Long 2013; Parrott 2012; Salih 2017), and, in particular, what makes a place familiar and feel like home (Dudley 2010, 2011; Hage 2010; Pechurina 2015; Mata-Codesal 2008; Boccagni and Vargas-Silva 2021). Scholars also focus on particular moments of community and coming together, for example to eat or celebrate, and what kind of emotions these events spark, such as feelings of belonging, hope, acceptance and home (Wise 2005; Johnston and Longhurst 2012). Affective spaces do not have to be three-dimensional. Virtual spaces can also be spaces of confidence, belonging and temporary home. For example, an article by Özlem Savaş points to the capacity of digital spaces to develop into 'affective digital media environments' in the context of migration (Savaş 2019, 5408).

One concept that I – like Savaş in this volume – find particularly helpful in studying the dynamic between environment, material objects and sensing bodies is that of 'atmosphere'. According to Friedlind Riedel, '"Atmosphere" refers to a feeling, mood, or *Stimmung* that fundamentally exceeds an individual body and instead pertains primarily to the overall situation in which bodies are entrenched' (Riedel 2019, 85). The concept of atmosphere directs the focus from the individual to the collective and understands feelings as 'collectively embodied, spatially extended, material, and culturally inflected' (Riedel 2019, 85). How individual bodies are affected by atmospheres varies and depends on one's prior experiences and personal background (Edensor and Sumartojo 2015, 257). People are not simply affected by atmospheres, they are part of their production. Bille and Simonsen argue for a focus on atmospheric practices: 'atmosphere is not only something humans *feel*, or that conditions perception, but it also simultaneously positions the felt space as something humans *do*' (Bille and Simonsen 2019, 304). Thus, they understand atmospheres as created by 'materiality and the presence and practices of people' (Bille and Simonsen 2019, 306).

This understanding of atmospheres enables migration researchers to look into important issues. Firstly, how do people on the move (re)produce homely atmospheres? As Edensor and Sumartojo argue, homely atmospheres are experienced unreflexively and often only become evident when disrupted (Edensor and Sumartojo 2015, 260). Migration or moving to another place may cause such a rupture. Secondly, atmosphere offers a new perspective on situations of community and how particular atmospheres are created or staged (Bille et al. 2015). In their chapters, Özlem Savaş and Andrea Verdasco focus on communal situations involving eating and drinking and how they create particular moods and feelings.

Savaş describes a community that forms around a rakı table in Berlin.[1] People who have recently left Turkey gather at the table, eating and drinking together in an affectionate atmosphere that enables and reinforces connectedness. The table, the food and the rakı form the material basis of connectivity and communication. In this atmosphere, people, things, tastes, smells, emotions, ritualised behaviour, narration and interactions unfold effects in their interplay. Without the arrangement of things and ritualised consumption, emotions are not possible, and without emotions, lasting relationships are not possible.

In her chapter, Andrea Verdasco uses the example of young refugees in a Danish shelter to show how the allotted pocket money is transformed to build and maintain social relationships with each other. The materiality of money is invested in the materiality of food, and by preparing and eating that food together, normality, continuity and social relations are created. Money is initially an object without sentimental charge, but in its transformed effect, commensality unfolds as an emotionally charged communal experience. This collective strengthens the ability to persevere in adverse and uncertain times.

Another perspective on migration and atmosphere opens up in Maike Suhr's chapter on the use of popular culture in exhibitions on migration. She describes the exhibition 'BITTER THINGS – Narratives and Memories of Transnational Families' (Berlin, 2018) in which pop culture media, especially songs, play a central role. Suhr argues that music and lyrics dissolve conventional forms of representation of migration, and create an atmosphere that develops 'powerful affectivity' and enables participation in emotional states such as abandonment, hope, future-oriented aspiration and attachment to family. However, pop culture also makes it possible to address irony and humour, which in turn subvert conventional clichés of victimhood and suffering. The objects thematised in pop songs appear as actants that essentially shape family relationships: they are mediators of tradition, nostalgia, aspiration, desire.

Relatedness through/in/by moving things

Migration processes disrupt relationships to people and places and thus people need to find ways to maintain connections and build new relationships. These efforts to stay in close contact with family, friends and particular places, while establishing new relationships in a new place, lead to a life in simultaneity (Levitt and Glick Schiller 2004). As migrants are embedded in multiple, transnational and transcultural relations

(Röttger-Rössler 2018, 238; Christensen and Jensen 2011), the questions arise: How do they negotiate multiple belonging? And how is this experienced emotionally (Röttger-Rössler 2018)? Indeed, the ways people maintain and (re-)create multiple belongings in the context of migration (Röttger-Rössler 2018; Pfaff-Czarnecka 2012; McKay 2007) and the role of materiality in that process have been important foci in migration research (Burrell 2008; Mata-Codesal and Abranches 2018; Fedyuk 2012). Using the term relatedness (Carsten 2000, 2007; Svašek 2018), we now look at how belonging is (re-)created through, in and by moving things.

Material objects are important in creating and maintaining relatedness. To stay connected to their former places of residence and to family and friends, migrants often take material artefacts with them (Svašek 2012a, 2012b; Povrcanović Frykman 2016a; Povrcanović Frykman and Humbracht 2013). At the same time, things are sent from one place to another, often between members of transnational families. These things – food parcels (Mata-Codesal and Abranches 2018; Camposano 2012), photographs (Fedyuk 2012) and money (McKay 2007) – have been discussed in the context of transnational motherhood and the creation of intimacy in transnational relationships. These studies show that material objects often play an important role in creating and maintaining intimacy across spatial distance.

Similarly, a number of studies show how communication technologies enable the building and maintaining of relatedness over space and time and create intimacy and co-presence (Wilding 2006; Baldassar et al. 2016; Madianou 2016). Here, material objects like telephones, smartphones and laptops mediate social relationships and create particular affective dynamics. In her chapter in this volume, Maruška Svašek focuses on these issues in the context of the Covid pandemic and shows how the possibilities of a long-distance family relationship are maintained via electronic media. The 'affective field' (Harris and Sørensen 2010, 150–1) of a virtual family meeting is shaped by software and hardware, and their susceptibility to malfunction. It is not only the other family members who trigger emotions thematised in the communication, but also the functionality – or lack of it – of the technology itself. The specific agency of communication technology has a massive impact on translocal sociality and care-giving practices, which in turn are indispensable for relatedness.

In many cases, particularly in forced migration, people are left with few – if any – possessions. During the processes of migration, they gradually acquire new things (Conlon 2011): papers, clothing, footwear, everyday items and so on. In her chapter, Magdalena Suerbaum looks at how three acquired material objects – the pram, the notebook and the plastic bag – create relatedness to the new place. Studying the mothering practices of women with a precarious legal status in Berlin, she argues that acquiring the material objects supports emplacing and feelings of belonging in the new context. These emotionally charged objects reveal the women's engagement in mothering practices and their efforts to conform to local ideals of mothering. At the same time, however, these objects illustrate the uncertainty that defines their lives.

Summary

This short overview shows how the study of emotion adds an important perspective to the understanding of the materiality of migration and the 'migrant experience' in general as multifaceted and complex (Boccagni and Baldassar 2015, 74). The study of emotion and affect allows scholars to ask not only how it feels to be a migrant in a particular context, but also how it feels to be part of a transnational family or to live in a camp or a new apartment. This approach shifts the attention to the ways in which material objects and environments trigger particular affects and emotions. At the same time, it allows researchers to look into how migrants use materiality creatively and actively to produce particular emotions and atmospheres, and familiar sensory experiences and memories. In other words, this approach allows scholars to look at how migrants create a feeling of being 'right with the world' (Dudley 2010, 4).

Note

1 Rakı is a liquor made of grapes and anise, considered a national drink in Turkey. The beverage is also very popular in Greece.

References

Abu-Lughod, Lila and Catherine Lutz. 1990. 'Introduction: Emotion, discourse, and the politics of everyday life'. In *Language and the Politics of Emotion*, edited by Catherine Lutz and Lila Abu-Lughod, 1–23. Cambridge: Cambridge University Press.

Ahmed, Sara. 2004. *The Cultural Politics of Emotion*. New York: Routledge.

Ahmed, Sara, Claudia Castañeda, Anne-Marie Fortier and Mimi Sheller, eds. 2003. *Uprootings/Regroundings: Questions of home and migration*. Oxford: Berg.

Baldassar, Loretta R. 2001. *Visits Home: Migration experiences between Italy and Australia*. Carlton, Victoria: Melbourne University Press.

Baldassar, Loretta R. 2007. 'Transnational families and the provision of moral and emotional support: The relationship between truth and distance', *Identities: Global Studies in Culture and Power*, 14(4): 385–409. https://doi.org/10.1080/10702890701578423.

Baldassar, Loretta. 2008. 'Missing Kin and longing to be together: Emotions and the construction of co-presence in transnational relationships'. In Transnational Families and Emotions, edited by Maruška Svašek, special issue of Journal of Intercultural Studies, 29(3): 247–66. https://doi.org/10.1080/07256860802169196.

Baldassar, Loretta, Mihaela Nedelcu, Laura Merla and Raelene Wilding. 2016. 'ITC-based co-presence in transnational families and communities: Challenging the premise of face-to-face proximity in sustaining relationships', *Global Networks* 16(2): 133–44. https://doi.org/10.1111/glob.12108.

Bille, Mikkel, Peter Bjerregaard and Tim Flohr Sørensen. 2015. 'Staging atmospheres: Materiality, culture, and the texture of the in-between', *Emotion, Space and Society* 15: 31–8.

Bille, Mikkel and Kirsten Simonsen. 2019. 'Atmospheric practices: On affecting and being affected', *Space and Culture* 24(2): 295–309. https://doi.org/10.1177/1206331218819711.

Boccagni, Paolo and Loretta Baldassar. 2015. 'Emotions on the move: Mapping the emergent field of emotion and migration', *Emotion, Space and Society* 16: 73–80. https://doi.org/10.1016/j.emospa.2015.06.009.

Boccagni, Paolo and Carlos Vargas-Silva. 2021. 'Feeling at home across time and space: A study of Ecuadorians in three European cities', *Population, Space and Place* 27(6). https://doi.org/10.1002/psp.2431.

Boddice, Rob. 2018. 'The history of emotions'. In *New Directions in Social and Cultural History*, edited by Sasha Handley, Rohan McWilliam and Lucy Noakes, 45–64. London: Bloomsbury Academic.

Böhme, Gernot. 2014. 'The theory of atmospheres and its applications', translated by A.-Chr. Engels-Schwarzpaul. *Interstices: Journal of Architecture and Related Arts* 15: 93–100.

Bourdieu, Pierre. 1977. *Outline of a Theory of Practice*. Translated by Richard Nice. Cambridge: Cambridge University Press.

Burrell, Kathy. 2008. 'Managing, learning and sending: The material lives and journeys of Polish women in Britain', *Journal of Material Culture* 13(1): 63–83. http://dx.doi.org/10.1177/1359183507086219.

Camposano, Clement C. 2012. 'Balikbayan boxes and the performance of intimacy by Filipino migrant women in Hong Kong', *Asian and Pacific Migration Journal* 21(1): 83–103. https://doi.org/10.1177%2F011719681202100104.

Carsten, Janet. 2000. 'Introduction: Cultures of relatednesss'. In *Cultures of Relatedness: New approaches to the study of kinship*, edited by Janet Carsten, 1–36. Cambridge: Cambridge University Press.

Carsten, Janet, ed. 2007. *Ghosts of Memory: Essays on remembrance and relatedness*. Malden, MA: Blackwell.

Christensen, Ann-Dorte and Sune Qvotrup Jensen. 2011. 'Roots and routes: Migration, belonging and everyday life', *Nordic Journal of Migration Research* 1(3): 146–55. http://doi.org/10.2478/v10202-011-0013-1.

Clough, Patricia Ticineto and Jean O'Malley Halley, eds. 2007. *The Affective Turn: Theorizing the social*. Durham, NC: Duke University Press.

Conlon, Deirdre. 2011. 'A fractured mosaic: Encounters with the everyday amongst refugee and asylum seeker women', *Population, Space and Place* 17(6): 714–26. https://doi.org/10.1002/psp.637.

Deleuze, Gilles and Felix Guattari. 2004. *A Thousand Plateaus: Capitalism and schizophrenia*. Translated by Brian Massumi. London: Continuum.

Dudley, Sandra H. 2010. *Materialising Exile: Material culture and embodied experience among Karenni refugees in Thailand*. New York and Oxford: Berghahn Books.

Dudley, Sandra H. 2011. 'Feeling at home: Producing and consuming things in Karenni refugee camps on the Thai–Burma border', *Population, Space and Place* 17(6): 742–55. https://doi.org/10.1002/psp.639.

Edensor, Tim and Shanti Sumartojo. 2015. 'Designing atmospheres: Introduction to special issue', *Visual Communication* 14(3): 251–65. https://doi.org/10.1177/1470357215582305.

Fedyuk, Olena. 2012. 'Images of transnational motherhood: The role of photographs in measuring time and maintaining connections between Ukraine and Italy', *Journal of Ethnic and Migration Studies* 38(2): 279–300. https://doi.org/10.1080/1369183X.2012.646422.

Fortier, Anne-Marie. 2000. *Migrant Belongings: Memory, space, identity*. Oxford: Berg.

Frykman, Jonas and Maja Povrzanović Frykman. 2016. 'Affect and material culture: Perspectives and strategies'. In *Sensitive Objects: Affect and material culture*, edited by Jonas Frykman and Maja Povrzanović Frykman, 9–28. Lund: Nordic Academic Press.

Hage, Ghassan. 2010. 'Migration, food, memory, and home-building'. In *Memory: Histories, theories, debates*, edited by Susannah Radstone and Bill Schwarz, 416–27. New York: Fordham University Press.

Harris, Oliver J. T. and Tim Flohr Sørensen. 2010. 'Rethinking emotion and material culture', *Archaeological Dialogues* 17(2): 145–63. https://doi.org/10.1017/S1380203810000206.

Johnston, Lynda and Robyn Longhurst. 2012. 'Embodied geographies of food, belonging and hope in multicultural Hamilton, Aotearoa New Zealand', *Geoforum* 43(2): 325–31. https://doi.org/10.1016/j.geoforum.2011.08.002.

Lambkin, Brian. 2008. 'The emotional function of the migrant's "birthplace" in transnational belonging: Thomas Mellon (1813–1908) and Andrew Carnegie (1835–1919)', *Journal of Intercultural Studies* 29(3): 315–29. https://doi.org/10.1080/07256860802169246.

Lefebvre, Henri. [1974] 1991. *The Production of Space*. Translated by Donald Nicholson-Smith. Malden, MA, and Oxford: Blackwell Publishing.

Levitt, Peggy and Nina Glick Schiller. 2004. 'Conceptualizing simultaneity: A transnational social field perspective on society', *International Migration Review* 38(3): 1002–39.

Löfgren, Orvar. 2016. 'Emotional baggage: Unpacking the suitcase'. In *Sensitive Objects: Affect and material culture*, edited by Jonas Frykman and Maja Povrzanović Frykman, 125–52. Lund: Nordic Academic Press.

Long, Joanna C. 2013. 'Diasporic dwelling: The poetics of domestic space', *Gender, Place & Culture: A Journal of Feminist Geography* 20(3): 329–45. https://doi.org/10.1080/0966369X.2012.674932.

Madianou, Mirca. 2016. 'Ambient co-presence: Transnational family practices in polymedia environments', *Global Networks* 16(2): 183–201. https://doi.org/10.1111/glob.12105.

Marschall, Sabine. 2019. '"Memory objects"': Material objects and memories of home in the context of intra-African mobility', *Journal of Material Culture* 24(3): 253–69. https://doi.org/10.1177%2F1359183519832630.

Massumi, Brian. 1995. 'The autonomy of affect', *Cultural Critique* 31: 83–109. https://doi.org/10.2307/j.ctv11smvr0.5.

Massumi, Brian. 2002. *Parables for the Virtual: Movement, affect, sensation*. Durham, NC: Duke University Press.

Mata-Codesal, Diana. 2008. 'Rice & coriander: Sensorial re-creations of home through food: Ecuadorians in a northern Spanish city', Working Paper 50, Sussex Centre for Migration Research, University of Sussex.

Mata-Codesal, Diana and Maria Abranches, eds. 2018. *Food Parcels in International Migration: Intimate connections*. Cham: Palgrave Macmillan.

Matt, Susan J. 2011. 'Current emotion research in history: Or, Doing history from the inside out', *Emotion Review* 3(1): 117–24. https://doi.org/10.1177%2F1754073910384416.

McGrail, Richard, Jesse Davie-Kessler and Bascom Guffin. 2013. 'Affect, embodiment, and sense perception'. Society for Cultural Anthropology. Accessed 20 August 2021. https://culanth.org/curated_collections/16-affect-embodiment-and-sense-perception.

McKay, Deirdre. 2007. '"Sending dollars shows feeling": Emotions and economies in Filipino migration', *Mobilities* 2(2): 175–94. https://doi.org/10.1080/17450100701381532.

Navaro-Yashin, Yael. 2009. 'Affective spaces, melancholic objects: Ruination and the production of anthropological knowledge', *Journal of the Royal Anthropological Institute* 15(1): 1–18. https://doi.org/10.1111/j.1467-9655.2008.01527.x.

Navaro-Yashin, Yael. 2012. *The Make-Believe Space: Affective geography in a postwar polity*. Durham, NC: Duke University Press.

Panagakos, Anastasia N. and Heather A. Horst. 2006. 'Return to Cyberia: Technology and the social worlds of transnational migrants', *Global Networks* 6(2): 109–24. https://doi.org/10.1111/j.1471-0374.2006.00136.x.

Parrott, Fiona R. 2012. 'Materiality, memories and emotions: A view on migration from a street in south London'. In *Moving Subjects, Moving Objects: Transnationalism, cultural production and emotions*, edited by Maruška Svašek, 41–54. New York and Oxford: Berghahn Books.

Pechurina, Anna. 2015. *Material Cultures, Migrations, and Identities: What the eye cannot see*. Basingstoke and New York: Palgrave Macmillan.

Pfaff-Czarnecka, Joanna. 2012. *Zugehörigkeit in der mobilen Welt: Politiken der Verortung*. Göttingen: Wallstein.
Povrzanović Frykman, Maja. 2016a. 'Conceptualising continuity: A material culture perspective on transnational social fields', *Ethnologica Fennica* 43: 43–56.
Povrzanović Frykman, Maja. 2016b. 'Sensitive objects of humanitarian aid: Corporeal memories and affective continuities'. In *Sensitive Objects: Affect and material culture,* edited by Jonas Frykman and Maja Povrzanović Frykman, 79–104. Lund: Nordic Academic Press.
Povrzanović Frykman, Maja and Michael Humbracht. 2013. 'Making palpable connections: Objects in migrants' transnational lives', *Ethnologia Scandinavica: A Journal for Nordic Ethnology* 43: 47–67.
Ramirez, Marcela, Zlatko Skrbiš and Michael Emmison. 2007. 'Transnational family reunions as lived experience: Narrating a Salvadoran autoethnography', *Identities: Global Studies in Culture and Power* 14(4): 411–31. https://doi.org/10.1080/10702890701578456.
Reckwitz, Andreas. 2012. 'Affective spaces: A praxeological outlook', *Rethinking History* 16(2): 241–58. https://doi.org/10.1080/13642529.2012.681193.
Reddy, William M. 2001. *The Navigation of Feeling: A framework for the history of emotions*. Cambridge: Cambridge University Press.
Riedel, Friedlind. 2019. 'Atmosphere'. In *Affective Societies: Key concepts*, edited by Jan Slaby and Christian von Scheve, 85–95. Abingdon: Routledge.
Rodaway, Paul. 1994. *Sensuous Geographies: Body, sense and place*. London: Routledge.
Röttger-Rössler, Birgitt. 2018. 'Multiple belongings: On the affective dimensions of migration', *Zeitschrift für Ethnologie* 143(2): 237–62. https://www.jstor.org/stable/26899773.
Salih, Ruba. 2017. 'Bodies that walk, bodies that talk, bodies that love: Palestinian women refugees, affectivity, and the politics of the ordinary', *Antipode* 49(3): 742–60. https://doi.org/10.1111/anti.12299.
Savaş, Özlem. 2019. 'Affective digital media and new migration from Turkey: Feelings, affinities and politics', *International Journal of Communication* 13: 5405–26.
Scheer, Monique. 2012. 'Are emotions a kind of practice (and is that what makes them have a history)? A Bourdieuian approach to understanding emotion', *History and Theory* 51(2): 193–220. https://www.jstor.org/stable/23277639.
Seigworth, Gregory J. and Melissa Gregg. 2010. 'An inventory of shimmers'. In *The Affect Theory Reader*, edited by Melissa Gregg and Gregory J. Seigworth, 1–25. Durham, NC: Duke University Press.
Svašek, Maruška. 2008. 'Who cares? Families and feelings in movement', *Journal of Intercultural Studies* 29(3): 213–30. https://doi.org/10.1080/07256860802169170.
Svašek, Maruška, ed. 2012a. *Moving Subjects, Moving Objects: Transnationalism, cultural production and emotions*. New York: Berghahn Books.
Svašek, Maruška. 2012b. 'Introduction: Affective moves: Transit, transition and transformation'. In *Moving Subjects, Moving Objects: Transnationalism, cultural production and emotions*, edited by Maruška Svašek, 1–40. New York: Berghahn Books.
Svašek, Maruška. 2018. 'Ageing kin, proximity and distance: Translocal relatedness as affective practice and movement'. In *Affect in Relation: Families, places, technologies*, edited by Birgit Röttger-Rössler and Jan Slaby, 31–49. Abingdon: Routledge.
Svašek, Maruška and Zlatko Skrbiš. 2007. 'Passions and power: Emotions and globalisation', *Identities: Global Studies in Culture and Power* 14(4): 367–83. https://doi.org/10.1080/10702890701578415.
Thrift, Nigel. 2008. *Non-representational Theory: Space, politics, affect*. Abingdon: Routledge.
Wilding, R. 2006. '"Virtual" intimacies? Families communicating across transnational contexts', *Global Networks* 6(2): 125–42. https://doi.org/10.1111/j.1471-0374.2006.00137.x.
Wise, Amanda. 2005. 'Home and belonging in a multicultural suburb', *Journal of Intercultural Studies* 26(1–2): 171–86. https://doi.org/10.1080/07256860500074383.
Yeoh, Brenda S. A., Shirlena Huang and Theodora Lam. 2005. 'Transnationalizing the "Asian" family: Imaginaries, intimacies and strategic intents', *Global Networks* 5(4): 307–15. https://doi.org/10.1111/j.1471-0374.2005.00121.x.

7

Rakı table conversations of post-Gezi migration from Turkey: emotion, intimacy and politics

Özlem Savaş

Shortly after I migrated to Berlin at the end of 2017, my path crossed those of many others who had recently left Turkey, at first with the colleagues who are signatories of the Academics for Peace's 2016 petition like myself. One day, three colleagues and I decided to drink rakı, the aniseed-flavoured spirit of Turkey, together, although we did not have intimate knowledge of each other back then. It was not an ordinary dining-out plan but a big step in friendship, because, as one of the many famous sayings about the rakı table goes: 'One does not sit at a rakı table with just anybody.' Still, we had already shared experiences of difficult times that gathered us around a rakı table.

We went to a Greek restaurant in Kreuzberg, which serves three rakı brands from Turkey and familiar meze dishes. When we saw the tray with the rakı bottle, ice and ouzo glasses coming towards us, we asked almost in panic if they had rakı glasses. Fortunately, they did. Over the next three years, we went to this restaurant so many times. Certainly, the atmosphere was not the same as what we had experienced at our favourite rakı restaurants in Turkey, where people drink rakı and engage in 'rakı conversation' at their tables. But what we were looking for was not to remember Turkey or bring it to Berlin through nostalgic feelings. Nor did any of us have the slightest personal or political interest in performing some kind of Turkishness. We were seeking some intimacy amid our feelings of loss and uprootedness. And we would not think of any social occasion other than a rakı table where we could find intimacy, because, as the famous saying goes, 'Rakı is the key to the heart.' With tears and laughter, we talked about everything: love and politics, childhood memories and future dreams, Turkey, Germany and the rest, our sorrows, anxieties, disappointments and hopes. Looking at those days, I can say that we built our close friendships at the rakı table, where we had a chance to get to know each other better. As another popular saying goes, 'One gets to know another person truly at the rakı table.'

This chapter focuses on the rakı tables of people who have recently left Turkey and relocated to Berlin; it explores their affective value, significance and potentialities for the experience of displacement. Falling between object and subject, material and immaterial, the rakı table can best be described as an intimate and affectionate atmosphere, which is created by persons, things, tastes, smells, emotions, rituals, narratives and interactions. The particular sensory, aesthetic, emotional, social and political feel of the rakı table holds a significant place in individual and collective memories in Turkey. But this chapter avoids simply and quickly associating rakı tables that are relocated to Berlin with nostalgic feelings or some sort of ethnic, national or 'migrant' identity performance. Rather, it explores how the rakı table, as the locus of intimate conversations that interweave the emotional and the political, embodies and shapes the affective political experiences and horizons of post-Gezi migration from Turkey.

Facing escalating political oppression and turmoil, a growing number of people – mostly academics,[1] artists, journalists and students – left Turkey in the years that followed the Gezi movement and have settled around the globe, especially in Berlin. As a crucial historical moment, the Gezi movement, the countrywide anti-government protests that started at Gezi Park in Istanbul in June 2013, has been employed as a keyword by various media texts, artistic works and public events that address new migration from Turkey, since impulses, needs or desires to leave the country have evolved from the escalation of political oppression in the years that followed. On the one hand, the Gezi movement has been a continuing source of hope for possible collectivities and activisms; on the other, the hope it sparked has been largely replaced by feelings of loss, disappointment and failure, which have prompted the decision to migrate.

Migration from Turkey to Germany has a long history, with various phases.[2] Consequently, the rakı table had already found its place in Berlin, through Turkish restaurants that are devoted to rakı and its cuisine, as well as some Greek, Syrian and Lebanese restaurants that include rakı and meze in their menus. New migrants from Turkey expand these public scenes of rakı by opening new restaurants and bars, but more importantly by appropriating the intimate and affectionate rakı table atmosphere into public events. Rather than gatherings in restaurants or homes, or at picnics, this chapter focuses on the reimagination and reconstitution of the rakı table in artistic and cultural events organised in Berlin; it examines the artistic performance 'Trautes Heim Glück Allein' (Home sweet home) by Candaş Baş and two events, 'Çilingir Sofrası' (Locksmith's table) and 'Rakı Prinzip – Intersection Sessions', that took place in the form of politically motivated public rakı tables.

The chapter is underpinned by my ongoing ethnographic research on the affective culture of post-Gezi migration from Turkey, which addresses emotional practices that mediate, circulate and archive the lived and felt experiences of political oppression, migration and relocation across media, artistic endeavours and public events, and explores their potentialities for affinities and collectivities both within and beyond a particular migration experience. The experience of new migration from Turkey can be characterised by the common, pervasive and interrelated affective states of loss, uncertainty and hope that encompass feelings of distress, disappointment, anger, fear, anxiety, grief and stuckness along with a sense of future possibilities and impossibilities. Rather than the role of emotions in the private realm of the everyday, which has been well researched in migration contexts (e.g. Skrbiš 2008; Svašek 2008), I focus on the significance and potentials of emotions in public and political spheres that are shaped and reshaped by the experience of migration. As suggested by a series of terms and concepts, including the 'cultural politics of emotion' (Ahmed 2014), 'public feelings' (Cvetkovich 2012), 'political emotions' (Staiger et al. 2010) and 'intimate public' (Berlant 2008), emotions, feelings and affects are collective, public and political, not 'merely' psychological, personal and private. On the one hand, emotions take shape as they move through social, public and political worlds (Stewart 2007); on the other, public and political spheres emerge not solely as ideological and cognitive formations, but as affective sites of emotional engagement and identification (Berlant 2008).

This chapter does not present a complete account of the affective culture of post-Gezi migration from Turkey, but rather brings together pieces on emotional/political practices around rakı tables that have 'naturally' emerged from my ethnographic research as the seemingly contradictory, yet interrelated, issues of our migration are welcomed and even suggested by rakı table conversations: emotion and politics, loss and affinity, hope and hopelessness. In what follows, I will firstly address how the rakı table is created and experienced as an intimate and affectionate atmosphere through its materiality, emotions, rituals and narratives. Secondly, I will discuss how the heartfelt conversations promised and invited by the rakı table have been redirected towards the emotional and political need to tell of experiences of political oppression, displacement and relocation. Thirdly, I will explore how the intimate rakı table atmosphere has been appropriated by public events as an emotional/ political source for opening up dialogue and affinity, and discuss the affective political potentialities of intimacy within and beyond the experience of post-Gezi migration from Turkey.

Rakı table atmosphere

Çilingir Sofrası, a public event organised in Berlin to discuss experiences of recent migration from Turkey, which I examine in detail later in this chapter, took place around rakı tables that were decorated with a specially designed tablecloth (Figure 7.1). The tablecloth is a top-view portrayal of the contents of a rakı table. While the visual representation shows the typical material arrangement of a rakı table, with plates, meze dishes and rakı glasses, explanations of the numbered plate-like items next to the images tell the larger story of the rakı table. Haphazardly placed on the tablecloth are the names of the invited artists, rakı and ice, mezes such as melon and cheese, anticipated feelings of melancholia and acts of laughter and tears, and the expected topics of conversation including politics, immigration, collective memory and future plans. As this portrayal demonstrates, a rakı table is neither simply the piece of furniture that holds the rakı and the meze dishes, nor merely the group of people sitting at the table. Rather, it is a particular sensory, aesthetic, emotional, social and even political experience, which is co-created by persons and things. Falling between objects and subjects, material and immaterial, the rakı table emerges and affects as a 'staged atmosphere' (Bille et al. 2015) through the co-present things, tastes, smells, emotions, rituals, narratives and interactions.

'Atmosphere' is the sense, feel or mood of a place, thing or situation (Bille et al. 2015; Riedel 2019). As Böhme (1993) argues, despite plentiful everyday vocabulary to characterise them, such as melancholic, joyful, calm or oppressive, atmospheres are indeterminate as to 'whether we should attribute them to the objects or environments from which they proceed or to the subjects who experience them' (114). To explain this intermediary status of atmospheres, Böhme attempts to liberate the ontology of the thing from the objective–subjective dichotomy by rejecting both the conception of a thing in its internal unity, closure and separation from the outside, and the idea that ascribes the existence of a thing merely to a cognitive subject. He suggests that a thing is present and presents itself through its 'ecstasies', that is, 'the ways in which it goes forth from itself'

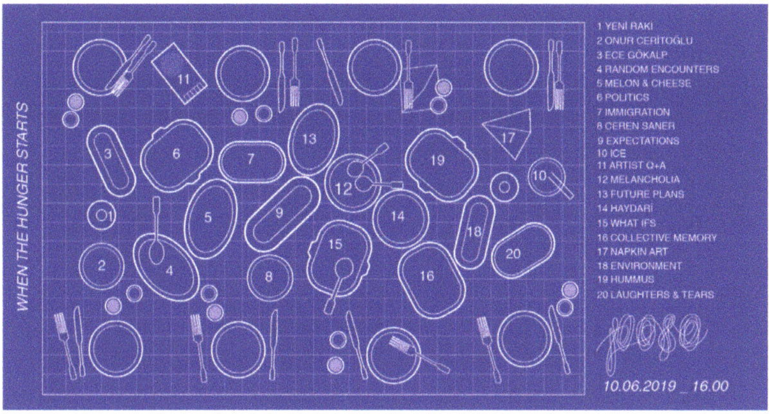

7.1 The tablecloth of Çilingir Sofrası, designed by Seda Gecü. https://www.pose-hello.com/cilingirsofrasi, public domain.

(Böhme 1993, 121), which include not only meanings and values ascribed by a subject, but also the thing's form, whose role is to externalise the thing to the perception, rather than enclosing it. By going forth from themselves, things 'radiate' atmospheres that become 'the common reality of the perceiver and the perceived' (Böhme 1993, 122). Böhme argues:

> Conceived in this fashion, atmospheres are neither something objective, that is, qualities possessed by things, and yet they are something thinglike, belonging to the thing in that things articulate their presence through qualities – conceived as ecstasies. Nor are atmospheres something subjective, for example, determinations of a psychic state. And yet they are subjectlike, belong to subjects in that they are sensed in bodily presence by human beings and this sensing is at the same time a bodily state of being of subjects in space.
>
> (Böhme 1993, 122)

A rakı table is formed by the rakı bottle, rakı glasses, ice and meze dishes, and by certain social and emotional anticipations which are brought to the table. As Edensor (2012) suggests, one of the significant co-creators of atmospheres is the 'anticipatory preparedness' of participating people, which emerges from cumulative past experiences, practices and conventions. Anticipations of the rakı table arise through a collective memory that has extended from the Ottoman period until today, as well as previous individual experiences. As Evered and Evered (2016) suggest, despite its consumption during the Ottoman Empire, particularly among non-Muslim minorities and members of *Bektaşi tarikatı* (a Sufi Islamic sect), rakı 'came to be viewed as the nation's preeminent drink' during the early years of the Republic of Turkey, as its particularity to Anatolia has done good service to 'the emergent nation seeking to distinguish itself' (44).[3] All sorts of narratives and representations of the rakı table, such as depictions of Ottoman *meyhanes* (rakı restaurants), photographs of Mustafa Kemal Atatürk drinking rakı (which decorate the walls of many rakı restaurants), rakı table stories of well-known authors, poets and artists, and films, songs and social media memes, have unfolded across various visual, literary and popular cultures. Well known for his books on rakı culture, Erdir Zat writes, in *Rakı: The spirit of Turkey* (2012), that rakı is a 'common cultural legacy of the various peoples living in Turkey' and 'an overriding identity that always paved the way for social interaction, creating sincere bonds irrespective of religion, language, nation, race or class' (21). This rather romanticised view of the rakı table overlooks the dynamics of inclusion and exclusion, particularly neglecting the gendered meanings of rakı (as a man's drink) that kept women away from at least the public scenes of rakı until the last few decades of the twentieth century. However, it points out the social significance of a strong and pervasive rakı culture for diverse people.

The culture of rakı includes a great number of idealised rituals and traditions about the aesthetics of the table,[4] foods that accompany rakı, and proper ways of drinking, eating, and interacting with others, all of which demand time, care, attention, respect and manners (Kesmez and Aydın 2014). Yet it is surely not a singular and coherent, but a highly plural, multiple and heterogeneous culture. The aesthetic, social and cultural practices of the rakı table, as well as its meanings and values, vary greatly between different socio-economic groups, lifestyles, geographical regions, and types of social occasion. Different food, aesthetics, social relations and cultural meanings evolve in diverse spaces of drinking rakı, such as luxury restaurants, cheap taverns, picnic sites, homes, fishing boats and many others.[5]

The distinguishing feature of the rakı table, which is common to the diverse spaces, practices and socialities, is the principle of sharing. What defines the intimate and affectionate character of the rakı table is sharing everything that comes to the table, not only rakı and meze, but also the conversation, which is indeed 'the most essential meze' (Kesmez and Aydın 2014). Mezes are tasted in small bites and rakı is drunk slowly, Zat (2012) suggests, because the aim of the rakı table is not to get full and drunk, but to spread flavours and conversations over hours. Belge (2012, 11) describes rakı as 'a great opener of new perspectives into all subjects and the opener of tongues'. Rakı table conversations continue throughout the occasion, evolving from chatting about everyday issues to telling love stories to discussing politics. Described as 'saving the country', political discussions are humorously accepted as indispensable to any rakı table. An anecdote about two Germans drinking rakı in Istanbul goes: 'As they are pouring their second glass, one of them asks, "Wolfgang, what do you think is going to become of Germany?"' (Belge 2012, 11).

Construed as heartfelt, honest, intimate and affectionate, rakı table conversations are distinguished from talk at other social gatherings. Rakı is called 'the key to the heart', which is one of the explanations for why the rakı table is named as çilingir sofrası (locksmith's table). Describing the rakı table as 'a gathering of hearts, a blending of souls', Zat (2012) writes that 'the focus of the rakı table is . . . the atmosphere of intimate conversation called *muhabbet* which, not coincidentally, is an Arabic word for affection, fondness and love' (112). In the past, the rakı table was also named the *hemdem* (cohesion through sharing) table, whose maxim was: 'The mystery of truth can be reached through conversation' (Zat 2014, 61). Therefore, the rakı table is felt as a great opportunity to build and strengthen intimacy, and a certain level of existing intimacy is required to sit together at the table.

Various narratives and images of the rakı table manifest how the rituals, feelings and meanings of the rakı table and its specific material and aesthetic qualities take shape through each other. The rituals of the rakı table do not simply revolve around, but are suggested or even imposed by, the things on the table. For example, by framing the occasion as a rakı table through its material presence, the rakı bottle 'assumes a dominant role over the dinner table' and 'begins to dictate' (Belge 2012, 10). Furthermore, the intimate and affectionate feel of the rakı table is co-created, expressed and supported by a particular material and aesthetic arrangement that is focused on the principle of sharing. As well as shared drink and food, special rakı glasses bring the idea of shared experience to the table. One research participant who migrated from Ankara to Berlin three years ago explains that 'the rakı glass represents everything on that table', including taste – rakı tastes different in different glasses, she suggests – ritual and companionship. Both rakı and water must be drunk from rakı glasses and a rakı glass should not be used to drink anything else, because 'it belongs to the rakı ritual'. Moreover, she tells me, 'Everyone sitting at a rakı table must have the same glasses. This brings aesthetic pleasure but also intimacy. Sameness of rakı glasses lays the ground for creating commonalities with the others sitting at the table.'

Co-created by specific aesthetic and material qualities and anticipations that stem from individual and collective memories, the rakı table atmosphere invites people into particular ways of being, doing, feeling, talking and interacting with the self, the others and the world. Abels (2019, 50) addresses music and dance as transitory techniques that 'can be used towards a flexing of the lived experience' that 'invites an intensification of the sensation of being in the world'. Through their power to reorganise time and space, music and dance serve as modes and practices of dwelling and 'making the world one's own' (Abels 2019, 50). In a similar fashion, the intensity of the rakı table experience promises particular modes of being in the world and intimate togetherness that are felt to be distinct from encounters and interactions that can take place at any social occasion. For example, unlike more ordinary plans of 'dining out' or 'having a drink', rakı table gatherings are arranged through phrases such as 'We need a rakı table' or 'Let's meet and speak at a rakı table'. One research participant describes the particular feel of the rakı table as follows:

> It is a table for very deep connections. You give your time to the table, sitting there for four to five hours. No rush. Time feels infinite. You just happen to be there and enjoy it, enjoy even the grief. You cry, laugh, and even sing. Fully transparent. It invites you to open yourself to the others. Eye to eye, heart to heart, shoulder to shoulder …

The collective and palpable feeling of intimacy is the main experience anticipated from the rakı table atmosphere, regardless of whether it can be achieved on every occasion. The concept of atmosphere, Riedel (2019) suggests, 'challenges a notion of feelings as the private mental states of a cognizant subject and instead construes feelings as collectively embodied, spatially extended, material, and culturally inflected' (85). Thus, affective intensities of atmospheres arise through their capacity to transcend individual bodies and distribute feeling among a group of bodies that becomes a felt collective (Riedel 2019, 85). As will be discussed in the rest of this chapter, the significance of the rakı table atmosphere for the experience of post-Gezi migration from Turkey stems from its potentiality to unfold and circulate feelings through intimate conversations.

Telling a story with a rakı glass in hand

How to drink rakı in Berlin is one of the most popular topics discussed in New Wave in Berlin,[6] a Facebook group founded and joined by individuals who have recently left Turkey. The group is focused on exchanging information and advice on a range of everyday issues such as bureaucratic processes, rental apartments, doctors, hairdressers and constructors, as well as restaurants that serve rakı and meze, and supermarkets that sell rakı and rakı glasses. Since it had been requested so many times, the group collaboratively prepared a list of Berlin restaurants at which to drink rakı. Moreover, some group members organised rakı evenings to get together. One of the rakı-related enquiries was posted by renk.Magazin (a German-Turkish magazine); it asked group members to leave a comment about the rakı table in order to get two invitations to a rakı dinner it organised in Berlin. Fifty-nine comments left on this post comprised an almost complete collection of famous sayings about rakı table, including:

> You won't die on the day you drink rakı!
> Sometimes rakı nourishes hopes all over again. As the poet says, if you are drinking rakı, there is something unfinished.
> To those who are far away, and those who are nearby; to those who make the impossible possible, who fill the eyes with tears.
> Rakı is drunk with the ones sitting next to you, but the glass is raised to the ones in your mind.

These well-known sayings that express the mixed sorrows and hopes of the rakı table utterly relate to the emotional/political experiences of post-Gezi migration from Turkey that oscillate between feelings of loss and a sense of future possibilities and impossibilities amid uncertainty and uprootedness. Despite the preoccupation of both scholarly and popular debates with the loss of a sense of belonging that results from migrating, migration is often preceded by loss that brings about the desire, need or impulse to leave, as in the case of post-Gezi migration from Turkey. One of the profound everyday experiences of the political oppression that has escalated in the years that followed the 2013 Gezi movement has been the sense of loss, caused by restrictions on and transformation of public spaces, the suppression of civic engagements, distrust of institutions and people, or simply the shutting down of a place, cultural event or website, not to mention the growing number of people who are leaving the country. In her essay 'I am here, simply standing', published on Kopuntu,[7] Sine Ergün (2017) describes the emotional/political atmosphere in Turkey as follows:

> The year 2017. Turkey. People constantly feel the impulse to leave or the obligation to do so. We are gathered around tables, making final decisions, and then 'But …', 'How …', 'Let's wait', 'What if it gets better?' I can't remember how many times we travelled the world, while sitting at how many rakı tables … Then, I watched my

> beloved ones leaving or being imprisoned, one after another. We carry on an insipid life with the ones who stayed. (My translation)

Various media spaces, artistic and literary works, and public events created by people who have recently left Turkey, express, circulate and archive the lived and felt experiences of migration, thereby creating an affective cultural sphere. Mostly, the first-person narratives of the intertwined experiences of political oppression, displacement and relocation unfold across journalistic interviews, essays, social media posts, talks, panels, exhibitions, film screenings, videos, photos and artistic performances. A striking example is the video series, titled 'Welcomed to Germany?' (2018), made by the video artist Özlem Sarıyıldız, who had herself migrated to Berlin in 2017. The video series brings together nine persons who had moved from Istanbul to Berlin in the previous five years, who all appear and talk at once in a single rectangular frame and talk about their own experiences, feelings and dreams, along with the others, while their voices and stories blend together. 'I realised that more and more of our spaces have closed down in Turkey,' says one participant, and another says, 'After a point, such a situation spits you out, annihilates you, wants you to leave.'

Proliferating narratives of post-Gezi migration from Turkey across various texts, spaces and performances manifest the profound need to tell 'what we have been through'. The act of recounting experiences of difficult times relieves traumas but also gains a political value and significance through its capacity to create a public memory. A research participant who has been writing a novel based on his experience of displacement suggests that telling these stories serves a political purpose: 'We should tell, share and put together our stories through any available means. What we have been going through should be visible and intelligible. It should be a history. Otherwise, if Turkey initiates another forced migration in the next twenty years, we all will be responsible for it.'

The emotional and political need to tell of experiences of displacement and relocation is at the heart of the value and the significance of establishing and sitting at rakı tables in Berlin. At many sorrowful and hopeful rakı tables I joined, we talked over and over again about our losses, angers, anxieties, disappointments and hopes, which take on a political character. As well as providing a sense of belonging within the experience of uprootedness, through its familiar sensory, aesthetic, emotional, social and political experience, the rakı table promises heartfelt, intimate and honest conversations. In other words, through the experience of post-Gezi migration from Turkey, the anticipation and experience of the rakı table as an intimate and affectionate atmosphere are redirected towards the emotional and political need to recount experiences of political oppression, displacement and relocation.

The act of telling a story with a rakı glass in hand has been turned into an artistic performance by the performance artist Candaş Baş, who migrated from Istanbul to Berlin in 2018. Titled 'Trautes Heim Glück Allein' (Home sweet home), the performance was premiered at the festival '#disPlaced – #rePlaced 2: Creating spaces and reflections between Berlin & Istanbul' in Berlin in April 2019. The performance is composed of episodes of conversation and contemporary dance, both performed with a rakı glass in hand (Figure 7.2). The artist's description of her performance is as follows:

> A picnic ... a date ... a date with a person she already has memories with ... a date with a total stranger ... maybe a blind date ...
> She listens to Turkish music and tells the story of her homeland through songs, through a conversation over Rakı.
> Rakı opens her heart ...
> She came here a while ago ...
> Rakı talks ...
> Her body talks ...
>
> (Baş 2019)

7.2 The performance 'Trautes Heim Glück Allein' by Candaş Baş. Radialsystem, Berlin, 12 April 2019. Courtesy of Candaş Baş.

Candaş Baş stepped onto the stage with shopping bags in her hands, walked towards a corner, spread a cover on the ground, and sat down. She calmly started setting a rakı 'table' on the stage, took a bottle of rakı and meze dishes from the bags and placed them on the cover. The moment she poured rakı into her glass, she started talking to an imaginary person accompanying her. She talked about the culture and rituals of the rakı table, explained the proper ways of drinking rakı, accompanied a song by the famous arabesque musician Orhan Gencebay, and told several stories and anecdotes about the rakı table. She had several phone conversations with her mother and talked about her troubles and struggles in Berlin, concluding with 'Don't worry mother, I am fine'. Several episodes of conversation and contemporary dance followed each other throughout the performance. When leaving the rakı 'table' towards the centre of the stage to dance, the artist took the glass with her and never dropped it. During the dance, the rakı glass and her bodily movements followed each other on a dark, empty stage. During our interview, Candaş Baş explained the place of the rakı glass in her performance:

> The glass was my entire connection with Turkey. I carried it on the top of my head; it became part of my hand. I could not break ties with it. The glass was the story of my past, my rituals, everything I brought with me. But I told my story in an empty space, in limbo, to someone who doesn't understand rakı culture at all, who doesn't even exist. I imagined the glass as my close friends, the ones that I had drunk rakı with, the ones that I had drunk rakı for, the ones that I lost. The glass represents my deep connections.

Candaş Baş describes her performance as 'a story of loneliness' that emerged from her 'profound need to tell'. Although she has met with many new people from many countries in Berlin, she does not have friends 'close enough to drink rakı with' or who 'know how to drink rakı and share a rakı table conversation'. Agreeing with the popular saying 'One does not sit at a rakı table with just anybody', she says:

> The rakı table is an important part of our culture of intimacy. That table is shared with very close friends, not with someone you have just met. Rakı, the çilingir, opens heart and tongue so much that at some point it discloses even things that you have hidden from yourself. A lot happened at those tables, I heard many stories. And we saved Turkey so many times. It has always been a political table;

sitting at that table has been a political stance itself. I have been missing all of it so much.

Candaş Baş's performance stages her personal experience of migrating by drawing on the anticipation and experience of the rakı table as the locus of intimate, honest and affectionate conversations. I am not able to comment on how the audience who are not familiar with the rakı table perceived the performance – which is worthy of further research – but the moment I saw the rakı bottle and the glass on the stage I expected to witness one of many emotional/political stories of our migration. The intertwining of the emotional and the political that completely describes the rakı table atmosphere is central to the affective experience of post-Gezi migration from Turkey, which is characterised by profound feelings that flow from the lived experience of politics and (re)shape political horizons. Therefore, the rakı table perfectly serves as a material and immaterial medium for the emotional and political need to recount felt experiences of political oppression, displacement and relocation.

Sitting together at the rakı table

The rakı table atmosphere interweaves the emotional and the political not only by inviting conversations that relate to both, but also, and more importantly, by suggesting ways of interacting intimately with others and dealing passionately with the world. Therefore, despite my knowing that a rakı table is conventionally or ideally shared by close friends, seeing public events organised in the form of rakı tables for the first time in Berlin has not been very surprising to me. As I will discuss here in connection with the two specific events that took place in Berlin, Çilingir Sofrası and Rakı Prinzip – Intersection Sessions, orchestration of the politically motivated public rakı tables rests upon the potentialities of an intimate and affectionate atmosphere for opening up dialogue and creating affinities among people who have not previously known each other personally.

Çilingir Sofrası was organised by Poşe, under 'Project Space Festival Berlin 2019: When the hunger starts', and took place in Hallo Machen, a rakı restaurant founded by a couple who had recently left Turkey (Figure 7.3).

Established by an artist and a film producer in Istanbul in 2018 amid the political and economic crises that have significantly restricted spaces for artistic and creative communities, Poşe serves as 'an open space for those who feel the need for dialogue and critique'.[8] A co-founder of Poşe,

7.3 Çilingir Sofrası, Hallo Machen, Berlin, 10 June 2019. https://www.pose-hello.com/cilingirsofrasi, public domain.

Larissa Araz, said in our interview that when they received an invitation from the Project Space Festival to organise a one-day event in Berlin, they wanted to address the experiences of artists who had recently left Turkey and relocated to Berlin. As they knew about the struggles of their friends and colleagues who had recently migrated, they aimed to facilitate conversations on 'why and how these artists decided to move and how this affected their practices'. The event started with inputs from three invited artists, Onur Ciritoğlu, Ece Gökalp and Ceren Saner, all of whom had recently moved from Istanbul to Berlin, and proceeded with open-ended conversations about experiences of new migration from Turkey. Larissa Araz said, 'Yes, we know that many people left Turkey. But if we do not talk about why it happened and what its consequences would be, and do not share our emotions about this migration, what, then, is the point?'

Çilingir Sofrası was organised around rakı tables, since, Larissa Araz tells me, 'these issues – disappointments after migrating, the difficult questioning of the migration decision, and the mixed emotions of joy and fear – could be discussed only at a rakı table'. This is because, she continues, 'after the second glass of rakı, something opens up with the key and you are just there with all of your good and bad'. The honesty of rakı table conversations is emphasised, and promised also by the event description of Çilingir Sofrası:

> Rakı can be seen as the master key for deep, insightful, long-lasting and honest conversations. One has to be prepared emotionally and physically to sit at a 'Çilingir Sofrası'; because, firstly, rakı is a strong drink and, secondly, once you start sipping your rakı, you will have no lies to tell.

Premised on the potential of the rakı table to open hearts and loosen tongues, Çilingir Sofrası attempts to orchestrate a public rakı table that can enable the addressing of difficult questions about difficult times through genuine conversations. It reimagines and reconstitutes the intimate and affectionate rakı table, which is conventionally shared by close friends, as a source for opening up public dialogue and affinity. Speaking about today's rakı tables in Turkey, Larissa Araz states that the collective feel of the rakı table is political in the sense that it allows coming together and facilitates conversation:

> Nowadays, just the ability to talk with each other is a form of resistance. Telling what we are going through and sharing it with someone else means leaving a mark in history. Amid the strong, ongoing depression in Turkey, there is a constant thirst for rakı tables due to our wish for coming together, sharing troubles and grief, and at least communally resigning ourselves to what we cannot change.

The emotional/political togetherness of a rakı table has been the evident goal of Rakı Prinzip – Intersection Sessions, which took place at bi'bak[9] in Berlin between 2017 and 2018 (Figure 7.4). Rakı Prinzip was founded in 2016 by Ariana Dongus, Freia Kuper, Yalın Özer and Elisa Pieper in order to create 'a "Counter-Stammtisch" in response to the rising visibility of right-wing positions in public'.[10] Aiming 'to push forward a collective discussion-culture' by 'bringing together various foreigners on one table for an evening', Rakı Prinzip sets up rakı tables at various places in Berlin. Focused on particular topics decided beforehand, including 'love', 'hate' and 'anger', these rakı tables invited people who wanted to join through an open call on Facebook, as well as inviting several people whose works relate to the topic to give short inputs. During our interview, Ariana Dongus described these events as 'the travelling table'.

When it moved to bi'bak under the name Intersection Sessions, the table of Rakı Prinzip was oriented towards the goal of building a network among people who work in the fields of art and culture. In a similar fashion to the previous events, each of the four sessions focused on a particular discussion topic – the public–private relationship, archives,

7.4 Rakı Prinzip – Intersection Sessions, bi'bak, Berlin, 14 June 2019. © Felix Kayser.

film-making and narratives of the future – and invited several people to give short inputs. The open call for participation addressed people who had recently moved to Berlin, especially those who 'had to escape armed conflict, political repression and prosecution'. The event description of Rakı Prinzip – Intersection Sessions states:

> The events brought together artists, cultural creators and other creative minds at a shared table, combining the intimate experience of a dinner with an informal discussion in a semi-public, semi-private setting ... The Rakı Prinzip is based on the vision of a vivid dinner culture that connects all kinds of different people together at a table.
>
> (bi'bak n.d.)

As well as migrants and refugees coming from various places to Berlin, many people who had recently left Turkey participated in Intersection Sessions, since they show a great interest in the events of bi'bak and perhaps also because of their attraction to the rakı table. Elisa Pieper explained in our interview that Rakı Prinzip was inspired by the ability of the rakı table to create intimacy and facilitate discussions in familiar terms:

> When I stayed in Turkey for a while, I experienced rakı tables with friends. It was the first time that I had experienced such a fusion of political and private discussions at the same table. I did not know about such a thing from my upbringing: sitting all together at a table on a street for hours, eating, drinking and discussing. I mean really discussing, but with a softness. Sharing the food and the conversation at that table creates intimacy. Experiencing this wonderful situation inspired us to create such a table.

As our conversation went on with how they experienced the sessions as organisers and moderators, I could not resist asking: 'But did it really feel like a rakı table?' Ariana Dongus replied that 'it was a major experience to take home'. Both Elisa Pieper and Ariana Dongus tell that participants in Intersection Sessions, around 30 to 40 people, not only engaged in small talk with each other, but also honestly engaged with the topics of discussion. Furthermore, by exchanging email addresses and phone numbers, participants kept in touch with each other after the sessions. Sitting at the table together for four hours, they explain, drinking rakı and sharing food, led to friendships, networking and even dates. Ariana Dongus describes the intimate atmosphere that evolved during Intersection Sessions as 'magic'. Elisa Pieper adds that the magic arose from sharing the food, which started an exchange among participants, blended intellectual and sensuous experiences, and created a relaxed atmosphere.

Both Çilingir Sofrası and Rakı Prinzip – Intersection Sessions stage politically motivated public rakı tables to open up encounters and conviviality among strangers, by bringing them together on the basis of shared experiences, interests and concerns such as engagement in artistic and creative endeavours and experiences of political oppression and migration. As Bille et al. (2015, 36) suggest, staged atmospheres are 'oriented toward ideals of how a place, event or practice should or could feel'. Atmospheres can be staged by orchestrating spaces, people and objects in particular ways to shape intended experiences, moods and emotions. However, they are open to ambivalence and contestation, as there is always uncertainty about the extent to which the participants feel and comply with the deliberately orchestrated atmosphere (Bille et al. 2015). Partly depending on expectations based on previous encounters with the situation and the participants' degree of familiarity with it, affective experiences of atmospheres are cultural and historical, rather than precognitive (Edensor 2012). However, Riedel (2019) argues that an affective atmosphere is so palpable that even 'those who are repelled by it or remain unaffected by it may nevertheless recognize the way in which a situation coheres in a distributed feeling, or sense its grip as a modulating force' (Riedel 2019, 92).

Regardless of whether it can be shared by all participants, the collective and palpable feeling of intimacy that is expected from a rakı table is what the public rakı tables orchestrated in Berlin seek to create. One of the few non-Turkish-speaking guests who attended 'Çilingir Sofrası', Nino Klingler (2019), points out the intimate atmosphere in his review of the event but also notes his disappointment with the conversations that turned out to be self-narratives rather than critical public discussions. He writes:

> Maybe it's the heat, maybe it's the drinks, but the stories start blending into each other. The ghosts of Turkey's recent past are conjured. ... This evening is not about information, it's about ritual. The intimacy, the confessional tone, like an AA meeting for the Turkey-addicted. 'My name is X and my story is ...' ... [T]here is a mild exhaustion in the room, a kind of collective daze enwrapping us, blunting the thoughts and suspending critical reflection. Twice something like a controversy emerges: Is the migrant artist doomed to be successful? Is Germany racist beyond redemption? ... But twice, no real discussion begins. Mildly frustrating, wasted potential.

Bille et al. (2015, 36–7) argue that 'simulations of atmospheres are not straightforwardly instrumental, and ... they do ... not simply reach an *end*, but unfold as a continuous process of reaching the *intensity* that the character of [a] play, an exhibition, a concert, a riot, a room, a ritual or a speech may seek to achieve'. Even though intimate and affectionate rakı table conversations might not evolve into more obviously public and political discussions with more or less envisioned outcomes, public rakı tables in Berlin pertain to potentialities for creating and sustaining affinities that can be brought by manifested, circulated and networked emotional/political experiences. They appropriate and relocate the rakı table atmosphere to create an 'intimate public' which 'flourishes as a porous, affective scene of identification among strangers that promises a certain experience of belonging' (Berlant 2008, viii).

As Gopinath (2010) suggests, affective texts, performances and spaces can open a doorway to momentary and enduring affinities, relationalities and intersections among diverse people, events and histories. Thus, feelings and emotions, including 'negative' ones, gain public and political significance in their potentiality to bring about new and alternative forms of publicness, collectivity and activism (Cvetkovich 2003; Gould 2009). Elsewhere (Savaş 2019), I discuss how digital media spaces of new migrants from Turkey that communicate, circulate and archive feelings serve as an affective political source for imagining and creating affinities and collectivities. In particular, Kopuntu, a digital media space and collective, is deliberately focused on affective experiences of post-Gezi migration, such as suffocation, uprootedness and expulsion, to create solidarity and affinity not only among people who have recently left Turkey, but also among diverse individuals and groups who might share similar political feelings, whether they flow from the experiences of authoritarianism, nationalism, patriarchy or capitalism. By staging an intimate and affectionate atmosphere that can potentially disclose and circulate similar emotional/political experiences, the public rakı tables orchestrated in Berlin invite the building of 'political friendships' (Arendt 1968), which are not confined to private spheres but unfold 'through political concern for the world that lies between people' (Canovan 1988, quoted in Mallory 2012, 25). Yet their potential to attract wider publics is limited not only by ambiguity in perceptions of staged atmospheres, but also by essentialising cultural policies and industries that confine creative endeavours by migrants to a sphere of 'migrant' art and culture (Kosnick 2016), in ways similar to those of scholarly studies that contain complex socialities, affinities, emotions and material cultures in supposed ethnic, migrant or diasporic communities.

In this chapter, I have attempted to explore the affective value and significance of rakı table conversations that are lost and refound within the experience of post-Gezi migration from Turkey. The rakı tables of people who have recently left Turkey are neither performances of some kind of ethnic, national or 'migrant' identity nor embodiments of nostalgia, which has been almost stereotypically associated with the migration experience. Rather, I argue, relocating the rakı table to Berlin as a material and immaterial medium pertains to the emotional/political need, desire and goal of exchanging experiences of difficult times and creating affinities with others through intimacy. The rakı table atmosphere shows a glimpse of the hoped-for possibility of intimacy and affinity amid lived and felt experiences of political oppression, migration and relocation. This potentiality can be realised as long as migration is regarded not as a bounded and exclusive category, but as a powerful affective political experience that can generate affinities and collaborations among diverse people on the basis of collective feelings such as loss and uncertainty, possibly transcending particular identities, places and histories as well as the migrant/non-migrant divide.

Notes

1 A particular case is that of the flight of academics who are signatories to the 11 January 2016 petition, 'We will not be a party to this crime!', publicly known as the Academics for Peace Petition. Signatory academics have been facing dismissal from their university posts, as well as trials, detention and imprisonment. For further information and opportunities for solidarity, see https://barisicinakademisyenler.net/ (accessed 21 August 2021).

2 Following the bilateral guest worker recruitment agreement in 1961 and authorisation of family unification in 1964, large numbers of people migrated from Turkey to West Germany. The political turmoil of the late 1970s that escalated with the 1980 military coup and the Kurdish conflict in the 1990s prompted political refugees and asylum seekers to leave Turkey, many arriving in Germany. The escalation of political oppression and turmoil, especially after the 2013 Gezi movement, initiated a new phase of migration, which has been described as Turkey's 'brain drain' (Lowen 2017) and 'loss of intellectual elite' (Bewarder and Drüten 2019) because of the high education levels and more urban origins (mostly Istanbul and Ankara) of these migrants.

3 As Evered and Evered (2016) discuss in great detail, the Anatolian history of alcohol production and consumption includes various examples of regulatory and prohibitory discourses and initiatives. Although grounded in public health discourses, the return of the regulatory initiatives by the AKP-led state, such as an increase in taxation and restriction of advertising, has been connected to social and political tensions, thereby reifying the secular–Islamic opposition (Evered and Evered 2016). Following Erdoğan's proclamation, 'Our national drink is ayran' (a yoghurt-based non-alcoholic beverage), at the Global Alcohol Policy Symposium organised by Green Crescent Turkey and the WHO in 2013, the public controversy fashioned the rakı table as the embodiment of opposition to and resistance to the government. For example, the ordinary self-presentation photos of rakı tables posted on social media have started to be captioned 'Our national drink is rakı'.

4 For example, Zat (2012) suggests that the tablecloth, napkins and plates should ideally be white in order to be in harmony with the milky-white colour of rakı when mixed with water.

5 An advertisement by Yeni Rakı, the leading rakı producer, represents diverse spaces and socialities for drinking rakı across a number of regions of Turkey: https://www.youtube.com/watch?v=l2Q2TL3lZLo (accessed 21 August 2021).

6 This group was closed in October 2020 and a new group with the same character has been opened under the name New Wave Berlin.

7 A digital media space and collective founded by individuals who have recently left Turkey (https://kopuntu.org/, accessed 21 August 2021).

8 https://www.pose-hello.com/ (accessed 21 August 2021).

9 Founded in 2014 as a non-profit organisation, 'bi'bak (Turkish: have a look) is a project space based in Berlin, with a focus on transnational narratives, migration, global mobility and their aesthetic dimensions' (https://bi-bak.de/about-us, accessed 20 September 2021).

10 https://www.facebook.com/rakiprinzip (accessed 21 August 2021).

References

Abels, Birgit. 2019. 'A poetics of dwelling with music and dance: *Le hip hop* as homing practice', *World of Music* 8(1): 49–64.

Ahmed, Sara. 2014. *The Cultural Politics of Emotion*, 2nd edition. Edinburgh: Edinburgh University Press.

Arendt, Hannah. 1968. *Men in Dark Times*. New York: Harcourt Brace.

Baş, Candaş. 2019. 'Trautes Heim Gluck Allein, premiered in Radialsystem DE 2019' (video description). Vimeo. Accessed 8 February 2021. https://vimeo.com/332816253.

Belge, Murat. 2012. 'Preface'. In *Rakı: The spirit of Turkey*, 9–11. Istanbul: Overteam.

Berlant, Lauren. 2008. *The Female Complaint: The unfinished business of sentimentality in American culture*. Durham, NC: Duke University Press.

Bewarder, Manuel and Carolina Drüten. 2019. 'Die Türkei verliert ihre intellektuelle Elite'. *WELT*, 7 February. Accessed 20 August 2021. https://www.welt.de/politik/ausland/plus188358129/migration-die-tuerkei-vergrault-ihre-intellektuelle-elite.html?wtrid=onsite.onsitesearch.

bi'bak. n.d. 'Raki Prinzip. Intersection Sessions'. Accessed 21 August 2021. https://bi-bak.de/de/archive/bi-baxchange/raki-prinzip/intersection-sessions-01.
Bille, Mikkel, Peter Bjerregaard and Tim Flohr Sørensen. 2015. 'Staging atmospheres: Materiality, culture, and the texture of the in-between', *Emotion, Space and Society* 15: 31–8. https://doi.org/10.1016/j.emospa.2014.11.002.
Böhme, Gernot. 1993. 'Atmosphere as the fundamental concept of a new aesthetics', *Thesis Eleven* 36(1): 113–26.
Canovan, Margaret. 1988. 'Friendship, truth, and politics: Hannah Arendt and toleration'. In *Justifying Toleration: Conceptual and historical perspectives*, edited by Susan Mendus, 177–98. Cambridge: Cambridge University Press.
Cvetkovich, Ann. 2012. *Depression: A public feeling*. Durham, NC: Duke University Press.
Edensor, Tim. 2012. 'Illuminated atmospheres: Anticipating and reproducing the flow of affective experience in Blackpool', *Environment and Planning D: Society and Space* 30(6): 1103–22. https://doi.org/10.1068%2Fd12211.
Ergün, Sine. 2017. 'Buradayım, öylece duruyorum' [I am here, simply standing]. *Kopuntu*, 2 June. Accessed 21 August 2021. https://kopuntu.org/2017/06/02 buradayim-oylece-duruyorum-sine-ergun/.
Evered, Emine Ö. and Kyle T. Evered. 2016. 'From *rakı* to *ayran*: Regulating the place and practice of drinking in Turkey', *Space and Polity* 20(1): 39–58. https://doi.org/10.1080/13562576.2015.1057003.
Gopinath, Gayatri. 2010. 'Archive, affect, and the everyday: Queer diasporic re-visions'. In *Political Emotions: New agendas in communication*, edited by Janet Staiger, Ann Cvetkovich and Ann Reynolds, 165–92. New York and Abingdon: Routledge.
Gould, Deborah B. 2009. *Moving Politics: Emotion and ACT UP's fight against AIDS*. Chicago: University of Chicago Press.
Kesmez, Melisa and Mehmet S. Aydın. 2014. *Rakı Cep Kitabı*. Istanbul: Overteam.
Klingler, Nino. 2019. 'Çilingir Sofrası'. Project Space Festival Berlin 2019. Accessed 21 August 2021. http://2019.projectspacefestival-berlin.com/en/cilingirsofrasi/?fbclid=iwar35sktndntoyabspzccub5ecewtzzf2lldw36_hatqpmcxp0sfgde6gype.
Kosnick, Kira. 2016. 'Cosmopolitan capital or multicultural community? Reflections on the production and management of differential mobilities in Germany's capital city'. In *Cosmopolitanism in Practice*, edited by Magdalena Nowicka and Maria Rovisco, 161–80. Abingdon: Routledge.
Lowen, Mark. 2017. 'Turkey brain drain: Crackdown pushes intellectuals out'. *BBC News*, 28 December. Accessed 21 August 2021. https://www.bbc.co.uk/news/world-europe-42433668.
Mallory, Peter. 2012. 'Political friendship in the era of "the social": Theorizing personal relations with Alexis de Tocqueville', *Journal of Classical Sociology* 12(1): 22–42. https://doi.org/10.1177%2F1468795X11433705.
Riedel, Friedlind. 2019. 'Atmosphere'. In *Affective Societies: Key concepts*, edited by Jan Slaby and Christian von Scheve, 85–95. Abingdon: Routledge.
Savaş, Özlem. 2019. 'Affective digital media of new migration from Turkey: Feelings, affinities, and politics', *International Journal of Communication* 13: 5405–26.
Skrbiš, Zlatko. 2008. 'Transnational families: Theorising migration, emotions and belonging', *Journal of Intercultural Studies* 29(3): 231–46. https://doi.org/10.1080/07256860802169188.
Staiger, Janet, Ann Cvetkovich and Ann Reynolds, eds. 2010. *Political Emotions: New agendas in communication*. New York and Abingdon: Routledge.
Stewart, Kathleen. 2007. *Ordinary Affects*. Durham, NC: Duke University Press.
Svašek, Maruška. 2008. 'Who cares? Families and feelings in movement', *Journal of Intercultural Studies* 29(3): 213–30. https://doi.org/10.1080/07256860802169170.
Zat, Erdir. 2012. *Rakı: The spirit of Turkey*. Istanbul: Overteam.
Zat, Erdir. 2014. *Rakı: Modern and unconventional*. Translated by Bob Beer. Istanbul: Overteam.

8

Cooking 'pocket money': how young unaccompanied refugees create a sense of community and familiarity at a Danish asylum centre

Andrea Verdasco

Introduction

> The room is filled with noise, with a mixture of languages making the soundscape. It is Thursday afternoon and, like every other Thursday, it is 'pocket money day' at Birkelunde asylum centre. A group of young Kurdish boys are loudly singing while an Eritrean group of girls and boys, who are sitting close by, are quietly looking down at their mobile phones. A group of Afghan girls have also separated themselves from the noise, and are sitting in the next room chatting. Meanwhile, the Red Cross staff are setting up the desks so that the young refugees may, in an orderly fashion, come and pick up their envelopes containing the pocket money. When the desks are set up, and the envelopes are ready to be handed out, organised alphabetically in different cardboard boxes, the young refugees start lining up.

This opening vignette describes an event that happened every other week in the same space, the ground floor of the refugee-only school a few hundred metres from the asylum centre for unaccompanied minors located in a rural town in Denmark. On this day, the young refugees[1] were handed their pocket money, that is, a small allowance granted by the

Danish government to asylum seekers to allow their basic needs to be covered. Different material objects carry deep significance for migrants and refugees both in their journeys, and later when they settle in a new country. For instance, many of the young refugees would always carry with them mobile phones storing important information and pictures of their loved ones. They would use them to communicate with their kin and networks through different applications, mostly Facebook and WhatsApp. Others, who did not own a phone, would carry a piece of paper on which they had scribbled a phone number they needed to call once they were safe somewhere in Europe. In spite of the places and spaces they went through in their perilous journeys to arrive in Denmark, this phone or piece of paper was the one thing they would never let go of. In this chapter, however, I will engage with a different kind of material object, one that initially is void of sentiment but when transformed acquires deep significance. I will examine how young refugees transform the materiality of the pocket money – in the shape of coins and banknotes – into food that allows them to create and negotiate a sense of continuity and normality, and to construct social relations. I argue that when they transform the money into food they are able to have a fleeting sense of normality, which gives them some continuity while they construct social relations.

On the basis of 12 months of ethnographic fieldwork among young unaccompanied asylum-seeking minors and refugees who were close to coming of age, and whose age was challenged by the state, I will use the pocket money as the ethnographic point of departure. I will follow the pocket money as it goes from the envelope and through the grocery stores, and is then transformed into cooked food. Thus, unlike the objects filled with meaning and sentiment that much of the literature engages with (see for example Povrzanović Frykman and Humbracht 2013; Sutton 2001), the 'pocket money' as an object is void of sentimental meaning, yet when transformed provides the opportunity to occupy spaces and places, and to construct meaningful forms of relatedness and a fleeting sense of normality.

In the context of migration studies the link between food and migration has been examined and has shown how essential food is to the migrant's experiences (see for example Tuomainen 2009; Lewis 2010; Sabar and Posner 2013; Abbots 2013). Food plays a significant role in the lives of migrants and refugees and can create a sense of belonging (Abbots 2016). Analytically, this chapter contributes to the body of literature on the anthropology of food and migration in the context of forced migration. Moreover, I will explore how the money is transformed into the materiality of food, enabling agency. Thus, I also seek to contribute to the literature that focuses on the socialities in refugeehood and youth agency.

I will first present an overview of the socio-political situation that framed the lives of my interlocutors at the time of my fieldwork in Denmark during the so-called 'refugee crisis' of 2015 and 2016. Next, I will provide an overview of the methodology used and how it intertwined with the materiality of doing research. Later, I will briefly present the literature on food and forced migration. I will then follow the pocket money to explore how young refugees transform this 'debt' into a sense of fleeting normality and homeliness through their agency and are able to experience a sense of normality and familiarity, and construct meaningful social relations.[2]

The context of a 'refugee crisis'

2015 was the year the so-called 'refugee crisis' peaked in terms of the numbers of refugees entering Europe.[3] In the midst of the political and media attention, with the endless images of people reaching the shores of Europe or crowding against the fences being erected across, mainly, eastern Europe, more than 95,000 unaccompanied asylum-seeking minors (UAMs) arrived in the European Union (EU) (EUROSTAT 2020). Until then, the EU received every year an average of 12,000 asylum applications from unaccompanied minors (EUROSTAT 2016). Of the estimated 95,000 UAMs a total of 2,144 sought asylum in Denmark. The Danish immigration authorities considered this a 'sharp increase' (Immigration Services 2017, 17) given the threefold increase with respect to the previous year. Not only in Denmark, but across Europe, unaccompanied minors became the fastest-growing category of refugees seeking asylum.

This 'sharp increase', as the Danish authorities considered it, had started back in 2009 when a larger than expected number of unaccompanied minors arrived from Afghanistan. This led the government to drastically change the conditions for minors coming of age. Whereas, formerly, unaccompanied minors would continue to be given special protection upon turning 18 years old by being granted extensions to their residence permits until a 'durable solution' could be found, from 2011 the legislation changed, and unaccompanied minors whose cases have been rejected must leave Denmark immediately upon turning 18 (see Lemberg-Pedersen 2015). Moreover, age assessments became common practice for older minors who claimed to be between 14 and 17 years. This discourse of mistrust regarding the ages of young refugees and their asylum claims meant that the discourse of care and protection had been overridden by discourses of criminalisation (see Vitus and Lidén 2010).

In Denmark, all asylum seekers, with very few exceptions, must live in an asylum centre for the duration of the asylum process. For many young refugees, their stay at an asylum centre was their first experience of everyday life within an institution. The majority of these centres are run by the Red Cross, although there has been a rapid increase in those managed by the different municipalities (see for example Whyte et al. 2019). In Scandinavian welfare societies the raising of children is highly institutionalised (Gilliam and Gulløv 2017), and many of the traits of this institutionalised system, which focuses on the individual, could also be found in the Danish asylum system for unaccompanied minors. At the centre each asylum seeker had an individual fridge and locker to keep their food in, and a lock for each. The staff at the centre and the teachers in the school would teach the young asylum seekers 'proper' social norms and values through everyday encounters. The young refugees were instructed in how to clean their rooms, take care of their hygiene, clean kitchen utensils and pronounce Danish words. Initially, there was considerable mistrust towards many of the Red Cross staff and teachers, which, over time, and through different activities including cooking together and, at times, sharing food was sometimes transformed into trust.

During the months of waiting at the residential centre, the young asylum seekers had a set routine associated with the centre's regime of protection. They were followed closely by a social protection system that included their Red Cross contact person and, when necessary, a nurse, a doctor or the centre's social coordinator. This was mostly a period of waiting, during which feeling stuck, and that time was not progressing (see Vitus 2010), was very common.

In 2016, there were 48 asylum centres in Denmark, of which nine were for unaccompanied minors. In this chapter, I focus on asylum seekers who lived at Birkelunde asylum centre, the largest Red Cross-run centre for unaccompanied minors, which, like most centres in Denmark, was located in a rural area (Whyte et al. 2019). In accordance with the policies of isolation that govern the Danish asylum and refugee systems it was largely detached from the wider society (see for example Larsen 2011). This is different to other European countries, Sweden for instance, where unaccompanied minors are placed from the outset in youth homes rather than asylum centres, where they are exposed to interaction with Swedes and attend mainstream schools (see Kaukko and Wernesjö 2017). Furthermore, the limited allowance the young asylum seekers received in the form of pocket money meant they could not afford mobility to other places. They therefore spent most of their time at school and the asylum centre, and participated in activities with a strong local nature.

The name given by the Danish authorities to this allowance – *lommepenge* – in its emic form literally means 'pocket money', and is to be used for short-term purposes, to get the asylum seekers by on a daily basis, while they wait for their individual case to be decided.[4] It is thus not meant to be used for savings or long-term projects. For the most part, the money covers the basic needs of food and at times clothes. However, there were some exceptions. Afwerki, one of the more disciplined Eritrean boys, managed to save part of his pocket money every month to buy a smartphone. This was something strongly praised by the Red Cross staff, who would keep reminding him how positive it was that he had saved to buy an individual good with the materiality of money. Thus, in terms of purchasing practices the pocket money was mainly used for food, an immediate need, and exceptionally to invest in a smartphone, which meant access to globalisation and globalised dispersed social relations.

Methodology

This chapter is based on 12 months of ethnographic fieldwork conducted between January 2015 and September 2016 in different locations in Denmark (see Verdasco 2018). My interlocutors entered the Danish asylum system classified as 'unaccompanied asylum-seeking minors', but they were on the boundaries of this legal category. Agewise some were close to turning 18, while the status of others was uncertain, as their ages were contested, and yet others were no longer minors, having become adults after several years in Denmark. In addition to the age-ascribed categories, they found themselves in different asylum-ascribed categories: some were waiting for their asylum outcomes as 'asylum seekers', others had had their cases rejected and were awaiting deportation, and yet others had been granted refugee status. I did not focus on one nationality or ethnicity; they were a heterogeneous group of young refugees from Syria, Afghanistan, Eritrea, Iraq, Iran, Somalia, Sri Lanka and Morocco. As I followed the life trajectories of my interlocutors, I incorporated new places in accordance with their mobility, adopting a 'processual approach to fieldwork' (Hastrup and Olwig 1997, 8). Despite the array of localities, rather than thinking of them as separate sites, I consider my field as one site. In my study, this geographical space was configured both by the social relations constructed by the refugees and by the asylum and refugee laws and policies that restricted their mobility. My field site expanded and contracted depending on the changing legal statuses of my interlocutors and related Danish asylum and refugee policies.

When one is doing research with young people, a position of authority as a researcher may divide one from them (Fine and Sandstrom 1988). Thus, as far as possible, I downplayed my position of authority and instead stressed what we had in common. Despite our gender and age differences, with me a woman in her thirties working with young people, many of whom were boys, through our interactions I realised that our main point of connection was that I too was a foreigner new to Denmark and like them struggling with the language, the food and the weather. As a result, I would often bring this up, and we would compare Denmark with our own traditions. I also used the materiality of clothes to downplay my age by wearing jeans, large jumpers and trainers. When food was served, I would always eat what they ate with them, and in class I would sit with them and engage in the activity the teacher was asking the students to do. For the most part interactions took place in English; however, as my fieldwork progressed, and my Danish improved, I used Danish to communicate with my interlocutors, as was the case with Yonas, whom I will introduce later.

Informed consent and the ethical principle of 'doing no harm' guided this research. In order to obtain consent from unaccompanied minors living at the Red Cross asylum centres I went through a background criminal check by the Danish police, a routine procedure for anyone working with minors in Denmark. I then introduced my project to the staff, who gave their informed consent, and later, and more importantly, so did the young refugees who were at the core of my research. I introduced myself and the research project multiple times as new asylum seekers arrived every week. However, consent is not something you gain once and for all; it was more of an ongoing and dynamic process (see Fluehr-Lobban 1998) in which, after an initial interaction, some of the young refugees decided they did not want to be a part of the research, while others, the interlocutors in this chapter, became full participants in the research.

The anthropology of food and forced migration

Food plays a critical role in refugees' everyday lives. Preparing and consuming food and feeding others are some of the most immediate and pressing concerns migrants face. Abbots (2012; 2016), who has studied how food affects migrant subjectivities in the Ecuadorian Andes and transnationally, explains that the processes of buying, cooking and eating food can provide security, empowerment and affiliation with others. Sharing meals or cooking together may facilitate the construction of group identities by way of creating social ties. However, foodways can also be a site of difference, marginalisation and uncertainty (Abbots 2016, 128) that may foster exclusion when others in the host country do not share the same tastes (see Bonfanti et al. 2019). Therefore, food can create community and cohesion as much as it can reveal political divisions and economic inequities. Food plays a significant role in 'anchoring' a migrant, while enabling the creation of new subjectivities and orientations (Abbots 2016).

Although it has been well established that food plays a critical role in the migrant's experiences, with a wealth of studies on the roles of food and identity (Ray 2004; Farquhar 2006; Frost 2008; Vallianatos and Raine 2008; Abbots 2012; Mata-Codesal and Abranches 2017), studies on food in the context of forced migration are scarce, and tend to focus on issues related to food security (Sabar and Posner 2013). There are, however, some notable exceptions. For example, Sabar and Posner (2013), who examined the foodways and culinary experiences of Sudanese and Eritrean asylum seekers living in Israel, argue that food and eating at their restaurants provided asylum seekers with a sense of familiarity, security, empowerment and certainty. They stress the critical importance of familiar foods in everyday survival strategies. Food, they explain, can provide one of the key mechanisms for interacting with hosts and with other migrants. The place we eat in, the act of eating and the food we eat are some of the main factors shaping our identities; thus, the analysis of people's foodways forms a unique prism for understanding human interactions (Sabar and Posner 2013). In a different asylum context, Vandevoordt (2017) explored how Syrian refugees create a sense of home in the hostile environment of the asylum system in Belgium. He posits that by eating and drinking their own food refugees could (re)gain autonomy, dignity and a collective sense of self. By hosting others and offering tea and snacks, they rearranged the subject definitions that were imposed upon them as receivers of the gift. Food, he argues, is of central importance to people who are forced to migrate, as most of the anchors that once provided ontological security to their lives, such as routines or objects, are left behind against their will. Eating and drinking therefore acquire a significant role in restoring a sense of intimacy, safety and normality (Seremetakis 1994; Vandevoordt 2017). In the context of Denmark, Larsen's (2011) study among newly arrived refugees examines how the interventionist welfare state practices of surveillance towards refugees' everyday lives included what food refugees eat. She explains that refugee parents were perceived as doing a poor job when they prepared their children's packed lunches for school, by not using the right kind of bread, that is, the bread that Danes eat (*rugbrød*, rye bread), and that a bad packed lunch meant bad parents. She explains that the refugee families' lack of familiarity with Danish bread contributed to an intensified institutional surveillance of the families by the school, kindergarten and municipal staff.

Taking the pocket money as the point of departure, the ethnography will examine the importance of foodways, food spaces and the acts of sharing food for young refugees living in asylum centres in Denmark. I now return to my field notes from that pocket money day.

Pocket money day: 'the exchange'

> I am standing next to Hejar,[5] one of the quieter Kurdish boys, as he patiently queues to pick up his envelope of pocket money. We are chatting about his day at school when I ask him what he uses the pocket money for. He explains that the money is to buy food and clothes. 'But I don't buy clothes all the time,' he clarifies. When I ask him if it is enough, he nods. When we get to the desk Hejar shows Jasper, the staff member, his asylum seeker's card. Jasper knows Hejar well but still needs to see his identification card. He looks up his name in a long list and asks him to sign next to his name. He hands Hejar a white envelope that has *Lommepenge* written on the front and, underneath, his name and the amount it contains. Hejar nods and moves away with his envelope. We make our way back to the asylum centre.

The above excerpt from my field notes explains how 'the exchange' of the envelope was carried out at an asylum centre for unaccompanied minors. The act of handing over the envelope reminds me of Mauss's exchange theory of the gift (Mauss [1950] 1990). Mauss explains that a gift is hardly ever 'pure', as it requires at some point a gift in return, a form of debt. I observed many of my interlocutors pick up their pocket money at different asylum centres, some for unaccompanied minors, others for adults waiting for asylum and others waiting for deportation: in all cases the exchange took a similar form, of a signature being given by the asylum seeker followed by the envelope being handed out by a Red Cross staff member. No money was expected in return from Hejar, or no 'pure' gift, but, as Mauss posited, the significant point of giving a gift is that it becomes a debt that comes with the obligation of a 'return gift'. In this case, in return the asylum seeker agreed to abide by the asylum rules and policies that deprive them of the possibility of working and require them to stay within the confines of the asylum centre. The act of accepting the pocket money means that Hejar agrees to becoming dependent on the state to buy his basic necessities. Moreover, I suggest that the 'gift' in the form of a debt was also intended to partly dispossess the young refugee of agency, understood as people's evolving capacity to act and influence their own life and to participate in society (Korjonen-Kuusipuro and Kuusisto 2019, 379). By accepting the 'gift' asylum seekers accept the policies of isolation and of not having the right to work, and hence not being able to participate in Danish society. This acceptance puts them in debt, and makes them dependent on a state that mistrusts their reasons for coming to Denmark, and for many of my interlocutors their identity as minors.

The anthropologist Inger Sjørslev posits that 'exchange implies social relations, and is embedded in processes that imply both material things and social relations' (Sjørslev 2020, 156). In her analysis of the materiality of debt, Sjørslev differentiates between 'vertical' and 'horizontal' relations. She explains that vertical relations are hierarchical, in opposition to horizontal relations, which are experienced as egalitarian (2020, 161). Hejar has a vertical relation with the state that gives the young asylum seeker money. When the exchange occurred, as Hejar gave his signature and was handed an envelope in return, the hierarchical vertical relation between young Hejar and welfare Denmark was further reinforced. However, as the ethnography will show, this vertical relation that structurally frames the lives of young Hejar and all asylum seekers in Denmark is transformed into meaningful social relations when the money leaves the envelope.

A trip to the Arab market

> On the ground floor of Birkelunde asylum centre is the office of the Red Cross staff, where the young boys and girls come throughout the day to ask questions or to hang out. The whiteboard outside the office shows the different activities scheduled for the week. Twice a week, including on Thursdays, there was a trip to the 'Arab market'. When we get back to the asylum centre there is a lot of movement, as some of the young refugees are using the kitchens, others are going in and out of their friends' rooms, and a small group is getting ready for the trip to the Arab market. I decide to join at the last minute. The minibus

> fits about 12 people, and today it is filled with Hejar's group of friends, some of the Kurdish boys, who are going to buy their groceries with the pocket money they have just received. I sit at the back and can see that one of the boys is collecting the money from each of them and pooling the money together. During the one-hour journey to the market they all talk loudly while also texting on their phones. Once at the 'market' – a small store filled with Middle Eastern products that cannot be found in Danish supermarkets – the Kurdish boys set about choosing what to purchase. They compare prices, and leave each with several white plastic bags containing large packs of rice, bread, canned food, vegetables and spices.

Migrants interact with speciality groceries at multiple levels. Historically, Abbots (2016) explains, 'ethnic' grocery stores have been a source of labour, employment and income, as well as being a place of definition between migrants and hosts. Mankekar (2005), who studied the significance of Indian grocery stores for a diasporic community in the San Francisco Bay area, explains that the stores are not only locations to purchase ethnic goods, but also social spaces where migrants can forge identity and community. She argues that ethnic grocery stores reproduce home, both materially and discursively. For the young Kurds, the Arab market was a place where they could create and negotiate a sense of community. At the store they roamed around and discussed, sometimes in pairs and at other times as a group, what products to buy. The visual display of the products, as well as the textures and smells of the produce, made this food space a familiar place where they could feel at ease as they spent almost an hour in the few square metres of the store discussing what to buy with their pooled money. This food space became an embodied experience with different sensory cues that together provided a sense of familiarity. They were also able to communicate with the owner of the store in a familiar language, in stark contrast to their experience of buying at Danish supermarkets where they relied on the Red Cross person to navigate the space and translate the ingredients the products contained (see Verdasco 2020).

Once at the asylum centre, they distribute the food into the individual lockers and fridges that have locks. There is no shared space they can use for their shared goods. When the money leaves the envelope, as I have suggested elsewhere (see Verdasco 2020), an act of de-individualising takes places (see Carsten 1989). As the money leaves the individual envelopes and is pooled it becomes a shared good of the community of friends which is used to buy food. The young refugees challenge the Danish welfare approach of valuing individualism and decide to transform the 'debt' into a 'shared good'. It is in the act of pooling their money that they break the individual relation vis-à-vis the state and create and invest in a community. When they go to buy food together, and later cook and eat together, 'matter' is transformed into a sense of community and belonging. The state, however, has an individual relation with each of the asylum seekers, and they are reminded of this by the materialities of the envelope, the locker and the fridge they each own.

However, this community of friends was not entirely harmonious and without conflict. The groups had hierarchies and leaders who decided who could be included and who was to be excluded (see Verdasco 2020). These leaders were known as 'alphas' by the Red Cross staff and would at times be troublesome. Rojan was one of the Kurdish alphas who went to the Arab market that day. When he stepped into the minibus, in spite of arriving last he got a front row seat as one of the other boys quickly moved to the back. At the market, Rojan was making most of the decisions with one other boy on the quantities to buy. Thus, as in a family in which the head of the household decides how the money is to be used, Rojan took this role.

Cooking money

Cooking in the kitchens was an activity that initially had no time restrictions. However, it was difficult for the night staff to maintain a quiet environment and some of the young refugees would use the kitchens at night. This translated into a lot of noise, which disrupted the sleep of others and the rhythm at the centre. Thus rules were put in place whereby the kitchens could only be used from 6 a.m. until 10.30 p.m., which was the curfew time for the young asylum seekers to be in their rooms.[6]

Studies on the importance of foodways among older refugees and asylum seekers explain that the process of preparing the food and the ritual stages of preparation are as important as the cooked meal (see for example Frost 2008; Sabar and Posner 2013). For many of the young male refugees at Birkelunde asylum centre, cooking was something new that they learned once they started living at the asylum centre, and therefore the preparation process was far less important, which allowed more space for doing things differently. When the young asylum seekers cooked together, especially the boys, there was a lot of improvisation on what ingredients and quantities to use. For the most part, they looked up videos on YouTube to find recipes. As Abbots (2016) notes, migration affords the opportunity for gender roles to be reconfigured. The young refugees' gendered identities were affected and transformed as they invested time in cooking, an endeavour that back in their home countries was reserved to women. Sabar and Posner's (2013) ethnography of male Eritrean and Sudanese asylum seekers explains how, through cooking and eating familiar foods, both as professional cooks and in their kitchens, these men renegotiated their identities in the context of forced migration. They explain how gendered roles were shattered and how men – be they alone, in groups or with their families – crossed gender roles that were once perceived as fixed (2013, 211). In a similar vein, the young refugees at Birkelunde asylum centre needed food not only as a basic necessity, but also to experience a sense of familiarity. It also allowed them to negotiate and invest in social relations that helped them navigate the asylum system and endure an everyday existence of uncertainties. Buying and cooking food together was something they enjoyed and that gave some meaning to the waiting time.

Because of the nature of my project, I was only allowed to do fieldwork in the house that hosted the older boys and not in the second house, which hosted the very young children and the girls; thus I cannot make a nuanced comparative appreciation of the differences between boys' and girls' eating and cooking habits. There were, however, a few exceptions, and four girls lived in the boys' house. These young women spent more time in the kitchens than the boys. Some, like Fatima, a Somali, knew how to cook and enjoyed spending time in the kitchen. Others like Amina, an Afghani, did not know how to cook and sought help from Red Cross staff who came from a similar region to learn new recipes that tasted like home (see Verdasco 2020). Although the boys did not directly seek out this kind of help, they would gather in the kitchens when they saw these 'cooking lessons' happening.

Eating together allowed groups of people who came from similar parts of the world and shared similar ideologies and upbringings to eat together. Thus the Kurdish groups would eat together, sometimes more than ten at the table, allowing age divisions to be dissolved when the younger boys joined the older ones. On these occasions an array of different dishes, many of them canned foods like sardines, was displayed on the table, from which they all shared.

However, food also reveals divisions and hierarchies, and eating not only created unity but also reinforced the differences between the groups at the centre. Thus, it was uncommon for anyone from a different ethnic background to sit down for a meal with the others, or even to share any of the common areas while eating.

I will now turn to how intergenerational relations were strengthened through the act of sharing of food, and how I was a part of this.

Sharing food

In several Danish asylum centres, including reception and deportation centres, cooking food and eating outside the canteen area were forbidden. At Birkelunde asylum centre, young refugees could cook their own food in the communal kitchens and eat together, often in their own rooms or in the common spaces away from the staff on the top floors of the centre. I was always offered food when the refugees were cooking or getting ready to eat: if they saw me walk by, they would immediately offer me a chair and ask if I would like to join them. During my fieldwork, I found myself having breakfast or dinner several times in the same day. Conversations with my interlocutors about food were recurrent, and those who were granted refugee status would invite me into their homes, where they would always invite me to eat: if not a meal there was always tea and snacks. Through 'foodtalk' (Sabar and Posner 2013, 201), my interlocutors could engage in talking about their families, kin and friends and life at home without having to directly speak about the loneliness, violence and deprivation they had endured.

On one occasion it was the birthday of Yonas, one of the Eritrean boys. Yonas was a tall, slender young man who was quiet when his group of friends were making a lot of noise, but very talkative when he felt at ease in one-to-one interactions. On this special occasion he had cooked an Eritrean dish and asked me and Laura, his Red Cross contact person, whom he was close to, if we would like to join him for food. I was hesitating over whether to stay longer at the centre that day, since I was getting a lift back to Copenhagen from another staff person, when Yonas walked into the office with a plate piled high with an Eritrean chicken dish with two generous pieces of chicken stacked at the top. He invited us into his room to have lunch. The rooms were not really adapted for eating, since there was not a lot of space and no dining table, only the two beds and side tables. However, Yonas set up the small side tables to create a dining space. I turn to my field notes from that day:

> Yonas places the table that barely fits between the two beds and Laura and I sit side by side on his bed. Yonas sits on the opposite bed where his friend and room-mate, Jemal, is lying to one side, covered with his duvet and looking at his phone. Jemal is Muslim and we are in Ramadan so he is fasting. Yonas doesn't pay much attention to him and we form a triangle around the food. He places the plate of food and a few slices of white bread on the table. As in Eritrea, we

> use bread as cutlery to dip into the sauce and grab the pieces of chicken. The dish is delicious and Yonas is really happy we have accepted his invitation. Both Laura and myself keep complimenting him on how tasty the food is. I ask him where he learned how to cook: 'From my mother and my sister,' he tells us. We talk about his family, religion and how food in Eritrea is very similar to that of Ethiopia. Yonas keeps encouraging us to eat: 'Eat, eat please, eat the chicken.' Laura laughs, 'You remind me of my mother.' I struggle with using the bread as cutlery and find my hands are filled with sauce and the chicken pieces keep escaping the bread. I look at Laura, who seems to be coping much more elegantly with clean hands while chatting in a lively manner.

Yonas's dish was an elaborate Eritrean one, normally eaten with another kind of Eritrean bread known as *injera*, a thick, spongy, sour pancake that is served on a large tray. Yonas did not have access to this bread; however, he decided that another kind of bread could serve the purpose just as well. The production of this hybrid dish showed creativity and agency (see Renne 2008). The chicken pieces were expensive and thus precious to Yonas, who purposely served two, one for Laura and one for me, and like a good host he kept encouraging us not only to keep eating, but specifically to eat the chicken. In his room with his cooked meal Yonas was the host and we became his guests. By hosting us he was able to make his room a place of his own where he ate familiar food, which gave him some continuity. By transforming the pocket money into a familiar meal, he transformed an individual exchange into a collective moment. Moreover, he was no longer the receiver of the 'gift', or the debt to be more accurate, but he was able to give. Yonas became the host and through the act of sharing food that he had cooked, and that tasted as it did at home, he was able to create what Vandevoordt (2017) calls intimate bubbles of homeliness, where home is not so much a place as 'a situation where people, objects, scents and tastes feel familiar, safe and warm' (Vandevoordt 2017, 616). When the pocket money is transformed into another 'matter', in this case a hot meal from home, this object is no longer foreign but, rather, brings a sense of social normality that enables the development of and investment in valuable social relations.

Several studies have shown that the sensorial experience of eating triggers detailed memories, which are key components of our identity (for example Sutton 2001). The materiality of food had the capacity to recall distant places and relations as we spoke about how his mother and sisters used to cook at home. Eating triggers memories of both home and those contained within it (Abbots 2016). While eating, Yonas opened up, talking about his brothers who were living in Israel. He also spoke about how he was raised as a Christian, the importance of religion in his life in Denmark and the church he regularly attended. Thus, eating, with its tastes, textures and smells, brought back memories that allowed Yonas to open up and talk about more intimate subjects such as family and religion.

It is also important to note that this dish requires preparation and time. Most of my interlocutors would make a real effort to find the right ingredients, which they could not normally find in the Danish supermarkets. The Eritrean dish tasted like home, but the bread did not; this is a reminder that he had a limited allowance, since we shared the cheaper kind of white bread that he could afford, which changed the taste of home. In the case of Yonas, his mother had taught him to cook when he was growing up, but he had never had to take care of cooking every day. As mentioned above, migration effectively obliterates the gendered roles of the young refugees who engage in cooking food. The act of eating allowed the relationship between Laura and myself to be strengthened, but it also made visible the cultural differences as I made every effort to eat the chicken 'properly'.

In spite of the efforts to create a sense of community and new social relations, the individual asylum cases dominated their existence. As we shared the meal, Jemal was also there, even though he did not want to participate in the eating. The creation of a community of friends and other forms of relatedness was not always possible, because the individual asylum cases framed and permeated their everyday lives. Jemal was not only fasting, he had also been living in asylum centres for longer than many of his friends since he was a 'Dublin case'. This meant that because he had close relatives in a different EU country, the Danish state was considering returning him to that country. Jemal wanted to stay in Denmark, mostly because of the meaningful forms of relatedness he had constructed, and while many of his friends had been granted asylum and moved to other municipalities, he was stuck at Birkelunde centre. His case helps illustrate that communities are not homogeneous or harmonious, that 'returning' the gift was not always possible, and that their understanding of themselves as individuals was imposed over their collective sense of identity by the state's restrictive framework of asylum policies linked to protracted waiting.

Becoming a host as a form of agency

In his account of Syrian refugees living in asylum centres in Belgium, Vandevoordt (2017) explains that, like me, he was always offered food and drinks when he met his interlocutors. Vandevoordt explains that when his informants became the hosts, in a sense they were engaging in subversive acts in relation to the Belgian state, whereby they shifted their position to become givers of the gift. In the case of my interlocutors, I do not think they intentionally engaged in eating and cooking as acts of subversion. I rather see these everyday acts of buying, cooking and eating food together as a form of exerting agency, seeking moments of normality, and constructing community. These forms of agency may not be intentional, proactive, or revolutionary in the sense of 'political' action (Cabot 2013). As Saba Mahmood (2005) suggests, agency should not be conceptualised only as a synonym of resistance to relations of domination, but 'as a *capacity for action* that specific relations to subordination create and enable' (Mahmood 2005, 18; emphasis added). Mahmood suggests that, rather than looking at subversion, we should explore 'the variety of ways in which *norms are lived and inhabited*' (2005, 23; emphasis added). In a similar vein, Durham is critical of an understanding of agency among youth that relies on Western assumptions constructed around the self. In her work among young Botswanans, she examines their capacity to create agency departing from open resistance. Mahmood (2005) and Durham (2008), in (radically) different contexts, are critical of looking at agency using Western assumptions and seeing it solely in terms of forms of resistance. Like them, I argue that by opening the envelopes and pooling their money to buy, cook and eat together the young refugees are agentive and show a capacity to construct social relations and search for the familiar in uncertain and precarious situations. When the young refugees *inhabit the norms* imposed by the system, of staying at the asylum centre and not having the opportunity to work, they are agentive. Some of these social relations are not 'vertical', to use Sjørslev's language, and may be defined as 'hierarchical', such as the relation between Yonas and Laura. Nevertheless, these social relations allow them to learn about Danish norms and values and how to navigate the system.

I argue that by spending time with Laura and me, Yonas showed that he wanted not only to share his food but to talk about his life back in Eritrea and how he experienced the world through his religion and his friends in Denmark. He also wanted to learn about our ways of viewing the world and gain a better understanding of Danish societal norms and values. The young refugees would use occasions such as birthdays, religious events or positive news on their asylum cases to create moments when food was shared and social relations were constructed and strengthened.

Conclusion

In this chapter, I have followed the pocket money from the individual site of the sealed envelope as it was pooled and transformed into the materiality of food. Following the money highlights the importance of food as the young refugees transform the individual 'gift' from the welfare state into a common good that allows them to spend time with peers and adults to construct and negotiate a sense of community and enjoy a sense of continuity and familiarity. When they enter familiar spaces such as the 'ethnic' grocery stores and then cook together and share their hot meals, they create a sense of familiarity in which the visual and linguistic cues, and the aromas, afford an embodied experience constructing bubbles of homeliness.

I posit that the pocket money creates a debt that places asylum seekers in a dependent hierarchical relationship vis-à-vis the state. By accepting the exchange, asylum seekers agree to abide by the rules and norms of the asylum regime. However, by transforming the money into a warm meal, and by inviting others to their table, the young refugees are able to turn around their status as guests to become hosts: they are no longer passively receiving but rather actively giving, thus being agentive. I further argue that food – buying and cooking it – affects and transforms their gendered subjectivities by prompting them to engage in activities that would otherwise remain outside the realm of their male identities. Thus, as Abbots (2016) notes, food enables the creation of new subjectivities and orientations. Moreover, the ethnography has revealed the young refugees' strong desire to socialise as they are constantly negotiating meaningful relations with both their peers and adults. Thus, 'unaccompanied' is an external category that bears little resemblance to their everyday construction of social relations. By following the food as it becomes a hot meal, I have reflected on how the refugees are able to create strong ties not only with their friends but also with adults who can help them navigate the system. By following the object of the money, and through the lens of foodways, it is possible to unfold aspects of the lived experiences of refugees that otherwise remain hidden.

Acknowledgements

I would like to thank the editors of this book for their insights and suggestions throughout the writing process. I would also like to thank my mother for taking care of my son so that I had the time to write this chapter. Finally, and foremost, I am indebted to the young refugees who lived in Birkelunde asylum centre, who gave me the gift of exploring their everyday lives while waiting in uncertainty.

Notes

1 I use the term 'refugee' inclusively to refer to people in all stages of the asylum process, except where it is relevant to differentiate people seeking asylum because of their restricted access to services and rights. This is reflective of the emic wording of my interlocutors, who called themselves refugees.
2 Parts of the ethnographic data used in this chapter were first published in Verdasco 2020.
3 Whether this can be termed a 'crisis' is a matter of discussion, since a crisis is defined by its pre- and post-crisis periods, and in this case it is not entirely clear where the boundaries between them lie (see Roitman 2014).
4 The pocket money received increased when the asylum seeker moved through the asylum-seeking process from Phase I to Phase II, that is, before and after the immigration authorities decided their case would be assessed in Denmark. In 2016, unaccompanied minors in Phase I received DKK 850 (€115) every fortnight, while those in Phase II received DKK 1,100 (€147).
5 The names of all informants and the asylum centre have been changed to preserve anonymity.
6 This time restriction was lifted during Ramadan so that refugees who were fasting could make use of the kitchens when they broke the fast during the night-time.

References

Abbots, Emma-Jayne. 2012. 'In the absence of men? Gender, migration and domestic labour in the southern Ecuadorean Andes', *Journal of Latin American Studies* 44(1): 71–96. https://doi.org/10.1017/S0022216X11001088.

Abbots, Emma-Jayne. 2013. 'Negotiating foreign bodies: Migration, trust and the risky business of eating in Highland Ecuador'. In *Why We Eat, How We Eat: Contemporary encounters between foods and bodies*, edited by Emma-Jayne Abbots and Anna Lavis, 119–38. Farnham: Ashgate.

Abbots, Emma-Jayne. 2016. 'Approaches to food and migration: Rootedness, being and belonging'. In *The Handbook of Food and Anthropology*, edited by Jakob A. Klein and James L. Watson, 115–32. London and New York: Bloomsbury Academic.

Bonfanti, Sara, Aurora Massa and Alejandro Miranda-Nieto. 2019. 'Whiffs of home: Ethnographic comparison in a collaborative research study across European cities', *Etnografia e Ricerca Qualitativa* 2: 153–74. http://doi.org/10.3240/94694.

Cabot, Heath. 2013. 'The social aesthetics of eligibility: NGO aid and indeterminacy in the Greek asylum process', *American Ethnologist* 40(3): 452–66. https://doi.org/10.1111/amet.12032.

Carsten, Janet. 1989. 'Cooking money: Gender and the symbolic transformation of means of exchange in a Malay fishing community'. In *Money and the Morality of Exchange*, edited by Jonathan Parry and Maurice Bloch, 117–41. Cambridge: Cambridge University Press.

Durham, Deborah. 2008. 'Apathy and agency: The romance of agency and youth in Botswana'. In *Figuring the Future: Globalization and the temporalities of children and youth*, edited by Jennifer Cole and Deborah Durham, 151–78. Santa Fe, NM: School for Advanced Research Press.

EUROSTAT. 2016. 'Almost 90,000 unaccompanied minors among asylum seekers registered in the EU in 2015'. Press release, 2 May. Accessed 23 August 2021. https://ec.europa.eu/eurostat/documents/2995521/7244677/3-02052016-AP-EN.pdf/19cfd8d1-330b-4080-8ff3-72ac7b7b67f6?t=1461935975000.

EUROSTAT. 2020. 'Asylum applicants considered to be unaccompanied minors by citizenship, age and sex'. Accessed 25 October 2021. https://ec.europa.eu/eurostat/web/products-datasets/-/migr_asyunaa.

Farquhar, Judith. 2006. 'Food, eating, and the good life'. In *Handbook of Material Culture*, edited by Christopher Tilley, Webb Keane, Susanne Küchler, Michael Rowlands and Patricia Spyer, 145–60. London: SAGE Publications.

Fine, Gary Alan and Kent L. Sandstrom. 1988. *Knowing Children: Participant observation with minors*. Qualitative Research Methods, 15. Newbury Park, CA: SAGE Publications.

Fluehr-Lobban, Carolyn. 1998. 'Ethics'. In *Handbook of Methods in Cultural Anthropology*, edited by H. Russell Bernard, 173–202. Walnut Creek, CA: AltaMira Press.

Frost, Nicola. 2008. '"Strange people, but they sure can cook!" An Indonesian women's group in Sydney', *Food, Culture and Society* 11(2): 173–89. https://doi.org/10.2752/175174408X317552.

Gilliam, Laura and Eva Gulløv. 2017. *Children of the Welfare State: Civilising practices in schools, childcare and families*. London: Pluto Press.

Hastrup, Kirsten and Karen Fog Olwig. 1997. 'Introduction'. In *Siting Culture: The shifting anthropological object*, edited by Karen Fog Olwig and Kirsten Hastrup, 1–14. London and New York: Routledge.

Immigration Services. 2017. 'Tal og fakta på udlændingeområdet 2016', Ministry of Immigration and Integration, Denmark. Accessed 23 August 2021. https://uim.dk/publikationer/tal-og-fakta-pa-udlaendingeomradet-2016.

Kaukko, Mervi and Ulrika Wernesjö. 2017. 'Belonging and participation in liminality: Unaccompanied children in Finland and Sweden', *Childhood* 24(1): 7–20. https://doi.org/10.1177%2F0907568216649104.

Korjonen-Kuusipuro, Kristiina and Anna-Kaisa Kuusisto. 2019. 'Socio-material belonging: Perspectives for the intercultural lives of unaccompanied refugee minors in Finland', *Journal of Intercultural Studies* 40(4): 363–82. https://doi.org/10.1080/07256868.2019.1628725.

Larsen, Birgitte Romme. 2011. 'Becoming part of welfare Scandinavia: Integration through the spatial dispersal of newly arrived refugees in Denmark', *Journal of Ethnic and Migration Studies* 37(2): 333–50. https://doi.org/10.1080/1369183X.2011.521337.

Lemberg-Pedersen, Martin. 2015. 'The rise and fall of the ERPUM pilot: Tracing the European policy drive to deport unaccompanied minors', Working Paper Series 108, Refugee Studies Centre, Oxford. Accessed 23 August 2021. https://www.rsc.ox.ac.uk/publications/the-rise-and-fall-of-the-erpum-pilot-tracing-the-european-policy-drive-to-deport-unaccompanied-minors.

Lewis, Hannah. 2010. 'Community moments: Integration and transnationalism at "refugee" parties and events', *Journal of Refugee Studies* 23(4): 571–88. https://doi.org/10.1093/JRS/FEQ037.

Mahmood, Saba. 2005. *Politics of Piety: The Islamic revival and the feminist subject*. Princeton, NJ: Princeton University Press.

Mankekar, Purnima. 2005. '"India shopping": Indian grocery stores and transnational configurations of belonging'. In *The Cultural Politics of Food and Eating: A reader*, edited by James L. Watson and Melissa L. Caldwell, 197–214. Malden, MA: Blackwell.

Mata-Codesal, Diana and Maria Abranches. 2017. 'Sending, bringing, consuming and researching food parcels'. In *Food Parcels in International Migration: Intimate connections*, edited by Diana Mata-Codesal and Maria Abranches, 1–21. Cham: Palgrave Macmillan.

Mauss, Marcel. [1950] 1990. *The Gift: The form and reason for exchange in archaic societies*. Translated by W. D. Halls. London and New York: Routledge.

Povrzanović Frykman, Maja and Michael Humbracht. 2013. 'Making palpable connections: Objects in migrants' transnational lives', *Ethnologia Scandinavica* 43: 47–67.

Ray, Krishnendu. 2004. *The Migrant's Table: Meals and memories in Bengali-American households*. Philadelphia: Temple University Press.

Renne, Elisha P. 2008. 'Mass producing food traditions for West Africans abroad', *American Anthropologist* 109(4): 616–25. https://doi.org/10.1525/aa.2007.109.4.616.

Roitman, Janet. 2014. *Anti-Crisis*. Durham, NC: Duke University Press.

Sabar, Galia and Rachel Posner. 2013. 'Remembering the past and constructing the future over a communal plate: Restaurants established by African asylum seekers in Tel Aviv', *Food, Culture and Society* 16(2): 197–222. https://doi.org/10.2752/175174413X13589681351692.

Seremetakis, C. Nadia. 1994. 'The memory of the senses, Part I: Marks of the transitory'. In *The Senses Still: Perception and memory as material culture in modernity*, edited by C. Nadia Seremetakis, 1–18. Chicago, IL: Chicago University Press.

Sjørslev, Inger. 2020. 'Money in the mattress and bodies in the market: Reflections on the material'. In *Who's Cashing In? Contemporary perspectives on new monies and global cashlessness*, edited by Atreyee Sen, Johan Lindquist and Marie Kolling, 156–64. New York: Berghahn Books.

Sutton, David. 2001. *Remembrance of Repasts: An anthropology of food and memory*. Oxford: Berg.

Tuomainen, Helena Margaret. 2009. 'Ethnic identity, (post)colonialism and foodways: Ghanaians in London', *Food Culture and Society* 12(4): 525–54. https://doi.org/10.2752/175174409X456773.

Vallianatos, Helen and Kim Raine. 2008. 'Consuming food and constructing identities among Arabic and South Asian immigrant women', *Food, Culture and Society* 11(3): 355–73. https://doi.org/10.2752/175174408X347900.

Vandevoordt, Robin. 2017. 'The politics of food and hospitality: How Syrian refugees in Belgium create a home in hostile environments', *Journal of Refugee Studies* 30(4): 605–21. https://doi.org/10.1093/jrs/fex017.

Verdasco, Andrea. 2018. 'Coming of age in asylum: Belonging, temporality and social relations among young refugees in Denmark'. PhD dissertation, University of Copenhagen.

Verdasco, Andrea. 2020. 'Everyday rituals of migration: Constructing relatedness and agency among young refugees in Denmark', *Ethnos* 85(3): 550–74. https://doi.org/10.1080/00141844.2019.1604558.

Vitus, Kathrine. 2010. 'Waiting time: The de-subjectification of children in Danish asylum centres', *Childhood* 17(1): 26–42. https://doi.org/10.1177%2F0907568209351549.

Vitus, Kathrine and Hilde Lidén. 2010. 'The status of the asylum-seeking child in Norway and Denmark: Comparing discourses, politics and practices', *Journal of Refugee Studies* 23(1): 62–81. https://doi.org/10.1093/jrs/feq003.

Whyte, Zachary, Birgitte Romme Larsen and Karen Fog Olwig. 2019. 'New neighbours in a time of change: Local pragmatics and the perception of asylum centres in rural Denmark', *Journal of Ethnic and Migration Studies* 45(11): 1953–69. https://doi.org/10.1080/1369183X.2018.1482741.

9
Circulating things, circulating knowledge: why popular culture matters in exhibitions on migration

Maike Suhr

> I got my balikbayan box, I waited for it for two months.
> I bet it's full of awesome stuff.'
>
> (Mikey Bustos 2013, 1:36)

Introduction

First video: a young man in the Philippines, excitedly ripping the tape off a huge package, to the music of Miley Cyrus's 'Wrecking ball', imagining all the goods his mother has sent him from overseas. Second video: a boy in a Romanian village, grieving over his parents' absence; their presents from abroad cannot comfort him. Third song, no video, but underlaid by a black-and-white image of a Greek folk singer from the 1970s. The song praises home over all potential foreign goods and wealth. What these three examples of pop music have in common, despite their differences in time, geography and language, is the stories they tell of labour migration from the perspectives of separated families.

The music videos (and in the latter case the audio) are part of the exhibition project 'BITTER THINGS – Narratives and memories of transnational families', developed by the Berlin-based project space bi'bak[1] (Turkish: take a look) in 2018. The exhibition explores family separation in the context of labour migration from the perspectives of both migrant workers and children, who are left in the custody of relatives or who are commuting between home and the parents' new place of work.

As a cultural actor working on issues of migration and global mobility on the intersection of arts, community and research, bi'bak conducted interviews with women migrant workers and children of labour migrants from various countries, and presented a selection of them as an audio installation which has been showcased in several exhibition spaces in Germany, Turkey and Romania.

The interview partners were either currently experiencing separation (both mothers and children), or, now grown up, reflecting on being left behind by their parents as children in the time of the recruitment agreements in the 1960s and 1970s. 'BITTER THINGS' thus depicts a continuum of the situations of families in labour migration from the 1960s until today, in which transnational models of the family appear to have become more rather than less common, not least because of the large number of migrant workers in the care sector, who are mainly women, and often have children at home.[2] The interviews are installed in 16 stations resembling phone booths, where, beside a telephone receiver, through which the interview can be listened to, objects are displayed which are related to the interviewees' accounts. The personal perspectives from the interviews are framed by a timeline that gathers together the political decisions that influenced families in their decision either to leave the children or to bring them to their new homes (or that made this decision impossible, for example when legal employment and therefore regular border crossing are restricted). A third element of the exhibition, upon which I will focus later, is a TV set showcasing pop songs and music videos from various countries, like those described at the beginning of this chapter, which refer to labour migration, family separation and the role of objects in transnational family relations.[3] In the following, the use of popular culture as a subject of cultural and societal enquiry in the exhibition 'BITTER THINGS' will be analysed with regard to the question of how migration can be narrated in exhibitions.

First, I give a brief introduction to the discourse on exhibiting migration and the – often problematic – representation of migration (hi)stories in museums and exhibitions. Second, I present an insight into the interviews and objects in the exhibition and then take a closer look at the displayed pop songs and their relation to the other elements of 'BITTER THINGS'. Based on 'BITTER THINGS', the perspective offered by popular culture for presenting alternative narratives about migration to those stereotypically repeated in exhibitions on migration (for example Baur 2009b; Lanz 2016; Poehls 2011) will be discussed.

Exhibiting migration

The 'musealisation' of migration and migration history is on the rise (see for example Korff 2005; Baur 2009a). The importance of a central immigration museum in Germany had been discussed over many years (Eryılmaz 2007; Motte and Ohliger 2004), until the Documentation Centre and Museum of Migration in Germany (DOMiD), a main actor in the endeavours towards such a museum, succeeded in its long-standing claim: in 2019 DOMiD got grant support and a space in Cologne for the construction of Germany's first museum of immigration. The immigration museum is, certainly, an important step towards 'adding a forgotten chapter and simultaneously compensating Germany's migrant population for lack of public acknowledgment and social recognition' (Wolbert 2010, 8). But besides the importance of a central immigration museum in Germany, there are many voices claiming that the state and history museums should be restructured by including migration history and (post-)migrant perspectives in their permanent exhibitions and thereby recognising movement and transnationalism as a vital part of Germany's society and of collective cultural memory. This position does not oppose the idea of a central immigration museum, as highlighted by Eryılmaz (2012, 33). It has been followed, for example, by the Historisches Museum Frankfurt (the Historical Museum, Frankfurt) with the establishment of the Stadtlabor (city lab) as a space where inhabitants of Frankfurt are involved in exhibiting the city's transnational history and presence, by the city museum in Stuttgart, and by neighbourhood museums such as the Kreuzberg Museum in Berlin (Gogos 2012, 15). Many exhibitions on migration today are not purely documentary or historical, but also contain artists' works. In this regard, the exhibitions 'Projekt Migration' (2005) and 'Crossing Munich' (2009) have been highlighted as interdisciplinary approaches to exhibition curation that include art, research and activism, and moreover narrating history from a migrant perspective (Bayer 2012, 55). 'BITTER THINGS', as an exhibition dealing with a historical but also current political issue, using tools of research as well as artistic interventions and practices of showcasing, and being displayed in art spaces as well as in the historical museum (Frankfurt), is placed on the intersection of arts, history and current political debates.

Problems of exhibiting migration

Addressing the issue of migration and global mobility in museums or exhibitions, be it through objects or immaterial sources, faces numerous problems. Too often exhibitions about migration and migrants have been made without letting the people with actual experience of migration speak. Through James Clifford's approach to 'museums as contact zones' (1997), which frames the ethnographic museum as a space for encounter and exchange with local experts, where, besides objects, immaterial stories and traditions can circulate, it also becomes clear for other types of museums that 'talking about' has to be replaced by constant collaboration. Moreover, the importance of appointing curators and museum management with migrant experience has to be stressed.

When it comes to the objects on display in existing migration museums, Joachim Baur observes an often seemingly meaningless collection of migrants' personal goods that creates an image of 'ostentatious colourfulness', which is used for 'staging multiculturalism' (2009b, 21, translated by the author). Gottfried Korff stresses the risk of generalisation and stereotypisation through the material representation of migration in the museum, since objects have a tendency to present meanings as fixed (2005, 7). Studies comparing international exhibitions on migration (for example Baur 2009a; Lanz 2016; Poehls 2011; Basso Peressut 2014) reveal that certain narratives, presentations and aspects, often materialised through objects, dominate the presentation of migration in museums and exhibitions. For example, movement is presented as linear rather than transnational and entangled (Baur 2009b) and the focus is often on the struggles of migrants, rather than their achievements (Klahn 2005), which, if at all, are presented as single stories of success, without examining the distinct meanings of success and achievement for different generations and societal groups as well as for migrants in comparison with non-migrants.

Moreover, throughout approaches that bring issues of migration to the museums, often the aim seems not to be to value the transnational society and to position Germany as a country in which immigration has always played a crucial role; instead, sociocultural attempts to bring visitors with a so-called migration background to the museum come into play. This socioculturalisation of exhibitions on migration all too often turns museums into institutions for integration (Van de Laar 2009), reproducing stereotypes through a mostly uncritical understanding of the term 'integration', and regarding migrants as a homogeneous group, presented as 'welfare cases' (Klahn 2005).

Narratives and objects in exhibitions on migration

While the question of whether there are 'typical objects of migration' (Vacca 2012, 52) remains more or less rhetorical, there are certainly, as Joachim Baur (2009a) shows in his study on migration museums, typical objects and narratives in *exhibitions* on migration. The recurring narratives and 'visual metaphors' (2009b, 18) include the voyage, all too often illustrated by a suitcase, and presented, as mentioned above, in a unidirectional way. Moreover, he defines the border, personal objects and belongings, and living spaces as typical concepts. Francesca Lanz (2016), with a focus on the design of migration museums, also highlights the voyage as a narrative that shapes the museums' spatial design. Kerstin Poehls (2011) examines the displaying of migration in temporary exhibitions and finds maps to be a predominant tool of presentation, and, like Baur, also finds various personal belongings donated to the museum and, again, the suitcase.

The focus on the voyage as a unidirectional movement denies the transnational, networked character of migration and thereby also neglects the perspectives of those who are not migrating, but nevertheless are part of migration experiences: the family members of those who leave their country to live and work abroad. Their countries are often deeply shaped by emigration movements. This perspective is highlighted by Andreas Gestrich and Marita Krauss (2007) and referred to in Baur's closing comments on an 'ideal' migration museum as a vital element in the representation of migration. Also, Eryılmaz (2004) stresses that migration museums should be 'presenting migration not only as a two-sided dynamic between country of origin and country of emigration, but as a multivocal and contradictory transnational process' (Eryılmaz 2004, 319). Taking into account these often one-sided narrations of migration in existing museums and exhibitions, a possible measure to broaden the image and to avoid stereotypisation could be, as Barbara Wolbert proposes, artistic interventions.

'On the need for art in exhibitions on migration'

In her essay 'Studio of realism' (2010), Barbara Wolbert argues that there is a 'need for art in exhibitions on migration'. In her eyes the problem of everyday objects in exhibitions on migration is that, through these objects and their related stories, immigrants are fictionalised as 'eternal migrants' while the personal objects, as mentioned above, are read by the audience as neutral and objective (Wolbert 2010, para. 30). Artists, on the other hand, 'insert a critical distance between the viewers and the objects' (Wolbert 2010, para. 30). Wolbert considers the exhibition 'Projekt Migration' and its transdisciplinary approach to be a 'benchmark exhibition' (Wolbert 2010, para. 4). Using selected objects from the exhibition as examples, she discusses the difficulties of a materialised representation of personal migration experiences: 'The objects – in a strict sense of the word – re-present the migrant workers and their families. The unchanged appearance of these items of everyday use evokes a sense of continuation of a reality of labor migration, which stretches migrant workers' past into the audience's presence' (Wolbert 2010, para. 18).

Concerning the biggest of the exhibited objects, one of the original Ford Transit vans, she questions the van's relevance within the collective memory of migrants, since it does not occur in any of the collection's family pictures featuring cars.[4] The Mercedes Benz, she proposes with regard to these photos, would be a much more suitable vehicle to display: it would put a focus on the aspirations and achievements of migrants in Germany instead of on the often narrated struggles.[5] But through an artistic intervention the Ford became a narrative object: on the licence plate it carried the word 'Transit', linking the model name to the term 'transit migration', and moreover opening a number of memories of holiday transit between Germany and Turkey. Through artistic interventions like this, she concludes, different narratives from those of the 'poor migrants', facing economic and cultural difficulties, can be established.

'BITTER THINGS'

In this section, I take a closer look at different elements of 'BITTER THINGS', finally coming to the sources of popular culture used in the exhibition. Following the proposed use of artistic interventions in exhibitions on migration, here I focus on the question of whether the use of popular culture can help to diversify narratives and images and add the perspectives of those who experience migration from the countries and places predominantly shaped by emigration. As Stuart Hall stresses in his 'Notes on deconstructing "the popular"' ([1981] 2002), 'Popular culture is one of the sites where this struggle for and against a culture of the powerful is engaged' (Hall [1981] 2002, 192), offering 'elements of recognition and identification … to which people are responding' (Hall [1981] 2002, 188). Popular culture can thus be regarded as an indicator of societal trends and issues. In a research project (MIGMA: Transnationalism from above and below: Migration management and how migrants manage) at the Peace Research Institute Oslo, pop culture is, in the field of migration research, regarded as a valuable source: 'Popular culture can give important insights into migration processes. Studying popular culture allows researchers to move beyond the host state perspective that remains so dominant in migration studies, and get a better understanding of migration experience and migrant perspectives' (Paasche and Carling 2017).

Where are the things in 'BITTER THINGS'?

The leading interest in 'BITTER THINGS' was to tell the stories of transnational families through objects, mainly presents, which play an important role in family relations. This interest emerged both from existing literature on the practice of gift sending in transnational families (for example Burrell 2016; Fresnoza-Flot 2009; Parreñas 2001), and from conversations with friends who have themselves experienced family separation due to labour migration. The idea of a more comprehensive exhibition was encouraged by a pilot programme of films and a reading on the topic in March 2017 at bi'bak.[6] In the films and stories selected for the programme, presents as well as communication technology[7] played a vital and often ambiguous role within the separated families, underlining the strategies Rhacel Salazar Parreñas (2001) identified for the negotiation of transnational mothering practices as a substitute for physical presence: 'the commodification of love; the repression of emotional strains; and the rationalization of distance, that is, they use regulation communication to ease distance' (Salazar Parreñas 2001, 371).

In the interviews, it often appeared that it was not so much specific objects that were relevant to the families as the practice of gift giving in general. But there was a difference between the interviews with people who experienced separation in the 1960s and 1970s and are now adults, and the accounts of young people who are experiencing separation today. For example, the interview partner Serpil[8] clearly remembered a dress, which she received from her parents at the age of four, recognising it as something special, and also stable, which would stay even when the parents were leaving again: 'I remember that I got a dress, with dots. And of course I was very happy. Really, extremely happy. That was like winning the lottery ... Then I thought: well, they will leave again, but I will keep the dress.'[9] The interview partner Berna also mentioned an object, which she had donated to DOMiD earlier: a picture book with a dedication from her parents, saying that they can hardly remember what she looks like after a long time of separation, during which all they could do was send presents: 'Our dear daughter, we apologize to you for missing the opportunity to hug you – we can't imagine what you look like now from the old photos – and to have to comfort you once again with these books. Your Mom and Dad' (Lippmann et al. 2018, 152).

It became obvious that, considering the greater number of objects that are circulating now in contrast with the 1960s and 1970s, for the younger people today the importance of the single item vanishes. For example, Gülnar from Uzbekistan tells of her teenage son, who wants her to send him several iPhone chargers, whereas she knows that he does not need more than one. 'He has a lot of wishes because I'm not there. I can't say "no" to his wishes. I just can't say: "One charger is enough, my son", for I'm living apart from him' (Lippmann et al. 2018, 130). Lenuța from Romania cannot (or does not want to) think of a specific present her mother has sent her. She mentions a doll, which she 'doesn't remember clearly' and adds that she does not expect her mother to send presents; instead she wants her to return.[10]

Comparing these accounts makes it clear that the chargers or the doll in their material presentation in the exhibition function rather as illustrative substitutes. The accounts moreover reveal an interesting ambivalence: not only is it stressed that money cannot replace the parents' presence (for example by Lenuța), it also, in some ways, can. It is not only Gülnar's case that illustrates this aspect from a present-day perspective; an audio letter recorded on cassette by Murat and his family for the boy's mother, who is working in Germany, sounds partly like a shopping list. For example, the cousin says: 'Bring me a pair of American jeans – if not, you don't need to come!' (Lippmann et al. 2018, 150).

But are the things in 'BITTER THINGS 'typical' objects for exhibiting migration? Compared with the exhibitions analysed by Baur, Poehls and others, it seems that the objects exhibited next to the interviews in 'BITTER THINGS' show a greater variety, from T-shirts to Gameboys to sanitary towels, while some, such as the smartphone, have become typical objects illustrating the stories of refugees in recent years. Without the interviews most of the objects cannot easily be understood, as the doll accompanying Lenuța's interview makes clear. They might confuse and provoke conversation or – in the frame of the exhibition – careful listening. To understand the object it is necessary to sit down and listen to the interviewees' accounts as a 'key' to reveal the object's status.

Not only through the interviews and objects, but also through the lens of films, pop music and literature, we came across recurring narratives and images beyond the suitcase, and beyond the voyage, the precarious working conditions and the difficulties of adapting to the new place. Most importantly, while the phone booths with their interviews and objects frame the individual accounts of transnational mothers and children, which can be listened to through a receiver, in an intimate and personal way, the songs are audible all over the exhibition space. They offer an insight into the collective memories of those countries, which are strongly shaped by emigration or people commuting to other countries to work – and into the circulating knowledge of these societies.

Narrative 1: Money can('t) buy me love

The first narrative that recurs throughout the selected pop songs from the Philippines to Romania, from the 1970s up to the present day, is that presents (and money) cannot substitute for the parents' presence, or, from a more nationalist perspective, goods and wealth cannot make up for the home country, as in the Greek folk singer Stelios Kazantzidis's song 'To psomi ths ksenitias' ('The bread of foreign lands') from 1975:

> The bread of foreign lands is dry
> Bitter tears I have shed upon it
> Better fresh bread and olives in the humble home
> Than thousands of goods in those bitter foreign lands.
> (Tsouf 2017; translated by Eleftheria Gavriilidou)

The Romanian child star Antonia Stoian directly addresses parents who work abroad:

> You parents, no matter what happens,
> Stay with your children
> Money can never replace
> Mummy and Daddy.
> …
> I don't want money for my well-being
> I want my mother next to me
> I can do without everything
> But not without my parents' love!
> (Arges Popular 2011; translated by Malve Lippmann)

A strong example, not presented in the exhibition but displayed in the accompanying side programme, is Romania's contribution to the Eurovision Song Contest 2015 by the band Voltaj (Eurovision Song Contest 2015). The song is connected to a short film by film-maker Sabin Dorohoi, telling the story of a boy whose parents left him with his grandfather to go to work in Vienna. No matter how generous the presents they send, the presents cannot make up for his parents, so finally he sets out to find them. The music clip ends with a link to a campaign started by the band to support children who are living without their parents in Romania. Here, clearly, a traditional understanding of parenthood is highlighted as the only good for the children. The children often appear as the voice reminding not only their own parents but a whole nation of the importance of a mother–child relationship. This notion is supported by traditional clothes, as worn by Antonia Stoian or the Ukrainian child star Violeta Timofieva, and the use of nature in the music videos. The village as a place of longing is visualised through traditional houses, farmers and animals. These images support a call for the allegedly natural, simple family life, which had already been addressed, though not yet visually, by Kazantzidis in the 1970s. Considering this moral pressure in countries such as Romania or Ukraine, where labour migration is not only widespread but can even be regarded as a crucial part of a global labour system that systematically outsources labour in care, construction work or the meat-processing industry to these countries, transnational parenthood and especially mothering becomes an emotionally challenging process, between 'here' and 'there'. As Ayşe Akalın (2018) emphasises, transnational mothers are often trying to fulfil two roles at the same time, that of the provider working abroad and that of the care-giver at home (Akalın 2018, 21). Considering the fact that the circulating pop songs are framing the mothers' absence as something unnatural, causing only pain for the children, might make the situation for transnational mothers even harder.

But these emotional accounts with a moral message are contrasted in the exhibition by a parody song by the Filipino-Canadian singer Mikey Bustos, whose Miley Cyrus parody was described at the beginning of the chapter. He does not hide his excitement over the cubic-metre-sized balikbayan box (repatriate box, also described by Glick Schiller et al. 1992), which he expects to be full of Canadian goods and money:

> I'm getting a balikbayan box,
> Sent to me from my Mom abroad.
> I will wait for a whole two months,
> All those pasalubong[11] coming to me,
> and I hope Canadian money.
>
> (Bustos 2013, 0:45)

When the content turns out to be rather disappointing, he says:

> I just want to say to my dear Mommy,
> I will always love you.
> But I got my balikbayan box
> And everything inside it sucks …
>
> (Bustos 2013, 2:46)

In the belletristic literature we collected for the accompanying anthology and readings, this different perspective comes to the forefront as well: in Stefano Polis's autobiographical memories *Milch in Papier* ('Milk in paper') (2011) gifts serve as an effective bait: with toys and sweets, the father, who has long been a stranger to his children, tries – with success – to make their new overseas home palatable. Halyna Kruk, too, in her story 'Ho paura' (2013), lets the protagonist, a migrant mother, recapitulate: 'For them you're the money-sender, the umpteen hundred-euro transfers, the voice on the phone that one asks to send this or that, you're the wish fulfilment machine' (Kruk 2013, 90; translated by John Barrett). As soon as the family has become accustomed to the new standard of living, it seems, the mother's new-found role as provider from afar cannot be reversed. Here, the children's role as victims is questioned; it becomes clear that for the parents, too, negotiating their position within the transnational family is a difficult process. Mikey Bustos's parody adds an unexpectedly light and even funny perspective on the situation. In his video the village too is visualised, not in romantic nature shots but looking rather dusty and dirty. The place of longing here is Canada, with all its brands and promising goods, but the longing is disappointed.

In all these sources, there is a tendency to blame the parents for leaving the country, for only sending presents instead of being there or for not sending the right presents. This notion could be found in the interviews as well: the pop music does not add a new perspective. But it frames the difficult aspect of blaming in a different way. It stresses the accounts from the interviewees as something more than personal memories, as notions that circulate in society and also reveal the expectations and images of motherhood that seem old-fashioned in an age of global mobility and migration.

Narrative 2: Evil lands

In a second recurring narrative in the songs, the nation (either the home country or the new place) is anthropomorphised as a responsible actor.

Here, not the parents but the countries or the politicians are held responsible for the family separation. Therefore, it can be regarded as a form of political protest, but often the perspective turns out to be rather determinist.

The above-mentioned Kazantzidis introduces his song by directly addressing the 'foreign lands', for which he uses the term 'Xenitiá'. Xenitiá, like the Turkish 'Gurbet', describes not only a geographical but also an emotional distance or the emotional state created by somebody being abroad:

> Furtive foreign lands you steal our young men
> Bad magic! You bewitch us with money
> You part mothers and children so heartlessly.
>
> (Tsouf 2017; translated by Eleftheria Gavriilidou)

The little-known Turkish folk singer Nebahat Yıldız dedicates her song 'Babamızı gönder Almanya' ('Germany, give us our father back') from the 1970s to the issue of family separation. It is not known if the singer has experienced migration herself, or if she joined in the trend of Gurbet Türküleri or Almanya Türküleri of the 1960s and 1970s. This was a genre of folk songs about migration which were interpreted by famous singers such as Cem Karaca or Metin Türköz. While these singers worked in Germany and experienced 'Gurbet' themselves, the genre was also adapted by non-migrants, since migration was also a pressing issue for people who stayed in Turkey at the time. The mother protagonist in Yıldız's song begs the country, Germany, for mercy:

> Germany, give us our father back
> Three kids and one widow are waiting for him
> The orphans are begging
> Germany, oh Germany!
> Have pity on these three kids
> And this poor mother whose heart is burning.
>
> (Yıldız n.d.; translated by Can Sungu)

As a very different account, the bi'bak team found by accident an amateur video of a song written and recorded by a Romanian boy (Unknown 2016; translated by Malve Lippmann).[12] The randomness of this teenager making up a song about the absence of his mother struck us, the curators, for it seems to stress the presence of the topic in Romanian society. Regarding the text, this song goes a step further by addressing the politicians in their responsibility:

Those making the laws,
And those creating all the troubles,
Don't think of those children,
Who have to grow up without their mothers.

In Ukraine, where the number of children whose parents work abroad is extraordinarily high, a song by the child star Violeta Timofieva, who wears traditional costumes and braids in her music videos, has a more nationalist tone. She holds her home country responsible for not offering enough work to keep the people, mainly the women, at home:

Without a mother and women, we will lose Ukraine.
A nation that so easily loses holy things can't be a nation!
Why do you need this money, you will ask
When souls are torn asunder.
But humans must survive
And the woman says: 'I must go.'
This truth is like a knife
That glistens with blood –
Why do you just look on and remain silent
My confused country?
(*Ukrainian Times* 2017; translated by Ivanna Zakharevych)

Addressing political responsibility in these songs is important for highlighting that it is not only personal stories and individual decisions, and therefore not the fault of parents, that lead to family separation. At the time of the recruitment agreements, and today, the economy and – especially – the health system are highly dependent on labour migration. Pop music serves here as a call for justice, and can even be regarded as protest. But on the other hand, the example of Antonia Stoian, who won a TV talent show with a song about her mother's absence, makes clear that the emotional issue also serves commercial purposes. It is this inconsistency and ambiguity that make the songs irritating, thereby raising awareness of the issue and its multilayered facets for exhibition visitors.

On the need for pop culture in exhibitions on migration

If we compare the popular culture in the exhibition 'BITTER THINGS' with the other elements such as interviews and objects, we can draw some conclusions about the use of popular culture in exhibitions on migration. Firstly, pop means similarity, through its typical use of references and intertextuality. In the case of Antonia Stoian, for example, the listener or viewer from another country is automatically confronted with the concept of a talent show, which is known all over the world for highlighting strokes of fate and emotional moments, leading to identification with the participants for many people. Seeing the separation of families in such a context underlines its position as an issue that moves the society, but also makes it more relatable for those exhibition visitors who have not experienced migration within their families.

Secondly, the interviews conducted are displayed intimately in the phone booths; they offer individual stories and personal insights, in which sometimes recurring and shared experiences can be identified. In contrast, the pop songs are audible in the whole room, in the background; they cannot be ignored or switched off but can instead be perceived as atmosphere, holding 'affective power', as Friedlind Riedel (2019, 3) puts it. More than personal accounts, the songs embody a 'circulating knowledge' and stress the presence and importance of the issue of family separation through migration in those regions strongly shaped by emigration, a perspective which, as mentioned before, has been missing in exhibitions on migration. In the context of the exhibition, next to the interviews of people explicitly speaking about their experiences (because they are asked to do so), they add meaning through their implicit casualness, their ordinariness, revealing that the topic is present in the societies shaped by emigration on an everyday level. Presented in the 'frame' of a TV set, the exhibition tries to catch this circulating memory and knowledge. Through its musealisation, the knowledge of pop culture is brought closer to the audience, and through bringing similarity to the fore it can create an understanding of the transnational span of the topic.

Thirdly, the songs support the relevance of the role of objects in transnational families. Whether framed as meaningless or promising, as traditional and nostalgic or new and alluring, objects appear as actants in these lyrics and videos and thereby manifest a 'materiality of migration' that, in its mediatised format, becomes manifest.

In the end, the limits of this brief analysis must be stressed. There are a lot of things we don't know about these songs collected for 'BITTER THINGS'. Since they have been selected largely by bi'bak, through mentions in other sources or the advice of friends from the regions, we don't know much about their reception in their countries of origin. Further research would require a systematised selection, accompanied by interviews on the reception and meaning of the songs, which could also be analysed through the YouTube comment section.

Notes

1 bi'bak (Turkish: have a look) is a project space based in Berlin, with a focus on transnational narratives, migration, global mobility and their aesthetic dimensions. The founders of bi'bak and artistic directors of the exhibition 'BITTER THINGS' are Malve Lippmann and Can Sungu, who also conducted the interviews quoted in this chapter. I have been working with bi'bak for several years and was involved in 'BITTER THINGS' as an editor and research assistant for the accompanying publication. bi'bak has been addressing the issue of transnational memory and pop culture in various projects, lately in the frame of Can Sungu's research about German-Turkish video culture in West Berlin, published as *Please Rewind: German-Turkish film and video culture in Berlin* (2020, Berlin: Archive Books).

2 The increased number of women in global (labour) migration is often referred to as the 'feminisation of migration' (see Castles and Miller 1998).

3 In addition to the exhibition, bi'bak developed a side programme, of screenings of international documentaries and fiction films related to the topic (see https://bi-bak.de/en/exhibitions, accessed 23 August 2021), and a publication, which, among other material, contains song lyrics as well as short stories and excerpts from novels that deal with the issue.

4 The Ford Transit occurs, contrary to Wolbert's observation, in many accounts collected by bi'bak for the previous exhibition 'Sıla Yolu – The holiday transit to Turkey and the tales of the highway' (2016–17). Nevertheless, her point, that objects can easily be loaded with meaning that is not always grounded in real experiences, becomes clear in this example.

5 For a deeper look into the car as a status object for both migrants and non-migrants in the 1960s and 1970s see Czycholl 2019.

6 More about the series can be found at https://bi-bak.de/en/archive/bi-bakino/zurueckgelassen-entwurzelt-versteckt (accessed 23 August 2021).

7 See for example the anthology *Skype Mama* of stories from Ukraine about transnational families and their ways of staying in touch (Brunner, Sawka and Onufriv 2013).

8 Names have been changed.

9 Unpublished interview by Malve Lippmann and Can Sungu, 2017, in preparation for the exhibition 'BITTER THINGS'. This interview was not selected for the exhibition.

10 See note 9.

11 Tagalog: 'souvenir, gift'.

12 This private video has since been deleted from YouTube.

References

Akalın, Ayşe. 2018. 'Doing care, the migrant way: Transnational mothering'. In *Bitter Things: Narratives and memories of transnational families*, edited by Malve Lippmann, Maike Suhr and Can Sungu, 19–27. Berlin: Archive Books.

Basso Peressut, Luca. 2014. *MeLa*: European Museums in an Age of Migrations: Cultural memory, migrating modernity and museum practices*. Milan: Politecnico di Milano. Accessed 23 August 2021. http://www.mela-project.polimi.it/.

Baur, Joachim. 2009a. *Die Musealisierung der Migration: Einwanderungsmuseen und die Inszenierung der multikulturellen Nation* [The musealisation of migration: immigration museums and the staging of the multicultural nation]. Bielefeld: transcript Verlag.

Baur, Joachim. 2009b. 'Flüchtige Spuren – Bewegte Geschichten: Zur Darstellung von Migration in Museen und Ausstellungen' [Fleeting traces – moving stories: On the depiction of migration in museums and exhibitions]. In *Inventur Migration: Tagungsdokumentation* [Inventory migration: conference documentation], edited by DOMiD, 14–26. Cologne: DOMiD.

Bayer, Natalie. 2012. 'Zur Notwendigkeit neuer Bilderproduktionen der Migration im Museum' [On the need for new image productions of migration in the museum]. In *Stand der Dinge: Sammlung und Darstellung der Migrationsgeschichte: Tagungsdokumentation* [State of things: collection and presentation of the history of migration: conference documentation], edited by Ahmed Sezer, 53–6. Cologne: DOMiD.

Brunner, Kati, Marjana Sawka and Sofia Onufriv. 2013. *Skype Mama*. Berlin: Edition.fotoTAPETA.

Burrell, Kathy. 2016. 'The recalcitrance of distance: Exploring the infrastructures of sending in migrants' lives', *Mobilities* 12(6): 813–26. https://doi.org/10.1080/17450101.2016.1225799.

Castles, Stephen and Mark J. Miller. 1998. *The Age of Migration*, 2nd edition. New York: Guilford Press.

Clifford, James. 1997. *Routes: Travel and translation in the late twentieth century*. Cambridge, MA: Harvard University Press.

Czycholl, Claudia Valeska. 2019. 'Auto und Fernseher: Die "private Praxis" der Fotografie von "Gastarbeiter*innen"' [Car and TV: the 'private practice' of photography by 'guest workers']. In *Das neue Zuhause: Haushalt und Alltag nach der Migration* [The new home: household and daily life after migration], edited by Hans Peter Hahn and Friedemann Neumann, 307–24. Frankfurt am Main: Campus.

Eryılmaz, Aytaç. 2004. 'Deutschland braucht ein Migrationsmuseum: Plädoyer für einen Paradigmenwechsel in der Kulturpolitik' [Germany needs a migration museum: plea for a paradigm shift in cultural politics]. In *Geschichte und Gedächtnis in der Einwanderungsgesellschaft: Migration zwischen historischer Rekonstruktion und Erinnerungspolitik* [History and memory in the immigrant society: migration between historical reconstruction and the politics of memory], edited by Jan Motte and Rainer Ohliger, 305–22. Essen: Klartext.

Eryılmaz, Aytaç. 2007. 'The political and social significance of a museum of migration in Germany', *Museum International* 59(1–2): 127–36. https://doi.org/10.1111/j.1468-0033.2007.00604.x.

Eryılmaz, Aytaç. 2012. 'Thesen zur Perspektive eines Migrationsmuseums' [Theses on the perspective of a migration museum]. In *Stand der Dinge: Sammlung und Darstellung der Migrationsgeschichte: Tagungsdokumentation* [State of things: collection and presentation of the history of migration: conference documentation], edited by Ahmed Sezer, 33–5. Cologne: DOMiD.

Fresnoza-Flot, Asuncion. 2009. 'Migration status and transnational mothering: The case of Filipino migrants in France', *Global Networks* 9(2): 252–70. http://dx.doi.org/10.1111/j.1471-0374.2009.00253.x.

Gestrich, Andreas and Marita Krauss. 2007. *Zurückbleiben: Der vernachlässigte Teil der Migrationsgeschichte* [Staying behind: the neglected part of migration history]. Stuttgart: Franz Steiner.

Glick Schiller, Nina, Linda Basch and Cristina Blanc-Szanton. 1992. 'Transnationalism: A new analytic framework for understanding migration', *Annals of the New York Academy of Sciences* 645(1): 1–24. https://doi.org/10.1111/j.1749-6632.1992.tb33484.x.

Gogos, Manuel. 2012. '"Wir graben den Schacht von Babel" – Kulturpolitische Grundlagen des Sammelns und Darstellens von Migration' ['We are digging the well of Babel': cultural political foundations of collecting and depicting migration]. In *Stand der Dinge: Sammlung und Darstellung der Migrationsgeschichte: Tagungsdokumentation* [State of things: collection and presentation of the history of migration: conference documentation], edited by Ahmed Sezer, 14–23. Cologne: DOMiD.

Hall, Stuart. [1981] 2002. 'Notes on deconstructing "the popular"'. In *Cultural Resistance Reader*, edited by Stephen Duncombe, 185–92. London and New York: Verso.

Klahn, Andrej. 2005. 'Zur Not auf vor den Reichstag' [In front of the Reichstag, if necessary], *kultur. west: Magazin für Kunst und Gesellschaft in NRW*, 1 November. Accessed 24 August 2021. https://www.kulturwest.de/inhalt/zur-not-auch-vor-den-reichstag/.

Korff, Gottfried. 2005. 'Fragen zur Migrationsmusealisierung: Versuch einer Einleitung' [Questions on the musealisation of migration: an attempt at an introduction]. In *Migration und Museum: Neue Ansätze in der Museumspraxis* [Migration and museum: new approaches in museum practice], edited by Henrike Hampe, 5–15. Münster: LIT.

Kruk, Halyna. 2013. 'Ho paura' [I'm frightened]. In *Bitter Things: Narratives and memories of transnational families*, edited by Malve Lippmann, Maike Suhr and Can Sungu, 85–90. Berlin: Archive Books.

Lanz, Francesca. 2016. 'Staging migration (in) museums: A reflection on exhibition design practices for the representation of migration in European contemporary museums', *Museum and Society* 14(1): 178–92. https://doi.org/10.29311/mas.v14i1.633.
Lippmann, Malve, Maike Suhr and Can Sungu, eds. 2018. *Bitter Things: Narratives and memories of transnational families*. Berlin: Archive Books.
Motte, Jan and Rainer Ohliger, eds. 2004. *Geschichte und Gedächtnis in der Einwanderungsgesellschaft: Migration zwischen historischer Rekonstruktion und Erinnerungspolitik* [History and memory in immigrant society: migration between historical reconstruction and the politics of memory]. Essen: Klartext.
Paasche, Erlend and Jørgen Carling. 2017. 'How migrants manage'. Department of Criminology and Sociology of Law, University of Oslo. Accessed 24 August 2021. https://www.jus.uio.no/ikrs/english/research/projects/migma/how-migrants-manage/index.html.
Parreñas, Rhacel S. 2001. 'Mothering from a distance: Emotions, gender, and intergenerational relations in Filipino transnational families', *Feminist Studies* 27(2): 361–90. https://doi.org/10.2307/3178765.
Poehls, Kerstin. 2011. 'Europe, blurred: Migration, margins and the museum', *Culture Unbound* 3(3): 337–53. https://doi.org/10.3384/cu.2000.1525.113337.
Polis, Stefano. 2011. *Milch in Papier: Kindheit und Jugend zwischen zwei Kulturen: Autobiographische Erzählungen* [Milk in paper: childhood and adolescence between two cultures: autobiographical stories]. Frankfurt am Main: Grössenwahn.
Riedel, Friedlind. 2019. 'Atmospheric relations: Theorising music and sound as atmosphere'. In *Music as Atmosphere: Collective feelings and affective sounds*, edited by Friedlind Riedel and Juha Torvinen, 1–42. Abingdon and New York: Routledge.
Vacca, Sandra. 2012. 'Modelle musealer Darstellung von Einwanderung' [Models of museal depiction of migration]. In *Stand der Dinge: Sammlung und Darstellung der Migrationsgeschichte: Tagungsdokumentation* [State of things: collection and presentation of the history of migration: conference documentation], edited by Ahmet Sezer, 50–2. Cologne: DOMiD.
Van de Laar, Paul. 2009. 'Erbe und das Leben der Anderen im Einwanderungsland' [Heritage and the life of others in the country of immigration]. Accessed 6 December 2020. https://docplayer.org/28349790-Erbe-und-das-leben-der-anderen-im-einwanderungsland.html.
Wolbert, Barbara. 2010. '"Studio of realism": On the need for art in exhibitions on migration history', *Forum: Qualitative Sozialforschung/Qualitative Social Research* 11(2) (art. no. 34). https://doi.org/10.17169/fqs-11.2.1483.

Songs and music videos

Arges Popular. 2011. 'Ai plecat mama departe', YouTube video, 04:35. 23 December. Translated by Malve Lippmann. Accessed 8 February 2021. https://www.youtube.com/watch?v=GpYDTQDqkgI.
Bustos, Mikey. 2013. 'Balikbayan box (Pinoy Wrecking Ball parody)', YouTube video, 4:12. 11 December. Accessed 24 August 2021. https://www.youtube.com/watch?v=WSMw7trHUcU&-index=26&list=PLg_aTjVGL1EP0McWqc-8NQFT1Kajwsvn6j.
Eurovision Song Contest. 2015. 'Voltaj – De la capăt/All over again – (Romania) 2015 Eurovision Song Contest', YouTube video, 03:00. 17 March. Accessed 24 August 2021. https://www.youtube.com/watch?v=WA3wOKHpzEU.
Tsouf, George. 2017. 'ΤΟ ΨΩΜΙ ΤΗΣ ΞΕΝΗΤΙΑΣ [The bread of Xenitiá] – ΣΤΕΛΙΟΣ ΚΑΖΑΝΤΖΙΔΗΣ (Stelios Kazantzidis)', YouTube video, 03:21. 26 April. Accessed 8 February 2021. https://www.youtube.com/watch?v=ICi8s-RyBnMk.
Ukrainian Times. 2017. 'Віолетта Тимофієва "Мати-емігрантка" автор пісні Ірина Лончина' [Violet Timofyva, 'Mati emigrant'. Song written by Irina Lonchina], Facebook Watch video, 5:13 mins. 29 November. Accessed 24 August 2021. https://www.facebook.com/watch/?v=546872542332167.
Unknown. 2016. 'O strofa pentru copii care au parintii la munca in strainatate', YouTube video, 00:59. 2 February. Translated by Malve Lippmann. Accessed 8 February 2021. https://www.youtube.com/watch?v=tsYXcCWBJSo&index=3&list=PLg_aTjVGL1EP0McWqc8NQFT1Kajwsvn6j.
Yıldız, Nebahat. n.d. *Babamızı gönder Almanya* [Germany, give us our father back]. Istanbul: Sevilen. Translated by Can Sungu.

10

Lockdown routines: im/mobility, materiality and mediated support at the time of the pandemic

Maruška Svašek

Introduction

In mid-March 2020, when my university in Belfast closed its doors and my diary began to show a confused picture of cancelled, postponed and digitised meetings, I spoke with my sister on WhatsApp about the impact of the coronavirus crisis on our lives, and our recent experiences of online teaching. Marianne is based in the Netherlands, our country of birth. She lives with her Dutch husband close to Rotterdam and teaches classical Indian music at the Rotterdam Conservatory. At the time, their 21-year-old daughter Milah studied art and photography and lived in rented accommodation, a 20-minute bike ride away from her parents. In line with Dutch government policy, Milah had to arrange 'socially distanced' meetings with her parents, and normal everyday physical interaction was no longer possible.

As I live in the UK, any chance that my sister and I would meet within the foreseeable future seemed zero.[1] Travel restrictions in both countries ruled out international travel, and the ban was not going to be lifted any time soon. Settled families, like ours, were in a relatively good position to deal with the crisis. Homeownership and steady jobs, which we continued to do from home, secured relatively comfortable lives in isolation, in both the UK and the Netherlands. Access to digital technology and financial security ensured ongoing long-distance communication, and guaranteed future get-togethers in post-pandemic times. Our situation was worlds away from the precarious circumstances faced by many migrants, asylum seekers and refugees (Cohen 2020; Ray 2020; Murphy 2021). Driven from their home regions and homelands by economic deprivation and political instability, and in numerous cases lacking legal status and a roof above their heads, many uprooted families found themselves in a highly vulnerable position, doubting whether they would ever meet their dispersed relatives, even in post-pandemic times.

Despite these vast differences, the Covid-19 crisis has posed challenges to all humans. The highly contagious disease has demanded new ways of coping with a radically changed dynamics of proximity and distance at a time when close contact can be deadly. Commenting on the crisis situation in Italy in March 2020, the sociologist Marco Pedroni argued that to gain a nuanced picture of the lockdown it is necessary to produce 'a microsociology of everyday lives', exploring people's 'individual routines'. Pedroni (2020) identified five contrasting factors that should be taken into account, dividing people into groups of:

1. people with *caring responsibilities* (children, old parents) vs. people without.
2. people required to *work outside* (doctors, nurses, couriers, cashiers etc.) vs. teleworkers.
3. people keeping their *job and salary* vs. people fearing they may lose it (or those who have already lost it).
4. people living in comfortable houses vs. those in confined tiny flats and *decaying public housing*.
5. people owning the cultural and economic resources to access and use *digital technologies* (e-shopping, entertainment platforms, devices for kids to be schooled online) vs. people with low or no resources.

This chapter adds a sixth division to the ones identified by Pedroni: the distinction between people whose family members *live nearby*, and those who live *at a geographical distance*. The transnational families at the centre of this chapter fit into the latter category.

'At a geographical distance' does not, of course, mean that relatives necessarily live in different countries. On the contrary, the imperative to stay at home during lockdown confronted both migrant and non-migrant families with a situation in which physical contact between members of different households was forbidden. While kin living at shorter distances from each other could potentially set up socially distanced meetings, the travel restrictions prohibited encounters between relatives who lived further apart. The pandemic, in other words, highlighted a commonality less obvious in pre-lockdown times: the fact that both migrant and non-migrant relatives often live in separate homes at some geographical distance.

Focusing on the interlinked themes of mobility, materiality and emotions, this chapter investigates how seven migrant women (including myself), living on the island of Ireland, dealt with the situation of forced quarantine during the first period of *deep lockdown* in March–April 2020, when governments put severe restrictions on people's physical movement. It investigates how the women, none of them key workers, attempted to create an ongoing sense of family life, providing care to distant relatives.[2] My understanding of care (Svašek 2008, 2010b, 2018) is informed by the work of Baldassar, Baldock and Wilding (2007), who, drawing on Finch and Mason (1993), have explored five dimensions of care: hands-on care, practical support, emotional support, financial support and accommodation provision, and have distinguished between 'virtual' and 'proximate' care practices (see also Kilkey and Merla 2014). This contrast gained particular relevance during deep lockdown. The analysis will investigate the provision of virtual emotional support at a time of increased human immobility, and examine how material artefacts, namely communication devices, afforded and mediated kin work at a distance.

When lockdown started in Northern Ireland and I found myself reaching out more regularly than usual to relatives in the Netherlands and the Czech Republic, I wondered how the pandemic was affecting the ways in which other transnational families used communication technologies. To what extent did the forced immobility produce new routines of long-distance emotional interaction and virtual care? Based on a series of digital interviews conducted between March and August 2020, the chapter focuses on the experiences of six migrant women, aged between 29 and 58, all living on the island of Ireland. Two are from the USA, and the others were born in Poland, Bulgaria, Germany and Finland. Adding an autoethnographic element, I also reflect on my own use of digital media during lockdown, comparing two technologies. I have changed the names and some of the details of the other women.

Emotions and virtual care in lockdown: polymedia environments

On 10 April, at around 10 a.m. UK time, 36-year-old Newtownards-based German Meike receives a WhatsApp text from her younger sister Else, who lives in Berlin. 'Can we talk?' Following local lockdown instructions, both started working from home when the numbers of people infected with Covid-19 increased sharply across Europe.[3] Since early March, they have had almost daily contact, keeping each other updated about the impact of the pandemic in Germany and the UK. When Meike reads Else's message she decides to take a brief break for a video call. Within seconds, her sister's image appears on the screen of her mobile. The cupboard behind her indicates that she is sitting at her kitchen table. The usual question, 'How are things?' (*Wie geht's?*), starts the conversation. After a few minutes of light-hearted banter, Meike detects signs of distress in her sister's voice. 'Is everything okay?' Else's face drops as she mentions rising tensions between herself and her husband, who also works from home in their tiny apartment. 'Wait a minute,' Meike interrupts, 'let's call on our laptops through Skype.' Soon the siblings look at each other on larger screens. While still unable to look into each other's eyes, they get a better sense of body language. 'I wish I could hug you!', Meike says, and blows a kiss at the camera. Else pushes her bottom lip out, demonstrating her distress. The projection of their own faces on the computer screens makes them hyper-aware of their performative actions. As Else discusses her problems, Meike listens carefully, nodding her head emphatically at the right moment and changing her facial expressions in expected ways. She then offers advice, but has to end the conversation after a few minutes as she is pressed for time, needing to finish a report for her boss. Her last comment is a joke that attempts to make her sister smile. Feeling a bit guilty, she follows up with a quick text to announce when she'll be able to continue the conversation: 'I'll call you tonight after dinner! ☺☺☺'. The three emojis are intended to lift her sister's mood.

The virtual exchange illustrates how, during deep lockdown, the research participants used different media to offer emotional support to their distant relatives, shifting between technologies and performative actions in 'polymedia' environments (Madianou and Miller 2012). Their choice of texting and video calls was informed by the specific possibilities and limitations offered by these technologies and the ways in which they created specific temporal experiences. As Nancy Baym (2010, 7) noted, 'temporal structure' is an important comparative dimension of virtual media.[4] In the exchange described above, the mix of synchronous and asynchronous engagement though rapid shifts between WhatsApp and Skype allowed for the interlinkage and break-up of shared time in reaction to family needs and work obligations. As with most of the other women in my research, the competing pressures of kin work and paid labour in pandemic circumstances affected Meike's normal work–leisure routine, as she now regularly inserted unplanned breaks in response to calls from distant relatives. Working from home, she had the freedom to shift rapidly between her job and family life, taking a flexible approach that allowed her to respond to an increased need for emotional support.

To explore the emotional dynamics of digital interaction, I draw on a multidimensional perspective that understands emotional processes as embodied experiences and discursively framed practices with performative dimensions (Svašek 2005a, 2005b). In the example above, the empathetic exchange was shaped by culturally constructed expectations that reinforced specific notions of mutual care obligation between close kin. The expectations did not just create a sense of emotional security (Else knew she could rely on her sister's support, and vice versa), but were also potentially felt as a burden. Meike's sense of guilt when she had to end the conversation clearly showed this tension.

Emotional repertoires that encode care-giving and care-receiving practices are often consciously performed when kin purposely enact the 'right' response and hide 'inappropriate' conflicting feelings (Svašek 2010b, 2018). These actions may be exaggerated in contexts of virtual exchange in response to the absence of physical proximity. Else consciously acted out her sadness, sticking out her bottom lip, and Meike used gestures to show support, blowing a kiss, and hiding feelings of work-related stress. Unlike involuntary physiological processes, such as a rising body temperature, these bodily activities were clearly learned. As Wetherell (2012, 160) argued, 'many complicated flows across bodies, subjectivities, relations, histories and contexts entangle and intertwine together' to generate emotions at specific affective moments.[5]

People, things and viruses as affective forces

Drawing on insights in research on material culture, materiality and agency (Bennett 2010; Gell 1998; Miller 1998) and recent debates in affect theory (Röttger-Rössler and Slaby 2018), this chapter explores how, in addition to people, all sorts of phenomena, including communication devices and viruses, constitute fields of interactive forces in relational scenes. My approach to affect and emotions does not, as those of some theorists have done, define affect as precognitive intensity, which becomes known through named emotions (see Wetherell 2012 and Wise and Velayutham 2017 for a critical discussion). In contrast, I employ the notion of affective relationality (Röttger-Rössler and Slaby 2018; Svašek 2018) to explore the interplay of forces within and between humans, and between human and non-human phenomena. From this relational perspective, stomach ache (causing pain, distress and anger), the act of blowing up a balloon when air pressure increases its size and triggers a smile on a child's face), a devastating virus (resulting in illness and death) and tapping on a phone (to send an upbeat text) are all processes in which affecting forces interact. Emotional processes emerge in, shape and are shaped by these unfolding dynamics (Svašek 2005a). In the example of Meike and Else, the threat of Covid-19 produced an increased need for emotional support, enabled and influenced by the technological possibilities and limitations of specific devices. This did not leave the sisters without affective agency. To maintain their long-distance relationship safely, they manipulated their phones and computers, adapting their emotional interaction to the circumstances.

In pre-pandemic research on transnational families, communication technology and care, I demonstrated that distant kin were often able to use multiple devices and digital platforms as connecting tools to create a sense of interconnected family life (Svašek 2010a, 2010b, 2018). Various technologies, including landlines, fax machines, mobile phones, computers, tablets and postal services, allowed them to stay in touch, express emotions, provide support and negotiate care arrangements (see also Baldassar and Merla 2014). The materiality of the devices was of crucial importance, as the artefacts, visibly present in people's everyday lives, were inherent forces in dynamic fields of translocal sociality. Particular devices had distinct capacities that generated and shaped a diversity of emotions and care-giving practices. These included the ability to remind owners of the existence of absent kin, confronting them with stored images (computers, smartphones, tablets) and recorded messages (computers, smartphones, tablets), and the possibility of calling for attention though ringtones (mobile phones and landlines) (Svašek 2018, 32). While synchronic technologies afforded immediate experiences of co-presence, asynchronic communication enabled intermittent discussions about care responsibilities between larger groups of kin living in different time zones.[6] Portability and accessibility were also important material factors that shaped the affective field. Mobile phones, for example, were easily carried around and used for frequent texting. This 'ambient virtual co-presence', described by Mizuko Ito and Daisuke Okabe (2005, 264) as 'a way of maintaining ongoing background awareness of others, and of keeping multiple channels of communication open', was not always welcomed by migrants, as it forced their attention away from locally lived lives.

In the case of Meike and Else, the materiality of the devices clearly mattered. Smartphone technology was needed to project texts and images across distance, and in the context of the pandemic the action of making one's voice heard in unreachable locations fed a sense of agency and mobility. Spatiality was equally important. The sisters always placed their mobiles next to their laptops, which allowed effortless movement between the devices. Size affected their emotional exchange as well, as the larger computer screens, placed directly in front of them, simulated physical co-presence. Furthermore, the webcam afforded simultaneous visual and aural input,[7] further shaping the affective environment (Hillis 1999, 2009; King-O'Riain 2015, 260).

Old and new routines in the face of im/mobility

The central question in this chapter is how, during the first lockdown period, different communication devices shaped old and newly emerging routines of long-distance sociality and emotional support. Bearing in mind Pedroni's five contrasting factors, all the research participants were settled, found themselves in relatively secure positions, were able to work from home, and felt responsible for the well-being of at least some relatives in the homeland. Four of the women had care obligations to young or teenage children. All had access to computers and mobile phones. Their lockdown routines showed a number of emerging patterns, described here as 'continuation', 'intensification', 'innovation' and 'distancing'.

'Continuation' alludes to the ongoing routines of pre-crisis activities. For migrant families, the need to communicate across geographical distance was, of course, already an unavoidable reality before the pandemic, shaping their translocal subjectivities (Baldassar et al. 2007; Baldassar 2007; Conradson and McKay 2007; Parreñas 2005; Ryan et al. 2014). Visibly present in the homes of the women, the devices were material reminders of lasting kin obligations and recurrent practices of mutual care. When I Skyped with Stella, a 47-year-old Bulgarian translator who had lived in Belfast for 20 years, she made exactly that point, saying: 'Being migrants, not much has changed. We normally talk on-line with family back home and have done so for a long time. It's been 15 years since we started using Skype.' For many years, she had video-called her parents every Sunday, keeping the tradition going with her dad after her mother died. As regular occurrences, her parents' virtual appearances in her Belfast home can be compared, at least in their predictability and moral and emotional intentionality, to rituals that many non-migrant families in Northern Ireland are engaged in, such as sharing a Sunday roast dinner. The digital get-togethers had nourished a relationship across three generations, strengthening the relationship between her children and their grandparents. The virtual routine was also part of a yearly rhythm of mobility that included annual visits to Bulgaria during the summer holidays. Unsurprisingly, the weekly virtual encounters continued during lockdown, especially when it became clear that they would have to cancel this year's trip.

Tiina, a 29-year-old Finnish student who was married to an Austrian IT worker, described her pre-crisis long-distance interactions with family and friends as follows:

> Both me and my husband have lived away from our home countries for almost ten years … Besides visiting everyone during the holidays, we both call our families at least once a week. I have gotten into a habit of calling one of my grandmothers, who lives in a residential home and misses me most from my family, twice a week. I stay in touch with the rest of the family mostly by sending an occasional picture or message in the family's WhatsApp group.

The exchange of messages and photographs, and their audible and visible appearance in concrete locations, linked up physically separate people and things in affective spaces of digital interaction. In addition to access to the internet, the availability and cost of particular technologies were influencing factors. As Tiina noted,

> Generally, we would also call my Austrian husband's grandparents, parents and brother around two times per week. For this purpose, I have kept my phone contract from my home country for the past two years, since I have free calls to all the EU countries due to free roaming. We are all used to staying in touch with each other by phone, Skype or WhatsApp.

Intensification

Tiina added that, compared with her pre-pandemic routines, 'it is surprising to notice how much Covid-19 has changed our ways of communicating with our family and friends'. Like Meike, Tiina intensified her mobile phone and internet use, communicating more frequently with a larger number of relatives and friends. She noted:

> The closure of schools in Austria changed our relations with my husband's family. Suddenly, his 11-year-old little brother would be

home all day and could not meet any of his friends or even grandmother who lives next door. He would also need help with some of his schoolwork and soon we noticed that instead of calling twice a week, we started talking with them at least twice a day.

Their laptops became important material entryways that allowed them to digitally access and become part of the boy's lifeworld, helping him to do his homework and fight boredom. 'To make it more fun', she said, 'we bought the same online game that he has (*Age of Empires 2*) and started playing with him, keeping Skype open so that we could talk as well.'[8] The boy missed visiting his 76-year-old grandmother, so they invited her to join in the game from her own computer. Tiina laughed, explaining, 'She is into computer games, though inexperienced in playing with other people. She's not very good at this game but that doesn't matter.' They were, however, able to communicate while playing. Tiina's husband advised the others on gaming strategies and his brother talked about 'absolutely everything'. The technology allowed them to be immersed in a shared activity and temporarily forget their forced immobility, playing in one team against the computer.

The 36-year-old Polish social worker Joanna noted that, at the beginning of lockdown, she had started using Skype and Messenger more frequently than before. She was concerned about her mother, a teacher, who was still going to work in Poland.

> I was worried that my mum would catch the coronavirus. Given that she is a heavy smoker and has hypertension, she is in a risk group. So at the beginning of that crisis I was calling her repeatedly over Skype. I was then very relieved when the government decided to close the schools.

She also contacted her sister to negotiate care arrangements.

> I started contacting my sister more often via Messenger because I was hoping my mum could possibly go over to where she lives, a small town, much safer than Warsaw. But unfortunately, the risk of travelling on public transport was too high.

Wondering how long it would be before her toddler would be able to see his granny, she regularly sent photographs of her son to her mother. Her mother found it hard to miss out on seeing her grandchild grow up, and the added insecurity of the pandemic made the situation worse. Decreased human mobility, in other words, was compensated for by an increased distribution of digital photographs and their potential as emotional triggers and repositories.[9] Looking at photos, however, was not the same as holding hands, and the striking difference generated mixed feelings. During my pre-pandemic fieldwork in 2010 and 2016, numerous elderly interviewees had noted that the sudden appearance of a photographic image of their grandchild on a screen, and the knowledge that the shot might have been taken only seconds ago, could trigger competing emotions. On the one hand, it triggered a warm sense of intimate belonging. On the other, it emphasised the limits of digital sociality and triggered painful feelings of longing and loneliness. Joanna hoped of course that the photographs of her child would most of all comfort her mother.

Covid-19 as mobile and motivating force

Betty, a 46-year-old American yoga teacher who lived in Larne, also intensified her contact with her relatives at home. She indicated that before the coronavirus crisis, she mostly texted older family members, as many did not have smartphones. She exchanged occasional calls with her younger sister and hardly ever used FaceTime. She was one of ten cousins. Eight lived in the USA, and one had moved to Sweden. Some years earlier, they had started organising a reunion in the USA every two years, and she travelled over from Ireland for that occasion. Otherwise, she was not in touch with them.

This routine changed when Jens, the Swedish husband, contracted Covid-19. The family was shocked, because the state of forced immobility had not stopped the very mobile virus from entering his body. All the cousins, concerned about his health, began sending frequent supportive messages to the family's Facebook page, participating in what Malcolm Parks (2011, 117–18) has called a 'virtual community'. The concept identifies groups whose members use social network sites to reinforce their relations, share ritual practices, bond emotionally, and engage in collective action, a process leading to an increased 'sense of belonging and group identification' (Parks 2011, 117–18). While the notion of 'community' has been widely debated (Amit and Rapport 2002) and has to be treated with care in relation to digital interaction (Postill 2008; Miller 2011, 181–6), regular online interaction did increase Betty's identification with the wider family network. This was partly enabled by Facebook's format, which allowed scrolling backwards and forwards between messages, photographs and other posts, irrespective of when contributions were made. This collapsing of time, in combination with the visual accumulation of messages and responses, intensified her sense of mutual interaction and support.

After Jens's recovery, the cousins looked for a way to meet up in shared time, and organised their first meeting on Zoom. At first, the technology felt alien. The fact that, realistically, only one person could speak at any one time seemed particularly unnatural.

> It was a bit awkward; we had to find a way of structuring the conversation. The first time, we took turns speaking, starting with the oldest cousin. The second time, the interaction was less structured, which made it more difficult, but it was still better than nothing. We felt closer together. I had never heard of Zoom before. Was it specifically invented for the lockdown situation?

Her question alludes to the rapid familiarisation process that has enabled migrants and non-migrants alike to overcome physical distance during the pandemic. While Zoom (and other technologies like MS Teams and Voov) were not new, many people only discovered their potential because of the travel restrictions.

Innovation

The need to come up with alternative means of long-distance support and emotional interaction was particularly felt when a distant family member became infected, as in the example above, or during regular annual celebrations that had structured family dynamics for generations. The Bulgarian, Stella, noted:

> During Easter, one thing really changed. We decided with my dad, my sister and her partner to have a shared Easter breakfast, using Skype conference. In both locations, we were sitting around the table with a laptop. It had no real resemblance to sitting together around the same table but it did create a sense of celebration. Communication was awkward because the sound quality was bad, but doing it marked the extraordinariness of Easter time. So the action was more important than the quality of the exchange.

The digitally mediated meeting emphasised the importance of ritual interaction to the dynamics of intergenerational sociality. As in the example of Meike and Else, the size of the laptops mattered. The devices were small enough to be placed on the dinner table, and large and powerful enough that the family could see and hear their distant kin. Other artefacts were also central to the occasion. Stella had baked a special Easter bread and the whole family had painted colourful Easter eggs. As objects that could be seen across distance, they were as important to the experience as the enabling laptops and internet connection.

During Easter, eggs were also central to long-distance exchanges between my sister and myself. On Easter day, my husband, my son and I painted an egg each, a common tradition in the Czech Republic and (less so) in the Netherlands. We had not done this for many years, but the activity helped us to break the humdrum of our confined lockdown lives. Inspired by the coronavirus crisis, my husband turned his egg into a bloke, smoking a cigarette through a mask. Our son created an internet star, complete with fake tan and ultra-blonde hair. I transformed my egg into a nasty-looking coronavirus. Relevant to the arguments made in this chapter, we photographed the eggs (Figure 10.1), and I sent the pictures to my sister through WhatsApp, wishing her happy Easter. The quick action of taking, attaching, uploading and sending photographs on a special family day reinforced the sense of care, not only for each other, but also for a shared family tradition. The reply of smiling emojis showed how we used humour and laughter to make light of a crisis situation.

Other forms of digital engagement with distant relatives that were newly introduced by the women in the study included meeting up for online quizzes and drinks, joining a variety of Zoom classes together, communication about imaginary visits to the homeland through Google Earth, and hanging out on Skype or Zoom, while being engaged in separate activities.

10.1 Three Easter eggs. © Maruška Svašek, 2020.

Innovation, reproduction and digital contexts

The ease of digital traffic and reproduction created its own rhythm. Once typed or photographed, little effort was needed to forward items or incorporate them into new media and posts. Maike remarked how easy it was to circulate photographs received from a relative within the wider German family network, adding new comments and symbols like hearts and thumbs-up. She explained that her extended family had eventually created a shared WhatsApp group to avoid cross-posting photographs. Some of the other women were concerned about the appearance of privately sent photographs and messages on publicly accessible social media sites. A funny, supportive joke, shared in a private group, could easily become an insulting statement in a new digital context. The impact of photographs could also change radically when they were reproduced in different formats. To illustrate this transitionary process, the next section briefly compares the significance of the photos of the three Easter eggs as WhatsApp messages with their affective force as visual elements in a longer and more complex blog post

At the start of lockdown, my sister Marianne, her daughter Milah and I decided to create a shared Google document to keep each other informed about the ways in which the crisis was affecting our lives. Referring to it as 'our blog' (*onze blog*), we anticipated that the string of contributions would help us reflect on the ups and downs of our isolation, and that our routine engagement, writing and reading each other's posts, would facilitate ongoing mutual support whenever we felt challenged or depressed by the situation. The contribution in which the photographs of the eggs appeared showed that this did indeed happen. It also illustrates how the pictures were newly contextualised, as they were incorporated into a more complex supportive chain of messages. In the post, the photographs of the eggs were three of five visuals in a short contribution that included a written text. The post started with a reference to a WhatsApp call I had made with my sister earlier in the day: 'As I said before, when we rang, beautiful picture and text!' My compliment referred to a photograph that she had uploaded some days earlier that showed an agricultural machine, standing in a typically Dutch landscape (Figure 10.2). The image was her visual comment on a photograph that I had posted some weeks before (Figure 10.3). Attempting to bring a playful element into the somewhat serious blog space, I had suggested that the three of us could create a growing series of photographs over time, each new picture reacting to the previously posted one. I took my first photo of two lonely swings, tied together by a signboard. The image indexed our local lockdown conditions, as all playgrounds had been closed because of the risk of infection. Reflecting my mood, a dark, grey sky above the Irish Sea completed the composition. Marianne's visual response repeated the theme of the abandoned landscape, but presented a more uplifting scene. Under a partially clouded sky that opened up with a promising blue patch, the machine parts seemed to be in intimate

10.2 Agricultural machine in the Netherlands. © Marianne Svašek, 2000.

10.3 Closed-down playground in Bangor, Northern Ireland. © Maruška Svašek, 2000.

conversation. Compared to my waiting swings, her landscape, complete with yellow flowers, reflected a sense of 'optimism after all'.

In the blog entry, my comment on Marianne's photograph was followed by a brief question and comment about online teaching and learning and a comment about an acquaintance who had broken down, saying that she had 'too much time to reflect' in isolation. A one-liner about 'the idiot Trump' was followed by a few sentences relating to our brother, who was stuck in India without a source of income, and with whom we were communicating through WhatsApp to organise his return to the Netherlands. The blog post ended with a reference to the painting of the Easter eggs and baking bread.

The blog, with its ability to incorporate digital photographs, was a particularly useful medium for creating a sense of ongoing communication and care. The routine of writing, taking pictures, posting, looking and reading created its own emotional rhythm, giving us time to react to each other's reflections and express appreciation, empathy and concern. This was also clear in the next post, in which Milah wrote how much she enjoyed reading the new entries, but missed our physical presence. At the time she was writing, her face-to-face contact with her parents was minimal because of new government regulations on social distancing. Responding to my comment about the friend who had cried, she reflected on her own emotional state, writing: 'I understand your friend, Marus, I think that everyone in quarantine is more intensely confronted with personal stuff, consciously or unconsciously. I find it hard, sometimes, but most of all I welcome it. I am slowly accepting that I am a dreamer who simply likes nature and silence.'

The shared Google Document format created an intimate digital space that also generated expectations. Disappointed when others had not posted for a while, we frequently reminded each other to create a new post and eventually stopped using it. The end of *onze blog* demonstrated that we had slowly become used to 'the new normal', my sister and I reverting to our usual (but now more frequent) WhatsApp texts and calls.

Distancing

This last section will give some examples of what I have called 'distancing', moments when some of the women in the study experienced alienation between themselves and their geographically distant relatives. Distancing counters the illusion of an unproblematic, happy digital world in which long-distance family relations always flourish.[10] Ashley, a 30-year-old American researcher, hit the nail on the head when she wrote:

> Weeks into my country's COVID-19 related shutdowns, and months into the global crisis, I've realized that my communications with my family haven't fundamentally changed during the pandemic. A lot of the discussion I see online romanticizes the notion of humans as social animals – discussing our deep-seated need for connection, suggesting that we turn to technologies like Zoom to make up for the lack of touch, of face-to-face conversation with those close to us. I find these discourses to be limited, and more than a little naïve … I have a family who can kindly be described as 'difficult', and so my own experience is much more complicated.

She described how, over the years, radically different views on politics and religion had resulted in a routine of social disengagement that, while not unloving, included little emotional interaction. 'I can (and often do) go many weeks at a time without contacting them – not out of malice, but out of genuine forgetfulness, because they're simply not a big part of my life.'

Covid-19 had, paradoxically, both intensified contact and reinforced a sense of distance. As Ashley noted, 'Just because you don't get on with someone doesn't mean you don't worry about them.' At the start of the pandemic, she started texting her parents a lot, and encouraged her mother to check up on her grandfather and advise him to give up weekly church visits. Ironically, she had not spoken to him for years, and might never see him again. In her own words, 'This is a man whose funeral I likely won't attend.'

Ashley's relationship with her mother-in-law was also strained. The latter was deeply disappointed in her son and daughter-in-law. She had expected them to share her values, live nearby and produce grandchildren. As a result, they had little contact, especially after the mother-in-law's recent remarriage. 'It seems', Ashley wrote in a reflective text, 'like the pandemic has reinforced the distance that's been growing there since her wedding. And honestly, this will make me sound like a bad person, but I am so relieved. I find her emails incredibly stressful and self-indulgent – walls of text littered with mundane details of her health.'

The other American interviewee, Betty, also alluded to a sense of alienation between herself and her relatives in the USA. Despite her renewed contact with her cousins, her relatives were much closer to each other than to her, as she was the only person in the family who had given up religion. Betty had mixed feelings when one of her relatives rang to talk about the recent death of an in-law who had been infected with Covid-19 and had died in an American hospital. Close to tears, the relative told her that they had gathered in the hospital car park, having to say goodbye by phone. A nurse in the hospital had held the phone to the dying woman's ear, which is another example of how communication technology has been used in new ways during the pandemic. Betty reacted with empathy, suppressing emotional ambiguity that emerged as she knew that 'she only called me because she could not get anyone else on the phone. She would have wanted to hear "she is in Heaven now". I couldn't say that, I'm not religious.'

Conclusion

The pandemic produced a situation in which a globally spreading coronavirus forced large numbers of human beings into spatial immobility as they attempted to counter its deadly impact. Like many others across the globe, the migrant women central to this chapter relied on communication technologies to 'move around' in virtual worlds to 'meet up' with distant kin. Their digital activities co-constituted an affective environment in which human and non-human agency shaped existing and newly emerging routines of virtual sociality and care. The unique situation can be understood as a triad of interacting affective forces that manifested themselves as dynamic assemblages of people, devices and viruses. I conceptualised the process as a relational field in which individuals continued to provide long-distance support in the changed socio-spatial, material and viral environment, not only drawing on pre-pandemic discourses, practices and embodied experiences of transnational family care, but also reacting to the specific opportunities and limitations posed by the lockdown and available technologies.

Their routines of long-distance care were partly driven by internalised moral discourses of family obligation. The women were also influenced by family-specific histories of care that produced specific desires and expectations around the provision and exchange of mutual support. As members of transnational families, they were used to the employment of communication devices for long-distance kin work, which meant that their bodies were already attuned to the affective possibilities of specific technologies. In pre-pandemic times, however, virtual rhythms of digital sociality existed in tandem with regular face-to-face interactions, including annual visits during holidays, and unplanned emergency visits at times of illness or death. As the threat of the virus and international travel restrictions disturbed their normal transnational movements, the lockdown called for additional communicative engagement.

To the women in the study, the situation of forced immobility generated an emotional need for increased contact, and led in all cases to an intensification of long-distance communication and care. Worries about the health of distant loved ones, concerns about rising mortality rates in the homeland, and anxieties about the exposure of distant kin to the disease encouraged more frequent virtual interaction, especially with elderly and vulnerable family members. The women all worked from home, and the easy accessibility of mobile phones and laptops motivated them to blend 'work time' and 'family time', a shift that increased expectations of frequent interaction.

The aggressive force of the virus had an enormous impact on the focus and content of the emotional interactions. The rapidly rising infection and mortality rates increased the women's urge to share concerns and regularly compare the situation on the island of Ireland with the situation in their homelands. When state borders and airports closed, they felt particularly powerless, fearing that it might be a long time before they would be allowed to travel internationally. In this regard, their situation was quite different to that of non-migrant locals who lived within a short distance of their kin, and who could easily organise socially distanced encounters. The situation of those living further apart was more akin to that of the migrant women. These non-migrant families, however, were able to meet up as soon as local restrictions were lifted. The migrant women, in contrast, were confronted with uncertainties about lengthy border closures. Furthermore, when travel restrictions ended temporarily, they were faced with the increased risk of contagion when travelling home. In addition to stress caused by physical immobility, these challenges increased the importance of long-distance communication with distant kin in their daily lives. As routines of digital engagement with family intensified, some tried technologies they had not used before, like Zoom and gaming. These innovations, which soon became familiar practices, provided new opportunities for translocal family life. Spending so much time in their homes, the women were in a position to experiment with virtual sociality and care, appropriating and mixing synchronous and asynchronous technologies.

The materiality of the devices affected old and new routines of interaction in multiple ways. The size of devices mattered, as mobile phones could be taken outside, and laptops and iPads were easily carried around the house, for example to show how home and garden spaces had been adapted to lockdown life, or how difficult it was to cope in a small kitchen. Larger screens enabled a more detailed gaze into the home spaces of distant kin. Portability enabled individuals to move into another room if a caller was in distress and needed personal attention. Spatial factors, such as the size of the house and the number of rooms, were also relevant, as those who lived in small apartments found it harder to find moments for private calls. Group-call features of Skype and Zoom encouraged get-togethers with larger groups of distant relatives. This was of particular use for ritual celebrations of birthdays and religious festivals. Visible signs of efforts made for others in virtually connected locations signalled a caring attitude. The resulting sense of togetherness was also enhanced through photos and films that were shared through family WhatsApp and Facebook groups, and captured aspects of social life in digitally interconnected separate lockdown locations. The illusion of co-presence was broken, however, whenever software or hardware problems occurred. Frozen screens, sound disturbances and blurred pixel faces reminded relatives of the reality of physical distance.

The affective field of long-distance family care produced a range of emotions, from joy and gratefulness, to irritation, sadness and guilt. The women in the study spoke about their longing for anticipated conversations, but also mentioned feelings of irritation caused by unwelcome calls and messages. Some referred to the moral and emotional burden of unrealistic expectations and noted that the pandemic had increased their sense of emotional distance from particular kin. Guilt about limited time for, or commitment to, specific relatives was also mentioned, as was disappointment about lapsing contacts, and ambiguous feelings about interactions with particular family members. So while the potential danger of the virus drove all the women in the study to take advantage of digital technology and use it to stay in touch with absent kin, their activities did not necessarily improve difficult relationships. Existing tensions, in other words, did not miraculously disappear when the affective force of the pandemic struck.

Notes

1 It was August 2021 before we managed to meet up in person.

2 The analysis draws on earlier research into transnational families and care practices, conducted in 2010 and 2016 (Svašek 2010b, 2018). This work focused on around one hundred European,

Indian, Iranian and Chinese transnational families, and analysed how relatives based in Northern Ireland used different technologies to demonstrate and negotiate practical and emotional support. This project employed multiple methods, including biographical interviews, focus groups, and participant observation in the Indian Community Centre in Belfast.

3 On 22 March, the German government and federal states prohibited gatherings of more than two people and imposed social distancing rules, requiring a minimum distance of 1.5 metres. Restaurants and services reliant on close contact, like hairdressers, had to close, and non-essential workers were encouraged to work from home. On 3 June, the German federal government agreed to allow travel to and from the UK (Connolly 2020), but Meike did not dare to travel to Berlin to see her sister.

4 Baym (2010, 7) identified six other comparative dimensions, namely 'interactivity … social cues, storage, replicability, reach, and mobility'.

5 See also Döveling et al. 2018, who use the term 'affect culture'.

6 Referring to Baron (1998), Carnevale and Probst (1997) and McKenna and Bargh (1998), Baym (2010, 8) argued that '[t]he beauty of synchronous media is that they allow for the very rapid transmission of messages, even across distance … [S]ynchronicity can enhance the sense of placelessness that digital media can encourage and make people feel more together when they are apart.' See also Madianou 2016 and Panagakos and Horst 2006.

7 As Rebecca Chyoko King-O'Riain (2015, 260) pointed out, 'Webcam use is visual and aural in real-time – one can see and hear the person with whom one is communicating as well as oneself simultaneously.'

8 In a study of Skype use in the Republic of Ireland, Rebecca Chiyoko King-O'Riain (2015, 256) used the term 'emotional streaming' to refer to practices that promote 'ongoing interaction over distance, which includes keeping Skype turned on for long periods of time'. She found: 'Through these attempts to try to recreate everyday practices via continuous use of Skype, transnational emotions of love and longing are deintensified.' See also King-O'Riain 2013.

9 See Elliott and Urry (2010) on 'emotional banking' and 'affect storage'.

10 Referring to Miller and Sinanan (2014), Rebecca Chyoko King-O'Riain (2015, 260) also found in her study of Skype use in Ireland that the availability of long-distance communication did not necessarily ensure strong kin relations and intimacy across distance.

Acknowledgements

I would like to thank the migrant women in this study for their cooperation and friendship, and the editors of this book for their constructive feedback.

References

Amit, Vered and Nigel Rapport, eds. 2002. *The Trouble with Community: Anthropological reflections on movement, identity and collectivity*. London: Pluto Press.

Baldassar, Loretta. 2007. 'Transnational families and the provision of moral and emotional support: The relationship between truth and distance', *Identities: Global Studies in Culture and Power* 14(4): 385–409. https://doi.org/10.1080/10702890701578423.

Baldassar, Loretta, Cora Baldock and Raelene Wilding. 2007. *Families Caring across Borders: Migration, ageing and transnational caregiving*. Basingstoke: Palgrave Macmillan.

Baldassar, Loretta and Laura Merla, eds. 2014. *Transnational Families, Migration and the Circulation of Care: Understanding mobility and absence in family life*. New York and Abingdon: Routledge.

Baron, Naomi S. 1998. 'Letters by phone or speech by other means: The linguistics of email', *Language and Communication* 18(2): 133–70. https://doi.org/10.1016/S0271-5309(98)00005-6.

Baym, Nancy K. 2010. *Personal Connections in the Digital Age*. Cambridge: Polity.

Bennett, Jane. 2010. *Vibrant Matters: A political ecology of things*. Durham, NC: Duke University Press.

Carnevale, Peter and Tahira M. Probst. 1997. 'Conflict on the Internet'. In *Culture of the Internet*, edited by Sara Kiesler, 233–55. Mahwah, NJ: Lawrence Erlbaum Associates.
Cohen, Jeffrey H. 2020. 'Editorial: Modeling migration, insecurity and COVID-19', *Migration Letters* 17(3): 405–10. https://doi.org/10.33182/ml.v17i3.986.
Connolly, Kate. 2020. 'Germany takes tentative steps back to normality as lockdown eases'. *The Guardian*, 20 April. Accessed 24 August 2021. https://www.theguardian.com/world/2020/apr/20/germany-takes-tentative-steps-back-to-normality-as-coronavirus-lockdown-eases.
Conradson, David and Deirdre McKay. 2007. 'Translocal subjectivities: Mobility, connection, emotion', *Mobilities* 2(2): 167–74. https://doi.org/10.1080/17450100701381524.
Döveling, Katrin, Anu A. Harju and Denise Sommer. 2018. 'From mediatized emotion to digital affect cultures: New technologies and global flows of emotion', *Social Media and Society* 4(1): 1–11. https://doi.org/10.1177%2F2056305117743141.
Elliott, Anthony and John Urry. 2010. *Mobile Lives*. London: Routledge.
Finch, Janet and Jennifer Mason. 1993. *Negotiating Family Responsibilities*. London: Routledge.
Gell, Alfred. 1998. *Art and Agency: An anthropological theory.* Oxford: Clarendon Press.
Hillis, Ken. 1999. *Digital Sensations: Space, identity, and embodiment in virtual reality*. Minneapolis: University of Minnesota Press.
Hillis, Ken. 2009. *Online a Lot of the Time: Ritual, fetish, sign*. Durham, NC: Duke University Press.
Ito, Mizuko and Daisuke Okabe. 2005. 'Technosocial situations: Emergent structuring of mobile e-mail use'. In *Personal, Portable, Pedestrian: Mobile phones in Japanese life*, edited by Mizuko Ito, Daisuke Okabe and Misa Matsuda, 257–74. Cambridge, MA: MIT Press.
Kilkey, Majella and Laura Merla. 2014. 'Situating transnational families' care-giving arrangements: The role of institutional contexts', *Global Networks* 14(2): 210–29. http://dx.doi.org/10.1111/glob.12034.
King-O'Riain, Rebecca C. 2013. 'Transconnective space, emotions and Skype: The transnational emotional practices of mixed international couples in the Republic of Ireland'. In *Internet and Emotions*, edited by Tova Benski and Eran Fisher, 131–43. New York and Abingdon: Routledge.
King-O'Riain, Rebecca C. 2015. 'Emotional streaming and transconnectivity: Skype and emotion practices in transnational families in Ireland', *Global Networks* 15(2): 256–73. https://doi.org/10.1111/glob.12072.
Madianou, Mirca. 2016. 'Ambient co-presence: Transnational family practices in polymedia environments', *Global Networks* 16(2): 183–201. https://doi.org/10.1111/glob.12105.
Madianou, Mirca and Daniel Miller. 2012. *Migration and New Media: Transnational families and polymedia*. London: Routledge.
McKenna, Katelyn Y. A. and John A. Bargh. 1998. 'Coming out in the age of the Internet: Identity "demarginalization" through virtual group participation', *Journal of Personality and Social Psychology* 75(3): 681–94. https://doi.apa.org/doi/10.1037/0022-3514.75.3.681.
Miller, Daniel. 1998. *Material Culture: Why some things matter*. London: UCL Press.
Miller, Daniel. 2011. *Tales from Facebook*. Cambridge: Polity.
Miller, Daniel and Jolynna Sinanan. 2014. *Webcam*. Cambridge: Polity.
Murphy, Fiona. 2021. 'Direct provision, rights and everyday life for asylum seekers in Ireland during COVID-19'. Social Sciences 10(4): 140. https://doi.org/10.3390/socsci10040140.
Panagakos, Anastasia N. and Heather A. Horst. 2006. 'Return to Cyberia: Technology and the social worlds of transnational migrants', *Global Networks* 6(2): 109–24. http://dx.doi.org/10.1111/j.1471-0374.2006.00136.x.
Parks, Malcolm R. 2011. 'Social network sites as virtual communities'. In *A Networked Self: Identity, community, and culture on social network sites*, edited by Zizi Papacharissi, 105–23. Abingdon: Routledge.
Parreñas, Rhacel S. 2005. 'Long distance intimacy: Class, gender and intergenerational relations between mothers and children in Filipino transnational families', *Global Networks* 5(4): 317–36. doi:10.1111/j.1471-0374.2005.00122.x.
Pedroni, Marco. 2020. 'Corona chaos: What the hell is going on in Italy?'. Medium, 13 April. Accessed 25 August 2021. https://medium.com/futurists-club-by-science-of-the-time/corona-chaos-what-the-hell-is-going-on-in-italy-931dbab6c6fe.
Postill, John. 2008 'Localizing the internet beyond communities and networks', *New Media and Society* 10(3): 413–31. https://doi.org/10.1177%2F1461444808089416.
Ray, Avishek. 2020. 'On the spectacle of walking: The migrant worker and the mobility regime', *Journal of Extreme Anthropology* 4(2): E25–E30. https://doi.org/10.5617/jea.7881.

Röttger-Rössler, Birgitt and Jan Slaby, eds. 2018. *Affect in Relation: Families, places, technologies*. Abingdon: Routledge.
Ryan, Louise, Amanda Klekowski von Koppenfels and Jon Mulholland. 2014. '"The distance between us": A comparative examination of the technical, spatial and temporal dimensions of the transnational social relationships of highly skilled immigrants', *Global Networks* 15(2): 198–216. https://doi.org/10.1111/glob.12054.
Svašek, Maruška. 2005a. 'Emotions in anthropology'. In *Mixed Emotions: Anthropological studies of feeling*, edited by Kay Milton and Maruška Svašek. Oxford: Berg.
Svašek, Maruška. 2005b. 'The politics of chosen trauma: Expellee memories, emotions and identities'. In *Mixed Emotions: Anthropological studies of feeling*, edited by Kay Milton and Maruška Svašek. Oxford: Berg.
Svašek, Maruška. 2008 'Who cares? Families and feelings in movement', *Journal of Intercultural Studies* 29(3): 213–30.
Svašek, Maruška. 2010a. 'On the move: Emotions and human mobility', *Journal of Ethnic and Migration Studies* 36(6): 865–80. https://doi.org/10.1080/13691831003643322.
Svašek, Maruška. 2010b. 'Who cares? Emotional interaction, support and ageing in transnational families'. Report for the Changing Ageing Partnership, Belfast: Queen's University.
Svašek, Maruška. 2018. 'Ageing kin, proximity and distance: Translocal relatedness as affective practice and movement'. In *Affect in Relation: Families, places, technologies*, edited by Birgitt Röttger-Rössler and Jan Slaby, 31–49. Abingdon: Routledge.
Wetherell, Margaret. 2012. *Affect and Emotion: A new social science understanding*. London: SAGE.
Wise, Amanda and Selvaraj Velayutham. 2017. 'Transnational affect and emotion in migration research', *International Journal of Sociology* 47(2): 116–30. https://doi.org/10.1080/00207659.2017.1300468.

11

The pram, the notebook and the plastic bag: mothering practices among migrants living in legal precarity in Berlin

Magdalena Suerbaum

This chapter deals with the pram, the notebook and the plastic bag. These everyday objects play an important role in the lives of four women who came to Germany to seek asylum shortly before or during the so-called refugee crisis in 2015–16. The women, whose relations to the pram, the notebook and the plastic bag I analyse in this chapter, are mothers and holders of a precarious legal status. By focusing on the women's use of these objects in their everyday lives as mothers coping with legal precarity, the chapter's aim is threefold: firstly, it traces their efforts to be in charge of their lives, their active decision-making and attempts of self-making. Secondly, I seek to highlight how motherhood transforms in meaning through the use of these objects. Thirdly, I show the objects' temporalities and how they mirror the precarious status of these women. The objects have a function and a deeper meaning for the women at a particular point in their lives and migration journeys. On the one hand, these objects are temporary, fragile and insecure; on the other hand, they all signify more enduring senses of belonging, purpose and self.

My arguments are based on findings resulting from 16 months of ethnographic fieldwork conducted in two phases, in 2017–18 and 2019–20, in Berlin. In the process of my fieldwork I met men and women from different countries of origin, with various legal statuses, from diverse socio-economic backgrounds. While I got to know asylum seekers from Afghanistan, Albania, Russia, Ethiopia, Vietnam and Colombia, I cultivated most of my long-term relationships with research participants with whom communication could take place in either English or Arabic. Since I stayed in touch with most of the research participants I met during the first fieldwork phase, I could follow and trace some trajectories for more than two years.

My ethnographic research took place in three contexts: a refugee shelter, a legal advice centre and a project dedicated to migrant mothers with their children. In these three contexts, I engaged in participant observation and consolidated relationships that allowed me to meet research participants individually for semi-structured interviews and, in some cases, biographical interviews. A significant part of my fieldwork can be defined as an 'ethnography by appointment'. Luhrmann (1996, vii), among others, uses the term 'appointment anthropology' to describe the part of her fieldwork that was mainly informed by meetings with numerous people individually. Likewise, Sloane-White (2017) applies the term in order to describe the challenges of researching corporate settings, and how contact with research participants was mainly established through appointment requests and rarely took place outside of business settings. During my previous fieldwork among Syrian refugee men in Egypt (Suerbaum 2020), 'ethnography by appointment' was the appropriate term to describe the regular meetings with Syrian men in different parts of the mega-city Cairo. Encounters occurred in accordance with Syrian men's schedules, were dependent on their invitations, and subject to the uncertainties, disruptions and changes that defined their lives. I faced a similar situation during my fieldwork in Berlin.

Apart from joining the women's group meetings, visiting families and socialising with people when I was in the refugee shelter, I met research participants individually at places and times they chose. During these individual meetings, I often accompanied them to their appointments at the *Jobcenter*,[1] the *Ausländerbehörde* (foreigners' registration office) or the *Sozialamt* (social welfare office). Being present during, before and after participants' appointments with the state authorities allowed me to get a deep sense of their emotions, worries and aspirations. I also learned about the objects that accompanied them in their day-to-day lives, witnessed how certain objects were elevated, and observed how the use of these objects evoked various emotions. The objects I am interested in and analyse throughout this chapter were purchased in Berlin, enabled the women to be mobile and to navigate life in the city, and were directly or indirectly related to their precarious legal status in Germany. In order to guarantee the anonymity of interlocutors, I make use of pseudonyms and disguise places of origin.

Among the emotionally charged, constantly used objects was the pram. It held an exceptional position, since it had the potential to bestow on a woman the status of a mother. Consequently, women, despite their precarious financial situations, invested a great deal of effort in buying one or getting access to a donated one. The second object I discuss in this chapter is the plastic bag filled with official documents and letters that many women carried with them. The plastic bag has the most direct connection to being a mother and holding a precarious legal status. Often, the papers that women produced from the bags were enquiries into the family situation by the youth welfare office, letters to parents sent by their children's schools, and requests for information to calculate child allowance. The contents of the plastic bag could evoke a plethora of emotions: powerlessness, fear, uncertainty and outrage about the interference of the German state. Finally, I engage with the notebook that was requested by the primary school that the daughter of one of my research participants attended. The notebook needed to be bought in preparation for the new school year. Finding the notebook of the correct size and style was about much more than a simple purchase: it was a success story, a feeling of being in charge, and a proof that one could be the committed and caring mother one aspired to be despite the language barrier and the novelty of the school system in Germany.

Basing my work on the assumption that 'maternal subjectivity emerges out of entanglements with the more than human' (Boyer and Spinney 2016, 1127), I trace how the above-mentioned objects were intimately related to these women's sense of motherhood. I argue that these objects relate not simply to their identity as mothers but also, and more precisely, to their identity as mothers with precarious legal status. The pram as an object of study and an indicator of different ideas of mothering and parenthood is not novel (see Clement and Waitt 2018; Jensen 2018; Boyer and Spinney 2016). In a similar vein, the materiality and meaning of legal documents, papers and official letters (Darling 2014; Hull 2012) and even the plastic bag (see Hawkins 2001) have been subject to research studies. I seek to add to these discussions how the pram, the plastic bag and the notebook relate to contexts of mothering in times of legal precarity. My aim is to present ethnographic vignettes in which objects of the everyday were elevated and signified the complex entanglement of forced displacement, legal precarity and motherhood.

Emphasising the condition of legal precarity among those who came to Germany to seek asylum, I follow Eule and colleagues, who make use of the term 'migrant with precarious legal status' (Eule et al. 2019, 25). The specific legal precarity of the women whose stories I present in this chapter is defined by their lack of access to long-term legal protection. One of the women whose cases I present in this chapter had received subsidiary protection (*subsidiärer Schutz*) in Germany and was thus less exposed to legal precarity. Another woman had held permission to remain pending the asylum decision (*Aufenthaltsgestattung zur Durchführung des Asylverfahrens*) since 2014, which severely restricted her rights. And the other two women received one *Duldung*[2] (temporary suspension of deportation), which lasted between one and six months, after another. The *Duldung* is not identical to a residence permit: it marks holders 'as neither fully "legal" nor fully "illegal"', and 'does not alter the fact that the person is obligated to leave the country' (Castañeda 2010, 253). Holding insecure legal statuses and living in 'permanent temporariness' (Tize 2020, 2) can cause continuous fear, stress and experiences of retraumatisation. Dimova (2006, 3) characterises holding a *Duldung* as an ordeal causing constant fear of deportation and traumatisation because of the uncertain future it creates. To the holder of an insecure legal status, such as a *Duldung*, frequent encounters with the *Ausländerbehörde* and other state authorities become a necessity, which adds another layer of stress and anxiety.

Studying materiality, emotions and motherhood in times of forced migration

Being or becoming a mother as a displaced person means the navigation of a complex (medical) system in a foreign country, often without familial support, standing up to new and specific responsibilities, and encountering the state in particular ways (Lowe 2019, 195). Motherhood in the context of forced displacement can be described as 'an ongoing performative process of becoming' that has various implications for one's future as a migrant, such as, in terms of onward migration, the potential to engage in strategic relationships, and belonging to broader familial networks (Lowe 2019, 199). Engagement in mothering practices as an asylum seeker often holds specific challenges, especially if mothers are separated from their children. It is the lack of social and political rights that severely hampers these women's relations with their families, since their legal status prohibits them from working and so makes it difficult to plan for the future (Madziva and Zontini 2012). Georgina Ramsay (2017) makes an important contribution to the study of motherhood in contexts of migration, by focusing on forced child removal. While pregnancy and child-rearing during flight gave several women a kind of purpose and agency, the forced removal of their children during resettlement in Australia through the intervention of youth welfare services caused a deep loss of meaning. In this context, motherhood is turned into a 'disciplining institution of biopolitics' through which the ability to integrate is judged (Ramsay 2017, 766).

In addition to literature dealing with mothering practices in times of forced displacement, this chapter is inspired by literature that examines materiality and emotions during (forced) migration. Studying such a context means 'a focus on objects, places, sensory perception and conceptions of time and space' (Dudley 2010, 1). There is a body of literature interested in objects '"carried over" by migrants as they form their new/old worlds in novel territories and contexts' (Basu and Coleman 2008, 328; see also Burrell 2008; Tolia-Kelly 2004; Mertus et al. 1997). Yet my focus in this chapter does not lie on objects that were 'carried over'. In fact, there were but a few objects in the lives of most of the women I met that came with them from their country of origin. Most of my interlocutors had not much more than official documents, such as birth certificates or a marriage certificate, from their country of origin or from the country in which they resided before coming to Germany, and even these documents were not always present. Deidre Conlon (2011, 721) argues that for asylum seekers the everyday is often marked by an absence of possessions and material objects that belonged to their pre-flight context. This absence of possessions is usually grounded in personal and material losses, since most asylum seekers were in their pre-migration lives immersed in commodity-laden cultures (Conlon 2011, 722). Conlon is interested in how the gradual accumulation of possessions can be understood as 'part of a training' (Conlon 2011, 723) and a process of emplacement enabling asylum seekers to manoeuvre 'physical environments as well as social and cultural spheres' (Conlon 2011, 723).

In a similar vein, I focus in this chapter on the everyday objects that defined forced migrants' day-to-day lives in Berlin and that had been purchased there. These were objects that the women thought they needed to be able to participate in everyday life. I am also inspired by Jonathan Darling's (2014) analysis of objects of relevance in contexts of forced migration: he focuses on the materiality of letters from the UK Home Office and discusses how they form relations between people, places and state institutions (Darling 2014, 485). I focus in this chapter on the everyday life of forcibly displaced mothers and on the objects that are part of this context. I suggest that the selected objects helped to emplace, embed and mobilise women who were both mothers and holders of a precarious legal status.

These objects were emotionally charged, reveal women's engagement in mothering practices, and display the uncertainty that defines their lives.

In an analysis of mothers' relations to specific objects of everyday life in the country of temporary settlement and the emotions they evoke, Sara Ahmed's conceptualisation of emotions is useful. Ahmed (2004) defines emotions as sticky and moving, as connecting and attaching. She argues that emotions denote a version of bodily change, and are relational, intentional and directional. They are culturally produced and thus demonstrate one's apprehension of the world. Ahmed (2004, 10) suggests the model of the 'sociality of emotions', through which she describes how emotions have the ability to shape and demarcate: 'Emotions create the very effect of the surfaces and boundaries that allow us to distinguish an inside and an outside.' Furthermore, she perceives emotions as 'sticky' when they connect to signs, figures and objects, and as spatial and directional, moving sideways, forwards and backwards, thus connecting past and present (Ahmed 2004, 45). In her model of emotion as affective economy, she stresses that emotions circulate and work as a form of capital. This means for the context of fear that it neither comes from within an individual nor is an inherent part of an object. It is when signs of fear circulate that others are read as fearsome (2004, 127).

It is useful to add to Ahmed's perspective Kay Milton's (2005) conceptualisation of emotions: with her argument that it is fruitful to understand emotions as an 'ecological phenomenon', Milton (2005, 202) foregrounds a perspective that locates emotions 'in the relationship between an individual and their environment', no matter whether this is a social or a non-social context (Milton 2005, 203). Furthermore, she highlights the fact that emotions cause learning, since the individual interprets and acts upon the information they get from their surroundings. It follows that the self can be regarded as 'a multiple, relational being-in-the-world that is captured by [one's] surroundings' (Svašek 2010, 868). This approach includes taking into consideration different temporalities and, crucially, memories and imagination (Svašek 2010, 868). The perception of emotions as circulating, sticky, and connected to both social and non-social contexts helps to bring together the complex aspects that define this study, which is a context of forced migration involving legal precarity, purchased objects that are deemed necessary for everyday life in the host country, and mothering practices. As for the temporal dimension I discuss in this chapter, I follow Megha Amrith (2021, 143) who stresses that migrants' 'shifting temporal horizons expose the stalled, asynchronous, sticky and non-linear forms of migrant lives, as well as the complex emotions that such temporalities (of aspiring, waiting, rupture, longing) engender'.

The pram: protector and connector

The pram is mobile, has the potential to roll, and can be pushed from one location to the next. Thus, the pram enables its owner to be a mobile person in everyday life. Pram strolling requires experience, coping strategies in manoeuvring the city, and interacting with others on the street (Jensen 2018, 590). Apart from carrying children, the pram can become a device that helps the fulfilment of domestic tasks, such as grocery shopping (Clement and Waitt 2018, 12). Most importantly, the pram is a carrier of meaning signifying parenthood and symbolising care (Jensen 2018, 584). It is an 'almost definitional artefact to the practice of early motherhood' (Boyer and Spinney 2016, 1119) and helps mothers to 'appear competent to themselves and others' (Miller 2005, 62, quoted in Boyer and Spinney 2016, 1120). Ultimately, it enables women to be 'good', 'in control' and 'prepared' mothers (Clement and Waitt 2018, 19).

All the women I met, no matter where they came from, placed immense importance on owning a pram. The prams I saw over the course of my fieldwork were in good shape, clean, fashionable and 'inhabited'. Mothers had hung bags of their belongings on the handle, and in the basket at the bottom they stored boxes of snacks, toys and blankets. My research partners transported their children in the pram when they went shopping, attended meetings or had appointments with the state authorities. They took the pram with them when they travelled by bus, underground or city train. Despite the difficulties of being in the city with a pram, such as out-of-order lifts in U-Bahn stations or the inability to board an already crowded bus, only one of the women who attended the women's group meetings was interested in a baby sling as a means of transportation for her child. However, she decided not to use it after she had tried it once for the women's group meeting. I noticed that new prams were picked with care, that mothers chose colours that matched the baby's gender, and that the prams were kept neat and tidy for as long as possible. Only on prams in which older children were transported did I recognise increased traces of use. Often, women who attended the women's group meetings would ask around for prams, for instance when their children had become too big for their current one or when they needed a double pram to transport an infant and an older sibling.

Consequently, I perceived the pram as a vehicle the women required to navigate the city, and which had to match their specific needs.

Having given an overall idea of pram use among the refugees and asylum seekers I met who were mothers, I introduce in what follows Susan, from a West African country. I expand on the analysis of the legal trajectories of Susan and Emilia in Suerbaum 2021. She had given birth to her daughter in Germany three months before I got to know her. We went together to the *Ausländerbehörde* (foreigners' registration office) to renew her *Schwangerschaftsduldung* (suspension of deportation based on pregnancy). Her pram was always at her side. Susan carried her daughter most of the time, but sometimes she would pass her over to me so that she could take a break, call her boyfriend or talk to others who were also waiting for their appointments. When we carried Susan's daughter in our arms, the pram would become the holder of our backpacks, jackets and the baby bag in which Susan had put nappies and wet wipes. We had to wait at the *Ausländerbehörde* for the whole day and were asked to move from the waiting area downstairs to a waiting room in one of the buildings. In this environment, the pram was a bulky companion. We had to queue, in front of and behind us families with prams and people in wheelchairs, for the lift, which had space for only one pram at a time. Nevertheless, the pram also brought us into contact with people in our surroundings: a security guard in the downstairs waiting area held the door open for us so that we could pass through with the pram and the baby in Susan's arms. The security guard's stern face lit up for a second as he helped us exit the waiting area. In a hostile, tense atmosphere the pram thus momentarily created a reason for friendly communication. In the upstairs waiting area of the *Ausländerbehörde*, the pram marked our seats and prevented other people who were waiting from coming too close. It guaranteed our space. However, when we finally entered the office of the official we had to deal with, everything seemed to take a bit longer: It took a while to manoeuvre all our belongings, especially the pram, into the narrow office. It seemed too tiny for the pram and Susan needed a minute to organise herself before she could focus on the conversation with the civil servant. After a challenging discussion, characterised by rejection and racist undertones, Susan received a new *Duldung* for six months.

Another time, when I visited Susan in the refugee shelter in which she was staying, which was located in a middle-class, homogeneous and predominantly white neighbourhood, my encounter with her pram was a different one. When I arrived, Susan gave me a tour of the former school which had been turned into a temporary refugee shelter before we entered her small room. Her daughter was tied to her back with a huge, colourful scarf and fell asleep after we had been walking around the building for a few minutes. Susan explained to me that it was common practice among mothers from her country of origin to carry their children on their backs. When Susan's daughter woke up we decided to go to the playground in the neighbourhood, and Susan chose the pram as a means of transporting her daughter. Self-confidently, she pushed the pram along the pavement, passing coffee shops, bookshops and nurseries, leading the way to the playground and chatting with me about the permanent legal status she hoped to receive soon. Even though she still held a *Duldung*, she was confident that she would soon get her daughter's German passport because of the father's permanent legal status in Germany. If her daughter received German citizenship, Susan would also get permanent permission to stay in Germany until her daughter turned 18. She kept saying proudly that her daughter was 'a German baby'. Upon arrival at the playground, she placed the pram next to all the others parked at the entrance, took her bag from the handle, and carried her daughter to the sandpit.

During our walk and our stay at the playground, and given Susan's preference for the pram over the scarf, I noticed the pram's performative dimension. In the public sphere, the scarf that is used to tie the child to her back is not Susan's preference, even if it helps her to calm her child inside the refugee shelter. Baby wrapping creates a 'mobile unit' of mother and child that allows the mother to focus on other tasks while also significantly decreasing the child's stress and insecurity (Russell 2014, 46; Becke and Bongard 2018, 81). Yet these advantages do not seem to trump the pram's symbolic and performative significance. Following Conlon's (2011) argument, I consequently came to perceive the pram as one of the accumulated material objects that assist Susan to immerse herself in the physical and cultural geographies that define her current place of living and parenting in a middle-class Berlin neighbourhood.

The broken pram

The pram is an object of movement and mobility. If it creates stasis and blockage unexpectedly or, on the contrary, goes too fast and becomes uncontrollable, the pram disrupts a (planned) journey and causes concern, unease and discomfort. Khadeeja, from an East African country, who held subsidiary protection status (*subsidiärer Schutz*) and was a regular attender of the women's group meetings, experienced such a situation. She had given birth to her second child six weeks ago and was participating in the weekly meeting for the first time after giving birth. We were sitting around the breakfast table and each woman said a few words about her current situation. When it was Khadeeja's turn, she burst into a desperate monologue: her husband had to leave home to go to work at four in the morning and Khadeeja felt troubled and stressed when she was with both children by herself. She was still recovering from her second caesarean section and was deeply disappointed that she had not been able to give birth to her son naturally. She said that she missed her mother and that she struggled with breastfeeding. Scared, she told the other women in the group that there was a lump in her breast and that she was afraid that she was ill. Her gynaecologist had checked the lump several times, yet Khadeeja could not get over her anxiety about being ill. On top of this, Khadeeja explained – and this is when she broke down in tears – that her pram had stopped working properly. In broken German she explained that one of the wheels would 'run away' when she used it. She felt that she could not control the pram any more, that it was not safe and that it had become 'too fast' for her. The group leaders eventually went out of the room with her and fixed the wheel of the pram.

Khadeeja's breakdown about the broken pram and the words she used to describe her problem shed light on her overall state: as a mother who had just had her second child she was still in a moment of adaptation. Life appeared overwhelming, intense and to be moving forward relentlessly. The pram, usually a reliable companion, stopped working and could not be controlled any longer. This experience not only relates deeply to her situation as a young mother of two children, but also speaks to the insecurity of her overall condition as a refugee who held subsidiary status in Germany. A couple of weeks later, Khadeeja was back with both her children to attend the women's group meeting. She seemed more at peace with herself and the new situation. Yet she came with new questions and concerns: she had to file an asylum application for her son and was surprised to have received an incomplete extract from the births register (*Auszug aus dem Geburtenregister*) for her son. Her name was mentioned on the document; however, there was an additional note stating that her identity was not proved (*Identität nicht nachgewiesen*). Her husband's name, as the father of the child, was not mentioned. Khadeeja wondered which office she had to turn to to get the information on the document changed and asked the group leaders why she had not received a proper birth certificate.

In the ethnographic vignettes I have presented, the pram held different roles: it was a connector, a door opener, a protector, a space maker, a supporter, but also an object that burdened its owner, created a sense of out-of-placeness, applied pressure and could easily turn from a companion into a threat. Consequently, using the pram was charged with different, even opposing emotions: on the one hand, it confirmed a woman's status as a mother and could consequently create pride and self-confidence. The pram was a marker of activeness, of being in charge and in control. On the other hand, however, it could evoke uneasiness and fear for the child and could, when broken, become a strong marker and reminder of one's challenging, uncertain situation as a mother navigating a context of forced displacement.

The plastic bag: a mobile vessel

In a similar vein to the pram, the plastic bag is mobile, with its potential to be carried around from one place to another, and acts as a vessel. From a gendered perspective, the use of plastic bags can hint at dominant gender ideologies, gendered divisions of labour and prevalent values in a gender system (Braun and Traore 2015). Among women vendors in Mali, Braun and Traore (2015, 864) detect, on the one hand, appreciation for the plastic bag because of its association with modernity and globalisation, and on the other hand rejection because of its 'poor performance' (Braun and Trarore 2015, 878) as an object created for single use only. Hawkins (2001) highlights the different associations plastic bags have for her, among them that they are objects of waste that evoke disgust. However, she also describes a movie scene in which the plastic bag becomes an object of aesthetics, and values the practicality of the plastic bag in her everyday life as a mother. Hence, she stresses that the plastic bag's 'movement through different categories, from container to rubbish, generates different attitudes and modes of relating' (Hawkins 2001, 7).

When accompanying mothers to different appointments with the German authorities, I could not help but notice the plastic bag that many of them carried with them. This plastic bag was usually of medium size, often previously white but now rather grey because of being worn and used. In this plastic bag, there was usually not one but a plethora of letters and documents. I would get a glimpse of the amount of paper in a bag when its owner was asked by a civil servant to produce a certain paper. Upon such a request, the owner of the plastic bag would frantically search it for the requested document. Once, when I shared my observation about the omnipresence of the plastic bag during appointments with the state authorities with the social worker who led the women's groups I regularly attended, she said that she had observed a similar trend and that she once tried to persuade a woman to use coloured folders for her papers instead.

She even organised the papers from the plastic bag for this woman. Yet this was met with resistance and disapproval and the woman abandoned the folders, putting all her papers back into the plastic bag.

In order to analyse the meaning of the plastic bag in which women who came to Germany to seek asylum carried their official papers, letters and documents, it is necessary to delve briefly into a discussion of emotions evoked by contact with state bureaucracies. Official documents issued by the state, such as identity papers revealing the holder's legal status, are not only instruments of bureaucratic organisations, but should be viewed as forming a bond between the state and its population. They mediate a specific image of the state (Sharma and Gupta 2006, 12). Following Das and Poole (2004, 15), encounters with the state through papers, such as identity cards or birth certificates, 'bear the double sign of the state's distance and its penetration into the life of the everyday'. Consequently, documents have the potential to evoke multiple and contingent affects in their holders, for instance fear, irony and wit (Navaro-Yashin 2007, 95). Papers similarly evoke emotions when they are absent or deemed useless, that is, when the validity of documents is routinely disputed or when people are left undocumented (Hull 2012, 253). Kelly (2006, 90), when analysing the relations of Palestinians in the West Bank with their identity documents, argues that, while identity documents usually distinguish between the legal and the physical person, Palestinians 'come to embody the indeterminacies of the documents that they hold'. Owning identity documents whose meanings and implications are unstable and unpredictable creates particular types of subjects, because of the apprehension, uncertainties and fears holders experience in relation to their documents and the legal statuses behind them (Kelly 2006, 92). Indeed, the meaning of their legal documents and the implications for their daily life were constantly present among the women I met. Their legal status had become a marker of everyday life, an omnipresent awareness, producing different emotions.

Once, I accompanied Hind, a mother of three from the Arab world to the district court. Hind's nationality is considered unresolved (*ungeklärt*) in Germany. When Hind, her husband and their son arrived in Germany in 2014, they applied for asylum and received a rejection. Their lawyer filed a suit. Ever since, Hind has held a permit to remain pending the asylum decision (*Aufenthaltsgestattung zur Durchführung des Asylverfahrens*),[3] which prohibits her from working and prohibits the receipt of child allowance. Every six months, the family needs to go to the *Ausländerbehörde* to renew their papers. Sitting in front of the civil servant at the district court, Hind produced a marriage contract and a UN card from her plastic bag. She had decided to come to the district court on that day to request renewed birth certificates for her younger daughter and her son. The birth certificates of her two children born in Germany do not state the father's name and there is a supplementary note after her own name saying that her identity is not proved (*Identität nicht nachgewiesen*). Such documents are issued if the civil registry office which is approached after a child's birth finds that the documents provided by the parents are not sufficient evidence of their identity. Since the father's name is not on the birth certificates, Hind's younger daughter and her son hold their mother's last name.

Hind took all the papers she had in her plastic bag and spread them on the table in front of the civil servant. Many papers, among them approved translations of the originals, were visibly old and well thumbed. Hind knew that she could not produce from her bag what the civil servant had already asked for repeatedly, namely a passport, an official marriage contract and her own birth certificate. Hind's two-year-old daughter sat next to her on the chair eating crisps from a small lunch box. Hind was visibly stressed by the appointment, especially after her daughter unintentionally spilt the crisps all over the desk, the documents and the floor. While Hind did her best to clean the table, sit her daughter in the pram and put the papers back into the plastic bag, the civil servant coldly explained the next steps of the procedure and expressed her doubts about the success of Hind's request for proper birth certificates for her son and daughter because of the lack of identity-establishing papers.

Often, when I met Hind during the women's group gatherings, she would take from her handbag the plastic bag filled with letters she wanted me to translate. Following the linguistic rules of bureaucratic documentation, these letters were barely comprehensible even to advanced German speakers. They were usually mixed with all kinds of mail, for example invoices and mailshots, that Hind transported unopened in the plastic bag. Speaking only a few words of German, Hind lacked the confidence to pick out the letters that required her attention and throw away the ones that were unimportant. As well as carrying the essential documents and certificates she possessed in Germany, the plastic bag was a vessel for the communications Hind did not understand. The plastic bag thus contained a mixture of documents: there were the letters that she could not identify herself as important or unimportant; then there were papers of temporary relevance (such as bills that needed to be paid); and finally there were documents of lasting importance, such as identification documents. Since Hind did not possess the 'correct' and required identification documents, such as a passport, she carried in her plastic bag 'replacement' documents, such as a marriage agreement and its approved translation, in the hope that they could make up for the missing ones. Consequently, Hind's plastic bag was a carrier of objects of existential importance, but also signified losses, absences and insecurities.

In contexts of asylum and forced migration, letters, papers and documents can become 'affectively loaded phenomena' (Navaro-Yashin 2007, 81). They are part of 'the fabric of everyday life' and turn into 'possessions critical to an individual's sense of self' (Darling 2014, 491). The plastic bag is highly significant for the women I met because of the existential meaning of its contents. The contents of the plastic bag marks the women's relation to the German state, is a determinant of the level of exclusion and inclusion they encounter, and is a proof of their efforts to be in charge of their lives. Similarly to the pram, the plastic bag is a means to be mobile. It allows movement and provides one with the possibility of carrying one's most important documents along to various locations. The plastic bag protects the papers from destruction and rain, and prevents the owner from losing one of them. A plastic bag is portable, resilient, waterproof, non-transparent and cheap. Furthermore, the plastic bag provides enough space to carry all the important documents (and the ones deemed important). The plastic bag is available: women can find one in the course of their everyday lives, for instance when they go grocery shopping. At the same time, however, the plastic bag, an object produced for single use, is insecure. The bag as a whole or its handles can tear and the bag's contents can easily fall out. Consequently, I suggest that the materiality of the plastic bag hints at the women's uncertain legal status in Germany, which often directly or indirectly affects their relationship with their children. It is an object of relevance at this specific moment in the women's lives and asserts the women's aspiration to create a future for themselves and their children in Germany.

The notebook: a success story

Emilia, a single mother of two children from a central African country, held a *Schwangerschaftsduldung* (temporary suspension of deportation based on pregnancy) for the permitted six months. After its expiration, Emilia had to struggle from one *Duldung* to the next, which meant that she had to go to the *Ausländerbehörde* with both her children every three months, sometimes even once a month, depending on the duration of the *Duldung* she received. Even though the child's father, from whom she was separated, acknowledged paternity and shared custody with Emilia, his residence in Germany could not secure a legal status for his children. He was married to an EU resident, but they had separated by the time his son was born. His residence in Germany was in question, and his unresolved legal situation severely affected Emilia and her children, who had to balance life from one *Duldung* to the next. Because the birth of her son was so recent and because she only held a *Duldung*, she could not attend German courses. This put Emilia in immense difficulty not only when she went to appointments with the social welfare office and the youth welfare office, but also when she had to deal with her daughter's primary school.

Often, Emilia asked me to translate letters from teachers which her daughter brought home. Once, on a hot summer's day, I met Emilia in an agitated and nervous state. Her daughter had brought home the list of items she had to purchase for the new school year. She showed me the list, which gave detailed information about the size, ruling, colour and number of the different notebooks. Her daughter needed a vocabulary book and several arithmetic and exercise books. The notebooks were listed in the following style: '2 notebooks in A4 format, ruling 3, margined'. Imagining the trip to the stationery shop, Emilia kept repeating: 'I pray that the salesperson in the shop is nice.' Eventually, Emilia and I agreed that I would accompany her to the shop a day later. At the shop, it took us two hours to scan the different notebooks on the shelves before Emilia found exactly what the school had requested. Emilia would not allow her daughter to take the list from her hands. She would check every item her daughter found and compared its description meticulously with the list. Of course, her daughter was drawn to the colourful writing materials that were available in the shop, but Emilia would not allow her to be distracted. Her priority was the requested notebooks and consequently she searched diligently through the shelves in the shop until she had found all the requested items.

A notebook is a basic, essential and required part of children's education and presence in the classroom. The notebooks on the list that Emilia's daughter had brought home from school were considered crucial for her successful participation in the next school year. Especially for children of primary school age, it is the responsibility of the parents to provide the child with the necessary school materials. Purchasing the correctly sized notebook created anxiety, pressure and insecurity in Emilia. The details and descriptions on the list caused an acute awareness of her own out-of-placeness as someone who had been exposed to a different school system with different rules and who still had not mastered the German language.

Finding the requested notebooks in the stationery shop consequently turned into a test to prove that she was a 'good' mother who knew how to abide by the rules of the German school system. Providing her daughter with materials for the new school year, Emilia could show her daughter and her daughter's teacher that she was reliable, committed and able to find her way. Following Georgina Ramsay's analysis of child removal among resettled refugees in Australia (2017), I argue that Emilia managed to perform deservingness of civic belonging through this purchase, since she adhered to implicit and explicit expectations of behaviour. She was able to prove in front of others that she conformed to the prevalent ideal of mothering a schoolchild and to normative care-giving practices. Thus Emilia's efforts can be seen as commitment to her child's future and consequent negotiations of when and how to conform to values prevalent in the host country (see Longman et al. 2013, 392). From the perspective of a mother with a precarious legal status in Germany and an uncertain legal trajectory ahead of her, the act of purchasing the correctly sized notebook relates to the 'pursuit of maximizing the child's feelings of belonging' and to the aim of 'making [her] children as well as [herself] into "good" and accepted citizens' (Longman et al. 2013, 391).

Conclusion

This chapter has engaged with three mundane objects, purchased by four women during forced displacement in Germany with the purpose of becoming mobile and active. They played a role in the women's attempts to become emplaced in Germany. The mothers purchased, used and interacted with and through these objects; in short, they lived with these objects in their everyday lives as forcibly displaced persons. Furthermore, these objects combined the women's precarious legal statuses with their positions as mothers. Hence, on the one hand these objects proved the women's commitment as mothers, and on the other hand they materialised their out-of-placeness; they bore witness to the women's struggles and efforts to be in charge of their lives and, at the same time, displayed their current insecurities and their uncertain futures.

Through engagement with these objects, motherhood transformed in meaning. The pram, for instance, was used to confirm the women's status as 'good' and 'caring' in the German public sphere and was consciously used for this endeavour. When broken, the pram could easily challenge self-confidence in one's position as a mother, reminding the women of the multiple struggles they faced on different levels. Motherhood also transformed in meaning when the women made use of the plastic bag as a vessel for carrying their papers to different state authorities and other appointments. The plastic bag reminded the women constantly of the instability and stuckedness that challenged them, affected their children similarly, and took their toll on the mother–child relationship. Finally, motherhood transformed in meaning during the act of purchasing notebooks. The successful purchase allowed the purchaser to feel pride and confidence in her ability to mother a child in the midst of adaptation, home-making and the creation of a feeling of belonging while living on inherently unstable (legal) ground.

The pram, the notebook and the plastic bag were charged with different emotions as they marked the women's complex positions as mothers living in Germany in legal precarity. They signified the exclusionary consequences of their legal status and their specific

Notes

1 The *Jobcenter* is a German state institution responsible for providing social support for unemployed people and those who work but cannot cover their basic living costs.

2 Holders of a *Duldung* have limited rights compared with those granted refugee status or subsidiary status. Their residence permit can be extended as long as protection claims remain valid (Leutloff-Grandits 2019).

3 The BAMF grants permission to asylum applicants to remain in the federal territory while the asylum procedure is pending. This entitles them to live in Germany until the asylum proceedings have been completed, that is, until a decision has been taken on the asylum application. The permission expires if the decision of the BAMF has become incontestable.

vulnerability as newcomers who were not yet able to speak German. However, these objects also materialised their struggles and efforts to become active participants and to take charge of their lives.

References

Ahmed, Sara. 2004. *The Cultural Politics of Emotion*. Edinburgh: Edinburgh University Press.

Amrith, Megha. 2021. 'The linear imagination, stalled: Changing temporal horizons in migrant journeys', *Global Networks* 21(1): 127–45. https://doi.org/10.1111/glob.12280.

Basu, Paul and Simon Coleman. 2008. 'Introduction: Migrant worlds, material cultures', *Mobilities* 3(3): 313–30. https://doi.org/10.1080/17450100802376753.

Becke, Sophia and Stephan Bongard. 2018. '"When I dey cry, my mother go carry me": Tücher als Care-Objekte in Kamerun'. In *Dinge als Herausforderung: Kontexte, Umgangsweisen und Umwertungen von Objekten*, edited by Hans Peter Hahn and Friedemann Neumann, 67–100. Bielefeld: transcript Verlag. DOI: 10.14361/9783839445136-005.

Boyer, Kate and Justin Spinney. 2016. 'Motherhood, mobility and materiality: Material entanglements, journey-making and the process of "becoming mother"', *Environment and Planning D: Society and Space* 34(6): 1113–31. https://doi.org/10.1177%2F0263775815622209.

Braun, Yvonne A. and Assitan Sylla Traore. 2015. 'Plastic bags, pollution, and identity: Women and the gendering of globalization and environmental responsibility in Mali', *Gender & Society* 29(6): 863–87. http://dx.doi.org/10.1177/0891243215602101.

Burrell, Kathy. 2008. 'Materialising the border: Spaces of mobility and material culture in migration from post-socialist Poland', *Mobilities* 3(3): 353–73. https://doi.org/10.1080/17450100802376779.
Castañeda, Heide. 2010 'Deportation deferred: "Illegality", visibility, and recognition in contemporary Germany'. In *The Deportation Regime: Sovereignty, space, and the freedom* of *movement*, edited by Nicholas De Genova and Nathalie Peutz, 245–61. Durham, NC, and London: Duke University Press.
Clement, Susannah and Gordon Waitt. 2018. 'Pram mobilities: Affordances and atmospheres that assemble childhood and motherhood on-the-move', Faculty of Social Sciences Papers 3775, University of Wollongong. Accessed 27 October 2021. https://ro.uow.edu.au/sspapers/3775.
Conlon, Deirdre. 2011. 'A fractured mosaic: Encounters with the everyday amongst refugee and asylum seeker women', *Population, Space and Place* 17(6): 714–26. https://doi.org/10.1002/psp.637.
Darling, Jonathan. 2014. 'Another letter from the Home Office: Reading the material politics of asylum', *Environment and Planning D: Society and Space* 32(3): 484–500. https://doi.org/10.1068%2Fd13067p.
Das, Veena and Deborah Poole, eds. 2004. *Anthropology in the Margins of the State*. Santa Fe, NM: School of American Research Press.
Dimova, Rozita. 2006. 'From protection to ordeal: *Duldung* status and Bosnians in Berlin', Working Paper 87, Max Planck Institute for Social Anthropology.
Dudley, Sandra. 2010. *Materialising Exile: Material culture and embodied experience among Karenni refugees in Thailand*. New York and Oxford: Berghahn Books.
Eule, Tobias, Lisa Marie Borrelli, Annika Lindberg and Anna Wyss. 2019. *Migrants before the Law: Contested migration control in Europe*. Cham: Palgrave Macmillan.
Hawkins, Gay. 2001. 'Plastic bags: Living with rubbish', *International Journal of Cultural Studies* 4(1): 5–23. https://doi.org/10.1177%2F136787790100400101.
Hull, Matthew S. 2012. 'Documents and bureaucracy', *Annual Review of Anthropology* 41: 251–67. https://doi.org/10.1146/annurev.anthro.012809.104953.
Jensen, Martin Trandberg. 2018. 'Urban pram strolling: A mobilities design perspective', *Mobilities* 13(4): 584–600. https://doi.org/10.1080/17450101.2017.1394683.
Kelly, Tobias. 2006. 'Documented lives: Fear and the uncertainties of law during the second Palestinian *intifada*', *Journal of the Royal Anthropological Institute* 12(1): 89–107. https://doi.org/10.1111/j.1467-9655.2006.00282.x.
Leutloff-Grandits, Carolin. 2019. 'Temporalities of refugee experience in Germany: Diversification of asylum rights and proliferation of internal boundaries', *Archivio Antropologico Mediterraneo* (online), Anno XXII 21(2). https://doi.org/10.4000/aam.2432.
Longman, Chia, Katrien De Graeve and Tine Brouckaert. 2013. 'Mothering as a citizenship practice: An intersectional analysis of "carework" and "culturework" in non-normative mother–child identities', *Citizenship Studies* 17(3–4): 385–99. https://doi.org/10.1080/13621025.2013.791540.
Lowe, Lucy. 2019. 'Refusing cesarean sections to protect fertile futures: Somali refugees, motherhood, and precarious migration', *American Ethnologist* 46(2): 190–201. https://doi.org/10.1111/amet.12759.
Luhrmann, Tanya. 1996. *The Good Parsi: The fate of a colonial elite in a postcolonial society*. Cambridge, MA: Harvard University Press.
Madziva, Roda and Elisabetta Zontini. 2012. 'Transnational mothering and forced migration: Understanding the experiences of Zimbabwean mothers in the UK', *European Journal of Women's Studies* 19(4): 428–43. https://doi.org/10.1177%2F1350506812466609.
Mertus, Julie, Jasmina Tesanovic, Habiba Metikos and Rada Boric, eds. 1997. *The Suitcase: Refugee voices from Bosnia and Croatia*. Berkeley and Los Angeles: University of California Press.
Miller, Tina. 2005. *Making Sense of Motherhood: A narrative approach*. Cambridge: Cambridge University Press.
Milton, Kay. 2005. 'Emotion (or life, the universe, everything)', *Australian Journal of Anthropology* 16(2): 198–211. https://doi.org/10.1111/j.1835-9310.2005.tb00034.x.
Navaro-Yashin, Yael. 2007. 'Make-believe papers, legal forms and the counterfeit: Affective interactions between documents and people in Britain and Cyprus', *Anthropological Theory* 7(1): 79–98. https://doi.org/10.1177%2F1463499607074294.
Ramsay, Georgina. 2017. 'Forced childlessness and ruptured personhood: The politics of motherhood for Central African refugee women resettled in Australia', *Anthropological Quarterly* 90(3): 743–70. https://doi.org/10.1353/anq.2017.0042.

Russell, Nancy Ukai. 2014. 'Aspects of baby wrappings: Swaddling, carrying, and wearing'. In *Wrapping and Unwrapping Material Culture: Archaeological and anthropological perspectives*, edited by Susanna Harris and Laurence Douny, 43–58. Walnut Creek, CA: Left Coast Press.

Sharma, Aradhana and Akhil Gupta. 2006. 'Introduction: Rethinking theories of the state in an age of globalization'. In *The Anthropology of the State: A reader*, edited by Aradhana Sharma and Akhil Gupta, 1–41. Oxford: Blackwell Publishing.

Sloane-White, Patricia. 2017. *Corporate Islam: Sharia and the modern workplace*. Cambridge: Cambridge University Press.

Suerbaum, Magdalena. 2020. *Masculinities and Displacement in the Middle East: Syrian refugees in Egypt*. London: I.B. Tauris.

Suerbaum, Magdalena. 2021. 'Embodying legal precarity: Living with ongoing short-term protection in Germany'. *International Migration*. http://doi.org/10.1111/imig.12903.

Svašek, Maruška. 2010. 'On the move: Emotions and human mobility', *Journal of Ethnic and Migration Studies* 36(6): 865–80. https://doi.org/10.1080/13691831003643322.

Tize, Carola. 2020. 'Living in permanent temporariness: The multigenerational ordeal of living under Germany's toleration status', *Journal of Refugee Studies* 34(3): 3024–43. https://doi.org/10.1093/jrs/fez119.

Tolia-Kelly, Divya. 2004. 'Materializing post-colonial geographies: Examining the textural landscapes of migration in the South Asian home', *Geoforum* 35(6): 657–88. http://dx.doi.org/10.1016/j.geoforum.2004.02.006.

Part IV

Taking and making place: engaging things

Introduction

Andrea Lauser

> [P]eople on the move, whether on the run from war, hunger or destruction, or, perhaps, simply looking for greener pastures elsewhere, do not move through an indifferent space. Rather, they move through places – and in moving through shape them and are in turn shaped by them.
>
> (Lems 2016, 321)

The point of departure for the last part of our volume is to approach the issue of 'place' and place-making as a fundamental mode of migratory – and indeed human – praxis. Inspired by philosophers like Lefebvre ([1974] 1991) and Certeau (1984), the spatial turn of the early 1990s was crucial for reconceptualising space away from an essentialising and territorialised understanding to a focus on its social production, appropriation, fluidity and movement. In this introduction, we draw on the conceptual and theoretical anthropological reflections on the cultural and social significance of mobility in a globally entangled and interconnected world and the consequential reformulation of anthropology as a self-reflexive and politically conscious discipline (Appadurai 1988, 1996; Gupta and Ferguson 1997a, 1997b; Clifford 1997; Malkki 1992, 1995, 1997). At the same time, we take up recent debates on the interrelations between mobility and immobility, emplacement and displacement (Turner in this volume; Jefferson et al. 2019; Glick Schiller and Salazar 2013), and home and exile (Dudley 2011; Brun 2015).

Here, we are especially interested in looking at what Annika Lems calls how 'being in- and out-of-place intersect, mingle and merge' (Lems 2016, 316). By focusing on people's everyday activities and engagement with the material world, our aim is to value people's lived experiences between – or rather 'betwixt and between' – emplacement and displacement. As Lems stresses, 'place does not cease to exist, even if it is experienced as a sense of deep and utter disruption (or displacement)' (Lems 2016, 320). This perspective raises questions about the links between place and memory, place and the sensual, place and movement, place and temporality and, therefore, the very interconnected dimensions we have discussed in the volume thus far. Furthermore, this perspective calls attention to migrant place-making practices which contribute to 'multiscalar city-making processes' (Çağlar and Glick Schiller 2018, 87).

We understand place not as a given, bounded physical structure but as shaped in complex ways, negotiated, approved and transformed in everyday interactions within a web of relations of humans, things and material surroundings. Thus, we perceive place-making as people's active and creative engagement with the places they inhabit (however fleetingly) in the form of everyday practices such as cooking, gardening, building, decorating and rearranging.

In the following, we approach place-making from three different – but interrelated – directions. We start with *camps as multifaceted spatial and material formations*, moving to notions of *home and home-making*, and finally to *routines and practices of togetherness and place-making*. Keeping in mind the focus on materiality, we connect these approaches with the contributions in this volume.

Camps: from space of exception to material assemblages

At first glance, camps offer relief and protection. But, as many studies emphasise, camps often turn into spaces of control and surveillance (Agier 2011; Martin et al. 2020). Martin, Minca and Katz argue that '[t]he camp is … a form of government of "exceeding" populations, often paradoxically interned in the name of their "protection"' (2020, 759). As an arena where the geopolitical and the everyday are linked, and mutually shaped, camps have taken many forms and functions, and are managed by multiple and changing actors and sovereignties.

Since about 2000, a new field of research in this area has emerged, 'camp studies' (Martin et al. 2020, 744).[1] With their specific infrastructures, camps produce paradoxical and ambivalent situations and settings, both spatially and materially. Many studies use Agamben's (1998) seminal conception of camps as exceptional spaces as a reference point, either to counter his arguments, or to revisit them and develop them further (Abourahme 2014, 202; Martin et al. 2020; Ramadan 2013). In this confrontation with Agamben's work, institutionalised camps have typically been understood as exceptional sites where people are reduced to 'bare life', abandoned outside the normal order of the state, and exposed to intensified sovereign powers. Some anthropologists, such as Agier, refer to camps as places of custody to keep the 'undesirables' in place, often neglected and in intolerable conditions. For Agier (2011, 4), 'There is no care without control', and the (undeclared) biopolitical role of these camps is also that of keeping the refugee bodies at a distance from the rest of society. Carna Brkovic (2020) argues that inadequate conditions and infrastructures are not an expression of exception but the result of 'governmental gaps'. State and non-state actors have limited mandates which sometimes result in unbearable and inhumane outcomes for the inhabitants of the camps.

More recent or 'post-Agambenian' studies – as Martin, Minca and Katz call them – emphasise camps as 'fields of possibility for political action' (Martin et al. 2020, 753; Ramadan 2013), as spaces of identity formation (Ramadan 2009), or as 'an assemblage of people, institutions, organizations, the built environment and the relations between them' (Ramadan 2013, 67). By looking at broader political and economic geographies and surrounding regions, including cities and border areas, these studies bring informal encampments and makeshift camps into focus. For example, in her analysis of graffiti in rural highway box culverts in Arizona, Gabriela Soto (2016) makes visible a recent history of migration beyond institutional camps, and illustrates migrants' place-making activities in 'non-places'.[2]

Through this research on camps, the focus has shifted to the people's agency, their strategies of resistance, and their everyday practices for coping with transient camp life (Bochmann 2018; Dudley 2011). For our focus, Abourahme's notion of the camp as a 'material assemblage' that is both 'object *and* process' (Abourahme 2014, 203, emphasis in original) is especially useful. Abourahme argues that, similarly to shanty towns, camp assemblages of buildings, infrastructures, tents, homes, people, institutions, social relations and everyday practices are contingent, in process and semi-formal, existing within a kind of liminality. Things such as electrical wiring and materials 'that go into the processes of their assemblage as a camp ... do not just play an enabling or intermediary role, they mediate action and practice in contingent and often unexpected ways' (Abourahme 2014, 3).

These processes become visible in the housing improvements and small enterprises in Greek refugee reception centres described in Nada Ghandour-Demiri and Petros Passas's chapter. In showing how humanitarian aid processes and the materiality of camps condition one another, Ghandour-Demiri and Passas emphasise different factors that affect the materialities of the camps and in turn people's material practices, from the camps' diverse infrastructures to the transient nature of the population. They argue that in order to survive and create a sense of normality, or enact and affirm cultural identities, residents use, circulate and (re)appropriate objects. Thus, the authors show the interrelationship between the camps' material infrastructure and people's place-making practices in everyday life, and the development of diverging forms of *homing* practices, a topic we turn to now.

Home and home-making

Another important strand in research into place-making is the study of home and home-making. This focus shifts attention to the numerous habitual and routine practices involving place, people and things and the way in which everyday activities shape place and places shape these everyday activities. Whatever the reason for it – to escape war or conflict, for work, or for love – mobility complicates the notion of 'home' (see Nowicka 2007) and can lead people to question what 'home' is and means. While spatially and temporally fixed notions of home continue to inform understandings of displacement, studies of (forced) migration have broadened the perspective to more fluid and dynamic conceptions of what home is (Dudley 2011; Brun and Fábos 2015; Nowicka 2007; Walsh 2006).

In her research on mobile professionals, Nowicka (2007) understands home as a 'set of relationships to both humans and things', as a process, and as something that has to be created. In short, she lends weight to the argument that home is a fundamental issue for people on the move and in the process of making place in new settings (Lems 2016; Hage 2010; Nowicka 2007). Brun and Fábos studied practices of home-making in protracted displacement, distinguishing between different dimensions of home as an idea and as a practice (Brun and Fábos 2015, 5).

Ghassan Hage understands home-building as building the feeling of being 'at home' (Hage 2010, 417). For Hage, home is an 'affective construct' that provides 'four key feelings: security, familiarity, community, and a sense of possibility or hope' (Hage 2010, 418). In a similar vein, in his extensive research on the 'migration–home nexus', Paolo Boccagni defines homes as possessing three key characteristics: security, familiarity and control: '[T]he home experience [thus] relies on a specific place, is potentially transferrable elsewhere, and draws on interpersonal relationships as much as material settings' (Boccagni 2017, 2). At the same time, the understanding of what these characteristics mean in practice – what makes a home adequate or ideal, secure or familiar – are culturally and socially shaped to a great degree, and therefore distinct. In these concepts of home, then, home comes into being through the processes of home-making or, as Boccagni phrases it, 'home-as-homing' (2017, 15).

Home-making involves 'different sets of practices' (Boccagni 2020, 8), including the improvement and beautification of space (Boccagni 2020, 9; Brun and Fábos 2015, 12), practices that enable cultural reproduction and continuity (Hage 2010; Boccagni 2020, 9), attempts to privatise space (Boccagni 2020, 9), daily routines, and the building of connections to people (Brun and Fábos 2015, 12). Material objects are involved in these processes in several ways, such as the acquisition and use of kitchen utensils that allow residents to cook familiar food, or blankets that can be hung up to separate spaces and provide more personal space.

In Rachel Barber's chapter, Mexican folk and popular art allows the American retirees to build connections and relationships to their new place of residence and the people living there. Barber analyses two particular types of aesthetic objects in the houses of the retirees, stressing the objects' roles as active agents in the social dynamics they are embedded in. She shows how the retirees acquire and display these objects out of a desire to establish relationships with the locals, and to represent themselves as 'friendly neighbours'. But Barber also shows that these connections do not transcend social and economic dynamics and are fundamentally economic. The folk art in the retirees' homes therefore reiterates and engages with the underlying, ambiguous social dynamics and economic asymmetries that mark their relationship with the local population.

Routines, practices of togetherness and place-making

These home- and place-making practices show how important routine practices can be in enabling feelings of familiarity, continuity and safety (Vandevoordt 2017; Dudley 2011; Nowicka 2007; Povrzanović Frykman 2016). Objects play an important role in these routine practices and create 'palpable connections between people and places' (Povrzanović Frykman and Humbracht 2013, 47). Taking things to a new place allows migrants to continue familiar practices, as in the case of a particular coffee maker described by Povrzanović Frykman and Humbracht (2013, 49). In other words, objects provide for 'uninterrupted pleasure and smoothness of everyday practices' (Povrzanović Frykman and Humbracht 2013, 50).

Residents in a camp or reception centre are often forced into a coincidental (close) coexistence with people of different origins, which is sometimes tense and conflict-laden. Several studies illustrate and describe how practices of togetherness and communality – including across ethnic and other differences – evolve around the joint preparation and consumption of food (Hage 2010; Wise 2011). Indeed, food and the practices connected to preparing and eating it are particularly effective in re-creating familiar experiences and homely feelings (Dudley 2011; Hage 2010; Vandevoordt 2017) and provide opportunities to come together, for commensality, or more general conviviality as a 'practice of living together with others' (Wise 2011, 82; Heil 2015). Intercultural situations centred on food have been studied between migrants with diverse backgrounds and between migrants and long-term residents and local populations (Hage 2010; Wise 2011), and as practices that foster 'intercultural conviviality' (Wise 2011, 83).

Being with each other and sharing a place with others is an important element in feeling at home (Boccagni and Vargas Silva 2021, 7). Situations of commensality allow people to overcome the temporal and spatial distance from their homes for a moment, both for a limited period of time and in an experiential way. The everyday social routines that develop, often around food, may be experienced as a kind of 'compensation' for displacement, helping people on the move to establish a feeling of belonging abroad by 'translating' their social practices of socialising or inviting a guest into their local-cultural possibilities. As Robin Vandevoordt (2017) shows, communal eating practices are also sites of (re)negotiating power relations and opportunities to become hosts and recover a sense of autonomy. Place-making in this sense is a communal activity connected to particular material practices.

In her chapter, Yaatsil Guevara González focuses on the social interactions surrounding everyday place-making activities, including the preparation and consumption of food and the allocation of resources in La 72 shelter in Tenosique in Mexico. Discussing interactions in the kitchen and dorm rooms, she shows how power relations are negotiated between people working in the kitchen and groups of 'old' and 'new' migrants. She shows that the kitchen is a place of power and privilege that keeps everyday life going, structures the commensal routines and creates inclusions and exclusions.

Summary

In this short introduction, we have looked at the materiality of migration from the perspective of place and place-making practices. The chapters in this part of the volume show how the particular materiality of specific places like shelters, camps or kitchens shape people's practices and how, in turn, people shape these places actively and creatively to create a sense of normality and familiarity. The examples demonstrate how migrants engage things in home-making practices, in daily routines and in order to produce situations of togetherness. In short, this perspective highlights place as a process, and as a constellation of people, material objects and surroundings, and migrants as important actors in place-making.

Note

1 The authors also provide a rich overview of camp genealogies and the origin of camps as institutions. See also Katz et al. 2018.
2 Soto refers to Marc Augé (1995).

References

Abourahme, Nasser. 2014. 'Assembling and spilling-over: Towards an "ethnography of cement" in a Palestinian refugee camp', *International Journal of Urban and Regional Research* 39(2): 200–17. https://doi.org/10.1111/1468-2427.12155.

Agamben, Giorgio. 1998. *Homo Sacer: Sovereign power and bare life*. Stanford, CA: Stanford University Press.

Agier, Michel. 2011. *Managing the Undesirables: Refugee camps and humanitarian government*. Translated by David Fernbach. Cambridge: Polity.

Appadurai, Arjun. 1988. 'Putting hierarchy in its place', *Cultural Anthropology* 3(1): 36–49. https://doi.org/10.1525/can.1988.3.1.02a00040.

Appadurai, Arjun. 1996. *Modernity at Large: Cultural dimensions of globalization*. Minneapolis: University of Minnesota Press.

Augé, Marc. 1995. *Non-Places: An introduction to an anthropology of supermodernity*. Translated by John Howe. London: Verso.

Boccagni, Paolo. 2017. *Migration and the Search for Home: Mapping domestic space in migrants' everyday lives*. New York: Palgrave Macmillan.

Boccagni, Paolo. 2020. 'At home in the centre? Spatial appropriation and horizons of homemaking in reception facilities for asylum seekers', HOMInG Working Papers 10_2020, ERC StG HOMInG, Università di Trento. Accessed 26 August 2021. https://erchoming.files.wordpress.com/2020/09/homing-wp-10_2020.pdf.

Boccagni, Paolo and Carlos Vargas Silva. 2021. 'Feeling at home across time and place: A study of Ecuadorians in three European cities', *Population, Space and Place* 27(6) (art. no. e24321): 1–13. https://doi.org/10.1002/psp.2431.

Bochmann, Annett. 2018. 'The power of local micro structures in the context of refugee camps', *Journal of Refugee Studies* 32(1): 63–85. https://doi.org/10.1093/jrs/fey018.

Brkovic, Carna. 2020. 'From sovereignty to mandate, and back again: Playing games with responsibility in a refugee camp in southeast Europe'. Paper presented at the conference 'Materializing the Transient', 13–16 May, University of Göttingen.

Brun, Cathrine. 2015. 'Active waiting and changing hopes: Toward a time perspective on protracted displacement', *Social Analysis* 59(1): 19–37. https://doi.org/10.3167/sa.2015.590102.

Brun, Cathrine and Anita Fábos. 2015. 'Making homes in limbo? A conceptual framework', *Refuge* 31(1): 5–17. https://doi.org/10.25071/1920-7336.40138.

Çağlar, Ayşe and Nina Glick Schiller, eds. 2018. *Migrants and City-Making: Dispossession, displacement, and urban regeneration*. Durham, NC, and London: Duke University Press.

Certeau, Michel de. 1984. *The Practice of Everyday Life*. Translated by Steven Rendall. Berkeley: University of California Press.

Clifford, James. 1997. 'Traveling cultures'. In James Clifford, *Routes: Travel and translation in the late twentieth century*, 17–46. Cambridge, MA, and London: Harvard University Press. Originally published in 1992 in *Cultural Studies*, edited by Lawrence Grossberg, Cary Nelson and Paula Treichler. New York: Routledge.

Dudley, Sandra H. 2011. 'Feeling at home: Producing and consuming things in Karenni refugee camps on the Thai–Burma border', *Population, Space and Place* 17(6): 742–55. https://doi.org/10.1002/psp.639.

Glick Schiller, Nina and Noel B. Salazar. 2013. 'Regimes of mobility across the globe', *Journal of Ethnic and Migration Studies* 39(2): 183–200. https://doi.org/10.1080/1369183X.2013.723253.

Gupta, Akhil and James Ferguson, eds. 1997a. *Anthropological Locations: Boundaries and grounds of a field science*. Berkeley: University of California Press.

Gupta, Akhil and James Ferguson, eds. 1997b. *Culture, Power, Place: Explorations in critical anthropology*. Durham, NC, and London: Duke University Press.

Hage, Ghassan. 2010. 'Migration, food, memory, and home-building'. In *Memory: Histories, theories, debates*, edited by Susannah Radstone and Bill Schwarz, 416–27. New York: Fordham University Press.

Heil, Tilmann. 2015. 'Conviviality: (Re)negotiating minimal consensus'. In *Routledge International Handbook of Diversity Studies*, edited by Steven Vertovec, 317–24. Abingdon: Routledge.

Jefferson, Andrew, Simon Turner and Steffen Jensen. 2019. 'Introduction: On stuckness and sites of confinement', *Ethnos* 84(1): 1–13. https://doi.org/10.1080/00141844.2018.1544917.

Katz, Irit, Diana Martin and Claudio Minca, eds. 2018. *Camps Revisited: Multifaceted spatialities of a modern political technology*. London: Rowman & Littlefield.

Lefebvre, Henri. [1974] 1991. *The Production of Space*. Translated by Donald Nicholson-Smith. Oxford: Blackwell.

Lems, Annika 2016. 'Placing displacement: Place-making in a world of movement', *Ethnos* 81(2): 315–37. https://doi.org/10.1080/00141844.2014.931328.

Malkki, Liisa. 1992. 'National geographic: The rooting of peoples and the territorialization of national identity among scholars and refugees', *Cultural Anthropology* 7(1): 24–44. https://doi.org/10.1525/can.1992.7.1.02a00030.

Malkki, Liisa. 1995. 'Refugees and exile: From "refugee studies" to the national order of things', *Annual Review in Anthropology* 24: 494–523. https://doi.org/10.1146/annurev.an.24.100195.002431.

Malkki, Liisa. 1997. 'News and culture: Transitory phenomena and the fieldwork tradition'. In *Anthropological Locations: Boundaries and grounds of a field science*, edited by Akhil Gupta and James Ferguson, 86–101. Berkeley and Los Angeles: University of California Press.

Martin, Diana, Claudio Minca and Irit Katz. 2020. 'Rethinking the camp: On spatial technologies of power and resistance', *Progress in Human Geography* 44(4): 743–68. https://doi.org/10.1177%2F0309132519856702.

Nowicka, Magdalena. 2007. 'Mobile locations: Construction of home in a group of mobile transnational professionals', *Global Networks* 7(1): 69–86. https://doi.org/10.1111/j.1471-0374.2006.00157.x.

Povrzanović Frykman, Maja. 2016. 'Conceptualising continuity: A material culture perspective on transnational social fields', *Ethnologia Fennica* 43: 43–56.

Povrzanović Frykman, Maja and Michael Humbracht. 2013. 'Making palpable connections. Objects in migrants' transnational lives', *Ethnologia Scandinavica: A Journal for Nordic Ethnology* 43: 47–67.

Ramadan, Adam. 2009. 'A refugee landscape: Writing Palestinian nationalisms in Lebanon', *ACME* 8(1): 69–99. https://acme-journal.org/index.php/acme/article/view/821/678.

Ramadan, Adam. 2013. 'Spatialising the refugee camp', *Transactions of the Institute of British Geographers* 38(1): 65–77. Accessed 27 October 2021. https://doi.org/10.1111/j.1475-5661.2012.00509.x.

Soto, Gabriella. 2016. 'Place making in non-places: Migrant graffiti in rural highway box culverts', *Journal of Contemporary Archaeology* 3(2): 174–95. http://dx.doi.org/10.1558/jca.31830.

Vandevoordt, Robin 2017. 'The politics of food and hospitality: How Syrian refugees in Belgium create a home in hostile environments', *Journal of Refugee Studies* 30(4): 605–21. https://doi.org/10.1093/jrs/fex017.

Walsh, Katie. 2006. 'British expatriate belongings: Mobile homes and transnational homing', *Home Cultures* 3(2): 123–44. https://doi.org/10.2752/174063106778053183.

Wise, Amanda. 2011. 'Moving food: Gustatory commensality and disjuncture in everyday multiculturalism', *New Formations* 74(1): 82–107. http://dx.doi.org/10.3898/NewF.74.05.2011.

12

Materiality, agency and temporariness in camps in Greece

Nada Ghandour-Demiri and Petros Passas[1]

Introduction

To an outsider, entering a refugee camp[2] in mainland Greece can bring a variety of uncommon sights and sensations, one of which is the degree to which the displaced populations residing within quickly alter the physical and architectural landscape of the camps. By changing the built and natural environments, they seek to improve their living conditions and, at times, create approximations of the lives they left behind in their countries of origin. The anthropology of materiality reveals interesting dilemmas about the nuance of refugee policy, practice and experience, the scope and success of humanitarian aid interventions aimed at restoring dignity and human rights to the displaced, and the motivations of institutional policy and practice. In a time of radical political polarisations, if a narrative of dependence dominates official channels and popular discourse concerning the European 'refugee crisis', a closer look at the materiality of migration shows that many of the prevailing stereotypes are devoid of any consideration for the agency of the displaced. And while this oversight is to be expected in popular media and discourse, a renewed look at how the materiality of refugee camps conditions and is conditioned by the humanitarian aid process can elucidate some of the above dilemmas, and so contribute to a more appropriate deliberation of their pragmatic and symbolic potency vis-à-vis institutional practices, and the production of knowledge that supports these practices.

In attempting to understand how an anthropology of materiality applies to the context of the refugee camps in Greece, it is important to concentrate on the mechanisms by which the lives of the displaced interact with conventionally conceived transitory infrastructures, and the policies and practices which create the latter. Doing this can shed light on details extraneous to the very policy discussions that formulate aid in the first place, despite their indisputable links to the refugee condition. These details include, on the one hand, how infrastructure projects are considered, designed and implemented by organisations that provide humanitarian aid, and, on the other, how objects and possessions are used, circulated and (re)appropriated by residents to survive, create a sense of normality, and enact and affirm cultural identities within the setting of refugee camps. In this way, we can consider how the agency of displaced persons residing in refugee camps intersects with formal material interventions, and the expressions and behaviours this engenders in humanitarian actors.

This chapter therefore attempts to connect a politics of materiality observed in refugee camps in mainland Greece with the potency of materials in regenerating personal and collective agency in adversity, by exploring the diversity of formal infrastructures established by the Greek government and humanitarian actors in Greece, and the agency of the displaced which emerges in this context. In order to orient the reader to the context, we begin by providing a presentation of the type of camps found in Greece and a brief sketch of the camp geographies from a materiality perspective, moving on to present ethnographic examples of how humanitarian practice is formulated, and then on to examples of material enactment of refugee agency, in particular the reappropriation and upcycling of aid infrastructure and associated, informal economies, ultimately arriving at some ideas about how to rethink the materiality of migration in the light of our observations and the conclusions we have drawn from them.

Research context and methodology

Research context

Since 2014, Greece has been the main gateway to Europe, experiencing unprecedented flows of displaced persons, which reached a peak of more than 850,000 arrivals in 2015 (UNHCR 2016).[3] Greece was primarily a transit country in people's journeys to northern European destinations, but the closure of the 'Western Balkan route' and the enactment of the European Union (EU)–Turkey statement in 2016 (European Commission 2016) resulted in a complete change in the situation: fewer people entered Greece via Turkey, and some people already in Greece were stranded. This situation put substantial pressure on the Greek asylum and reception system, which was not prepared to accommodate or process the number of displaced persons who remained within the country's borders.

Therefore, in April 2016, at the request of the Greek government, the European Commission took the unprecedented step of deploying its Directorate-General for European Civil Protection and Humanitarian Aid Operations (DG ECHO) on EU soil for the first time. The deployment of DG ECHO, the EU's donor arm for funding humanitarian aid in non-EU countries, brought attention to the fact that the problem was a European one in nature, called out the inability of the Greek government to respond using existing national resources, and de facto implicated the involvement of international non-governmental organisations (INGOs) pre-approved to work with DG ECHO funding (European Commission 2020). In 2016, funding was rapidly allocated in two initial phases (early spring and midsummer 2016), and in total 29 projects were funded to the amount of €644.5 million (European Commission 2018). Between 2016 and 2018, with EU funding, the United Nations High Commissioner for Refugees (UNHCR), the International Organization for Migration (IOM) and INGOs upgraded nearly all the camps in Greece from basic tented camps to 'containerised' camps. In mid-2018, planning began for the eventual phase-out of DG ECHO and the reallocation of all EU funding for Greece to the DG HOME[4] Asylum, Migration and Integration Fund (AMIF) emergency assistance (EMAS) grant scheme. The EMAS grant scheme can only fund national governments and UN agencies, and so funding for all refugee response activities had to be disbursed directly to IOM and UNICEF, and indirectly to other international and national NGOs (via the aforementioned UN agencies). The efforts resulted in the establishment of a new paradigm for providing aid in all the mainland open accommodation centres, in the form of Site Management Support (SMS)[5] led by IOM. Its main element was intended to be the 'harmonisation' of infrastructure and service provision in all the camps in mainland Greece. It is against the backdrop of this funding shift, and within the spirit of harmonisation described above, that the present research is situated. At the time of writing, the 32 camps on the mainland are administered by the Greek government's Reception and Identification Service (RIS),[6] and the majority of services are provided by IOM and two humanitarian INGOs: the Danish Refugee Council (DRC) and Arbeiter-Samariter-Bund (ASB). Additionally, other local and international NGOs are contracted to provide specialised services, including child protection and non-formal education. These include Terre des Hommes (TdH), ARSIS, Solidarity Now and European Expression.

Research methodology

This chapter draws on the authors' experiences as scholar practitioners who worked as researchers and humanitarian aid workers in various NGOs in Greece between 2015 and 2020, and primarily with the Danish Refugee Council between 2018 and 2020. During this period, both authors were able to gain in-depth knowledge on the context, humanitarian operations and politics of aid, and to collect observations on the process of programming infrastructure interventions and materiality in almost all the open accommodation centres on the mainland. Practising anthropology with the support of NGO legitimacy, logistics and resources has given us privileged access to situations and knowledge which would otherwise have been impossible. Through our positionality, we were able to be 'observant participants' (Gow 2008; Mosse 2005; Rottenburg 2009) in the wide spectrum of engagement with the context, conducting verification exercises, taking part in and leading senior coordination and management meetings of key actors, preparing proposals and budgets, negotiating with Greek government authorities and the European Commission, recruiting and training staff, monitoring and evaluating services in the camps, and conducting interviews with displaced persons. While we are aware of the differences between academia and practice, and the biases that each can engender, we believe that through our experiences of, access to and interaction with key forums of humanitarian decision-making and practice, we can contribute meaningfully to an in-depth understanding of the humanitarian aid context in Greece and its effects. Moreover, we are both proficient in Greek, French and Arabic, which allowed us a wide degree of access with different stakeholders and displaced persons, enriching the research and providing insights beyond the professional spaces of our everyday employment.

At the time of the research and writing of this chapter, since we were both employed by the Danish Refugee Council in Greece, it became important to infuse our own perspectives, beliefs and values with a healthy dose of reflexivity, while remaining critical of the organisational practices and policies we were engaged in creating or formulating. Our research is therefore situated between a critical engagement with humanitarian practice, the ongoing professional dilemmas of applied work, and individual efforts to find practical solutions that would ameliorate the living conditions of the displaced. The methodological approach employed thus draws inspiration from anthropological studies of the humanitarian and development sectors that examine the complex interplay of policy and practice (Mosse 2005; see also Agier 2011; Malkki 1995; Nolan 2013; Peteet 2005; Sanyal 2014; Smirl 2015; Ward et al. 2020). Our analysis also draws on anthropological archaeology and material culture studies (Abourahme 2015; Appadurai 1986; Barry 2018; Basu and Coleman 2008; Dudley 2010; Kiddey 2020; Kopytoff 1986; Hamilakis 2016; Hicks and Mallet 2019; McGuire 2020; Mould 2018) that shed light on the material, sensual and temporal experiences that migration entails in the spatial and politicised context of refugee camps (see Agier 2011; Feldman 2015; Kandylis 2019; Minca 2015; Ramadan 2012; Sanyal 2014; Singh 2020). Furthermore, our methodology leans heavily on the realisation that our professional access provides us with privileged access to the 'complex set of institutions, flows and actors' involved in shaping the politics of humanitarian aid and materiality in Greece (Olivier de Sardan 2005). The meeting of these methodological influences helps elucidate how, in combination with an ethnography of materiality, an ethnography of the institutional practice of humanitarian aid can be used to challenge key assumptions about materiality, avoid the essentialisation of material practices and contribute to future humanitarian practice able to channel lessons learned from them into more effective programme delivery methods.

Camp geographies

Demographic particularities of the displaced population in Greece

A striking feature of refugee camps in Greece is the transience and diversity of the populations that inhabit them. While the capacity of a camp may remain fixed for a long time, there is often a high turnover in the camp population, including sudden departures and unexpected arrivals. For example, since late 2018, it has become increasingly common for camps in the mainland to have to receive at short notice (that is, without sufficient time to prepare, or set up emergency accommodation) hundreds of people from the Reception and Identification Centres (RICs) as a way of decongesting the islands. Displaced persons stay in a camp for a few days or up to four years, a duration that is not predetermined but depends on an amalgam of bureaucratic and legal procedures, governmental decisions and, ultimately, luck. They live in a state of lasting temporariness and waithood (Brun 2015; Katz 2017; Martin

2015; Martin et al. 2019; Pallister-Wilkins 2020). This uncertainty about the duration of stay and about what comes afterwards leaves people in a state of 'permanent impermanence', which affects their relation to the space they live in (Sayigh 2005). In other words, a person who remains in a space for a few days might not 'invest' in it emotionally and materially to the same extent as a person who remains for years.

Another particularity of the refugee camps in Greece is the diversity of ethnic and cultural backgrounds of their residents. This, together with the transient nature of the population, makes it somewhat difficult in seemingly permanent camps for one ethnic community to emerge (as is the case with Palestinian camps in Lebanon, Syrian camps in Jordan, Rohingya camps in Bangladesh and Karenni camps in Thailand). In fact, such a situation is generally avoided by the Greek government in order to ensure that these camps remain places of temporary stay and to prevent their transformation into ghettos, despite the fact that over the years some camps have become mono-ethnic, and others have been planned this way.[7]

Typology and legal framework of accommodation infrastructure

At the outset of the 'refugee crisis', a number of formal accommodation centres were established throughout Greece. According to Directive 2013/33/EU on standards for the reception of asylum seekers, accommodation means 'any place used for the collective housing of applicants' (Article 2), and should 'guarantee an adequate standard of living' (Article 18) (European Parliament and Council 2013). These accommodation centres, however, represent one variation of formal accommodation for displaced persons in Greece. Other variations include: RICs, transit camps on the mainland (e.g., IOM's open centre for migrants registered for assisted voluntary return and reintegration), open accommodation centres, hotels (e.g., IOM's FILOXENIA project), apartments (e.g., UNHCR's ESTIA accommodation scheme), detention centres (e.g., the Amygdaleza detention facility), and other types of formal shelters for particularly vulnerable persons, such as unaccompanied minors and survivors of sexual and gender-based violence (e.g., the Shelter for Women Victims of Violence and their children of the City of Athens). However, the predominant types are the RICs and the open accommodation centres, where the great majority of the displaced reside.

Furthermore, Greek legislation (Law 4375/2016) distinguishes between RICs and open temporary facilities of reception or accommodation (*Hellenic State Gazette* 2016), the former operating predominantly in border regions and responsible for the initial registration of all displaced persons entering Greece. The open accommodation centres, on the other hand, are meant to provide accommodation to asylum seekers and other third-country nationals until their asylum claims can be processed by the Greek Asylum Service. The chapter focuses on the open accommodation centres, as the fieldwork research took place in the 26 of those centres that were operational in 2019, and in other ones previously operational but now closed.

Material origins and the practice and policy of material harmonisation

Many of the open accommodation centres in Greece were initially established by the Hellenic armed forces and were located primarily on decommissioned military bases, warehouses or brownfields, and consisted of tents without any kind of ground covering. Others were located on campsites that belonged to different ministries and were originally intended for use as summer camps by the children of the employees of those ministries. Finally, there was an eclectic mix of camps adhering to no set definition, situated in schools, hotels and other social service infrastructures (e.g., Tsepelovo, Konitsa, Volvi).

The initial establishment and the material quality of camps were closely related to the criticality of need, and it is thus worth noting that different approaches taken by different actors in the early planning of sites have resulted in both positive and problematic outcomes, each conditioning the subsequent materiality of camps in different ways. Thus, most camps look and feel different; some are older than others, some have only tents (Nea Malakasa, Serres-Kleidi), some have only old buildings (an abandoned hotel in Thermopylae, an old music school in Doliana, empty rented houses in Volvi, an old car dealership in Volos), some have primarily prefabricated containers (Koutsochero, Kato Milia, Skaramangas, Katsikas), and some have a mixed infrastructure, which can lead to inequalities in service provision (see Figures 12.1 to 12.4). An important effect of these differences is that the type of existing land ownership infrastructure and the nature of specific camps 'processed' by humanitarian aid policy formulation in Greece determine the possibilities for infrastructural and material interventions. In other words, while in some camps it is possible to build new concrete structures to accommodate more people, in others it is not possible or allowed. The same applies to material interventions made by residents. For example, while the residents in Koutsochero were able to create a tea house with a fountain (see Figures 12.5 and 12.6), this was not possible in a camp like Nea Malakasa (which was built in early 2020 as a highly securitised detention camp that has only tents and limited electricity and water provision).

Furthermore, over time, as the material infrastructure of a camp changes, new shelters – tents, Rubb halls (large, relocatable tent-like structures often used in situations of emergency) and more permanent structures – are built or set up to accommodate more people, the present infrastructure changes (it is painted, or extended), disappears (is removed or stolen), burns or decays, and elements of materiality shift and new potentialities are either opened or closed. Thus, when we say open accommodation centres are the predominant type of camp, it is important not to essentialise these camps but to recognise their inherent differences, their evolution over time, how they affect their residents (especially given the residents' transfer from one camp to another by the authorities), and how these differences create and shape expressions of materiality.

12.1 Tents in Nea Kavala camp, northern Greece, June 2019. © Ghandour-Demiri

12.2 Main building of Oinofyta camp (former plastics and chemical factory), near Attica, Greece, October 2019. © Nada Ghandour-Demiri.

12.3 Main building of Volos camp (former car dealership), central Greece, April 2021. © Nada Ghandour-Demiri.

12.4 Containers/prefabricated housing units, Skaramangas camp (the largest camp in mainland Greece, located on a dock of the Hellenic navy, in a shipyard area), Attica, May 2020. © Nada Ghandour-Demiri.

12.5 Restaurant/tea house with fountain (before), Koutsochero camp, central Greece, 2019. © Nada Ghandour-Demiri.

12.6 Restaurant/tea house with fountain (after), Koutsochero camp, central Greece, 2019. © Nada Ghandour-Demiri.

In the early years of the response, when UNHCR was leading the process of upgrading the tented camps into containerised shelters, significant efforts were made to create a framework to manage all shelter and water, sanitation and hygiene (WASH)-related structural interventions in the camps. These efforts, at an institutional level, were strongly supported by the fact that DG ECHO employed at least one technical adviser with a civil engineering background, and thus the in-house capacity of the European Commission was facilitative towards the establishment of material standards in camps, via donor-led technical discussions and field visits. With DG HOME funding in 2019, and the leadership of the Site Management Support (SMS) programming passing to IOM (and later to RIS as well, with the support of NORCAP[8]), independent project-led efforts were made to collectively standardise broader elements of the SMS programme, via the organisation and facilitation of various harmonisation workshops aimed at creating a blueprint for a more harmonised SMS programme. However, in the absence of a donor leadership, the workshops failed to define the operational details required to create infrastructure standards, particularly the application of standards relating to the minimum shelter typologies required in the Greek context.[9] Similarly, the issue of standards emerged in long-standing discussions with DG ECHO and RIS, and initial efforts to harmonise shelter types within camps – something that was agreed by all actors – were ultimately abandoned in favour of plans to create what we have called 'two-track' accommodation modalities within camps.[10]

The above information, gathered primarily from high-level project coordination meetings, demonstrates the fundamentally ad hoc nature of formal infrastructure interventions in the camps in Greece, both in the lack of a clear policy concerning the establishment and operation of camps, and in the lack of any common practice concerning the nature of material humanitarian interventions within them. This is important, because the two main issues impacting the infrastructure management of camps relate to the constant material changes associated with the transient nature of the population (capacity changes, degradation of materials), and the intractable challenge of defining shelter capacity, the impacts of which have effects on expressions of materiality in the camps. Each of these issues will be explored in turn, as they each impact the resulting materiality in different ways.

With regard to the first issue, the main elements of material change in the camps relate to the addition of new shelter spaces (via new constructions or the repurposing of containers initially used as offices), the frequent turnover of shelter units and the upkeep required to keep them functional, the damage frequently inflicted on the infrastructure of communal spaces, and the frequent movement of displaced persons to new shelter spaces not assigned to them. Similarly, shelter capacity was a contentious issue in Greece between 2016 and 2020. Multiple negotiations between UN agencies and the Greek government, supported by NGOs and mediated by the SMS working group, led to the establishment of shelter standards, issued by the government in 2016. Despite this, however, we were able to identify numerous examples of a failure to apply harmonised standards, especially between camps in Attica and Thessaloniki, until late 2019. In mid-2019, this issue was addressed by IOM, and substantial work was done to establish internal clarity (among SMS actors, and subsequently with the Greek government) about how square metres should be calculated in all of the distinct shelter types. Efforts are perpetually frustrated by the need to bring more displaced persons from the islands, and therefore to create additional spaces in existing camps already full to capacity.

Considering the above, we conclude that the lack of any overarching policy concerning the standards required to accommodate displaced persons in Greece for extended periods of time, the nature and diversity of camps, and the variegated services and amenities available and found within them have created the perfect environment for expressions of materiality to flourish in a myriad of new and interesting ways. The remainder of this chapter is dedicated to examining them.

Reappropriation and upcycling of aid infrastructure

In his introduction to the *Social Life of Things*, Arjun Appadurai argues that things have social lives in the sense that their meaning changes as they circulate in and out of different 'regimes of value' (1986, 15). To understand materiality in the humanitarian context, we must track the social lives of materials, their entangled relationships with people, and explore how practices such as reappropriation and upcycling affect their value and meaning. Appadurai's approach is particularly helpful, as it lays the ground for understanding how humanitarian aid infrastructure acquires and loses value throughout its life cycle.

Within the framework of diverse camp geographies and experiences of temporariness and waithood, displaced persons reappropriate and upcycle humanitarian aid infrastructure and commodities to survive, create a sense of normality, or enact and affirm cultural identities. In upcycling, as opposed to recycling, the focus is on improving rather than dissolving; it is the creative repurposing of materials. Humanitarian aid infrastructure acquires another value when reappropriated or upcycled by camp residents. And the biography of materials further contributes to their value (Graeber 2001; Kopytoff 1986): the fact that they once belonged to aid agencies, the government or the military adds to their value as upcycled items, as does the human agency that is incorporated in them through their upcycling (Petridou 2020). David Graeber in his anthropological theory of value demonstrates this by explaining that a thing's value does not rely primarily on the thing itself but on its history (2001).

Furthermore, the process of reappropriation and upcycling has both material and non-material (social) outcomes. At first, we observe the material changes and outcomes. Displaced persons reuse and transform materials to improve functionality and better suit their needs. These material changes can also affect how they feel, live, and interact with their living environment and each other. Because of the limited availability of resources, and restrictions from camp authorities on possible or 'legal' interventions, they acquire and upcycle all kinds of materials provided by aid agencies as part of other material programme interventions. For example, fabrics that provide shade from the sun are stripped from communal areas and distribution points, metal sheets and wooden panels are (re)moved to create private shading areas or partitions and extensions of prefabricated shelter units (see for example Figure 12.7). Women hang blankets on the metal fence in communal WASH areas to protect themselves from the men's gaze (Figure 12.8). Crates are transformed into additional storage space or fridges by attaching them to windows externally, and using them to store vegetables in winter, because of the limited space indoors and because the fridges provided are too small. Pipes, sinks, fire hoses and even traffic cones are used to create private toilets (to avoid using communal WASH facilities) or to provide an added level of material comfort and normality otherwise not provided for in the shelter units.

There are so many examples of such material practices and interventions, in which aid infrastructure is upcycled, that it would be impossible to analyse each one at length in this chapter. We will therefore focus on two common practices observed in camps, which highlight the ways in which camp residents reappropriate, upcycle or trade aid infrastructure and humanitarian commodities: the creation of makeshift gardens, and the informal economies shaping and shaped by materiality. All these practices must be understood as both material and social (Steigemann and Misselwitz 2020).

Makeshift gardens and the agency of the 'uprooted'

Many camps in Greece lack trees and greenery, are located in deserted areas, exposed to bad weather conditions, and lack shade. The 'uprooted' residents, or displaced, often create their own gardens, from placing a few flowerpots on a windowsill to cultivating the small plot of land around

12.7 Reuse of materials to extend balconies, Thermopylae camp, central Greece, October 2019. © Nada Ghandour-Demiri.

12.8 Blankets upcycled for privacy in the communal WASH area (between women's and men's toilets/shower facilities), Nea Malakasa camp, near Attica, Greece, May 2020. © Nada Ghandour-Demiri.

12.9 Makeshift garden, Schisto camp, Attica, Greece, May 2020. © Nada Ghandour-Demiri.

their shelter. Sometimes aid infrastructure is reused for these gardens. For example, materials that initially served a different purpose are upcycled to create flowerpots or create small fences around private gardens (see Figure 12.9). While gardens inherently imply an intention to stay for a while (Shamma 2020), this is not always the case for camp residents-gardeners in Greece as they cannot be sure when they will be able or required to change shelter or leave the camp. Nevertheless, makeshift gardens are a common phenomenon in refugee camps on the mainland, a sign of *sumud* (the Arabic word for steadfastness), as Jawad,[11] a Palestinian refugee, told us once.

Through gardening, camp residents create a sense of home and privacy (protecting the residents from the passer-by's gaze) or find a way to pass the time. Some of these gardens are used to cultivate fruits and vegetables, reflecting the need for self-sufficiency and survival. The gardens are also a way of decorating and beautifying the ugly and impersonal aid infrastructure. Within such contexts, 'decorating spaces is a valuable and vital aspect of living, coping and supporting people's sense of identity and pride' (Nabil et al. 2018). The act of gardening, however, is not always tied to higher pursuits. Ali and Mousa, two of the very first residents in the camp of Katsikas, confided that they simply created the garden because Ali was a farmer and had nothing else to do all day.

In the design phase of newly built camps in Greece, spaces for gardens were rarely envisioned, and even when they were, they were not put into practice.[12] However, with time and experience, the need for gardening is now slowly being taken into consideration. For example, in the camp of Koutsochero in central Greece, many residents created gardens outside their containers. Sometimes the vegetation blocked the passageways between containers. During the design of a new section of Koutsochero camp in mid-2018, the Danish Refugee Council planned that the prefabricated containers or shelters would be placed so as to leave a small plot of land in front to use as a garden. This worked well, and people used them extensively, and appreciated this adaptation. At the same time, this 'improvement', based on people's needs in one section, created imbalances in the shelter provision throughout the camp.

In her study of gardens as migration projects in southern California, Pierrette Hondagneu-Sotelo argues that 'gardens are constitutive elements of society' (2014, 12). Rather than being passive environments, 'garden sites and gardening practices help shape the social world' in which they are located (Hondagneu-Sotelo 2014, 13). In the context of refugee camps in Greece, makeshift gardens and gardening practices are an important material and social element in the lives of their 'owners'. We should, however, be careful not to romanticise or generalise the effect of gardens on camp residents. Not all residents may be interested in gardening, or have the privilege or luck of having a small space next to their shelter to cultivate (for example people residing in buildings that held more than one household, or in rooms without balconies or even windows). Yet, sometimes and when the opportunity arises, makeshift gardens are a material enactment of refugee agency.

'Informal' economies and the trading of humanitarian commodities

Reappropriation of aid infrastructure is apparent in mechanisms of 'informal' economies in the camps. Aid infrastructure and humanitarian commodities are often subject to informal exchange and trading. For example, the sale of prefabricated containers or shelter units is not uncommon, especially when a family leaves a camp and bequeaths its belongings to other residents. The removal and sale of various commodities and materials provided by humanitarian aid actors – such as refrigerators, stoves, chairs and lamps – is a relatively frequent phenomenon. Additionally, aid infrastructure is used to create shops, either from scratch or as extensions of people's shelters. While shops in camps are considered illegal by the Greek authorities, makeshift restaurants, food markets, barber shops, bakeries and butcheries can be found in almost all the camps in mainland Greece (Figures 12.10 and 12.11). The need for such 'informal' markets often emerges because of the isolated location of the camps, and the difficulty in reaching the nearest urban centre. Through these makeshift shops the camps are in a way transformed into a small village, creating a sense of normality and self-sufficiency, and enhancing the possibilities for social interaction between residents. Especially in camps where communal spaces are not provided by the camp management, residents often build their own makeshift spaces to gather and interact (for example the makeshift tea house with a fountain in Koutsochero, Figures 12.5 and 12.6).

Through this reappropriation and adaptation of objects, displaced persons negotiate their relationship with the material world in the camp, in an effort to maintain their dignity and normality in a non-normal situation. It is a form of politics that challenges the material support provided as humanitarian aid. As Newhouse eloquently states, 'these semi-licit efforts to achieve sustenance, invest in the future, and exert autonomy also serve as a public reminder that humanitarian assistance fails to meet the minimum standard to ensure human persistence, and that refugees aim for something more than mere survival' (Newhouse 2015, 2303).

Most of these material practices are often described within accounts of informality or irregularity, and are hence distinguished from the 'formal' and 'official' interventions of the state or humanitarian organisations. This creates a presupposed hierarchy of 'formal' as the norm, tidy and regulated, versus the 'informal' as abnormal, uncontrolled and even dissenting (Banks et al. 2020, 225; Lutzoni 2016, 7). The concept of informality is particularly helpful for making sense of such material practices. Informality, within urban studies, is often associated with processes and phenomena that take place outside formal procedures or planned and regulated areas (Banks et al. 2020; Lutzoni 2016; Roy 2005). It incorporates the spatial aspect, as well as the social, economic and political underpinnings.

In Greece, the official reactions of authorities (and humanitarian actors) to such 'informal' material interventions are often ambivalent. On the one hand, there are instances of such practices being explicitly forbidden, criticised and torn apart. The reasons for this may include the fact that they pose a risk (for example a fire hazard, such as electrical connections), bluntly challenge and 'disrespect' the camp authorities (for example unauthorised occupation of spaces), or are perceived as unnecessary and meaningless. On the other hand, there are occasions when such initiatives are accepted, or even celebrated and admired, especially when they reflect inventiveness and talent, beautify spaces or propose a functional solution to an issue.[13] The specific tolerances of camp managers or other actors were able to significantly influence expressions of materiality. Thus, while in some camps, such as Kato Milia, there are almost no extensions or supplementary structures, camps like Nea Kavala and Skaramangas are replete with them. As a result, a wide spectrum of informality appears, with blurry lines between 'formal' and 'informal', 'legal' and 'illegal', and leading to various degrees of legitimacies. In fact, it is precisely the correlation between these seemingly oppositional perspectives and practices that should be the centre of attention. As Lutzoni writes in his study on informality in urban design,

> it is not the single formal or informal processes that determine the positive outcome of the planning and design process for urban space, but rather the quality of the relations existing between the two spatial concepts. The informal, placing itself in a dialectical relation with the formal, configures relational spaces and defines a meeting point between two different ways of structuring society.
> (Lutzoni 2016, 10)

12.10 Restaurants area, Skaramangas camp, Attica, Greece, May 2020. © Nada Ghandour-Demiri.

12.11 Barber shop (extension construction), Nea Kavala camp, July 2020. © Ghandour-Demiri

We should be wary of ascribing the generalised trope of material interventions to resistance and instead try to distinguish the motivations behind each of these practices (Varley 2013). In the Greek context, where camps are transient spaces with limited opportunities for long-term political organisation, these practices are often ways in which the displaced manage from day to day the failures of the humanitarian apparatus. We must therefore be careful not to romanticise and glorify the way displaced persons in camps use materiality to negotiate spaces, economies and politics. In fact, recognising the limitations of agency can help us identify the ways in which agency is prevented or repressed (Banks et al. 2020).

Conclusion

When we consider the diverse geographies of the open accommodation centres in Greece and the extent to which materiality plays a central role in affirming the way in which displaced persons live and experience the camp settings, some immediate conclusions emerge concerning the interlinkages between the design of aid programming, the governance of refugee camps and the agency of displaced persons. Most salient is how initial camp infrastructure and governing structures critically affect the subsequent possibilities for material interventions and the articulation of agency by displaced persons. While expressions of agency were observed in all camps, they were strongly tempered by the layout, infrastructure and management of the camps, which considerably affected the nature of material interventions.

A question thus emerges about the ways in which a predetermined analytical emphasis on the material world of camps can help humanitarian practitioners ameliorate the living conditions for the refugees a priori, and what links such an emphasis can foster to encourage resilience among displaced populations. This is in no way meant to suggest that the camp settings should be romanticised, or that the refugee experience should be essentialised via the application of programmatic decisions meant to channel agency into predetermined channels, but rather that engagement with camps should foster the creation of an awareness that the material interventions employed also speak to the shortcomings of aid delivery, and thus offer opportunities to reflect on how better to design it. While such an approach might be advised against, or discouraged, because of the temporariness of the stay in the open accommodation centres, which affects how material interventions are made, there is ample evidence of an ongoing and supra-personal transference of materiality, in which items and solutions are often transferred from one owner to another, or reappropriated.

Thus materiality is an important element that needs to be incorporated in strategies of humanitarian intervention, as well as in debates about whether camps are spaces of protection or detention, and whether they preserve refugee rights or erode them (Feldman 2015, 251; see also Lischer 2005; Paszkiewicz and Fosas 2019; Rosenberg 2011; Shearlaw 2013). The dynamism that approaches to materiality in camps engender underscores the importance of assessing camps not only for the quality of humanitarian activities in support of shelter construction and their impact on the welfare of displaced persons, but also for potentialities of materiality in channelling the agency of displaced persons towards a more positive and equal ownership of the humanitarian process.

Notes

1 During the research and writing process of this chapter, both authors were employed by the Danish Refugee Council. However, the content of this chapter does not necessarily reflect the views of the organisation.

2 The terms 'refugee camp' and 'open accommodation centre' are used interchangeably here, and refer to spaces temporarily hosting refugees and migrants in mainland Greece, as opposed to Reception and Identification Centres (RICs) on the islands. Refugee camps in mainland Greece are also known as 'sites' or 'open refugee accommodation centres' by the Greek government, and 'long-term accommodation centres' by the International Organization for Migration (IOM).

3 For clarity, the term 'displaced persons' will be used in this chapter to refer to asylum seekers, refugees and migrants. In the context of this research, the term refers primarily to displaced persons who have arrived in Greece within the recent 'refugee crisis' (i.e., from 2014 onwards).

4 DG HOME is the Directorate-General for Migration and Home Affairs of the European Commission. It is the EU-level ministerial body responsible for migration policy, internal security, external borders, and dialogue and cooperation with non-EU countries.

5 Site management support (SMS) is the collective of humanitarian actions undertaken by non-government actors (usually UN agencies and NGOs) to support the state's management of the open accommodation centres in Greece. SMS covers a wide range of activities, including the management of arrival, reception and departure procedures, the provision of welcome kits and other non-food items to new arrivals and vulnerable beneficiaries, the care and maintenance of shelter and water, sanitation and hygiene (WASH) facilities and the reinforcement of community participation and accountability mechanisms. It is something like what in other contexts is called camp coordination and camp management (CCCM). The 2019 SMS project was titled 'Improving the Greek reception system through site management support and targeted interventions in long-term accommodation sites', and the 2020 one 'Supporting the Greek authorities in managing the national reception system for asylum seekers and vulnerable migrants', both led by IOM and funded by DG HOME.

6 RIS only appointed a camp manager to every open accommodation centre in mainland Greece in May 2020. Previously, the only camps being formally managed by RIS were Eleonas, Schisto and Diavata; some other camps had RIS representation without formal decision-making authority, and some had no RIS representation whatsoever.

7 With the exception of the creation of Yazidi-only camps, there does not appear ever to have been an overarching strategy at RIS for promoting or avoiding the creation of open accommodation sites with specific ethnic compositions. Early in the response there were some camps that became exclusively mono-ethnic (for example Schisto for Farsi-speakers), but this

course was later reversed as the need to transfer displaced persons from the islands trumped any competing priority concerning their ethnicity. Likewise, anecdotal comments by key RIS staff, for example suggesting that Africans have a 'calming effect' on other camp residents, appear to indicate a general lack of attention to this matter.

8 NORCAP is the funding mechanism established by the Norwegian government and operated by the Norwegian Refugee Council. It provides governments globally with expertise seconded to the humanitarian, development and peace-building sectors. In Greece, NORCAP has funded numerous posts in the Reception and Identification Service (RIS).

9 For example, whether all prefabricated shelter units should have individual WASH units or each dedicated living space should have its own kitchen. In Skaramangas, there are containers which are divided into two, mostly separate, parts, but there is only one kitchen, located in one part, so that the residents of the part without a kitchen have to access the other part, while the residents of the part that has a kitchen can only enter their own part.

10 In this case, 'two-track' means having prefabricated shelter units in the same camp with widely divergent specifications: for example, some containers have bathrooms and kitchens while others have no such amenities, so that displaced persons residing in the latter units have to use communal spaces dedicated to those functions (communal toilets, showers and kitchens). It should be noted that it was widely accepted that in some camps that had pre-existing buildings (e.g. Alexandria), an element of 'two-trackedness' was inevitable, and that discussions of this nature were restricted to ensuring the avoidance of prefabricated container units with different specifications in the same camp.

11 Names have been changed to protect research participants' identities.

12 Numerous camp 'redesigns' included provision for garden areas, for example UNHCR's plans for Katsikas camp and the Ministry of Migration Policy's plans for Vassilika camp. None of these, or other utopian versions of camps, were constructed.

13 Since March 2020, a new legislative text has provided for the opening of small shops in RICs and open accommodation centres, as long as the municipalities play a leading role in their establishment. However, no form of 'legalisation' of irregular shops in the camps has happened up to the time of writing. The legislative text can be found in the *Hellenic State Gazette*, 30 March 2020, p. 1283, Article 43. Accessed 26 August 2021. https://www.gsis.gr/sites/default/files/2020-03/ΠΝΠ%20A75.pdf.

References

Abourahme, Nasser. 2015. 'Assembling and spilling-over: Towards an "ethnography of cement" in a Palestinian refugee camp', *International Journal of Urban and Regional Research* 39(2): 200–17. https://doi.org/10.1111/1468-2427.12155.

Agier, Michel. 2011. *Managing the Undesirables: Refugee camps and humanitarian government*. Cambridge: Polity.

Appadurai, Arjun, ed. 1986. *The Social Life of Things: Commodities in cultural perspective*. Cambridge: Cambridge University Press.

Banks, Nicola, Melanie Lombard and Diana Mitlin. 2020. 'Urban informality as a site of critical analysis', *Journal of Development Studies* 56(2): 223–38. https://doi.org/10.1080/00220388.2019.1577384.

Barry, Kaya. 2018. 'Art and materiality in the global refugee crisis: Ai Weiwei's artworks and the emerging aesthetics of mobilities', *Mobilities* 14(2): 204–17. https://doi.org/10.1080/17450101.2018.1533683.

Basu, Paul and Simon Coleman. 2008. 'Introduction: Migrant worlds, material cultures', *Mobilities* 3(3): 313–30. https://doi.org/10.1080/17450100802376753.

Brun, Cathrine. 2015. 'Active waiting and changing hopes: Toward a time perspective on protracted displacement', *Social Analysis* 59(1): 19–37. https://doi.org/10.3167/sa.2015.590102.

Dudley, Sandra H. 2010. *Materialising Exile: Material culture and embodied experience among Karenni refugees in Thailand*. New York: Berghahn Books.

European Commission. 2016. 'EU–Turkey statement, 18 March 2016' (press release). Accessed 26 August 2021. https://www.consilium.europa.eu/en/press/press-releases/2016/03/18/eu-turkey-statement/.

European Commission. 2018. 'Evaluation of the operation of Regulation (EU) 2016/369 on the provision of emergency support in the Union'. Accessed 26 August 2021. https://ec.europa.eu/echo/sites/default/files/esi_evaluation_final_211118.pdf.

European Commission. 2020. 'Humanitarian partners'. Accessed 26 August 2021. https://ec.europa.eu/echo/partnerships/humanitarian-partners_en.

European Parliament and Council. 2013. 'Directive 2013/33/EU of the European Parliament and of the Council of 26 June 2013 laying down standards for the reception of applicants for international protection (recast)', *Official Journal of the European Union*, L 180/96. Accessed 27 August 2021. https://eur-lex.europa.eu/legal-content/EN/TXT/PDF/?uri=CELEX:32013L0033&from=EN.

Feldman, Ilana. 2015. 'What is a camp? Legitimate refugee lives in spaces of long-term displacement', *Geoforum* 66: 244–52. http://dx.doi.org/10.1016/j.geoforum.2014.11.014.

Gow, David D. 2008. *Countering Development: Indigenous modernity and the moral imagination*. Durham, NC, and London: Duke University Press.

Graeber, David. 2001. *Toward an Anthropological Theory of Value: The false coin of our own dreams*. New York: Palgrave.

Hamilakis, Yiannis. 2016. 'Archaeologies of forced and undocumented migration', *Journal of Contemporary Archaeology* 3(2): 121–39. https//doi.org/10.1558/jca.32409.

Hellenic State Gazette. 2016. 'N.4375/2016 Οργάνωση και λειτουργεία Υπηρεσίας Ασύλου, Αρχής Προσφύγων, Υπηρεσίας Υποδοχής και Ταυτοποίησης και άλλες διατάξεις' [N.4375 / 2016 Organisation and operations of the Asylum Service, Refugee Authority, Reception and Identification Service and other provisions], 3 April. *The Greek Ombudsman*. Accessed 28 January 2021. https://www.synigoros.gr/resources/docs/n-4375-2016.pdf.

Hicks, Dan and Sarah Mallet. 2019. *Lande: The Calais 'Jungle' and beyond*. Bristol: Bristol University Press.

Hondagneu-Sotelo, Pierrette. 2014. *Paradise Transplanted: Migration and the making of California gardens*. Oakland: University of California Press.

Kandylis, George. 2019. 'Accommodation as displacement: Notes from refugee camps in Greece in 2016', *Journal of Refugee Studies* 32(1): i12–i21. https://doi.org/10.1093/jrs/fey065.

Katz, Irit. 2017. 'Between *Bare Life* and *Everyday Life*: Spatializing Europe's migrant camps', *Architecture_MPS* 12(2): 1–20. https://doi.org/https://doi.org/10.14324/111.444.amps.2017v12i2.001.

Kiddey, Rachael. 2020. 'Reluctant refugee: An activist archaeological approach to alternative refugee shelter in Athens (Greece)', *Journal of Refugee Studies* 33(3): 599–621. http://dx.doi.org/10.1093/jrs/fey061.

Kopytoff, Igor. 1986. 'The cultural biography of things: Commoditization as process'. In *The Social Life of Things: Commodities in cultural perspective*, edited by Arjun Appadurai, 64–91. Cambridge: Cambridge University Press.

Lischer, Sarah Kenyon. 2005. *Dangerous Sanctuaries: Refugee camps, civil war, and the dilemmas of humanitarian aid*. Ithaca, NY: Cornell University Press.

Lutzoni, Laura. 2016. 'In-formalised urban space design: Rethinking the relationship between formal and informal', *City, Territory and Architecture* 3 (art. no. 20): 1–14. https://doi.org/10.1186/s40410-016-0046-9.

Malkki, Liisa H. 1995. 'Refugees and exile: From "refugee studies" to the national order of things', *Annual Review of Anthropology* 24(1): 495–523. https://doi.org/10.1146/ANNUREV.AN.24.100195.002431.

Martin, Diana. 2015. 'From spaces of exception to "campscapes": Palestinian refugee camps and informal settlements in Beirut', *Political Geography* 44: 9–18. https://doi.org/10.1016/j.polgeo.2014.08.001.

Martin, Diana, Claudio Minca and Irit Katz. 2019. 'Rethinking the camp: On spatial technologies of power and resistance', *Progress in Human Geography* 29(4): 743–68. https://doi.org/10.1177%2F0309132519856702.

McGuire, Randall. 2020. 'The materiality and heritage of contemporary forced migration', *Annual Review of Anthropology* 49: 175–91. https://doi.org/10.1146/annurev-anthro-010220-074624.

Minca, Claudio. 2015. 'Geographies of the camp', *Political Geography* 49: 74–83. https://doi.org/10.1016/j.polgeo.2014.12.005.

Mosse, David. 2005. *Cultivating Development: An ethnography of aid policy and practice*. London: Pluto Press.

Mould, Oli. 2018. 'The not-so-concrete Jungle: Material precarity in the Calais refugee camp', *Cultural Geographies* 25(3): 393–409. https://doi.org/10.1177%2F1474474017697457.

Nabil, Sara, Reem Talhouk, Julie Trueman, David S. Kirk, Simon Bowen and Peter Wright. 2018. 'Decorating public and private spaces: Identity and pride in a refugee camp', *Extended Abstracts of the 2018 CHI Conference on Human Factors in Computing Systems*, 21–6 April, Montreal. http://dx.doi.org/10.1145/3170427.3188550.

Newhouse, Léonie S. 2015. 'More than mere survival: Violence, humanitarian governance, and practical material politics in a Kenyan refugee camp', *Environment and Planning* 47(11): 2292–307. https://doi.org/10.1068%2Fa140106p.

Nolan, Riall, ed. 2013. *A Handbook of Practicing Anthropology*. Chichester: Wiley-Blackwell.

Olivier de Sardan, Jean-Pierre. 2005. *Anthropology and Development: Understanding contemporary social change*. London: Zed Books.

Pallister-Wilkins, Polly. 2020. 'Moria hotspot: Shelter as a politically crafted materiality of neglect'. In *Structures of Protection? Rethinking refugee shelter*, edited by Tom Scott-Smith and Mark E. Breeze, 71–82. New York: Berghahn Books.

Paszkiewicz, Natalia and Daniel Fosas. 2019. 'Reclaiming refugee agency and its implications for shelter design in refugee camps'. In *Proceedings of the 1st International Conference on Comfort at the Extremes: Energy, Economy and Climate, Dubai, 10–11 April 2019*, edited by Susan Roaf and Will Finlayson. Heriot Watt University, Dubai, Ecohouse Initiative. Accessed 28 August 2021. https://windsorconference.com/wp-content/uploads/2019/04/CATE2019_Proceedings-compressed.pdf.

Peteet, Julie. 2005. *Landscape of Hope and Despair: Palestinian refugee camps*. Philadelphia: University of Pennsylvania Press.

Petridou, Elia. 2020. 'Refugee life jackets thrown off but not away: Connecting materialities in upcycling initiatives'. In *Exploring Materiality and Connectivity in Anthropology and Beyond*, edited by Philipp Schorch, Martin Saxer and Marlen Elders, 228–46. London: UCL Press.

Ramadan, Adam. 2012. 'Spatialising the refugee camp', *Transactions of the Institute of British Geographers* 38(1): 65–77. https://doi.org/10.1111/j.1475-5661.2012.00509.x.

Rosenberg, Tina. 2011. 'Beyond refugee camps, a better way', *New York Times*, 6 September. Accessed 28 August 2021. https://opinionator.blogs.nytimes.com/2011/09/06/beyond-refugee-camps-a-better-way/.

Rottenburg, Richard. 2009. *Far-Fetched Facts: A parable of development aid*. Translated by Allison Brown and Tom Lampert. Cambridge, MA: MIT Press.

Roy, Ananya. 2005. 'Urban informality: Toward an epistemology of planning', *Journal of the American Planning Association* 71(2): 147–58. https://doi.org/10.1080/01944360508976689.

Sanyal, Romola. 2014. 'Urbanizing refuge: Interrogating spaces of displacement', *International Journal of Urban and Regional Research* 38(2): 558–72. https://doi.org/10.1111/1468-2427.12020.

Sayigh, Rosemary. 2005. 'A house is not a home: Permanent impermanence of habitat for Palestinian expellees in Lebanon', *Holy Land Studies* 4(1): 17–39. http://dx.doi.org/10.3366/hls.2005.4.1.17.

Shamma, Yasmine. 2020. '"Heaven is green": The ecoglobalism of refugee desert gardens', *Journal of Narrative Theory* 50(3): 321–38. https://doi.org/10.1353/jnt.2020.0013.

Shearlaw, Maeve. 2013. 'Are refugee camps the best solution for people fleeing a crisis?', *The Guardian*, 25 July. Accessed 28 August 2021. https://www.theguardian.com/global-development/2013/jul/25/refugee-camps-solution-people-fleeing-crisis.

Singh, Ashika L. 2020. 'Arendt in the refugee camp: The political agency of world-building', *Political Geography* 77 (art. no. 102149): 1–9. https://doi.org/10.1016/j.polgeo.2020.102149.

Smirl, Lisa. 2015. *Spaces of Aid: How cars, compounds and hotels shape humanitarianism*. London: Zed Books.

Steigemann, Anne Marie and Philipp Misselwitz. 2020. 'Architectures of asylum: Making home in a state of permanent temporariness', *Current Sociology* 68(5): 628–50. https://doi.org/10.1177/0011392120927755.

UNHCR. 2016. '2015 year-end report, Greece'. Accessed 28 August 2021. https://reporting.unhcr.org/sites/default/files/pdfsummaries/GR2015-Greece-eng.pdf.

Varley, Ann. 2013. 'Postcolonialising informality?', *Environment and Planning D: Society and Space* 31(1): 4–22. https://doi.org/10.1068%2Fd14410.

Ward, Michael, Cristina Paleacovschi, Kasey M. Faust, Carl F. Weems and Nell Gabiam. 2020. 'Evaluating the role of infrastructure components and demographics on social capital in refugee camps', *Journal of Management in Engineering* 36(3): 1–11. http://dx.doi.org/10.1061/(ASCE)ME.1943-5479.0000754.

13

A retouched relationship: North American retirees' quest for connection through popular art in Mexico

Rachel Barber

In Chapala, along the banks of Mexico's largest lake, is a series of towns that foreign migrants have flocked to for over 50 years. Not forced from their country by civil unrest, political persecution or the search for lucrative employment, the migrants who live in the Lakeside Chapala area are primarily North American retirees whose motive for moving is to enjoy the temperate climate and greater purchasing power the area offers (Lardiés Bosque and Montes de Oca 2014; Lizárraga 2008; Migration Policy Institute 2006). In spite of the fact that retirees' economic precarity in their country of origin is a factor in their decision to move south (see Bender et al. 2018; Hayes 2015; Lardiés Bosque and Montes de Oca 2014; Lizárraga 2008), upon arriving in their new country of residence they find themselves in a position of affluence compared with the local population. As Michaela Benson (2014) notes, the relative privilege retired migrants enjoy is often taken for granted as a static structural inequality. Nevertheless, while retirees' relative affluence deeply conditions the interactions they have with the local community, it does not fully define the character of this asymmetric relationship. Foreign retirees are actively engaged in negotiating these social dynamics in the face of both their structural privileges and their cultural limitations.

At first glance, there is little evidence of this process of social negotiation in Chapala. In the foreign community of Lake Chapala, few North American migrants speak Spanish and there is minimal socialisation with the local Mexican community. Yet, despite this limited contact with Mexican society and a lack of initial interest in and knowledge of Mexican culture, an overlooked change in Chapala's foreign community indicates a more complex process of sociocultural adaptation: a widespread new taste in Mexican folk and popular art. Guided by Pierre Bourdieu's understanding of taste as an inherently social phenomenon, that 'functions as a sort of social orientation, a "sense of one's place"' ([1984] 2010, 468), this chapter sets out to explore the intersections between retirees' new-found interest in Mexican folk and popular art and their negotiations of social dynamics in Mexico. I specifically seek to highlight the social significance of two particular types of aesthetic object: first, portraits of local Mexicans and their function in defining an ambiguous social relationship between North Americans and Mexicans in Chapala, and second, artisanal objects and the personal connection they enable these retirees to have with Mexican artisans.

These two new consumption habits illustrate the distinct social significances that objects can take on as a result of the ongoing dialogue between their material properties and sociocultural circumstances. Following what Geismar and Horst (2004) call a 'relational approach', which stresses objects' role as active agents in the social dynamics they are embedded in, I hope to illustrate the specific ways in which these two categories of object, by virtue of their formal, material and representational characteristics, interact in distinct ways with the concrete social circumstances in which they are consumed. By attending to these different features of the objects themselves on the one hand, and the social dynamics surrounding their consumption on the other, we can gain insight into how these popular and artisanal objects alternately reflect, redefine and negotiate the asymmetrical relationship between North Americans and Mexicans in the Chapala area.

Painting a relationship: a positive redefinition of Mexican–North American relations in Lake Chapala

To apprehend the intersection between North American retirees' appreciation of Mexican folk art and their social position and relations in Chapala, it is necessary to situate ourselves in the particular context of the foreign community in Lake Chapala. While there are no exact numbers of how many foreign retirees live in the Chapala area, it is considered to house the largest community of US retirees outside the United States (Schafran and Monkkonen 2011; Truly 2002), and estimates from the past 20 years place the numbers of the total retiree population between 7,500 and 10,000 (Croucher 2009). The foreign community is characterised by a certain degree of heterogeneity: we find retirees from different regions of Canada and the United States, a mix of full-time residents and part-time snowbirds and sweatbirds, who winter and summer in the zone, and different social classes. Some live exclusively on their pensions, while others could have retired in North America comfortably but chose to move to enjoy the temperate climate or to retire early. In spite of this internal diversity, members of the foreign community share a common position in relation to the local population of Chapala: they are generally retired, white North Americans who speak little or no Spanish and whose income is at least twice that of the average local Mexican.[1] The language barrier and economic asymmetry condition the relationships that retirees form with the local population. Most of the interactions that the retired migrants have with Mexicans are limited to service staff: their maids, gardeners and handymen and the waiters in the restaurants they frequent.

Rather than acknowledge the economic asymmetry and communicational barriers that mark their relations with the Mexican population, North American retirees tend to de-emphasise the tensions inherent in this relationship. In the more than 20 semi-structured interviews I conducted and the many informal conversations I had, I never heard any negative characterisations of Mexicans. Mexicans were unvaryingly described as friendly, warm, welcoming and helpful. These uniformly positive characterisations of Mexicans go hand in hand with retirees' descriptions of their relationship with Mexicans as one of harmonious coexistence.

An oft-repeated discourse that presented this image of a cordial and peaceable relationship between Mexicans and North American retirees was one that described them as 'neighbours' in Chapala. Interviewees often spontaneously compared Chapala to the towns where they grew up in the United States in the 1950s:

> For those of us who grew up in the fifties, it's like being what it was back in the fifties, where all the neighbours knew everybody. It's just, we walk to get this, we walk to get our meat.
>
> (Melody)

> I think it's very family-oriented. It reminds me of the US 50, 60 years ago when I was growing up.
>
> (Donna)

> Now, you know you walk to the store, and it's your same little store. 'Hi.' We chat a little bit. You run into this person and that person because it's such a small town and everybody's walking. '*Hola Mari, hola José Luis*.'
>
> (Susan)

In these descriptions, US migrants project a nostalgic vision of neighbourly feeling lifted from their childhood memories of the United States onto their new Mexican home. The emphasis placed on a sense of community – going to 'your same little store' and greeting the familiar faces of your neighbours – represents a way of assimilating the new setting of an undeniably foreign location. In equating Chapala to their childhood homes, retirees present a narrative of natural and automatic belonging in Mexico.

However, this characterisation of the Chapala area as a unified and harmonious community passes over important cultural and economic differences that complicate relations between North American retirees and Mexican locals. While the distance that separates these two populations is obliquely hinted at, as when Donna mentions that she does not know all her neighbours' names, it is ultimately brushed off as unimportant and is not considered to impede a sense of shared community where everyone is a friendly face who 'looks after' you. We can appreciate the tensions that the narrative of the 'friendly neighbour' adeptly smoothes over by considering a certain type of popular art found in the foreign community of Chapala.

This art form could be categorised as genre painting, a type of painting that depicts scenes from everyday life. An unusual characteristic of the genre paintings popular in the foreign community of Chapala are that they often portray local characters that the retirees recognised. Melody, who has lived for the past five years in Ajijic, the hub of the foreign community in Chapala, owns a portrait of Conchita, who wove cloth by the banks of Lake Chapala before she got arthritis, and a second of Pedro Loco, a Canadian who moved to Chapala, who Melody described as 'pretty much drunk all the time but an interesting character'. Later, Melody's good friend Jude points out a painting in her house in a similar style, identifying its subject as 'Chris, the fellow that sells these baskets around town'.

The couple Ron and Ann, who spend three months of the year in the Chapala area, showed me an identical painting of the same local basket seller which they have in their home in Virginia:

Ron: That's Crescencio, who lives in Guadalajara, and comes to Ajijic every day carrying his hats and baskets and things like that. So we asked Louise to make a painting of that. Well she did and this is the original. She then copied it and if you walk around Ajijic you can see the same picture on pocketbooks and all sorts of other things like that she used. And he's such a nice man, I don't know if you ever crossed him, when he's walking around town.

Ann: He's such a sweet man.

Rachel: Oh wow, and what made you come up with the idea of having a painting done of him?

Ann: Because I liked him so much and I just thought it would make a very interesting painting. And you know, he has this sweet face. And so Louise thought it was a good idea, too.

As Ron says, these images of local vendors are wildly popular, with the same 'sweet face' of the local basket seller reproduced in paintings and on pocketbooks and mugs throughout the foreign community of Chapala. This widespread interest in acquiring images of local characters is a surprising new practice. In Canada and the United States, people do not own paintings of casual acquaintances in the neighbourhood. And yet, in North American homes in Chapala, genre paintings of local Mexicans have become a fixture. While retirees' desire to establish a connection with their new Mexican surroundings certainly seems an important motivation behind this new interest, it is worth delving deeper into the type of relationships portrayed in these genre paintings of Mexicans.

Louise Neal Pedroza, a US retiree and the artist who painted Ron and Ann's picture of Crescencio, the basket seller, offers a good point of reference for analysing this art form. Pedroza's paintings depict a certain class of people and scenes: they are primarily workers, people of indigenous descent and children. They are in the act of selling their work in the street or fishing in Lake Chapala, or in the market, or in picturesque, folkloric scenes in which they are captured dancing, praying or playing music. They are presented showing their merchandise, constructing a wall, brick in hand, carrying their fishing net, all smiling for the photo that Pedroza takes of them and bases her paintings on. They are painted with gouache in bright, glowing colours, which appear even more luminous against the black background that characterises most of the paintings.

These upbeat colours and the depiction of Mexican subjects in public spaces, practising their trade or posing for the camera, echo the narrative in which Mexican locals are presented as friendly neighbours. This interpretation is underscored in the captions that accompany the photos of Pedroza's paintings uploaded on her Facebook page, like 'Lady selling corn husk flower' (Figure 13.1): 'This lady sells her beautiful handmade corn husk flowers at the Wednesday market on calle Revolucion. She is always set up where the market starts, off the carretera. What a beautiful lady, always wearing a smile and so friendly!!' (Pedroza 2018).

13.1 Lady selling corn husk flower. © Louise Neal Pedroza, used with permission.

13.2 Maria Margarita Martinez de Moya. © Louise Neal Pedroza, used with permission.

Here and elsewhere, Pedroza highlights the cordial relations that she has with the subjects of her paintings, as well as the casual familiarity that comes from seeing them regularly in the neighbourhood. In the caption for the painting 'Maria Margarita Martinez de Moya' (Figure 13.2), Pedroza writes: 'This little lady sweeps calle Javier Mina – We see her every day working and making the street look beautiful!!' (Pedroza 2019).

These paintings transmit a sense of everyday familiarity and warmth, if not exactly closeness. They represent cordial, pleasant relations, a painted version of the narrative that presents local Mexicans as friendly neighbours. However, a central element in the representation of Mexican locals that the neighbour discourse smoothes over is made manifest in these paintings: the choice to depict members of the Mexican working class. This choice of subject and the manner in which they are represented form part of a tradition of genre painting that dates back to the sixteenth century. John Berger ([1972] 1990, 104) describes the significance that owning genre paintings (specifically those depicting members of the lower class) had in this earlier period:

> These people belong to the poor. The poor can be seen in the street outside or in the countryside. Pictures of the poor inside the house, however, are reassuring. Here the painted poor smile as they offer what they have for sale ... They smile at the better-off – to ingratiate themselves, but also at the prospect of a sale or a job. Such pictures assert two things: that the poor are happy, and that the better-off are a source of hope for the world.

Berger highlights the fundamentally economic nature of the relationship that subtends these paintings, an observation that applies just as well to the relationship that the retired North Americans have with the local vendors portrayed in the paintings they own. The cordial atmosphere the paintings establish through depictions of a smiling, friendly subject arise from circumstances in which a possible or concluded economic transaction is taking place.

We can appreciate the similarity in tone between the *Fisher Boy* (Figure 13.3) that Berger refers to, painted by the baroque Dutch artist Frans Hals, in which a young, smiling fisherman offers his wares, and the painting 'Building a house in San Antonio' (Figure 13.4), in which Pedroza portrays 'our good friend Luciano along with his brother laying brick for a new house. He built the house we use [*sic*] to live in and we loved it!! He has built lots of the homes near us' (Pedroza 2013). In both paintings, we see happy workers who reflect the perception held by many North

13.3 *Fisher Boy*. Painting by Frans Hals, 1630–2. Wikimedia Commons, public domain.

13.4 Building a house in San Antonio. © Louise Neal Pedroza, used with permission.

Americans in Chapala that 'the foreigners help the economy and help with employment and the Mexicans are very much aware of that and are grateful in turn for us, to us. So it is a mutually beneficial relationship' (Regina).

In line with this view, the paintings convey the idea that the economic transactions that frame the relations that North American migrants have with Mexicans ultimately constitute a relationship in which North Americans provide economic support in exchange for the gratitude of the Mexican workers, thus distorting the standard formulation of an economic relationship based on payment for services rendered. The emphasis on cordiality and friendliness reformulates the economic subtext into something more personal, reinforcing the image of a happy community that the neighbour narrative suggests. By means of these personal and approachable portraits, rather than depicting Mexicans as the exotic 'Other', these genre paintings construct a convivial relationship between North American retirees and local Mexicans in Chapala.

To fully appreciate the strategic importance of the positive image of a friendly community that these genre paintings convey, it is important to recognise not only the underlying economic dynamics that are de-emphasised in these portraits, but also the deep social divisions that exist in the Chapala area. There are many gated communities in the zone that are populated mainly, if not entirely, by North American retirees. Some of these gated communities have a policy of requiring Mexicans to leave the premises in the evening because they are assumed to be workers, which actively reinforces the economic division that separates Mexicans from North Americans. The many volunteer-run clubs and charitable organisations in the foreign community tend to have exclusively North American members. While their charitable efforts are aimed at improving the lives of needy locals, it is rare for Mexicans to participate as equal members. Major organisations in the area, like the Lake Chapala Society, which was established in 1955 and continues to serve as a hub for retirees' socialising and volunteering activity, are currently making efforts to include the local Mexican community. However, one local Mexican I interviewed, Roberto, described the confusion occasioned by his participation in a meditation group at the Lake Chapala Society: when he arrived at the session on his bicycle, the North American members 'found it strange that I would come and sit next to them. They thought I was the gardener or something [laughs].'

As this contextualised look into the popularity of genre painting among the North American retirees of Chapala reveals, these portraits do not constitute a facile, abstract assimilation of 'Mexicanness' into retirees' homes in Chapala, but represent a more complex engagement with the underlying, ambiguous social dynamics, economic asymmetries and stark social divisions that mark these migrants' relations with the local population. These paintings, hand in hand with narratives that characterise the relationship between North American retirees and Mexican locals as one between neighbours, serve to redefine a potentially tense and conflictive coexistence as an unequivocally pleasant relationship. However, this redefinition, while it casts this intercultural relationship in a positive light, does not alter the underlying economic structure that moulds North Americans' relations with Mexican locals. North American retirees' interactions with Mexicans remain largely limited to street vendors, domestic employees and service staff, an aspect that these portraits reflect, and present in cordial terms, muting, but not bridging or transforming, this cultural difference and economic inequality. However, a second object of consumption, Mexican folk art, reveals a different manner in which material objects mediate social relations, presenting a potential point of connection between the culturally different and economically unequal positions held by North American retirees and Mexicans.

Situating folk art consumption

Certain features, particular to artisanal objects, make them a unique class of cultural goods. As a concrete manifestation of an inherited tradition that involves a particular technique, shared aesthetic sensibilities and shared practical uses, folk art is intimately linked to its culture of origin. Research on foreigners' interest in folk art has highlighted the ways in which the aura of authenticity has tended to eclipse the original significance the artisanal object held in the culture that produced it. James Clifford argues that in the institutional settings of museums the classificatory order according to which objects are organised and displayed both replaces previous categories that endowed them with meaning and also transforms objects themselves into representations of entire cultures, 'a "Bambara mask", for example, becoming an ethnographic metonym for Bambara culture' (Clifford 1988, 220). Tourists' interest in buying 'authentic' foreign artefacts is described in similar terms, in which the tourist's conception of authenticity is an abstracted and subjective vision of what they consider to be 'genuine'. The buyer 'does not have to understand the symbolism or the iconography of the item, he [*sic*] only has to find it aesthetically acceptable and visually authentic. Closeness to what is believed to be traditional by the collector's reference group is the goal' (Graburn 1976, 14). Cultural authenticity is thus exposed as being less an objective trait inherent in folk art and more a Western imagining of what tradition looks like. In a similar vein, García Canclini considers that the ethnic qualities of folk art (*artesanía*), when bought by tourists, become reduced to a simplified interpretation of ethnic groups' 'typical' features. The author argues that this is due to the fact that national culture appears to be a 'compact, undifferentiated whole for the tourist' if it is not accompanied by information about the groups who make up the nation and their confrontations with colonisers and other ethnic groups (García Canclini 1982, 128).

Tourists' valorisation of folk art thus tends to be characterised as a process of decontextualised appropriation, in which the original meaning and value that the artisanal objects hold for the communities who make them are cannibalised and made to fit into Western schemas of significance. While to a certain extent the displacement of objects necessarily implies a shift in their meaning, it is also important to question these accounts of folk art consumption in which the artisanal object is moulded so completely to a Western vision of the 'Other' or as an arbitrary marker of authenticity. In the case of the North Americans who move to the Lake Chapala area to retire, the Mexican, indigenous 'Other' is no longer at such a remove and the function of the artisanal object of signifying an authentic experience is not necessarily the same factor that drives their acquisition of folk art. The above treatments of folk art collecting and tourist purchases hinge upon the abstraction of the artisanal object that occurs when it enters a different sociocultural sphere, whether in a museum, a souvenir shop or a private home. No longer embedded in the social structure, traditions and practices of its place of origin, folk art comes to stand in for a fuzzy idea of ethnic peoples and cultures themselves, an emblem of Westerners' own conception of the 'Other' and proof of their authentic experience in a foreign land. But what changes when the tourist stays? For one thing, the folk art she purchases is no longer brought home to the States and displayed to visitors as evidence of her travels abroad. Now home *is* abroad.

It is certainly tempting to discount the change in place as minimal. In the foreign community of Chapala, foreigners tend to socialise with other foreigners, fluency in Spanish is rare, and a strong institutional framework exists within the foreign community that assists foreigners with practical issues and provides a social network through clubs and volunteer organisations. Furthermore, numerous studies on international retirement migration indicate that retirees living in established migrant communities evidence little cultural adaptation or integration into the local community (Gustafson 2001; King et al. 1998; O'Reilly 2007, 2017;

van Laar et al. 2014). Nonetheless, rather than jump to the conclusion that the widespread consumption of Mexican folk art within the foreign community in the Chapala area is no different from tourists' interest in souvenirs for the authenticity they imagine they embody, we should ground this new taste in the social dynamics in which it occurs. By virtue of living in Mexico, the North American residents in Chapala have to redefine their social and cultural relationship to their new country. They are not on vacation, but at home. As a result, the sociocultural divide held to be self-evident in analyses of tourists' and collectors' displacement of the significance of the artisanal object from a foreign cultural sphere of meaning to their own is no longer at such a geographical distance. The move to Chapala at the age of retirement entails not only a new vantage point from which the Mexican local is seen, but also a re-evaluation of one's own social position in relation to this new social environment.

Against prevailing analyses of foreign consumption of folk art as an abstract process in which the significance the artisanal object has in its place of production is switched for an entirely different one, in which the object is an arbitrary signifier of authentic 'foreignness', we should consider the concrete social dynamics in which this new cultural consumption occurs, and a unique material feature of the artisanal object that tends to be overlooked in analyses of folk art consumption, namely its production by hand. While pointing out that artisanal objects are handmade may appear to be a superfluous description of what an artisanal object is simply by definition, this handmade quality leads us to consider a connotation folk art holds that is not merely cultural. Octavio Paz writes: 'Made by hand, the artisanal object is imprinted, concretely and metaphorically, by the fingers that formed it' (1994, 68). Here Paz highlights the fact that the handmade production of artisanal objects connects them in the first instance not to a culture, but to the 'fingers that formed it', in other words to the actual person who made it. In a passage that evokes this same emphasis on the human labour behind the artisanal object, Jean Baudrillard writes: 'The fascination of handicraft derives from an object's having passed through the hands of someone the marks of whose labour are still inscribed thereupon: we are fascinated by what has been *created*, and is therefore unique, because the *moment* of creation cannot be reproduced' ([1968] 1996, 76)

These reflections on the significance of the handmade quality of artisanal objects – a material feature of folk art that is obvious and at the same time easily overlooked – prove useful in the analysis of the particular significance that Mexican folk art acquires for North American retirees in Chapala.

Made by hand: a potential connection through the artisanal object

While most of the North American retirees I encountered in the Chapala area expressed an interest in Mexican folk art, a subgroup of individuals had a more sizeable collection of artisanal objects and shared a criterion of appreciation of folk art that is rooted in a particular feature tied to its handmade nature. Marianne, the founder of the Feria Maestros del Arte, a Mexican folk art fair that brings artisans to Chapala from all over Mexico, expresses this criterion of valorisation in her explanation of why she loves artisanal objects:

> It's not that it's just beautiful, it's not that I can say 'Oh, I've got all these things'; it's that every single piece, I know where I got it. I know whose hands made it, there's a story behind it, and that's one nice, wonderful thing about the Feria too: you buy from the *maestro* or the *maestra*.

13.5 Artisans presenting their work at the 2019 Feria Maestros del Arte. © Feria Maestros del Arte, 2019, used with permission.

When Marianne emphasises the importance of where she got her folk art, she is referring not to the region or to the fact that it is a Mexican product, but to the experience of being in the artisan's workshop, seeing him or her at work, and buying the artwork directly from the artisan. These interactions, as well as the marks of the artisan that live on in their products, offer concrete moments in which North American retirees can establish a sense of connection to Mexican artisans. As Marianne says, it is also an important feature that she seeks to cultivate in the Feria she organises, where all the artisans sell their own work in person and interact directly with the North American buyers (Figure 13.5).

The emphasis that Marianne places on the handmade quality of folk art, particularly her appreciation of knowing 'whose hands made it', echoes Octavio Paz's vision of the importance of the mark left on the artisanal object by the 'fingers that formed it'. 'Made *by* hands,' Paz goes on to explain, 'the artisanal object is made *for* hands: not only can we see it, but we can also touch and feel it' (1994, 68).

The palpable nature of folk art that Paz points out was evident in the tours I filmed of North Americans' homes in Chapala: one retiree touched nearly every object that he showed, stopping in front of a Huichol yarn painting to trace the placement of the threads (Figure 13.6). Another caressed the lacquered gourd that she showed me and invited me to do the same to appreciate its smoothness. Judy, who has a large collection of

13.6 Tracing the yarn lines. © Rachel Barber.

13.7 Touching the 100-year-old hat, stiff with sweat. © Rachel Barber.

Mexican folk art acquired during the more than 15 years she has lived in the country, also urged me at different moments to feel the objects:

> I love these hats so much. Come up close with your camera because they're a hundred years old. Look at how they've been sewn. And the sweat is still on them. Just think of who wore them and worked. A hundred years ago. I just love them. They're really stiff. You should put your hand on one just to feel it. (See Figure 13.7.)

On another occasion she said:

> The copper's all from Santa Clara. From a really wonderful man named Angel Puzo. I was actually doing some cleaning in my house and I put a big dent in it. And I took it back to him in Santa Clara del Cobre and asked him if he would fix it for me. And he did and then I asked him, 'How much do I owe you?' 'Oh, nothing.' He's a very sweet man. And he said, 'But I haven't had any business in the last, I don't know, like, four months,' he said. 'Could you buy something?' So we bought this. Just put a hand out and feel it. It's really heavy. But anyway, he's a lovely, lovely man. (See Figure 13.8.)

13.8 Judy letting me feel the heaviness of the copper fish. © Rachel Barber.

These quotations allow us to appreciate that the act of feeling an object is not purely physical, and nor is it a personal, isolated experience. As Paz (1994) notes, 'Folk art's transpersonal character is expressed directly and indirectly through sensation: the body is participation. To feel is … above all, to feel *with* someone' (68). However, unlike the anonymous 'someone' Paz refers to here, the retired North Americans who appreciate the hands that formed their pieces are seeking out and valuing a connection with particular Mexican artisans through the artisanal object.

This aim of establishing a personal, meaningful connection with particular artisans is made clear by retirees' repeated emphasis on the importance of their face-to-face interactions with artisans as well as by their inclusion of personal details and anecdotes about the artisans when the retirees show their folk art. Judy referred to various artisans as her friends and tended to personify her artisanal objects as these artisan friends when she presented them: 'And this [a lithograph in her room] is an artist that was a friend of ours in Oaxaca. Fernando Olivera. A wonderfully sweet man'; 'And this [an abstract crucifix] is my friend again. That guy that did the work in tin'; 'Here's my friend Cecilia [presenting a *rebozo* (a traditional Mexican shawl)]. The only *rebozos* I own are hers.'

Judy's frequent emphasis on the individual artisan, as well as her characterisation of artisans as friends, was echoed in many of the other filmed house tours. This appreciation of the artisan was not limited to the presentation of the objects in the home, but was also presented as a key factor behind North American retirees' process of acquiring folk art. Marianne characterises this process as driven primarily by her connection to the artisans behind the objects.

> I don't go out and say I want this giant beautiful plate, but I know José Luis Cortez, and when he gives it to me it's just another wonderful piece of art that I can add to my collection, and when I look at it I think of him and his wife and that's kind of the story behind a lot of my folk art.

As Marianne reveals here, in the decision to acquire a piece, an interest in a certain type of folk art with a particular set of aesthetic features is secondary to the personal connection she has with the artisan. As she hints in the quotation, this personal connection is particularly evidenced when the artisanal object was acquired as a gift. Mauss states in his famous essay 'The Gift': 'We can see the nature of the bond created by the transfer of a possession. … [T]his bond created by things is in fact a bond between persons, since the thing itself is a person or pertains to a person' ([1925] 1967, 10). Judy stresses this bond when she shows a small ceramic vase that an artisan gave her, and turns it over to show the dedicatory note on the bottom: 'To Judy, with love. María Refugio Medrano.'

However, this bond is not without its complications. The gift, as Mauss ([1925] 1967, 70) notes, is not a simple category of object:

> Our terms 'present' and 'gift' do not have precise meanings … Concepts which we like to put in opposition – freedom and obligation; generosity, liberality, luxury on the one hand and saving, interest, austerity on the other – are not exact and it would be well to put them to the test … It is a complex notion that inspires the economic actions we have described, a notion neither of purely free and gratuitous prestations, nor of purely interested and utilitarian production and exchange; it is a kind of hybrid.

Marianne's collection of folk art provides a good example of some of the ambiguous shades of meaning that artisans' gifts take on. While Marianne previously collected masks and *catrinas* (farcical skeleton figures), now her goal is to own one piece of art from every artisan who has come to the Feria. Although the Feria hosts 85 artisans every year, Marianne's goal is feasible in part because many of the artisans have given her pieces of their art over the years.

> Some of my other pieces that are just really meaningful to me are Martín Ibarra's things that he's gifted me. The piece up here [points to the crucifix above the door], the dragonfly, and the virgin on the left. I've known Martín for many years now, he was at the very first Feria and he's just a wonderful soul.
>
> (Marianne)

While Marianne emphasises the significance of the work in connection with the relationship and history she has with the artisan, the personal connection the objects make manifest must also be situated within the particular social dynamics that frame their relationship. Given that Marianne started the Feria 19 years ago, has continually been on its board of directors, and has been actively involved in choosing which artisans participate every year, it is difficult to disentangle her official role in the organisation from the personal relationship she has with the artisans. There is a tension inherent in her roles as Feria founder, in which she acts as patron of the artisans, and personal friend, which the ambiguous nature of the gift underscores. The artisanal object is freely given by the artisan, but, considering the context, there is also a sense of duty and interest that accompanies the artisan's choice to give it.

A study on Anglo-American patron involvement in promoting the folk art of artisans of Mexican descent in New Mexico emphasises the murky character of the relationship between the artisan and the patron. The friendships that certain patrons and artists formed existed side by side with patrons' function of offering artisans 'an economic and social link to individuals who possessed much more familiarity with and access to the institutions of the superordinate society' (Briggs 1986, 216).

North Americans' relative economic wealth in Mexico poses complications similar to those of the ideal of a freely reciprocated friendship and meaningful personal connection. North Americans' role as folk art consumers and patrons forces them to grapple with the advantages their economic resources afford them, and, in more general terms, with how that shapes their position in Mexico and their relation to Mexicans. While folk art offers a connection to Mexicans that North American migrants treasure, and which their limited proficiency in Spanish tends to hinder otherwise, the fact that this connection is made possible by their spending power represents an uncomfortable fact that North American migrants attempt to negotiate.

At times, the role of benefactor is embraced: North American retirees have founded numerous volunteer associations in the area that provide children with clothes and poor families with food, medical support and school tuition. Many of the North Americans interviewed also mentioned instances in which they had personally supported individuals, paying the school expenses of their housekeepers' children, covering employees' and artisans' medical bills, buying household items for acquaintances and directly offering financial support on seeing the squalid state of artisans' living conditions. However, at other moments, North American migrants seek to establish a cross-cultural connection that these asymmetrical economic relations disturb. Marianne's extended description of the artisan Martín Ibarra subtly reveals her negotiation of the problematic economic aspect of North American folk art buyers' relationship with artisans:

> He also told me he can tell how much people love his work by the way they handle it. And I just love hearing things like that – that, you know, more important than the money they make, it's that their art creates in somebody else something special, a memory, or just admiring the workmanship. Having talked to him, that's more meaningful to him than anything. That's what most of these artists live for, and the reason they want to continue their work is because they like to please people. And they love it when people compliment their work. They're just very special people to me.

The explicit opposition that is proposed between economic gain and the personal connection fostered by the artisanal object ('creates in somebody something special', 'a memory', 'admiring the workmanship', 'having talked to him') points to the projected desire of Marianne rather than the expressed feelings of the artisan. Describing the main motive for working as an artisan as the aim to 'please people' is a very particular reading of artisanal tradition that posits the happiness of the folk art consumer as a central motivation for folk art production. Through this framing of folk art's significance, the uncomfortable fact that the relationship between folk art consumer and artisan is a commercial one is momentarily smoothed over.

We find a very similar example of this projected desire for a reciprocated relationship that transcends communicational barriers and economic asymmetries in the case of Melody, a US retiree who has resided in Ajijic for five years, in her explanation of the significance of a rug she considers her most prized artisanal object.

> I met the son and then the mom, who – their father, or their husband – wove it and so it means a lot, that personal thing, and the hours and hours they spent doing it. And they're just as proud to know that you bought it. That you love it as much as they liked doing it. And I think it's so neat, even though the family who wove these rugs, the mom didn't speak any English, and my Spanish is … no, but we could communicate. You know, always a hug, always a whatever, we don't know what each other's saying, but at least we – she knows that I appreciate her and her family.

Despite Melody's inability to communicate with the woman who made the rug, she characterises the act of purchasing it as something that transcends this communicational barrier and goes far beyond a mere economic transaction. It is presented as even more than an opportunity to meet the artisan who made it. In describing how her love for the object parallels the love that went into making it and how this fact is recognised and appreciated by the artisan, she converts the artisanal object into the mediator of a relationship. Melody's love of the object she buys is transmuted into an appreciation of the artisan, and the artisan – according to Melody – recognises and reciprocates this feeling.

While the communication barriers and economic premises that frame North American retirees' interactions with Mexican artisans may lead us to question the depth of the relationships that Melody, Marianne, Judy and others claim and cherish through the artisanal objects they have acquired, it becomes clear that the importance these objects are assigned stems from these relationships, however one-sided they may be. In her essay on the utility and importance of material culture in historical studies, Leora Auslander (2005) makes an observation that is particularly pertinent to these retirees' unique appreciation of their artisanal objects: 'intimate things are crucial objectifications of intimate relationships' (1020). For this particular group of folk art enthusiasts in Chapala, the value assigned to their artisanal possessions is tied to the capacity of the artisanal object, being intimately bound to the artisan who made it, to objectify the intimate relationships with Mexican artisans that these retirees long to have.

Conclusion: art's potential and limitations in negotiating an asymmetrical relationship

This chapter has presented two art forms and the distinct ways in which they are consumed with the aim of altering the separate and unequal socio-economic position that North American retirees occupy in Chapala in comparison with the local Mexican population. By contextualising North American retirees' appreciation of these artistic objects within the social and economic circumstances that these individuals find themselves in, we find that these objects take on a meaning that is a far cry from the arbitrary marker of authentic 'foreignness' that compels the average tourist to buy folk art. Rather than being an emblem of authentic difference, the genre paintings of Mexicans and the artisanal objects that these retirees purchase are valued for connoting an authentic connection. In the face of economic asymmetries and communication barriers, these objects become important tools for both defining and demonstrating North American migrants' relationships with Mexican locals.

While Bourdieu's conception of taste as a sense of social orientation and classification is a fundamental text that this enquiry's understanding of cultural consumption's social significance is premised on, we find that these North American retirees' consumption of genre paintings and Mexican folk art goes beyond the straightforward signalling of social position and belonging that Bourdieu posits. These new tastes are intimately tied to the new social circumstances the North American retirees find themselves in, but, rather than reproducing these conditions or serving as a form of social ascension, these tastes are primarily geared towards redefining the nature of the asymmetrical relationship between North American retirees and Mexicans.

In the case of the genre paintings of Mexican locals, this redefinition echoes a narrative in which North Americans and Mexicans are described as neighbours. Both the visual and verbal presentations of the relationship in these terms emphasise the cordiality that reigns in the community, silencing the problematic aspects of North Americans' presence in Chapala. These problematic aspects range from historical tensions between North Americans and Mexicans to local conflicts stemming from North Americans retirees' inability to communicate in Spanish and their superior economic status in Chapala. These factors create a significant gulf between retired foreign migrants and Mexican locals that runs counter to the social harmony and personal connection that retirees highlight in their consumption of genre paintings and folk art. As I argued in my analysis of the portraits of local Mexicans that are popular among North American retirees, these class dynamics and social tensions are visually represented. While the portraits reveal the economic asymmetry that complicates Mexican-North American relations in Chapala, inequality is not altered through this cultural consumption. The representation of this asymmetry is simply recast in a far more complimentary light.

North American migrants' appreciation of Mexican folk art on the basis of the connection it offers with Mexican artisans seems to present a means of forging personal connections that circumvent the asymmetries that complicate North Americans' relationships with the local Mexicans they employ and primarily interact with. The artisanal object's handmade nature lends itself to the creation of a bond between the North Americans who feel and appreciate the objects and the artisans who crafted them with their own hands. However, the material connection the artisanal object offers does not transcend social and economic dynamics; the reciprocated friendship that North American retirees seek to establish with Mexican artisans through their consumption of folk art is encumbered by the socially unequal positions they occupy as patrons and beneficiaries, as well as the economic relationship they have as buyers and sellers.

Notes

1 Calculations based on the average monthly income of MXN 12,493 (Observatorio Laboral n.d.) in the state of Jalisco (where Chapala is located) reported in Mexico's National Survey of Occupation and Employment in 2020, compared with the average benefits, MXN 28,557 (USD 1,503), that American retirees received from the Social Security Administration in 2019 (Social Security Administration 2020).

References

Auslander, Leora. 2005. 'Beyond words', *American Historical Review* 110(4): 1015–45. https://doi.org/10.1086/ahr.110.4.1015.

Baudrillard, Jean. [1968] 1996. *The System of Objects*. Translated by James Benedict. London and New York: Verso.

Bender, Désirée, Tina Hollstein and Cornelia Schweppe. 2018. 'International retirement migration revisited: From amenity seeking to precarity migration?', *Transnational Social Review* 8(1): 98–102. https://doi.org/10.1080/21931674.2018.1429080.

Benson, Michaela. 2014. 'Negotiating privilege in and through lifestyle migration'. In *Understanding Lifestyle Migration: Theoretical approaches to migration and the quest for a better way of life*, edited by Michaela Benson and Nick Osbaldiston, 47–68. New York: Palgrave Macmillan.

Berger, John. [1972] 1990. *Ways of Seeing*. London: BBC and Penguin Books. Accessed 29 August 2021. https://archive.org/details/waysofseeing00john.

Bourdieu, Pierre. [1984] 2010. *Distinction: A social critique of the judgement of taste*. Translated by Richard Nice. New York: Routledge.

Briggs, Charles L. 1986. 'The role of *Mexicano* artists and the Anglo elite in the emergence of a contemporary folk art'. In *Folk Art and Art Worlds*, edited by John Michael Vlach and Simon J. Bonner, 195–224. Logan: Utah State University Press.
Clifford, James. 1988. *The Predicament of Culture: Twentieth-century ethnography, literature, and art*. Cambridge, MA: Harvard University Press.
Croucher, Sheila. 2009. *The Other Side of the Fence: American migrants in Mexico*. Austin: University of Texas Press.
García Canclini, Néstor. 1982. *Las culturas populares en el capitalismo*. Mexico City: Nueva Imagen.
Geismar, Haidy and Heather A. Horst. 2004. 'Materializing ethnography', *Journal of Material Culture* 9(1): 5–10. https://doi.org/10.1177/1359183504041086.
Graburn, Nelson H. H. 1976. 'Introduction: Arts of the Fourth World'. In *Ethnic and Tourist Arts: Cultural expressions from the Fourth World*, edited by Nelson H. H. Graburn, 1–30. Berkeley and Los Angeles: University of California Press.
Gustafson, Per. 2001. 'Retirement migration and transnational lifestyles', *Ageing and Society* 21(4): 371–94. https://doi.org/10.1017/S0144686X01008327.
Hayes, Matthew. 2015. 'Moving south: The economic motives and structural context of North America's emigrants in Cuenca, Ecuador', *Mobilities* 10(2): 267–84. https://doi.org/10.1080/17450101.2013.858940.
King, Russell, Anthony M. Warnes and Allan M. Williams. 1998. 'International retirement migration in Europe', *International Journal of Population Geography* 4(2): 91–111. https://doi.org/10.1002/(SICI)1099-1220(199806)4:2%3C91::AID-IJPG97%3E3.0.CO;2-S.
Lardiés Bosque, Raúl and Verónica Montes de Oca. 2014. 'Migración internacional de jubilados en España y México'. In *Vejez, salud y sociedad en México: Aproximaciones disciplinarias desde perspectivas cuantitativas y cualitativas*, edited by Verónica Montes de Oca, 365–415. Mexico City: UNAM.
Lizárraga, Omár. 2008. 'La inmigración de jubilados estadounidenses en México y sus prácticas transnacionales: Estudio de caso en Mazatlán, Sinaloa y Cabo San Lucas, Baja California Sur', *Migración y desarrollo* (11): 97–117. Accessed 29 August 2021. http://www.scielo.org.mx/scielo.php?script=sci_arttext&pid=S1870-75992008000200005.
Mauss, Marcel. [1925] 1967. *The Gift: Forms and functions of exchange in archaic societies*. Translated by Ian Cunnison. New York: Norton.
Migration Policy Institute. 2006. 'America's emigrants: US retirement migration to Mexico and Panama'. Accessed 29 August 2021. https://www.migrationpolicy.org/sites/default/files/publications/americas_emigrants.pdf.
Observatorio Laboral. n.d. 'Panorama profesional por estados'. Accessed 29 August 2021. https://www.observatoriolaboral.gob.mx/static/estudios-publicaciones/Panorama_profesional_estados.html.
O'Reilly, Karen. 2007. 'Intra-European migration and the mobility–enclosure dialectic', *Sociology* 41(2): 277–93. https://doi.org/10.1177/0038038507074974.
O'Reilly, Karen. 2017. 'The British on the Costa del Sol twenty years on: A story of liquids and sediments', *Nordic Journal of Migration Research*, 7(3): 139–47. http://doi.org/10.1515/njmr-2017-0017.
Paz, Octavio. 1994. 'El uso y la contemplación'. In *Obras Completas, Volumen VI. Los privilegios de la vista I: Arte moderno universal*, 2nd edition, 63–74. Mexico City: Fondo de Cultura Económica.
Pedroza, Louise Neal. 2013. 'Building a house in San Antonio'. Photograph. 30 July 2013 Accessed 29 August 2021. https://www.facebook.com/louisenealpedrozapaintingsontinwithgouache/photos/a.491034274312008/491040650978037/?type=3&theater.
Pedroza, Louise Neal. 2018. 'Lady selling corn husk flowers'. Photograph. 22 June 2018. Accessed 29 August 2021. https://www.facebook.com/louisenealpedrozapaintingsontinwithgouache/photos/a.491034274312008/1757809477634475/?type=3&theater.
Pedroza, Louise Neal. 2019. 'Maria Margarita Martinez de Moya'. Photograph. 28 July 2019. Accessed 29 August 2021. https://www.facebook.com/louisenealpedrozapaintingsontinwithgouache/photos/a.2336811876400896/2336813556400728/?type=3&theater.
Schafran, Alex and Paavo Monkkonen. 2011. 'Beyond Chapala and Cancún: Grappling with the impact of American migration to Mexico', *Migraciones internacionales* 6(2): 223–58. Accessed 29 August 2021. http://www.scielo.org.mx/scielo.php?script=sci_arttext&pid=S1665-89062011000200008.
Social Security Administration. 2020. *Fact Sheet: Social Security*. Accessed 29 August 2021. https://www.ssa.gov/news/press/factsheets/basicfact-alt.pdf.

Truly, David. 2002. 'International retirement migration and tourism along the Lake Chapala Riviera: Developing a matrix of retirement and retirement migration behaviour', *Tourism Geographies* 4(3): 261–81. https://doi.org/10.1080/14616680210147427.

van Laar, Sanne, Ine Cottyn, Ronnie Donaldson, Annelies Zoomers and Sanette Ferreira. 2014. '"Living apart together" in Franschhoek, South Africa: The implications of second-home development for equitable and sustainable development'. In *Contested Spatialities, Lifestyle Migration and Residential Tourism*, edited by Michael Janoschka and Heiko Haas, 190–203. New York: Routledge.

14

Place-making in the transient: things that matter in the everyday lives of Honduran refugees at the La 72 shelter

Yaatsil Guevara González

As I was finishing this chapter, in October 2020, a caravan COMPOSED of thousands of Honduran young people, adults, children and families has left San Pedro Sula, Honduras, in transit towards Mexico and the United States. This population is fleeing hunger and a systematic violence that has plagued this country for decades. This exodus is not, however, the first of its kind. In October 2018, hundreds and eventually thousands of Honduran people organised themselves and moved forward, in a collective and massive way, towards the neighbouring country of Guatemala. There, Guatemalans and Salvadorans, populations equally plagued by poverty and violence, joined the so-called ‘caravans’. The main goal of these caravans is to arrive together in the United States, or in Mexico, in search of a more peaceful life, either through legal means such as asylum or migratory regularisation, or through (temporary) settlement without legal migratory documentation. Most, if not all, of the people that form the caravans lack official documents to support their legal migratory stay in either Mexico or the United States.

The phenomenon of migrant caravans transiting through Mexico is a collective action that, among other things, has forced both civil society and the Mexican state to discuss the Central American exodus openly. The forced disappearance of migrants in transit (Nyberg Sørensen and Huttunen 2020), the violation of their human rights, and the corruption that exists at the various levels of government, drug cartels and local populations along the Mexican migratory routes, are only some of the problems associated with this phenomenon. The 2018 caravans were not the first attempt to cross Mexican territory en masse. Since 2011, various activists and human rights defenders have initiated collective actions, including the 'Via Crucis Migrante' caravan (Vargas Carrasco 2018). Mainly organised by Catholic Church activists who denounced abuse, violence and the forced disappearance of migrants in transit along the migration routes, the 'Via Crucis Migrante' was organised in the form of caravans that departed from strategic border crossing points on Mexico's southern border to state capitals or to Mexico City. These caravans were used mainly by Central Americans to cross the country more collectively and safely. As these caravans advanced, more and more people joined in. Without doubt, the desire for a dignified and safe transit through Mexico has been the fundamental motor for the permanence of these kinds of social movements.

But most Central Americans who flee towards Mexico and the United States do not travel with the caravans. It is estimated that three to four hundred thousand Central Americans cross the southern border of Mexico each year, either to continue to the United States or to settle within Mexican territory (Rodríguez Chávez 2016; Masferrer et al. 2018). Since the beginning of this century, the number of Central Americans, especially Hondurans, fleeing has increased exponentially (Frank-Vitale and Martínez d'Aubuisson 2021). In the United States, these migratory flows have been deemed 'humanitarian crises' or 'national security' problems (Galli 2018). At a policy level, they have been used to justify the intensification of interdiction and migration control practices within US territory, as well as the militarisation and securitisation of the USA–Mexico border. Furthermore, the United States has been a fundamental actor in financing transnational border regulation policies, from its involvement in 'development' plans for Mexico and Central America, such as the Merida Initiative or the Plan Puebla-Panama (now Proyecto Mesoamerica) (Galemba 2018), to its most recent binational agreements with Guatemala and Honduras to declare them 'safe third countries' (Homeland Security Department 2019; 2020). Moreover, Mexico has followed the same precept, obeying the political and economic interests that it has with its neighbour to the north. The Mexican state has become an accomplice of migratory 'necropolitics' (Mbembé 2003; Varela Huerta 2017) and an executor of systematic violence against the Central American population that seeks refuge in its territory. One emblematic example of the Mexican state's necropolitics is the San Fernando massacre. In August 2010, 72 people, mainly transit migrants from Central America, were massacred by members of a drug cartel, probably with protection and assistance from the Mexican army (Varela Huerta

2017). This unfortunate event served as a watershed in urging the Mexican state to put the issue of Central American transit migration on its political agenda in a more vehement manner. However, despite the issuance of a new (more liberal) migration law in 2011, in recent years Mexico has strengthened and militarised its border with Guatemala more than ever before (Coraza de los Santos and Arriola Vega 2018). Through national security programmes, anti-drug-trafficking programmes and programmes to 'prevent' the clandestine crossing of its southern border, Mexico has found official reasons to deport a yearly average of at least a hundred thousand Central Americans during the last ten years (Dirección de Estadística 2019).

Although the routes and conditions of transit migration through Mexico are heterogeneous and influenced by diverse factors, there is a common ground that marks the reality of Central American refugees and migrants in transit through Mexico: transit has become daunting and violent: it is slow, fragmented and uncertain. To mitigate the risks of kidnap, trafficking, rape and death, Central Americans nowadays fragment their trajectories (Collyer 2010); that is, interruptions and pauses within the journey have become increasingly frequent. On the one hand, interrupting their journeys can delay migrant persons and force them to face more challenges. On the other hand, sometimes the interactions that happen in places of waiting become tools for knowledge exchange, which may increase their chances of reaching their destination. Increasingly, the periods of time that people must wait to move from one point to another along this migratory route have become longer. Journeys that previously lasted days or weeks are now routes of indefinite waiting and horizons of despair. Along migratory routes, solidarity and advocacy initiatives for transit migrants have emerged, in the absence of state policies of care or protection. Independent support groups, soup kitchens (*comedores*), food and clothing dispensaries, or even more institutional initiatives, such as migrant shelters (*casas de migrantes*) can be identified along the migratory routes. This 'rescue industry' (Agustín 2008), also called the 'hospitality corridor' (Olayo-Méndez et al. 2014), extends throughout Mexican territory and mitigates to some extent the impacts of the necropolitical governmentality of Central American transit migration.

Migrant shelters play a central role in the landscape of extreme violence that characterises migratory routes through Mexico. Some militants of the Catholic Church, principally those influenced by liberation theology, have become actively involved in the fight for migrants' and refugees' human rights as they transit through Mexico. Since the late 1980s, this faction of the Catholic Church has founded migrant shelters where humanitarian aid (food, shelter and basic medical attention) is provided. In northern Mexico, especially along the US border, these migrant shelters have traditionally been concerned with supporting and receiving Mexicans deported from the United States, although they have also begun to support Central American deportees who have been returned to Mexico under a changing US border policy (Diamond et al. 2020). Furthermore, because of the 'Remain in Mexico' programme implemented from January 2019 by the then US president Donald Trump, thousands of people seeking asylum in the USA were forced to process their asylum applications in Mexican territory. This situation brought great challenges to migrant shelters located along the USA–Mexico border.[1] In southern Mexico, especially along the Guatemalan border, migrant shelters focus on sheltering Central American and Caribbean refugees and, more recently, all kinds of transit migrants from the Global South (Guevara González 2015). Since 2006, the number of migrant shelters operating throughout the country has grown strikingly, and there are currently nearly a hundred groups and organisations dedicated to providing humanitarian aid to transit migrants (Li Ng 2020). Increasingly, these migrant shelters have become temporary homes for asylum seekers arriving in Mexico from Honduras, Guatemala and El Salvador (Candiz and Bélanger 2018). In 2013, the Comisión Mexicana de Ayuda a Refugiados (COMAR; the Mexican Commission for Aid to Refugees) registered 1,296 asylum petitions from citizens of those three countries. Six years later, in 2019, approximately 43,026 asylum applications were registered (Comisión Mexicana de Ayuda a Refugiados 2020), an increase of more than 4,500 per cent in less than a decade. In southern border states such as Chiapas and Tabasco, the number of asylum petitions has grown exponentially. As a result, migrant shelters have gradually set up their facilities and rules to attend to the needs of these people, some with more success than others. Nowadays, many migrant shelters offer legal advice and accompaniment during asylum procedures, and others have even incorporated special care units for families, members of the LGBTIQ community, unaccompanied minors, etc. This operational shift in the shelters has created opportunities for migrants to find new strategies for surviving and for venturing into Mexican territory.

Far from organised social movements, far from caravans and the media, thousands of people create quotidian tactics and strategies for surviving uncertainty and prolonged waiting periods while living in migrant shelters. Thus I am interested in describing how migrant shelters can be conceived as places of ambivalence, where hope and despair, happiness and sadness, individuality and collectiveness, cruelty and mercy, and movement and stillness, entangle. I analyse empirical data derived from extensive ethnographic work carried out in the years 2014, 2015 and 2016 in a migrant shelter in Tenosique, Tabasco, Mexico, a city located approximately 60 kilometres from the Mexican–Guatemalan border[2] (see Figure 14.1). In the next section of this chapter, 'Practising place while doing nothing', I share some examples of place-making practices and the different meanings that inhabitants of that shelter give to some of the areas that constitute it. In a further section, 'Things that matter', I examine how migrant persons[3] assign new meanings to the material world surrounding them. What are the things and objects that become important? What are the 'things that matter' when people live under these conditions? In the same section, I follow Henare, Holbraad and Wastell's postulates about how it can be that (milk) 'powder is power' (Henare et al. 2007). Throughout this chapter, I depict some daily experiences and events that take place in two key places of the shelter: the women's dormitories and the kitchen. In these places, power relations and negotiations around food, objects, intimacy and solidarity arise as main constitutive elements embodying the shelter's social life. The chapter concludes with a brief discussion about the interweaving ambivalences towards materiality, time passing and everyday banalities in forced migration contexts.

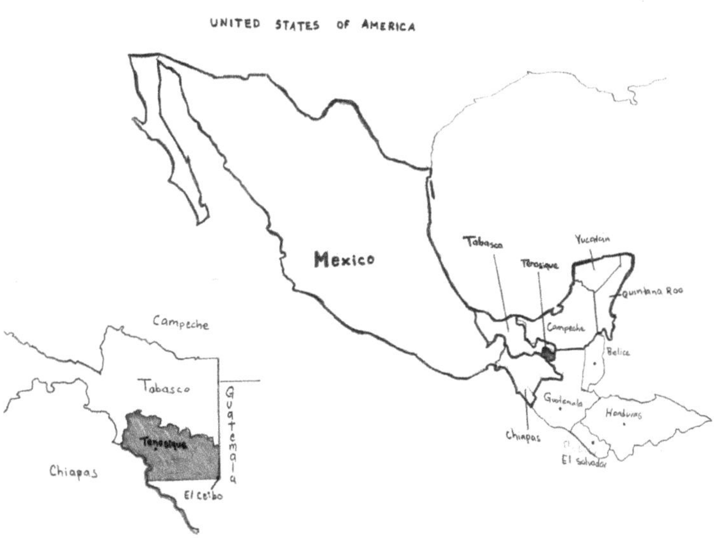

14.1 Tenosique, Tabasco, Mexico. Drawing © 'Chino', 2020. Chino was a resident at La 72.

Practising place while doing nothing

Tenosique is characterised as a transit city with a high traffic of goods, drugs and persons (Arriola Vega 2014). Until mid-2020,[4] the presence of the goods train, used as a means of transport by migrant persons, together with the construction of Mexican–Guatemalan highway networks from the beginning of the twenty-first century, transformed it into a principal node within the migratory route. This city is home to the migrant shelter 'La 72 Hogar Refugio para personas migrantes' (La 72), which until 2017 was the only migrant shelter in the state of Tabasco. La 72 was founded in 2011 to provide humanitarian assistance for Central Americans fleeing from their countries and arriving in Tenosique. The shelter emerged without assured funding and with limited human resources, like most others of its kind. Little by little, the shelter became a rich landscape of humanitarian aid for migrant persons, mainly Honduran. Both the physical and aesthetic appearance and the operational rules have changed over time. From 2014 to 2016, for example, accommodation for LGBTIQ persons and unaccompanied minors was built, and several care units, mainly related to asylum accompaniment, were created. The operation and management of the shelter have also changed drastically over time, but at the times when I conducted most of my research the permanent staff consisted of one or two Catholic friars coordinating the shelter, national and international volunteers, and a semi-permanent staff in charge of critical or sensitive care units, such as migratory regularisation, accompanying people seeking asylum to hearings, or care of vulnerable groups. The Mexican state is not involved with the shelter, although it does receive assistance or collaboration from some international organisations, namely the UNHCR, Médecins Sans Frontières (Doctors Without Borders), Asylum Access and the International Committee of the Red Cross. Still, any policy changes need to be carried out in consultation with the management of the shelter. The management is defined as the coordinators and the direction of the shelter.

Since 2014, the number of migrant persons arriving at the shelter looking for food, rest, shelter and refuge has increased considerably. During 2019, the shelter received about 15,700 people[5], and some of these did not use the shelter just as a transit place but lived there for months or years. Although this shelter is one of the most flexible in Mexico in terms of its rules of operation, it nevertheless has significant similarities to carceral management. In the case of La 72, times for taking a shower, eating, sleeping, getting up, cleaning the shelter, and entering and leaving the shelter are defined by the staff. Women and children, men, unaccompanied minors and members of the LGBTIQ community have separate accommodation. In addition to the dormitories, the shelter has a chapel, a wide corridor where people rest during the day, administrative offices, a room where basic pharmaceutical supplies are provided, a room where clothing is provided to new incomers, a kitchen, a dining room, an open space with four open-sided shelters with roofs of dried palm leaves (*palapas*), and a recreational court normally used for playing football or basketball or for collective events. But regulating daily life in confined places like La 72 is complex. Beyond organisational structures, matters like psychological stress and limited privacy merge together in a place where the boundaries between the private and public spheres are practically non-existent, which gives rise to daily struggles. Immobility and prolonged periods of waiting further exacerbate the situation.

Of course, social life inside the shelter is entangled with occurrences outside it. For example, even if inhabitants can enter and leave the shelter whenever they want (within the scheduled times), because of the continual migration raids carried out randomly by agents of the Instituto Nacional de Migración (INM; the National Migration Institute) in the city, many people prefer to spend the whole day inside the shelter, which government agents like the INM cannot enter. Nevertheless, for asylum seekers it is quite different. While their asylum claims are being reviewed, these people are given an official document which, if inspected by an agent of the INM, prevents them from being deported. Consequently they are slightly more 'mobile' than others, feeling more able to leave the shelter. Still, many of them prefer not to leave the shelter because of the daily hostility they experience while interacting with local actors. For these reasons, a significant proportion of the shelter's inhabitants spend most of their time inside this place.

For migrant persons, the shelter is mainly conceived as a *place for passing*, to stop, rest, recover and continue their path to the north. Hardly any of the inhabitants I met could imagine spending more than a couple of days there. However, as the days go by, the shelter becomes a *space* that serves *as a platform for knowledge exchange*. Strategies about how to cross Mexico, stories and narratives from others who have been deported several times, and information coming from the shelter's personnel, can play a central role in encouraging residents to reconsider or reorganise their journeys. Consequently, many people reassess or abandon their initial plans and use the time at the shelter to re-evaluate their transit strategies. Some years ago, few people considered staying in Mexico at this early stage of their journey. Nowadays, it has become very common for people to abandon their plans of continuing towards the north. Marina[6] was one of the people who originally planned to spend only one or two nights in the shelter. She was born in Honduras and fled her country in 2016, when she was 52 years old. First she decided not to seek asylum in Mexico, because she thought the procedure was too cumbersome and would force her to stay for too long in Tenosique. Her initial plan was to reach the United States. Since she did not have a migratory permit to stay in Tenosique, she preferred to stay at the shelter instead of going to the city. But as time passed this situation prevented her from getting any kind of job and earning money to cover her basic expenses. Although the shelter provides three meals a day and a place to sleep, any additional expenses must be covered by the migrant persons themselves.[7] So some months after her arrival Marina sought asylum in Mexico. Her petition was denied after she had been waiting over six months for a resolution. Finally, in 2017, after living at the shelter for over a year, she decided to continue her journey to Mexico City. In 2018, she managed to get a residence permit. Only in summer 2020 was she able to move to another city in northern Mexico. Four years after fleeing her country, she has not yet reached her destination country.

When I met Marina for the first time, in May 2016, she spent her time talking with other women, sitting in the *palapas*, in the corridor or in the dining area. When I met her again in November 2016, she had initiated her asylum application and went outside the shelter more often. She worked sporadically on domestic tasks for other people. But when I asked her or anybody else the routine question, 'What are you doing?', the most common answer was 'Nothing', 'Nothing, just killing time'. But what does 'nothing' mean? What is like 'to do nothing' for months and months under temporary confinement or mobility constraints? Just like Marina, dozens of other people inhabited the shelter's places while 'doing nothing' and 'killing time'. Small groups of women sharing their personal histories in the women's dormitories, LGBTIQ individuals – usually engaged in cooking or taking care of the kitchen – managing the shelter's food, men sitting in the *papalas* arranging their future journeys with guides or smugglers (Guevara González 2018b) – all these interactions were happening while people were 'doing nothing'.

But social interactions also produce new ways of self-positioning, transform power relations and build new hierarchies. These were reflected in the women's dormitories in constant disputes about who slept where, on the basketball court in endless negotiations about how to form teams, in the *palapas* in debates about Protestants and Catholics, in the unaccompanied minors' dormitories in inevitable acts of solidarity or betrayal, in the kitchen in confrontations about who was in charge of what, and all of this while waiting. The ball bouncing on the walls, the shouts of men playing football, children running, the gathering of small groups, or people lying in the corridors resting or chatting about their utopias and dystopias, all these mundane things made up a day of 'nothing going on' at the shelter. This 'endotic' life (Perec 1997), that which is not exotic or astonishing (the latter being, for example, when a train passes, or when the INM carries out a raid) but the ordinary and mundane, forms a complex laboratory of power and gendered relations, of emerging identities, of temporary belongings, of practices of resistance through the everyday. Furthermore, as time passed, the transient life of the shelter's inhabitants was inevitably attached to the shelter's places. Tim Cresswell asserts that 'places are constantly being made through gathering/ weaving/assembling and constantly being pulled apart. Among the things that are gathered in place are objects (materialities), meanings (narratives, stories, memories etc.) and practices' (2017, 321). La 72 is a place constituted and demarcated by the entanglements of objects, experiences, narratives and daily practices that emerge from social life in spatial constraint.

Things that matter

A woman with her mouth covered with tape is drawn on a piece of wood, and, next to it, the words 'Indignation. The tender fury'. This sign hangs on the door of the women's accommodation and delimits the women's territory. A large building ventilated by six windows, and protected by metal bars and a sliding door, further increases the confinement experienced by those living in La 72. In September 2014 the women's dormitory was occupied by about 30 women, some of them with children and babies. Although the number of women varied daily, that average was generally maintained. The sleeping area was a large room in which mats were placed on the floor nightly and collected and stacked the next morning, except for six mattresses that were always kept in the same place. These 'permanent' or 'given' places stirred up constant disputes between the 'old' and the 'new' women. 'The old women', as the women categorised themselves, were those who had been living at the shelter for months, most of them asylum seekers. These distinct notions of temporality in the same place – for some a transient home, for others a place to spend a night – caused daily confrontations. Although there was no official established rule about the distribution of mats and mattress, 'the old women' arranged the placement of the mattresses and to whom they belonged. If some 'old woman' left, then they decided who took over the free sleeping space. They would also explain to 'the new' how and where to place their mats. New arrivals frequently came to staff to complain about the differential treatment of 'old' and 'new' women in the dormitories. This example shows how mundane actions, such as going to bed, caused negotiations, expectations and belongings across place and time. Women living at the shelter for longer periods performed a kind of territoriality, creating a platform for the formation of power hierarchies in the management of the dormitory. This example also shows how powerful objects and daily utensils can become when people are living under conditions of prolonged uncertainty and endless waiting. Since the 'old women' had their 'own' place, after a couple of weeks they began to accumulate objects that added to their comfort: mosquito nets, pillows, spoons, electric grills, microwaves, electric kettles, blenders, hair irons, small pieces of furniture, fans. The accumulation of objects in addition to the formation of groups of 'old' and 'new' women caused continual disputes in the dormitories. Through objects and temporality new hierarchies in the dormitories were built. In this way, artefacts and objects, such as mattresses, electric fans or mosquito nets, represent the practices of doing place and the entanglements existing between materiality and everyday life in confined spaces.

Wooden boxes usually used to transport vegetables are reused in women's dormitories as lockers: some are colourfully painted, some still have traces of their former use. In these boxes hanging on the walls of the dormitory's corridor, women leave their belongings in a kind of 'open cupboard' (Figure 14.2). This space reveals the mundane life at the shelter. A recycled grocery box containing lipstick, underwear, deodorant, a photo and baby formula is the first personal (involuntary) encounter between the persons inhabiting the bedrooms and the outsiders (like shelter staff, or volunteers). To the bystanders in the corridor, the 'immediate' daily life of the women who live in the shelter for days, weeks or months is packed into those open and visible boxes. In that space, belongings in daily use exhibit the life of the other; those belongings reveal what may be the most important, the most needed for the owner of each closet. In this way, they represent the entanglement of materiality and human life, objects and human practices together in everyday life: photos representing longing and memories, baby objects that suggest motherhood, lipstick and deodorant that shed light on personal care and hygiene. Iris, a 38-year-old Honduran woman, never wanted to use the wooden boxes; she constantly said to me: 'I am not crazy about putting

14.2 Women's dormitories at La 72. Tenosique, Tabasco, Mexico. © Yaatsil Guevara González, 2014.

my things there [in the wooden boxes] … and then have the others talk about what I wash with and what I perfume with. I prefer to have everything under my bed.' In such circumstances, when people are living under prolonged uncertainty, 'objects become symbols of belonging, status and remembrance' (Guevara González 2018a). Another example that shows the importance of encounters between humans and objects of great significance is the shelter's kitchen. This is one of the most powerful places in the shelter. Food for all the inhabitants is prepared there three times a day. Women and children, LGBTIQ community members and men queue shortly before 8 a.m., 2 p.m. and 7 p.m., to receive their daily meals. In this act, the shelter's multiple dynamics crystallise and turn into a normative environment that gives rise to commensal time. Queue jumping, for example, is a reason for receiving – in front of everyone – a warning, coming either from the friars or from migrant persons themselves. The result would be 'temporary microclimates' (Ehn and Löfgren 2010) of social judgement, collective irritation, scolding, mocking and whistling. With this example I want to point out how, through mundane daily events, such as queuing, events at the shelter around food and the kitchen become central to its social life.

Everyday life interactions that emerge around cooking, feeding and eating are intrinsically embedded in notions of place-making. If we follow Barthes's assertion that food is 'a system of communication, a body of images, a protocol of usages, situations, and behavior' (Barthes 2013, 24), then it is also necessary to think about the sense of place that derives from that system. The shelter's food is served every day through a serving hatch onto a long counter which constitutes part of the kitchen's main structure (Figure 14.3). A folding metal grille which is opened and closed by the kitchen team on shift indicates when food time begins or ends. Thus, both the metal grille and the counter represent a clear borderline between those who belong and do not belong in the kitchen. Thus, the kitchen's architecture itself is a material tool for group membership and group exclusion, and for the emergence of processes of 'othering' in everyday life. Social relations and exchange at the shelter are fragmented here through a tangible material, which invites insiders (in this case, kitchen staff) or outsiders (the rest of the shelter's inhabitants) to rearrange their sense of collectiveness through one essential element: food.

Food for the whole shelter – about two hundred people – is prepared in one large wood-burning stove. The kitchen coordinator – who is usually an asylum seeker and a long-term inhabitant of the shelter – decides what food to cook and how, and allocates the tasks among the shifts, each of which is usually composed of five or six people. Most of the kitchen staff were part of the LGBTIQ community, families, or women and men seeking

14.3 Kitchen at La 72. Tenosique, Tabasco, Mexico. © Yaatsil Guevara González, 2014.

asylum, meaning people staying for several months at La 72. Food was collected every day by volunteers and friars from the town's groceries; those donations mostly consisted of tomatoes, carrots, potatoes and occasionally seasonal fruit. Sometimes there were donations of non-perishable food items such as maize flour, beans and rice. Just occasionally other, more 'luxury' items were received, for example milk powder and instant coffee, some cereal products, tins of tuna, biscuits, spices or bottles of juice. The ability to store food gave the kitchen staff access to highly valued food products, such as tuna, coffee powder and biscuits. This food arrived seldom and in small quantities, so it was not shared with the whole population of the shelter. Although the staff of La 72 had prohibited the kitchen teams from consuming these products to avoid some kitchen staff having more privileges than others, these items were constantly 'stolen' or disappeared. This situation provoked disputes and tensions among kitchen staff, causing gossip and enmities. Food has, as Appadurai writes, the 'capacity to mobilize strong emotions' (Appadurai 1981, 494).

The kitchen is a place where boundary-making practices are performed. The entanglements between place, gender, food and emotions give rise to the (re)production of temporal power hierarchies and inequalities in everyday interactions. A look at ethnographic evidence should illustrate this last assertion. During the first month of my stay at the shelter in 2014, I mostly participated in kitchen activities, and it was there I met Louis. One day, a dispute arising from a situations similar to the one described above caused a delay at lunchtime. Here is an excerpt from my fieldnotes:

> Today I helped in the kitchen. I helped Louis, he is Honduran, and he is seeking asylum in Mexico. It seems that he got it and he will have the final decision soon. He was in charge of the kitchen today. Yesterday the kitchen was in chaos, we served the meal at 2.30 because the voluntary kitchen group, constituted mainly of LGBTQI community members, well, they argued yesterday, they were fighting, and the team got divided. Some left their assigned tasks and in effect the food was prepared by three persons, instead of six or seven.[8]

Through his role as kitchen coordinator, Louis's power in the shelter increased over time. He was in charge of making decisions that assured the kitchen's functionality with little intervention from the friars; that is, he was in charge of determining what tasks should be done, how and by whom. On the one hand, he had to resolve the dynamics between different members of the kitchen staff; that is, the role of moderator was embedded in his social position. But on the other hand, this autonomy was accompanied by daily tensions and arguments between him and other kitchen staff, particularly when new LGBTIQ people arrived. The delay mentioned in the last example originated during a dispute between two members of the kitchen team. These two people were assigned a shared task, and while carrying it out they started to dispute vociferously, and both left. Since their relations with Louis were already tense, they did not care about their kitchen responsibilities. The result was that several other people abandoned the kitchen staff and there was a delay in the serving of lunch, since there were not enough people to cook and serve. Delaying lunchtime was a big event at the shelter that day. Here, the kitchen turned into an interpersonal place in which to share emotions, personal stories and dreams. In this way, as Meah and Jackson argue, 'kitchens can … be intensely personal spaces in which encounters with food and other objects play a role in mobilising the sensory, haptic and kinetic dimensions of memory, through a combination of taste-, sound- and smellscapes and mundane activities which are embedded in the rhythms of everyday life' (2016, 514). Another important event was the serving of the food. This was one of the kitchen staff's favourite tasks. The reason was the power interrelations involved in this activity, that is, the giving and receiving practices. Since there were people living at the shelter for prolonged periods, small temporal communities emerged. These were sometimes favoured by some people in the kitchen; that is, instead of receiving one cup of soup, they received one and a half, and one more tortilla than originally stipulated. Furthermore, sometimes there were people who had emotional bonds to others, as relatives, friends or transitory partners dating at the shelter. In this context, intimacy and affective relations intertwined with food. The food itself then represented a central amalgamating element to create either solidarities or enmities.

Moreover, although everyday activities around food, such as peeling vegetables and preparing and serving the dishes, may seem to be insignificant, mundane activities, they can, as Ehn and Löfgren affirm, 'constitute a strong force in social life, not just as compensatory resting places but as tools needed to keep everyday life going' (Ehn and Löfgren 2010, 209). Personal stories are narrated in front of concrete sinks while people chop vegetables, or morning incidents are gossiped about while they stir the beans on the stove; that is, the kitchen's mundane activities play a role in stimulating remembering and nostalgia, but also in keeping temporary aspirations alive and coping with the notion of a suspended life at the shelter. For some of the people who volunteer in the kitchen, that place turns into a temporal refuge to diminish uncertainty, worry and anxiety.

Conclusions

In her very well-known paper 'A global sense of place', Doreen Massey writes: 'what gives a place its specificity is not some long internalized history but the fact that it is constructed out of a particular constellation of social relations, meeting and weaving together at a particular locus. If one moves in from the satellite towards the globe, holding all those networks of social relations and movements and communications in one's head, then each "place" can be seen as a particular, unique, point of their intersection. It is, indeed, a meeting place' (Massey 1994, 154). By asserting this, Massey highlights the social relations and meanings derived from interactions between diverse social constellations. In this sense, La 72 can also be conceived as a 'meeting place' where disputes, negotiations and solidarities intertwine. It is a place marked by the fluidity and diversity of social relations coming together; but it is also a place that represents what Appadurai calls 'expressions of the crystallization of global moments' (Appadurai 2017). Here, La 72 as place is the materialisation of moments of confluence and fixity through current lived experiences and memories, and through intersections of temporal living in transit and immobility.

The people living in the shelter appear to spend their time doing 'nothing'. But precisely this 'wasted time' hides utopias, dystopias and 'small' things that are created and imagined in everyday life. Interactions between bodies and objects within women's dormitories create a bricolage of feelings, opinions, struggles and activities in this confined space. Orvan Löfgren asserts that 'everyday life is full of small utopias and dystopias, small tiny heritage items, ideas and dreams, and they're all synchronised in the present' (Löfgren 2015, 2:14). Could these cabinets showing everyday belongings be the reflection of those small utopias, dystopias and dreams that these women imagine in the present?

Things missing from the kitchen, verbal confrontations, thefts, disputes over sleeping places and gossip were part of everyday life at the shelter. So were solidarity, empathy, collectiveness and mutual support. Cohabitation in this space was full of contestations and ambivalences. Flows of emotions, utopias, dreams and narratives constituted everyday interactions between inhabitants coming from various and multiple social backgrounds. Mobile phones, clothes, toiletries (deodorant and toothpaste the most coveted), money and USB memory sticks were always the most envied objects. In this spatial context, some objects were precious treasure representing not only materiality, but also intimacy and memories coexisting in this public and private place. Thus, objects, as

Nigel Thrift suggests, 'must be understood as involved in multiple overlapping negotiations with human being[s] and not just as sets of passive and inanimate properties' (Thrift 2010, 292). For many migrant persons, a pair of jeans is not just a simple pair of jeans. They manage how to get them, how to sew or mend them, how to wash them, and how to keep them safe in a place where proper cloth is one of the scarcest objects.

The human interactions that took place at the shelter generated kinds of 'temporary microclimates', following Ehn and Löfgren (2010, 50). The microclimates formed at La 72 show, among other things, the importance of territoriality, belonging and self-positioning practices. There is also, because of the vulnerability and the unstable social terrains, a 'need for attachment of some sort, whether through place or anything else' (Massey 1994, 151). For some, La 72 becomes a kind of transient home, where a collective 'sense of time slowing down' (Griffiths 2014) takes place because of the impossibility of crossing Mexico. But it seems that time passing then becomes the contrary of passivity. Accordingly, experiences, negotiations, expectations, belongings, utopias and imaginations that emerge during migrants' immobile life entangle and materialise in the social life of the shelter. Furthermore, by exploring the meanings of the life of 'doing nothing', we get closer to understanding the complexity of the interweaving of what Simon Turner calls 'carceral junctions' (Turner 2020) by highlighting the multiple interfaces taking place in refugee camps or migrant shelters.

Notes

1 As from February 2021, the new president of the United States of America, Joe Biden, has put an end to this programme.

2 The ethnographic work was part of my doctoral studies. During 2014–15 the first phase lasted six months. In 2015, I visited the shelter for one month, and finally during 2016 I stayed for two weeks. During my visits I volunteered at the shelter, mainly accompanying migrants to appointments, or serving as an observer in order to protect their human rights. The main methods used were participant observation, narrative and biographical interviews, recordings of diverse everyday events and the writing of diaries and field notes. The data set was analysed following a situational analysis approach (Clarke 2005).

3 I use the term *migrant person* to refer to asylum seekers, recognised refugees and transit migrants living at the shelter.

4 After approximately 50 years, the 'Ferrocarril del Sureste' (south-east railway) train stopped operating in 2020, because of the new government's new plans to build the controversial tourist passenger train called *El tren maya* ('the Mayan train').

5 Statistical data obtained from internal sources at La 72.

6 All names have been changed.

7 Unlike in some European countries, such as Germany, asylum seekers in Mexico do not receive any social or economic support from the state. Each asylum seeker must make arrangements for his or her daily survival for the duration of the asylum process.

8 Excerpt from my field notes, 19 September 2014.

References

Agustín, Laura María. 2008. *Sex at the Margins: Migration, labour markets and the rescue industry*. London: Zed Books.

Appadurai, Arjun. 1981. 'Gastro-politics in Hindu South Asia', *American Ethnologist* 8(3): 494–511. https://doi.org/10.1525/ae.1981.8.3.02a00050.

Appadurai, Arjun. 2017. 'Globalization today and its historical predecessors: The traps of comparison over time'. Workshop, Bielefeld University, Germany, 14 December.

Arriola Vega, Luis Alfredo. 2014. 'Migration, violence, and "security primacy" at the Guatemala–Mexico border'. In *Binational Human Rights: The U.S.–Mexico experience*, edited by William Paul Simmons and Carol Mueller, 112–25. Philadelphia: University of Pennsylvania Press.

Barthes, Roland. 2013. 'Toward a psychosociology of contemporary food consumption'. In *Food and Culture: A reader*, edited by Carole Counihan and Penny Van Esterik, 3rd edition, 23–30. New York: Routledge.

Candiz, Guillermo and Danièle Bélanger. 2018. 'Del tránsito a la espera: El rol de las *casas del migrante* en México en las trayectorias de los migrantes centroamericanos', *Canadian Journal of Latin American and Caribbean Studies/Revue Canadienne des Études Latino-Américaines et Caraïbes* 43(2): 277–97. https://doi.org/10.1080/08263663.2018.1467533.

Clarke, Adele E. 2005. *Situational Analysis: Grounded theory after the postmodern turn*. Thousand Oaks, CA: Sage Publications.

Collyer, Michael. 2010. 'Stranded migrants and the fragmented journey', *Journal of Refugee Studies* 23(3): 273–93. https://doi.org/10.1093/jrs/feq026.

Comisión Mexicana de Ayuda a Refugiados. 2020. 'Boletines estadísticos de solicitantes de refugio en México 2013–2020'. Mexico City: Mexican Government. Accessed 30 August 2021. https://www.gob.mx/comar/articulos/boletin-estadistico-de-solicitantes-de-refugio-en-mexico-182244?idiom=es.

Coraza de los Santos, Enrique and Luis Alfredo Arriola Vega. 2018. 'Introducción'. In *Ráfagas y Vientos de un Sur Global: Movilidades recientes en estados fronterizos del sur-sureste de México*, edited by Luis Alfredo Arriola Vega and Enrique Coraza de los Santos, 5–13. New York: Peter Lang, and San Cristóbal de Las Casas, Chiapas: El Colegio de la Frontera Sur.

Cresswell, Tim. 2017. 'Towards *topopoetics*: Space, place and the poem'. In *Place, Space and Hermeneutics*, edited by Bruce B. Janz, 319–31. Cham: Springer. https://doi.org/10.1007/978-3-319-52214-2_23.

Diamond, Megan, Luke Testa, Carissa Novak, Kathryn Kempton-Amaral, Thalia Porteny and Alejandro Olayo-Méndez. 2020. 'A population in peril: A health crisis among asylum seekers on the northern border of Mexico'. Cambridge, MA: Harvard Global Health Institute. Accessed 30 August 2021. https://www.bc.edu/content/dam/bc1/schools/sw/pdf/A_Population_in_Peril_HGHI_BCSSW.pdf.

Dirección de Estadística. 2019. 'Extranjeros presentados y devueltos'. Extranjeros devueltos ante la autoridad migratoria, según continente, país de nacionalidad y sexo, 2011–2019. Mexican Government, Mexico City, dirección de estadística, series históricas. Accessed 1 November 2021. http://portales.segob.gob.mx/es/PoliticaMigratoria/Series_historicas.

Ehn, Billy and Orvar Löfgren. 2010. *The Secret World of Doing Nothing*. Berkeley: University of California Press.

Frank-Vitale, Amelia and Juan José Martínez d'Aubuisson. 2021. 'The generation of the coup: Honduran youth at risk and of risk', *Journal of Latin American and Caribbean Anthropology* 25(4): 552–68. https://doi.org/10.1111/jlca.12512.

Galemba, Rebecca B. 2018. '"He used to be a *Pollero*": The securitisation of migration and the smuggler/migrant nexus at the Mexico–Guatemala border', *Journal of Ethnic and Migration Studies* 44(5): 870–86. https://doi.org/10.1080/1369183X.2017.1327803.

Galli, Chiara. 2018. 'No country for immigrant children: From Obama's "humanitarian crisis" to Trump's criminalization of Central American unaccompanied minors', CIRI Research Brief Series 6. Center for Comparative Immigration Studies, University of California San Diego. Accessed 30 August 2021. https://escholarship.org/uc/item/5bg545kf.

Griffiths, Melanie B. E. 2014. 'Out of time: The temporal uncertainties of refused asylum seekers and immigration detainees', *Journal of Ethnic and Migration Studies* 40(12): 1991–2009. https://doi.org/10.1080/1369183X.2014.907737.

Guevara González, Yaatsil. 2015. 'Migración de tránsito y ayuda humanitaria: Apuntes sobre las casas de migrantes en la ruta migratoria del pacífico sur en México', *Forum for Inter American*

Research, FIAR 8(1): 63–83. Accessed 30 August 2021. https://pub.uni-bielefeld.de/record/2775517.

Guevara González, Yaatsil. 2018a. 'Inmovilidades en tránsito: Vida cotidiana de migrantes irregularizados y personas refugiadas en Tenosique, Tabasco'. In *Ráfagas y Vientos de un Sur Global: Movilidades recientes en estados fronterizos del sur-sureste de México*, edited by Enrique Coraza de los Santos and Luis Alfredo Arriola Vega, 39–58. New York: Peter Lang, and San Cristóbal de Las Casas, Chiapas: El Colegio de la Frontera Sur.

Guevara González, Yaatsil. 2018b. 'Navigating with coyotes: Pathways of Central American migrants in Mexico's southern borders', *ANNALS of the American Academy of Political and Social Science* 676(1): 174–93. https://doi.org/10.1177/0002716217750574.

Henare, Amiria, Martin Holbraad and Sari Wastell. 2007. 'Introduction: Thinking through things'. In *Thinking through Things: Theorising artefacts ethnographically*, edited by Amiria Henare, Martin Holbraad and Sari Wastell, 1–31. New York: Routledge.

Homeland Security Department. 2019. 'Agreement between the government of the United States of America and the government of the Republic of Guatemala on cooperation regarding the examination of protection claims', *Federal Register*, 20 November. Accessed 30 August 2021. https://www.federalregister.gov/documents/2019/11/20/2019-25288/agreement-between-the-government-of-the-united-states-of-america-and-the-government-of-the-republic.

Homeland Security Department. 2020. 'Agreement between the government of the United States of America and the government of the Republic of Honduras for cooperation in the examination of protection claims', *Federal Register*, 1 May. Accessed 30 August 2021. https://www.federalregister.gov/documents/2020/05/01/2020-09322/agreement-between-the-government-of-the-united-states-of-america-and-the-government-of-the-republic.

Li Ng, Juan José. 2020. 'Mapa 2020 de casas del migrante, albergues y comedores para migrantes en México' [2020 map of migrant houses, shelters and soup kitchens for migrants in Mexico], 2 March. Observatorio Migración México. BBVA Research. Accessed 30 August 2021. https://www.bbvaresearch.com/publicaciones/mapa-2020-de-casas-del-migrante-albergues-y-comedores-para-migrantes-en-mexico/.

Löfgren, Orvar. 2015. 'Living in the past, the present and the future: Synchronizing everyday life'. Keynote speech at the conference of the International Society for Ethnology and Folklore, 21 June. (Video.) https://www.siefhome.org/videos/sief2015.shtml.

Masferrer, Claudia, Víctor M. García-Guerrero and Silvia E. Giorguli-Saucedo. 2018. 'Connecting the dots: Emerging migration trends and policy questions in North and Central America'. *Migration Policy Source*, 7 March. Migration Policy Institute. Accessed 30 August 2021. https://www.migrationpolicy.org/article/connecting-dots-emerging-migration-trends-and-policy-questions-north-and-central-america.

Massey, Doreen B. 1994. 'A global sense of place'. In *Space, Place and Gender*, 146–56. Cambridge: Polity Press.

Mbembé, Achille. 2003. 'Necropolitics', *Public Culture* 15(1): 11–40. https://doi.org/10.1215/08992363-15-1-11.

Meah, Angela and Peter Jackson. 2016. 'Re-imagining the kitchen as a site of memory', *Social & Cultural Geography* 17(4): 511–32. https://doi.org/10.1080/14649365.2015.1089587.

Nyberg Sørensen and Laura Huttunen. 2020. 'Missing migrants and the politics of disappearance in armed conflicts and migratory contexts'. *Ethnos*. https://doi.org/10.1080/00141844.2019.1697333.

Olayo-Méndez, Alejandro, Stephen Nathan Haymes and Maria Vidal de Haymes. 2014. 'Mexican migration-corridor hospitality', *Peace Review* 26(2): 209–17. https://doi.org/10.1080/10402659.2014.906887.

Perec, Georges. 1997. *Species of Spaces and Other Pieces*, edited and translated by John Sturrock. London: Penguin Books.

Rodríguez Chávez, Ernesto. 2016. 'Migración centroamericana en tránsito irregular por México: Nuevas cifras y tendencias', CANAMID Policy Brief Series PB14, CIESAS, Guadalajara, Mexico. https://doi.org/10.13140/RG.2.2.28698.44483/1.

Thrift, Nigel. 2010. 'Understanding the material practices of glamour'. In *The Affect Theory Reader*, edited by Melissa Gregg and Gregory J. Seigworth, 289–308. Durham, NC: Duke University Press.

Turner, Simon. 2020. 'Stuckness and connectedness in camps'. Keynote speech at the conference 'Materializing the transient: Ethnographies and museums in the study of (forced) migration', University of Göttingen, 15 May.

Varela Huerta, Amarela. 2017. 'Las masacres de migrantes en San Fernando y Cadereyta: Dos ejemplos de gubernamentalidad necropolítica', *Íconos: Revista de ciencias sociales* 58: 131–49. https://doi.org/10.17141/iconos.58.2017.2486.
Vargas Carrasco, Felipe de Jesús. 2018. 'El vía crucis del migrante: Demandas y membresía', *Trace* 73: 117–33. Accessed 30 August 2021. https://journals.openedition.org/trace/2840.

Index

www.ingramcontent.com/pod-product-compliance
Lightning Source LLC
LaVergne TN
LVHW052005260926
848888LV00022B/190
* 9 7 8 1 8 0 0 0 8 1 6 1 1 *